I Found God in Me

I Found God in Me

A Womanist Biblical Hermeneutics Reader

EDITED BY

Mitzi J. Smith

▲ CASCADE *Books* · Eugene, Oregon

I FOUND GOD IN ME
A Womanist Biblical Hermeneutics Reader

Cascade Books
An Imprint of Wipf and Stock Publishers
199 W. 8th Ave., Suite 3
Eugene, OR 97401

www.wipfandstock.com

ISBN 13: 978-1-62564-745-0

Cataloging-in-Publication data:

I found God in me : a womanist biblical hermeneutics reader / edited by Mitzi J. Smith.

xii + 314 p. ; 23 cm. —Includes bibliographical references.

ISBN 13: 978-1-62564-745-0

1. Womanist biblical interpretation. 2. Bible—Feminist criticism. 3. Bible—Black interpretations. I. Title.

BS521.4 I5 2015

Manufactured in the U.S.A.

Permissions

We, the editor and the publisher, are grateful for permission to reprint the following copyrighted material. Please note that, in some cases, the current copyright holder is different from the original publisher.

"Womanist" from *In Search of Our Mothers' Gardens: Womanist Prose* by Alice Walker. Copyright © 1983 by Alice Walker. Reprinted by permission of Houghton Mifflin Harcourt Publishing Company. All rights reserved.

© Katie Geneva Cannon, "Womanist Interpretation and Preaching in the Black Church," *Katie's Canon: Womanism and the Soul of the Black Community* (New York: Continuum, 1995), 113–121. Used by permission of Continuum, an imprint of Bloomsbury Publishing Inc.

© Kelly Brown Douglas, "Marginalized People, Liberating Perspectives: a Womanist Approach to Biblical Interpretation, *Anglican Theological Review* 83:1 (2001) 41–47. Reprinted by permission of the *Anglican Theological Review* and of Kelly Brown Douglas.

© Clarice J. Martin, "Womanist Interpretations of the New Testament: The Quest for Holistic and Inclusive Translation and Interpretation," *Journal of Feminist Studies in Religion* 6:2 (1990) 41–61. This essay is reprinted with the permission of the author who holds the copyright.

© Madipoane Masenya (Ngwana' Mphahlele), "An African Methodology for South African Biblical Sciences: Revisting the *Bosadi* (Womanhood) Approach," *OTE* 18:3 (2005) 741–51. Used by permission of *Old Testament Essays*.

© Mitzi J. Smith, "Minjung, the Black Masses, and the Global Imperative: A Womanist Interpretation of Luke's Soteriological Hermeneutical Circle," *Reading Minjung Theology in the Twenty-first Century*, ed. Yung Suk Kim and Jin-Ho Kim (Eugene, OR: Wipf and Stock, 2013). Reproduced by permission of Wipf and Stock Publishers.

© Mitzi J. Smith, "'Give Them What You Have': A Womanist Reading of the Matthean Feeding Miracle (Matt 14:13–21)," *Journal of the Bible and Human Transformation* 3:1 (September 2013) 1–22. Used by permission of Sopher Press.

© Mitzi J. Smith, "'Knowing More Than is Good for One': A Womanist Interrogation of the Matthean Great Commission, excerpted from *Teaching All Nations: Interrogating the Matthean Great Commission* edited by Mitzi J. Smith and Jayachitra Lalitha (Minneapolis: Fortress, 2014). Reproduced by permission of Augsburg Fortress Publishers.

© JoAnne Marie Terrell, *Power in the Blood? The Cross in the African American Experience* (Eugene, OR: Wipf and Stock, 2005). Chapter 5, pp. 126–143 reprinted by permission of the author who holds the copyright.

© Renita Weems, "Re-Reading for Liberation: African American Women and the Bible," *Feminist Interpretation of the Bible*, Sylvia Schroer & Sophia Bietenhard, eds. (London: T. & T. Clark, 2003).

Contents

Contributors

Katie Geneva Cannon (PhD, MPhil, Union Theological Seminary) is Annie Scales Rogers Professor of Christian Ethics at Union Presbyterian Seminary in Richmond, Virginia. Rev. Dr. Cannon was the first African American woman ordained in the United Presbyterian Church (USA). She focuses her work in the areas of Christian ethics, womanist theology, and women in religion and society. She has lectured nationally on theological and ethical topics and is the author or editor of numerous articles and seven books including *Katie's Canon: Womanism and the Soul of the Black Community* and *Black Womanist Ethics*.

Lynne St. Clair Darden (PhD, Drew University) is Assistant Professor of New Testament at the Interdenominational Theological Center in Atlanta, Georgia. She is a contributor to *Teaching All Nations: Interrogating the Matthean Great Commission* (Fortress, 2014).

Kelly Brown Douglas (PhD, Union Theological Seminary) is Professor of Religion at Goucher College. She specializes in womanist theology and sexuality and the black church. Dr. Douglas is the author or editor of numerous articles and books including *Sexuality and the Black Church, What's Faith Got to Do With It?* and *Sexuality and the Sacred*. She has been honored as Womanist Legend by the Black Religious Scholars Group at the Womanist Legends Gala and was the first recipient of the Anna Julia Cooper Award from the Union of Black Episcopalians.

Febbie C. Dickerson is a PhD candidate at Vanderbilt University. She also received an MDiv degree from Vanderbilt University and is ordained clergy. Febbie's research interest includes the special Lukan material and the depiction of women in Luke-Acts. Her publications are "The Canaanite Woman (Matthew 15:22–28): Discharging the Stigma of Single Moms in the African American Church," in *Matthew: Texts @ Contexts* (Fortress, 2013) and "The

Ten Commandments in an African American Community," in *Global Perspectives on the Bible* (Pearson, 2013).

Wil Gafney (PhD, Duke Divinity School) is Associate Professor of Hebrew Bible at the Brite Divinity School in Fort Worth, Texas. She is the author of *Daughters of Miriam* and a general editor of *The Peoples' Bible* and *The Peoples' Companion to the Bible*. Her volume *Womanist Midrash* is forthcoming. An Episcopal priest, the Rev. Gafney does the work of biblical scholarship and interpretation in Jewish and Christian congregations as well as in the academy.

Clarice Martin (PhD, Duke University) is Jean Picker Professor of Philosophy and Religion at Colgate University in Hamilton, New York. She is a graduate of San Francisco Theological Seminary (MDiv) and the Duke University Graduate School of Religion (PhD). Her teaching and research interests include early Christianity, the late antique mediterranean (200–800 CE), modern religious thought, ethics, and philosophy, and africana women's history, literature, and thought. She has numerous publications, including *Pentecost 2*. Dr. Martin is the proud mother of six children, and resides in Manlius, New York.

Madipoane J. Masenya (DLit et Phil, Biblical Studies) is chair of the Department of Old Testament and Ancient Near Eastern Studies at the University of South Africa (UNISA). She is the author or co-author/editor of three books and numerous articles, including *How Worthy is the Woman of Worth? Re-Reading Proverbs 31:10–31 in African-South Africa* (Peter Lang, 2004) and *African Women, HIV/AIDS and Faith Communities* (Cluster, 2003).

Yolanda M. Norton is a fourth year doctoral student in Hebrew Bible and Ancient Israel at Vanderbilt University where her current research interests include womanist interpretation and narrative and literary criticism. In particular, her current work is focused on the books of Genesis and Ruth, and how each text treats foreign women. She is concerned with the ways in which insider-outsider paradigms in Scripture influence constructions of identity such that they vilify and/or oppress women of color who encounter the biblical canon in the modern world. She holds MDiv and MTS degrees from Wesley Theological Seminary in Washington, DC, where she received both the C. C. Goen Award for Church History and the Award for Excellence in Biblical Interpretation. She is also ordained clergy in the Christian Church (Disciples of Christ), having been ordained at New Covenant Christian Church (Disciples of Christ).

Kimberly Dawn Russaw is a doctoral candidate at Vanderbilt University studying the Hebrew Bible and Ancient Israel. While her research interests are varied, Kimberly examines daughters in the Hebrew Bible in her dissertation. Kimberly is an active member of both the Society of Biblical Literature and the American Academy of Religion, and has presented and published in numerous scholarly and ecclesial contexts.

Mitzi J. Smith (PhD, Harvard) is Associate Professor of New Testament and Early Christian Studies at Ashland Theological Seminary-Detroit. Dr. Smith is the author of *The Literary Construction of the Other in the Acts of the Apostles: Charismatics, the Jews, and Women*, co-editor of *Teaching All Nations: Interrogating the Matthean Great Commission*, and a contributor to *True to Our Native Land: An African American New Testament Commentary*, *The Revised Women's Bible Commentary*, *Reading Minjung Theology in the Twenty-first Century*, and *The Handbook of Women Biblical Interpreters*.

JoAnne Marie Terrell (PhD, Union Theological Seminary) is the Associate Professor of Ethics and Theology at Chicago Theological Seminary. She is the author of *Power in the Blood? The Cross in the African-American Experience* and is an ordained elder in the African Methodist Episcopal Zion Church. Dr. Terrell is a Womanist scholar whose research interests include: Christian origins and their potential for enhancing future developments in black, feminist and womanist theologies.

Renita J. Weems (PhD, Princeton Theological Seminary) is founder of *Something Within*, a monthly e-newsletter and blog that explores issues of faith in the context of the daily challenges women face. An ordained minister in the African Methodist Episcopal Church, Dr. Weems served for two years as the William and Camille Cosby Professor of Humanities at Spelman College in Atlanta, Georgia. She spent nearly two decades as a Professor of the Hebrew Bible at the Divinity School at Vanderbilt University in Nashville, Tennessee. Dr. Weems has written numerous books and articles, including, *What Matters Most: Ten Passionate Lessons from the Song of Solomon* and *Showing Mary: How Women Can Share Prayers, Wisdom and the Blessings of God*. Her *Listening for God: A Minister's Journey through Silence and Doubt* won the Religious Communications Council's prestigious Wilbur Award.

Introduction

"I found God in Myself & I loved her / I loved her fiercely"
—Ntozake Shange[1]

The seeds of womanism were planted in me at Howard University School of Divinity (HUSD) in Rev. Dr. Kelly Brown Douglas's womanist theology class. In Dr. Douglas's course we read womanist theologian Delores Williams's *Sisters in the Wilderness*,[2] a womanist reading of the Hagar narrative—a story of surrogacy, survival, and quality of life that speaks to the experiences of African American women. We were exposed to Dr. Douglas's *The Black Christ*[3] wherein she argues that the black Christ can be found wherever black women and men engender wholeness in the black community as a whole; that the black Christ of womanism will lift up the existence of Christ in the lives of the poorest black women; and that the black Christ must reflect the interests of not just black men (the failure of black theology) but of the entire community. Douglas's *Sexuality and the Black Church*[4] raised our consciousness about sexism and heterosexism in the black church, and their connection to the historical control of black bodies in American slavery and beyond. Equally formative was Dr. Emilie Townes's *Breaking the Fine Rain of Death*,[5] in which she calls for communal

1. Ntozake Shange, *For Colored Girls Who have Considered Suicide / When the Rainbow is Enuf* (New York: Scribner) 71–72.

2. Delores Williams, *Sisters in the Wilderness* (Maryknoll, NY: Orbis, 1995).

3. Kelly Brown Douglas, *The Black Christ* (Maryknoll, NY: Orbis, 1994).

4. Kelly Brown Douglas, *Sexuality and the Black Church: A Womanist Perspective* (Maryknoll, NY: Orbis, 1999).

5. Emilie Townes, *Breaking the Fine Rain of Death: African American Health Issues*

lament and repentance, similar to the Old Testament prophet Joel, regarding the health care crisis and the systemic disparities of quality and access to care for the poor and for African Americans. A womanist ethic of care necessitates the creation of opportunities for healing and wholeness.[6]

My introduction to womanist biblical interpretation prepared the soil of my soul for the seeds of womanism. At HUSD in Dr. Cain Hope Felder's New Testament class we, of course, read both Drs. Renita J. Weems and Clarice Martin's articles in *Stony the Road we Trod*.[7] In her essay Dr. Weems explores black women's relationship to the Bible as sacred text and the reading strategies they use in light of their marginalization. In Dr. Martin's essay she analyzes the household codes in the disputed Pauline letters, arguing that while the black church has rejected "slaves obey your masters" it has failed to critique the subordination of women to men; the code pertaining to women's submission remains universally binding. Also, Dr. Weems's book *Just a Sister Away*,[8] a reader-response and feminist biblical interpretation of women in the Bible to which she adds the concerns and experiences of black women, gives us insightful and relevant readings of stories about women in biblical texts. A lifelong insight for me from Weems's seminal book has been the idea that no matter our station in life, we all may at any time find ourselves in a position to exploit or oppress another human being; we all have potential victims. And we can be passive participants in our own exploitation.

Since my seminary days, more womanist scholars have earned doctorates in religion and society, Bible, theology, and ethics, and as a result womanist scholarship has multiplied. More recently, we have witnessed the publication of two womanist readers: *Womanist Theological Ethics. A*

---

and a Womanist Ethic of Care (Eugene, OR: Wipf & Stock, 2006).

6. The topic of health care disparities particularly interested me, since I had written my master's thesis at The Ohio State University on the connection between high mortality rates in all cancers for African Americans in Ohio cities with large black populations and the proximity of quality health care facilities, fear of doctors, and individual and systemic racisms.

7. Renita J. Weems, "Reading *Her Way* through the Struggle: African American Women and the Bible," in *Stony the Road We Trod: African American Biblical Interpretation*, ed. Cain Hope Felder (Minneapolis: Fortress, 1991) 57–77; Clarice Martin, "The *Haustafeln* (Household Codes) in African American Biblical Interpretation: 'Free Slaves' and 'Subordinate Women,'" 206–31.

8. Renita J. Weems, *Just a Sister Away: Understanding the Timeless Connection between Women of Today and Women in the Bible* (West Bloomfield, MI: Walk Worthy, 2005). Of course, Weems has since written several other books including *Battered Love: Marriage, Sex, and Violence in the Hebrew Prophets* (Minneapolis: Fortress, 1995); and *Listening for God: A Minister's Journey through Silence and Doubt* (Touchstone, 2000).

Reader, edited by Rev. Drs. Katie Cannon, Emilie Townes, and Angela Sims,[9] and consisting of essays by seven African American female theologians and ethicists and one biblical scholar, Dr. Renita Weems. Prior to 2011 Dr. Layli Phillips edited *The Womanist Reader*,[10] a multi-disciplinary volume containing articles by womanists of color (African, African American, Asian, and Latina or Mujeres) and black male feminists scholars of religion, literature, psychology, anthropology, education, social work, history, and more.

After writing a third womanist essay in the fall of 2013, which appears in *Teaching all Nations: Interrogating the Matthean Great Commission*,[11] and is reprinted in this volume, I felt it was time for a womanist biblical hermeneutics reader. There now exists a number of institutions, including my own, which offer courses dedicated to womanist biblical interpretation or that include womanist biblical interpretation as a subject within other courses. In addition, there is also a *critical mass* of black women biblical scholars doing or interested in doing womanist work to necessitate and allow for the compilation of a womanist *biblical hermeneutics* reader. By *critical mass* I do not mean that our numbers in the academy have risen to a level comparable to those of white feminist biblical scholars, because they have not. Nor do I mean that we do not still need to encourage and nurture a larger cohort of womanist biblical scholars; this is greatly needed. But we do have a significant number of black women biblical scholars (and other women of color) who are doing womanist biblical interpretation that we can collectively impact and contribute to biblical studies, womanist studies, and other disciplines through the production of a womanist biblical hermeneutics reader. As black feminist Patricia Hill Collins argues, "*mass* does not necessarily mean large numbers of people, as in 'mass' culture and 'mass' media. Instead, *mass* can mean some sort of political threshold associated with action."[12]

I Found God in Me constitutes an attempt to fill a pedagogical, political, and spiritual void and/or function. This womanist biblical interpretation reader brings together eight classic essays, one new essay on womanist interpretation, six new original womanist readings of biblical texts, plus three reprints of womanist biblical interpretation readings written within the last three years. *I Found God in Me* can be used as a text in courses on womanist

9. Katie Geneva Cannon, Emilie M. Townes, and Angela D. Sims, eds., *Womanist Theological Ethics: A Reader* (Louisville: Westminster John Knox, 2011).

10. Layli Phillips, ed., *The Womanist Reader* (New York: Routledge, 2006).

11. Mitzi J. Smith and Lalitha Jayachitra, eds., *Teaching all Nations: Interrogating the Matthean Great Commission* (Minneapolis: Fortress, 2014).

12. Patricia Hill Collins, *Fighting Words: Black Women and the Search for Justice* (Minneapolis: University of Minnesota Press, 1998) 243.

biblical hermeneutics, womanist theology, womanist ethics, and in New and Old Testament introductory or upper level courses in institutions that recognize the importance of incorporating diverse voices and methodologies into courses and curriculums; that such a spiritual and political perspective and practice fosters pedagogical excellence. Over the years, I realized the need for a womanist biblical hermeneutics reader whenever I have taught womanist biblical hermeneutics at Ashland Theological Seminary (face-to-face, and online). I have been at a loss to find a critical mass of essays that demonstrate, concretely, for students diverse methodologies or multiple approaches for doing womanist biblical interpretation. This is a prophetically political endeavor, as well, not merely an academic one, in that the authors unapologetically confront in their essays issues of oppression such as racism, sexism, classism that impact black women's lives and other women of color and their communities. This project takes for granted the legitimacy and viability of womanist biblical interpretation as a discipline, even as some reject it as normative biblical studies, and disingenuously regard it even as racist that we audaciously start with and concern ourselves with the lives of black women and our communities. *I Found God in Me* is a spiritual project, as evidenced in the title, in that through our individual essays and in our collective writing we are doing the work that our souls must have, as womanist ethicist Dr. Emilie Townes puts it.[13] We are doing that which we believe God has called us to do, to be, and to say. Through our soul work, we hope to connect with, to touch in transformative, healing ways the souls of our sisters and communities. And we do this work, as multi-generational womanist biblical scholars in this space, sharing space with the voices of our elders who have and continue to teach, inspire, and feed our souls.

Seminal voices in the field of womanist biblical interpretation are biblical scholars Drs. Renita Weems and Clarice Martin. These we consider first generation, pioneers in the discipline of womanist biblical hermeneutics.[14] Both Weems and Martin wrote pivotal essays in Cain Felder's *Stony the Road we Road* as mentioned above. This first generation paved the way for the inclusion of black women's voices and work in the area of biblical interpretation generally. We celebrate Weems and Martin as we continue to do

---

13. Emilie M. Townes, "Ethics as an Art of Doing the Work Our Souls Must Have," *Womanist Theological Ethics*, ed. Katie Geneva Cannon and Angela D. Sims (Louisville: Westminster John Knox, 2011) 35–50.

14. The African American biblical scholars I name as womanist biblical scholars do not necessarily identify themselves solely using the adjective "womanist." For some African American biblical scholars "womanist" refers more to a methodological or interpretive approach that they use from time to time, but it is not their only approach to biblical interpretation.

the work they began of critically reading texts, contexts, cultures, readers, readings, and worlds. We continue to affirm that behind the text, in the text, and in front of the text we find the politics of androcentricism, patriarchalism, (neo)colonialism, sexism, classism, heterosexism, othering, and other forms of hierarchy and difference that silence, exploit, and delegitimize certain voices, peoples, and cultures. While we hold the biblical text to be sacred, we reserve the right to struggle with it and to read it in ways that affirm the multiplicity of black women's experiences, especially in ways that privilege God's interaction with and revelation to and in black women.

Second generation womanist biblical scholars[15] include Drs. Gay Byron, Cheryl Anderson, Valerie Bridgemann, Madeline McClenney-Sadler, Margaret Aymer, and Raquel St. Clair; all are Old Testament scholars, with the exception of Aymer and St. Clair who are New Testament scholars. Dr. Byron's text *Symbolic Blackness and Ethnic Difference in Early Christian Literature*[16] examines the discursive use of Egypt/Egyptian, Ethiopia/Ethiopian and blacks/blackness through ethno-political rhetorics; such images Byron argues came to represent extremes within early Christianity. Dr. Bridgemann has explored black women as prophetic preachers and contributed to the *Africana Bible,*[17] the first African American Commentary on the Old Testament/Hebrew Bible in which she wrote commentaries on Jonah and Nahum, co-edited the *Introduction to the Prophets,* and also functioned as an associate editor on the project. Dr. Anderson analyzes women and violence in the Old Testament law codes, in her book *Women, Ideology and Violence.*[18] Dr. Margaret Aymer's book *First Pure, then Peaceable. Frederick Douglass Reads James*[19] examines how nineteenth-century abolitionist and former slave Frederick Douglass read the Epistle of James, particularly James 3:17, as a darkness reading, reading through the darkness of his circumstances. Aymer centers Douglass as reader and not the Bible. I place Drs. Aymer and St. Clair among the second generation of womanist biblical scholars, but in actuality they may bridge second and third generation womanists.

15. These categories (i.e., second, third, and fourth generation) are not fixed and may not accurately reflect how each womanist biblical scholar sees herself in relationship to others or the field. The categories are somewhat fluid. But they assist in talking about the development of womanist biblical scholarship in a cursory way.

16. Gay H. Byron, *Symbolic Blackness and Ethnic Difference in Early Christian Literature: Blackened by the Skins* (New York: Routledge, 2002).

17. Hugh R. Page, Jr., *The Africana Bible: Reading Israel's Scriptures from Africa and the African Diaspora* (Minneapolis: Fortress, 2010).

18. Cheryl B. Anderson, *Women, Ideology and Violence* (London: T. & T. Clark, 2005).

19. Margaret Aymer, *First Pure, then Peaceable: Frederick Douglass Reads James* (New York: T. & T. Clark, 2008).

I first met Dr. St. Clair at a SBL luncheon for underrepresented minorities; I was applying to doctoral programs and she was a doctoral student. St. Clair's book *Call and Consequences* is the first womanist biblical interpretation monograph published by an African American female biblical scholar. Building upon the work of womanist theologians like Drs. Delores Williams and JoAnne Terrell, St. Clair argues that suffering is a consequences of following one's call, just as Jesus suffered as a result of his ministry. God does not call us to enter into his pain but to partner with him in ministry. Agony (pain and suffering) are not required for discipleship or ministry. Pain as recognized, named, and transformed agony is a consequence of discipleship. Dr. St. Clair's mentor and advisor at Princeton Theological Seminary was African American biblical scholar Brian K. Blount (a former student of Dr. Cain Hope Felder) who provided the intellectual and spiritual space and mentorship for St. Clair to engage in womanist biblical interpretation as her dissertation project. Unfortunately, in many institutions African American and womanist hermeneutics are not considered biblical studies but theology or hermeneutics. Therefore, black women and other women of color pursuing doctoral degrees in biblical studies are too often discouraged from writing doctoral dissertations on womanist interpretation; they must have a willing mentor, advisor, and departmental and institutional support, and such continue to be rarities. Of course, the lack of a womanist scholar within the institution plays a role as well. Dr. St. Clair also wrote an essay entitled "Womanist Biblical Interpretation" in the first African American commentary on the New Testament, *True to Our Native Land*, edited by Dr. Blount.[20] (Unfortunately, Dr. St. Clair was unable to participate in this womanist biblical interpretation reader as she was preparing to give birth to her first child.) A number of the first, second, and third generation womanist biblical scholars contributed to the first African American commentaries of the Bible, *True to Our Native Land* and *The Africana Bible*.

Third generation womanist biblical scholars such as Drs. Stephanie Buckhanon Crowder, Wil Gafney, Nyasha Junior, Love Sechrest, and myself generally did not begin to do womanist biblical interpretation until after we published our first academic books. Most of us could, with the blessings of our advisors, departments, and institutions, use feminist biblical interpretation in our dissertation projects; however, this was and remains generally more acceptable in the guild than the use of an overarching womanist interpretive lens. This means that third generation womanist biblical scholars have had to develop a womanist hermeneutical lens beyond the

20. Brian K. Blount, ed., *True to Our Native Land: An African American New Testament Commentary* (Minneapolis: Fortress, 2007) 54–62.

dissertation project and/or the first published book. Dr. Wil Gafney's Womanist Midrash is in the process of being published. Dr. Gafney served as an editor of the *Africana Bible* and has presented a number of papers on womanist biblical interpretation or midrash. Her first book, however, was an exhaustive treatment of women prophets in the Hebrew Bible, *Daughters of Miriam*.[21] Since publishing my first book based on my dissertation, *The Literary Construction of the Other in the Acts of the Apostles: Charismatics, the Jews, and Women*,[22] I struggled to find my voice as a womanist biblical scholar, to do the work my soul has for me and for my communities. The soul-searching journey resulted in the publication of three womanist essays, all of which are reprinted in this volume, and two new original essays. Other womanist biblical scholars are also working on or are completing womanist biblical interpretation projects to be published in the very near future.

Some of those among the fourth and most recent generation of womanist biblical scholars are publishing womanist biblical hermeneutics monographs based on their dissertation projects. Fourth generation womanist biblical scholars include Drs. Lynne St. Clair Darden, Shanell Teresa Smith, Kimberly Dawn Russaw, Febbie Dickerson, Yolanda Norton, Vanessa Lovelace, and others of whom I may not be aware or whose names I might have inadvertently omitted. Drs. Darden and Smith are both publishing womanist readings of Revelation. All of the fourth generation scholars mentioned above wrote essays for this volume, except Dr. Shanell Teresa Smith, for who the timing of this book conflicted with that of her upcoming womanist reading of the book of Revelation. Some womanist biblical scholars, such as Drs. Nyasha Junior, Love Sechrest, Gay Byron, Valerie Bridgemann, Stephanie Buckhanon Crowder, Madeline McClenney-Sadler, and Cheryl Anderson could not participate in this reader because they were occupied with other womanist biblical scholarship, womanist activist projects, or other publishing commitments. May God continue to bless the fruit of their labors.

With *I Found God in Me* we hope to continue to "empower African American women as critical readers, as agents, and as shapers of discourse by uncovering the program and agenda of both biblical texts and dominant cultural readings. . . . The point here clearly is to decenter for marginalized readers the privileged status of dominant readings and the dominant community of readers."[23] Influenced by both black liberation theology and

21. Wilda C. Gafney, *Daughters of Miriam: Women Prophets in Ancient Israel* (Minneapolis: Fortress, 2008).

22. Mitzi J. Smith, *The Literary Construction of the Other in the Acts of the Apostles: Charismatics, the Jews, and Women* (Eugene, OR: Pickwick, 2011).

23. Weems, "Re-Reading for Liberation," 57.

feminist biblical criticism, womanist biblical interpretation is engaged in a political liberationist project aimed at dismantling oppressive structures and obliterating racism, sexism, classism, heterosexism, and other isms. Simultaneously, African American women and other women of color insist that neither feminism nor black theology can be held to represent the universal experience of black people or of women of color in general.[24] Unlike black men and white women, black women and other women of color, as black feminist Patricia Hill Collins has argued, experience sexism, racism, and classism as interlocking systems of oppression.[25] Womanist biblical scholars cannot analyze biblical texts, contexts, readers, or interpretations solely on the basis of gender or race. Womanist biblical hermeneutics prioritizes the communal and particular lived experiences, history, and artifacts of black women and other women of color as a point of departure, a focal point, and an overarching interpretative lens for critical analysis of the Bible and other sacred texts, contexts, cultures, readers, and readings.

Ntozake Shange wrote a poem for her brown and black students at California State College at Long Beach Upward Bound, students "with everything moving against them." Shange called that poem "somebody / anybody sing a black girl's song." And it continues with " bring her out / to know herself . . . / but sing her rhythms / carin / struggle / hard times / sing her song of life / she's been dead so long / closed in silence so long / she doesn't know the sound of her own voice / her infinite beauty . . . her signs . . . her possibilities, a righteous gospel . . . let her be born."[26] Womanists believe that we are the somebody, the anybody, who must "sing a black girl's song" because things are "moving against" us: male-center and other-centered texts, oppressive interpretations that justify the maiming and killing of our spirits and our bodies, androcentric narratives relegating us to the background and to silence, readings that marginalize us. We sing, write, and speak from the margins for the margins and for those who are outsiders within the periphery—the doubly marginalized, the black woman called to preach in the black church, the single black mother, the motherless black child, the pregnant unwed mother striving to find a home in the black church. We testify that the God in us is great, compassionate, courageous, audacious, loving, nonjudgmental, and empowering. It is our hope that this volume will assist our readers in finding and loving the God within and affirm the God that resides in others.

24. Ibid., 55.

25. Patricia Hill Collins, *Black Feminist Thought: Knowledge, Consciousness, and the Politics of Empowerment* (New York: Routledge, 1991) 34.

26. Shange, *For Colored Girls Who have Considered Suicide*, 2.

As Ntozake Shange transformed the disparate poems she created as solo voices to be performed by herself as a solo spoken-word artist into the play, the choreopoem, *For Colored Girls Who Have Considered Suicide when the Rainbow is Enuf*, she states that "the personal story of a woman became every woman, the solo voice becoming many. Each poem fell into its rightful place, a rainbow of colors, shapes, and timbres of voice, my solo instrument blossoming into a cosmic chamber ensemble." This reader is a collection of solo voices that speak to, about, and in some ways, for an ensemble of women of color who share the historical legacy of belonging to a once colonized people who still struggle under neo-colonialism, who strive to live under the oppressive umbrella of racism, sexism, heterosexism, classism, and other isms. Just like Shange's poem, this is a woman-centered book about colored girls, for colored girls, and other readers who care about the lives and voices of colored girls as human beings upon whose bodies/ souls and voices can be seen and heard the image and voice of God. It is about interpreting biblical texts in ways that are true to the shared and particular struggles, experiences, needs, desires of colored girls and in ways that are liberating, truth-telling, and prophetic. It is a volume that affirms and testifies to the presence of God in black women's lives and being. This volume is a declaration that God's image is not monochromatic nor is God's voice monotone. God is a colorful God who loves equally the many colors she creates. God speaks in tunes and tones that resonate with the oppressed and marginalized, particularly with the lived experiences of black women and other women of color.

Part One, "Alice Walker's *Womanist* and Womanist Interpretative Theory," of *I Found God in Me* begins with Alice Walker's definitions of womanist. The essays in Part One are reprints of significant and seminal essays on womanist interpretation and/or theory written by womanist scholars. New Testament scholar Dr. Clarice Martin's essay, "Womanist Interpretations of the New Testament: The Quest for Holistic and Inclusive Translation and Interpretation," addresses womanist concerns regarding translation and interpretation of biblical terminology, as well as the significance of class in the biblical narrative. In her essay "Re-Reading for Liberation: African American Women and the Bible," Old Testament scholar Dr. Renita Weems argues for the significance of stories; that "reading the Bible for liberation is grounded in the acknowledgement and respect for the otherness of those whose otherness is silenced and marginalized by those in power." In her essay "Womanist Interpretation and Preaching in the Black Church" ethicist Dr. Katie Geneva Cannon addresses the negative and derogatory portrayal of females in black preaching and offers a strategic "womanist critical evaluation process" for eliminating such representations. Womanist theologian

Dr. Kelly Brown Douglas's essay, "Marginalized People, Liberating Perspectives: A Womanist Approach to Biblical Interpretation," argues for biblical interpretation that considers the presence and impact of interlocking and interactive structures of oppression in society and in our churches and the need to read from the perspective of those most marginalized. Womanist theologian Dr. JoAnne Marie Terrell's essay, "Our Mothers' Gardens: Discrete Sources of Reflection on the Cross in Womanist Christology" contextualizes and conceptualizes a hermeneutics of sacrifice in a quest for a holistic spirituality. I contributed one new essay in this section entitled, "'This Little Light of Mine': The Womanist Biblical Scholar as Prophetess, Iconoclast, and Activist." Dr. Madipoane Masenya's essay, "An African Methodology for South African Biblical Sciences: Revisiting the *Bosadi* (Womanhood) Approach," is included to facilitate a point of dialogue with our sisters on the continent of Africa. Dr. Masenya, having evolved from employing feminist-liberationist and womanist interpretative approaches, now self-defines her hermeneutical approach as a *bosadi* (womanhood) methodology that foregrounds Africa and African-South African women's contexts in which the Bible is taken seriously (as a source of faith and transformation and as a human book) and is read through the lens of African-South African women's experiences that include apartheid, post-apartheid, racism, sexism, classism, HIV/AIDS, and land possession among other oppressions.

Part Two, "Reading the Bible as a Womanist Biblical Scholar" consists of womanist readings of biblical texts by womanist biblical scholars, PhDs and doctoral students, of the Old Testament/Hebrew Bible and the New Testament. The readings of Old Testament texts are weaved together with New Testament essays. Three of the essays are reprints and six are new original essays. I shall provide a synopsis of each essay in this section, including the reprints.

In chapter 8, "A Womanist Midrash of Zipporah," Dr. Wil Gafney interprets biblical and rabbinic literature about the story of Moshe (Moses) and Tzipporah (Zipporah) using a womanist lens that prioritizes the experience of black women. Gafney recovers Zipporah as an African woman whose character functions in a multiplicity of roles, including motherless daughter, clergy spouse, divorcee, shepherd, survivor, and matriarch. Zipporah, Gafney argues, "transcends and transforms stereotypes that are often applied to black women."

In chapter 9, "Fashioning Our Own Souls: A Womanist Reading of the Virgin-Whore Binary in Matthew and Revelation," Dr. Mitzi J. Smith reads the virgin-whore binary of difference found in Matthew's prologue and in the parable of the Ten Virgins as well as in Revelation, chapters 17–18 through the lens of African American women's history as indentured servants, slaves, and up to the present. Smith argues that black women have always been perceived and treated as Jezebels or as whores. The virgin-whore binary of difference functions for the benefit of men and to control women's bodies and sexuality. Historically, racism, sexism, classism, capitalism, and religious dogmatism have united to debase black women. Smith also discusses how violence is connected to the virgin-whore binary. Black women particularly should reject the imposition of this binary and choose to name their own experiences in ways that promote healthy self-esteem and affirm black women as created in the image of God.

In chapter 10, "A Womanist-Postcolonial Reading of the Samaritan Woman at the Well and Mary Magdalene at the Tomb," Dr. Lynne St. Clair Darden provides a womanist-postcolonial scripturalization of John's Gospel through the lens of the Samaritan Woman in chapter 4 and Mary at the Tomb in chapter 20. Darden suggests that the unfolding of these two stories highlight the imperial/patriarchal ambivalence that is evident throughout this text, a text that at first reading may seem to be presenting a radical, alternative world.

In chapter 11, "Minjung, the Black Masses, and the Global Imperative: A Womanist Reading of Luke's Soteriological Hermeneutical Circle," Dr. Mitzi J. Smith discusses Minjung theology as a theology that recognizes Jesus' concern for and ministry for/among the masses; she then discusses the historical and contemporary issue in the black community about the responsibility of successful African Americans to the masses. Smith argues that African Americans are not free until the masses are free and that the two are integrally linked. She then uses the relationship between successful individuals in the African American community and the masses as a lens for reading the relationships among the crowds or masses in Luke's Gospel, those who Jesus heals from the crowds, and Jesus.

In chapter 12, "Wisdom in the Garden: The Woman of Genesis 3 and Alice Walker's *Sophia*," Kimberly Dawn Russaw interrogates the idea of wisdom, identifies the markers of wise individuals in ancient Near Eastern and ancient Israelite literature, maps the markers of a wise individual onto the woman of Genesis 3, and finally bridges Wisdom Literature with womanism by considering how the character of Sofia Butler from Alice Walker's book *The Color Purple* meets the requirements for a wise individual. Russaw recovers the woman of Genesis 3 as a wise woman and a protowomanist that black women can draw wisdom from and with whom she compares Sophia's character in Alice Walker's *The Color Purple*.

In chapter 13, Dr. Mitzi J. Smith's essay, "'Knowing More than is Good for One': A Womanist Interrogation of the Matthean Great Commission," discusses knowledge production in African American communities,

particularly by African American mothers who must teach their children to
know more than their white counterparts in order to survive. Through this
epistemological lens Smith argues for reading Matthew's Jesus differently
than through the iconic lens of the so-called Great Commission and she
calls into question the very nomenclature and its use to subordinate social
justice to teaching.

In chapter 14, "Silenced Struggles for Survival: Finding Life in Death
in the Book of Ruth," Yolanda Norton contributes a womanist reading of
the book of Ruth through the lens of the trope of the "strong black woman."
Norton argues that the book of Ruth functions to affirm the normative
power structures within Israel as superior to non-Israelites, like the Moabite
daughter-in-law of Naomi, Ruth. Ruth as the perpetual outsider forsakes
her own culture, country, and biological family, assimilates, takes risks, and
sacrifices so that Naomi might survive and have an heir. In the book's reception history, white male norms have been, overtly and covertly, prescribed
to the disadvantage of black women. The story of Ruth, Norton argues, has
served for Christian black women as a mimetic paradigm of the woman
who risks her own health to serve as the care-taker and surrogate for others.

In chapter 15, "'Give Them What you Have': A Womanist Reading of
the Matthean Feeding Miracle (Matt. 14:13–21)" Dr. Mitzi J. Smith draws
upon the experiences of black women like Harriet Tubman who used the
few resources they had to positively impact the lives of others as a framework for reading the story of the feeding of the five thousand. Using Yung
Suk Kim's theory of human transformation she demonstrates how the disciples became aware of their status as no one before God, someone relative
to God, and finally someone for others. Transformation occurs when we
enter into loving relationships with our neighbors.

In chapter 16, "Acts 9:36–43: The Many Faces of Tabitha, A Womanist
Reading," Febbie C. Dickerson argues that too often womanist interpretation is essentialized foregrounding struggle and survival as black women's
history and experience and does not consider the particularity of black
women's lives as well. She also asserts that since womanist thought to date
has generally been done by womanist theologians and ethicists rather than
womanist biblical scholars, the use of historical critical methods together
with womanist hermeneutics has been almost nonexistent. Dickerson
reads the story of Tabitha/Dorcas using a womanist biblical hermeneutics
informed by attention to literary and cultural constructs. For Dickerson, it
is Tabitha, and not Peter, who functions like Jesus; she "sacrificed for others, died, and was raised." Dickerson rescues Tabitha from conventional,
stereotypical readings of her as the helpless poor widow whose presence
elevates Peter.

I am eternally grateful to all my womanist sisters who thought it not robbery to participate in this project, as well as the sisters who could not participate but who offered words of encouragement, who prayed for me and this project, and assisted me in any way they could. I am thankful for the assistance of my younger sister Lenora Smith and my former graduate assistant MarShondra Scott Lawrence. I dedicate *I Found God in Me* to my mother Flora Carson Smith (1929–2009) who constantly encouraged me, as an extremely shy teenager, to speak up and out, reciting to me 1 John 4:4: "Greater is he that is in you than he that is in the world." Flora Smith was a proto-womanist who believed always in God and the God in me, who prayed without ceasing, who expressed courage, audacity, and faith whenever her back was against the wall, who loved her children and the people, and who taught me through her example to strive to do the same.

Mitzi J. Smith

Part One

Alice Walker's *Womanist* and Womanist Interpretative Theory

Alice Walker's *Womanist* (1983)[1]

1. From *womanish*. (Opp. of "girlish," i.e., frivolous, irresponsible, not serious.) A black feminist or feminist of color. From the black folk expression of mothers to female children, "You acting womanish," i.e., like a woman. Usually referring to outrageous, audacious, courageous or *willful* behavior. Wanting to know more and in greater depth than is considered "good" for one. Interested in grown-up doings. Acting grown up. Being grown up. Interchangeable with another black folk expression "You trying to be grown." Responsible. In charge. *Serious.*

2. *Also*: A woman who loves other women, sexually and/or nonsexually. Appreciates and prefers women's culture, women's emotional flexibility (values tears as natural counterbalance to laughter) and women's strength. Sometimes loves individual men, sexually and/or nonsexually. Committed to survival and wholeness of entire people, male *and* female. Not a separatist, except periodically, for health. Traditionally universalist, as in: "Mama, why are we brown, pink, and yellow, and our cousins are white, beige, and black?" Ans.: "Well, you know the colored race is just like a flower garden, with every color flower represented." Traditionally capable, as in: "Mama, I'm walking to Canada and I'm taking you and a bunch of other slaves with me." Reply: "It wouldn't be the first time."

3. Loves music. Loves dance, Loves the moon. Loves the Spirit. Loves love and food and roundness. Loves struggle. Loves the Folk. Loves herself. *Regardless.*

4. Womanist is to feminist as purple to lavender.

1. "Womanist" in *In Search of Our Mothers' Gardens: Womanist Prose* by Alice Walker (San Diego: Harcourt Brace, 1983).

CHAPTER ONE

Womanist Interpretations of the New Testament

The Quest for Holistic and Inclusive Translation and Interpretation[1]

CLARICE J. MARTIN

The subject of "womanist biblical interpretation" has come to the fore in recent years in conjunction with the growing body of literature on "womanist theology" in general. The term "womanist" was coined by Alice Walker in her book *In Search of Our Mothers' Gardens*. Describing the courageous, audacious, and "in charge" behavior of the black woman, the term "womanist" affirms black women's connection with both feminism and with the history, culture, and religion of the African American community. Womanist literature represents the ongoing academic work of womanist scholars in a variety of disciplines, including theology, ethics, sociology, and biblical studies.[2]

1. Clarice J. Martin, "Womanist Interpretations of the New Testament: The Quest for Holistic and Inclusive Translation and Interpretation," *Journal of Feminist Studies in Religion* 6:2 (1990) 41–61. This essay is reprinted with the permission of the author.

2. Alice Walker, *In Search of Our Mothers' Gardens: Womanist Prose* (New York: Harcourt Brace, 1983) xi. See the works of Katie G. Cannon, *Womanist Ethics* (Ithaca, NY: Scholars, 1988); Toinette M. Eugene, "Moral Values and Black Womanists," *Journal of Religious Thought* 49 (Winter–Spring 1988) 23–24; Jacquelyn Grant, "Womanist Theology: Black Women's Experience as a Source for Doing Theology, with Special Reference to Christology," *Journal of the Interdenominational Theological Center* 13:2 (Spring 1986) 195–212; Renita J. Weems, *Just a Sister Away: A Womanist Vision of Women's Relationship in the Bible* (San Diego: LuraMedia, 1988); Delores S. Williams, "Womanist Theology: Black Women's Voices," *Christianity and Crisis* 47 (March 1987) 66–70. For a fuller listing of womanist scholarship see the helpful essay by womanist

One discipline where womanist theological reflection is especially welcome is biblical studies. What concerns do womanist biblical interpreters bring to the translation and interpretation of the Bible? How does their interrogation of the text differ from that of their white feminist colleagues? These questions will be explored in this essay in preliminary fashion. Not meant to be an *ultimatum verbum* (the last word) for all womanist biblical scholars, but only *primum verbum* (first word) by one, it highlights some of the critical and methodological concerns and overarching interests of womanist biblical interpreters.

If, as theologian Delores Williams notes, womanist theologians bring black women's social, religious, and cultural experience into the discourse of theology, ethics, and religious studies,[3] they also bring black women's social, religious, and cultural experience and consciousness into the discourse of biblical studies. Thus, African American women's historical struggles against racial and gender oppression, as well as against the variegated experiences of classism, all comprise constitutive elements in their conceptual and interpretive horizon and hermeneutics; for experiences of oppression, like all human experience, affect the way in which women decode sacred and secular reality.[4]

In addition to importing gender, race, and class concerns to the task of biblical interpretation, womanist theologians have addressed the issue of linguistic sexism with increasing urgency.[5] Womanist biblical interpretation,

theologian Kelly D. Brown, "God Is as Christ Does: Toward a Womanist Theology," *Journal of Religious Thought* 46:1 (Summer–Fall 1989) 7–16.

3. Williams, "Womanist Theology," 67.

4. Theo Witvliet, *The Way of the Black Messiah: The Hermeneutical Challenge of Black Theology as a Theology of Liberation* (Oak Park, IL: Meyer Stone, 1985) 61.

5. While there is not a plethora of literature on the subject by black women, black female and male academics and clergy are adopting and promoting inclusive language usage. See Yvonne Delk, "A Call to Wholeness," in *The Word and Words Beyond Gender in Theological and Liturgical Language*, ed. William D. Watley (Princeton, NJ: Consultation on Church Union, 1983) 1–5; Angelique Walker-Smith, "Exclusive Language Reflects Inner Beliefs," *Christianity and Crisis* 45:7 (April 29, 1985) 164–65. For examples of inclusive language usage in sermons, see sermons by ethicist Katie G. Canon, "The Patience to Wait" and "On Remembering Who We Are," in *Those Preachin' Women: Sermons by Black Women Preachers*, ed. Ella Pearson Mitchell (Valley Forge, PA: Judson, 1986) 43–50, 84–90. Sociologist Cheryl Townsend Gilkes has documented the use of female imagery for God in African American homiletical discourse in "Some Mother's Son, Some Father's Daughter: Gender and the Biblical Language in Afro-Christian Worship Tradition," in *Shaping New Visions: Gender and Values in American Culture*, ed. Clarissa W. Atkinson, Constance H. Buchanan, and Margaret Miles (Ann Arbor, MI: UMI Research Press, 1987) 86. I have explored some dimensions of the issue in "Inclusive Language and the Brief Statement of Faith: Widening the Margins of Our Common Confession," in *To Confess the Faith Today*, ed. Jack L. Stotts and Jane

then, has a "quadruocentric" interest ("four-fold," from the Latin *quadru*, meaning "four") where gender, race, class, and language issues are all at the forefront of translation (the science of expressing the original meaning as accurately as possible) and interpretation (the process of bringing together the ancient canonical texts with new, changing situations) concerns,[6] and not just a threefold focus where gender, class, and language concerns predominate almost exclusively, as is often the case in white feminist biblical interpretation and translation.

In this essay I will examine the ways in which womanist concerns about the translation and interpretation of biblical terminology are focused. I will also examine the ways in which presuppositions about the significance of class in biblical narrative have been operative in contemporary biblical interpretation.

Doulos, Doule: Servant or Slave?

The tremendous proliferation of literature on inclusive language in ecclesial and academic discourse in recent decades[7] has reawakened our interest in the complexities of the translation of biblical terminology. Assessing the appropriate meaning of a particular Hebrew or Greek term, and rendering it with some fidelity in English, remains a thorny problem for interpreters. For example, the King James Version of the Bible describes Jesus and his disciples as walking "through the corn" in Matt 12:1. As they walked, they began to "pluck the ears of corn to eat." The twentieth-century student of the Bible may be tempted to imagine the itinerate group "strolling through a cornfield, stripping off a ripening cob, pulling back the husk and silk, to

---

Dempsey Douglas (Louisville: Westminster John Knox, 1990) 107–29; in my work, *Communicating a Liberating Word: Inclusive Language and African American Religious Discourse* (Louisville: Westminster John Knox, 1991) I explore inclusive-language usage in African American social and religious history.

6. These abbreviated definitions of the terms "translation" and "interpretation" are based on discussions by Letty M. Russell and Sharon H. Ringe. See Russell's introduction in *The Liberating Word: A Guide to Nonsexist Interpretation of the Bible* (Philadelphia: Westminster, 1976) 20; and Ringe, "Bible Authority and Interpretation," In *The Liberating Word*, 29.

7. These are not the only arenas where inclusive language concerns have begun to alter the way we conceptualize the use of gendered language. Casey Miller and Kate Swift (*The Handbook of Non-Sexist Writing for Writers, Editors and Speakers*, 2d ed. [New York: Harper & Row, 1988]) note that when the first edition of their work appeared in 1980, efforts to eliminate linguistic sexism had already gained support from a wide assortment of national and local organizations (1–2).

nibble on the tender kernels."[8] But in fact, the Greek term for "corn," *stachys*, should probably be rendered "grain," as it is in the Revised Standard Version of the Bible (the RSV uses the phrases "grainfields" and "heads of grain" respectively in Matt 12:1). "Grain" in biblical usage is a generic term used to indicate the seed of cultivated cereal grasses such as wheat, barley, millet, and sorghum (these grains were ground into flour as a major component of bread products—compare Deut 33:28 in the KJV and the RSV).[9]

One of the more debated translation issues is the translation of the Greek term *anthropos*. Translators have regularly rendered *anthropos* as "man," concealing women or rendering them invisible under a blanket of male linguistic hegemony. Like blacks who must constantly "imagine" themselves as represented in so-called generic representation of Americans by all white groupings (whether on television or in other media) women must constantly "imagine" themselves as represented in so-called generic representations of all humanity in biblical traditions that are punctured by the almost exclusive usage of male gendered pronouns. The real point, of course, is that *anthropos* does not always mean "man" or "men." As had been amply demonstrated (and as some common sense would dictate) *anthropos* does have a more generic meaning. It can mean "human, person, people, or humanity."[10] The Oxford Annotated RSV does grant this sense in the translation of Rom 2:9: "There will be tribulation and distress for every human who does evil." According to the *Greek-English Lexicon of the New Testament*, *anthropos* also has a generic meaning in Matt 5:13, but the RSV translates the term as "man" when it records the familiar words:

> You are salt of the earth; but if the salt has lost its taste, how shall
> its saltiness be restored? It is no longer good for anything except
> to be thrown out and trodden under foot by *men*. (Italics mine.)

Surely the more generic usage of *anthropos* is indicated and appropriate in the Oxford Annotated Bible for such texts as the Matt 5:13 pericope, as well as for such texts as Titus 2: "the grace of God has appeared for the

8. Nancy A. Hardesty, *Inclusive Language in the Church* (Atlanta: John Knox Press, 1987) 75.

9. See "Stachys," William F. Arndt and F. Wilbur Gingrich, *A Greek-English Lexicon of the New Testament and Other Early Christian Literature* (Chicago: University of Chicago Press, 1973) 773; Robert M. Good, "Corn," in *Harper's Dictionary of the Bible* (New York: Harper & Row, 1985) 189; Robert A. Coughenour, "Grain," in *Harper's Dictionary of the Bible*, 358.

10. Arndt and Gingrich, *A Greek-English Lexicon*, 67–68. All Scripture citations in this essay are taken from the *New Oxford Annotated Bible with the Apocrypha: Expanded Edition Revised Standard Version*, ed. Herbert G. May and Bruce M. Metzger (New York: Oxford University Press, 1977) unless otherwise indicated.

salvation of all *men*"; the text in 1 Tim 2:4, which says: "God desires all then to be saved"; and 1 Tim 4:10: "we have our hope set on the living God who is the Savior of all *men*, especially of those who believe." Nance Hardesty hits the mark when she says of the androcentric rendering of *anthropos* in these verses in the RVS, that the God described in those passages "does not offer much hope for me as a woman!"[11] The problem with these texts is that the translation of *anthropos* in these examples does not render in English what the Greek texts intended.

The task of faithfully rendering biblical terminology in English and assessing ideological import and sociopolitical impact on communities of women and men is a major concern to womanist biblical interpreters. This is particularly the case with the Greek term *doulos*, usually translated "slave." As I have pursued my own research and study of the New Testament over the years, I have been asked frequently if *doulos* should be rendered "slave" or "servant" in modern translations of the Bible. The post-sixties era, with the rise of liberation theologies and the recognition of how one's social location affects the interpretive task, has sharpened the *question* of how people of color and women "hear" certain texts, and with this comes some concern about whether the term "slave" is in some sense offensive to the African American reader, given our "involuntary" participation in our nation's legacy of slavery. Does it recall an image that is painfully reminiscent of that legacy? Is the use of the term *infradignitatem* (beneath one's dignity)? Would it not be better, people ask, to translate *doulos* regularly as the more euphemistic "servant"? This writer personally responds with a resounding No! for at least two reasons.

First, *doulos* in Greco-Roman parlance *is* generally translated as "slave." Arndt and Gingrich note that the use of "servant" for "slave" is largely confined to biblical translation and early American times.[12] *Doulos* and its cognates describe the "status of a slave" or "an attitude corresponding to a slave."[13] For slaves, the rendering of service is not a matter of choice—they must perform whether they like it or not because they are subject to an alien will, the will of the owner. Human autonomy is set aside and an alien will takes complete precedence over one's own.[14] The word "servant" usually suggests an element of submission. The *American Dictionary* has a threefold definition of a servant:

11. Hardesty, *Inclusive Language in the Church*, 80.

12. Arndt and Gingrich, *A Greek-English Lexicon*, 20.

13. Karl Heinrich Rengstorf, "doulos, douleuo, douleia, douloo, kaiadouloo, doula-gogeo, ophthomodoulia," in *Theological Dictionary of the New Testament*, ed. Gerhard Kittel, trans. Geoffrey W. Bromiley, vol. 2 (Grand Rapids: Eerdmans, 1974) 261.

14. Ibid.

1. Someone privately employed to perform domestic services. 2. Someone publicly employed to perform services, as for a government. 3. Someone expressing submission, recognizance, or debt to another: your obedient servant.[15]

That the condition of the slave was usually not "voluntary" is clear from the definition of "slave" in the dictionary:

1. One bound in servitude to a person or household as an instrument of labor. 2. One who is submissive or subject to a specified person or influence. 3. One whose condition is likened to that of slavery. 4. A machine or component that is controlled by another machine or component.[16]

A widescale translation of *doulos* as "servant" would promote an unrealistic and naively "euphemistic" understanding of slavery. First of all, "servant" is a euphemism. In their book, *Kind Words: A Thesaurus of Euphemism*, Judith S. Neaman and Carole G. Silver note that the word "euphemism" comes from the Greek *eu*, "good" and *pheme*, "speech" or "saying," and thus means literally "to speak with good words or in a pleasant manner." Thus, "euphemizing is generally defined as substituting an inoffensive or pleasant term for a more explicit, offensive one, thereby veneering the truth by using kind words."[17] According to Joseph M. Williams, euphemisms are formed when unpleasant elements of response attach themselves strongly to particular words. One then substitutes another word free of negative associations.[18] Euphemisms can be formed by borrowing words from other languages. For example, we may use the word *halitosis* for "bad breath." Euphemisms may also be formed by a process called "widening," where a more abstract word is substituted for a term that has become too painful or vivid—"we move up the ladder of abstraction." An example of "widening" is seen in the renaming of "cancer" as a "growth."[19]

In actuality, "servant" is a euphemism for "slave," a point confirmed by Hugh Rawson in his book, *A Dictionary of Euphemisms and Other Doubletalk*.[20] According to Rawson, "servant" was a euphemism in colonial

15. *The American Heritage Dictionary of the English Language*, s.v. "servant."

16. *American Heritage Dictionary*, s.v. "slave."

17. Judith S. Neaman and Carole G. Silver, *Kind Words: A Thesaurus Of Euphemisms* (New York: Facts on File, 1983) 1.

18. Joseph M. Williams, *Origins of the English Language* (New York: Free Press, 1957) 202–3.

19. Neaman and Silver, *Kinds Words*.

20. Hugh Rawson, *A Dictionary of Euphemisms and Other Doubletalk Being a Compilation of Linguistic Fig Leaves and Verbal Flourishes for Artful Users of the English*

America that went out of fashion in the early nineteenth century because white servants, who weren't actual slaves, refused to accept the same label as black "servants," who were in fact slaves. ("Servant" had been widely used for black slaves for some time, even though they were "slaves" and the terms "servant" and "black" had become fairly synonymous.) In an essay published in *The History Book Club News* in 1775, it was noted that William Penn (1644–1718) was a slaveholder, "but he used the less pejorative term 'servant' instead of slave."[21] Euphemistic translations of *doulos* should be eschewed, then, because they do not always convey fully the etymological sense of the term. In the final analysis, every single occurrence of *doulos* in the New Testament must be examined within its particular literary and scoiohistorical context to determine the author's intention in the use of the term, including any nuance which should be assigned to it.

A second and related problem with "servant" is that it minimizes the full psychological weight of the institution of slavery itself. I have always been troubled by exegetical arguments and interpretations of slave existence in the Common Era that suggest ancient slavery was only a sporadically stressful interruption in an otherwise "quiet," normal existence.

In his book *The Special Context of the New Testament,* Derek Tidball says the following about Paul's posture toward slavery:

> In the first place, the institution of slavery was such an integral part of the social fabric in Paul's day that it would have been difficult for Paul or others to conceive of social organization without it. . . . By the time of Paul it was not a severe and cruel institution. Of course there were exceptions . . . but the experience of most slaves was different. *In Carcopina's memorable phrase, "with few exceptions slavery in Rome was neither eternal, nor, while it lasted, intolerable."* . . . There was no widespread discontent about slavery. So, to the early church the question of the abolition of slavery was probably insignificant. . . . What Paul offers to Christian slaves is a totally new appreciation of their value as persons. They are no longer "things" but people who have a standing and status before God (1 Cor. 7:20). In Christ the slave is a free man. . . . If only, Paul argues, they grasp this greater fact, slavery becomes inconsequential. *A slave can remain happily a slave and still serve the Lord in spite of his social limitations.*[22] (Italics mine)

Language (New York: Crown, 1981) 13, 16.

21. Ibid., 251.

22. Derek Tidball, *The Social Context of the New Testament: A Sociological Analysis* (Grand Rapids: Baker, 1984) 114–16.

In order to adequately address Tidball's idyllic notion of the "happy slave" in the first century of the Common Era it is necessary and appropriate to document the fact that the institution of slavery was not, in fact, as innocuous as he wants to portray it. Such a task is easily undertaken, and there is no dearth of literature on the subject.[23] While a full-scale discussion of Greco-Roman slavery is not possible here, I would make a few brief observations about Greco-Roman slavery pertinent to the present discussion.

First, that slavery was an integral part of the social fabric of Paul's day is not in dispute, but the thesis that it was not a "severe and cruel institution" has been challenged in recent years. In *Slaves and Masters in the Roman Empire*, K. R. Bradley argues that while harmonious relationships may have existed between masters and slaves, one must be cautious in concluding that such intimacy was necessarily characteristic of the master-slave relationship. While "simple, constant animosity between slave and slave master is too naïve a concept to have had universal applicability or meaning," the less human side of Roman slavery should not be romanticized:

> But although the harmonious relations attested between some slaves and their masters should not be lost sight of, they were not in all likelihood characteristic of the Roman slave system as a whole. . . . The essential brutality of the slave experience in the Roman world and especially the kind of harsh pressures to which slaves were constantly exposed as a normal part of their everyday lives . . . must be understood. . . . It is vital to understand something of the less elevated, less humane side of Roman social relations, of which the depressed conditions under which most slaves lived provide abundant illustration.[24]

Roman slave owners may have treated their slaves generously, but generosity alone did not, in Bradley's words, "secure the elite ideal of servile *fides* and *obsequium* that is to guarantee social stability. . . . Generosity had to be tempered with either force or the threat of force in order for control to be maintained, and a climate of fear over those of subordinate social position had to be created. . . . 'Fear in the slaves produced greater loyalty,' so it was said." Slaves were subjected to a number of indignities: capricious sexual abuse (slaves could be used as or sold for prostitutes, and they could be

23. H. Bellen, *Studien zur Slavenflucht im romischen Kaiserreich* (Wiesbaden: Steiner, 1971); M. I. Finley, *Ancient Slavery and Modern Theology* (New York: Penguin, 1983); Orlando Patterson, *Slavery and Social Death* (Cambridge: Harvard University Press, 1982); Alan Watson, *Roman Slave Law* (Baltimore: Johns Hopkins University Press, 1987).

24. K. R. Bradley, *Slaves and Masters in the Roman Empire: A Study in Social Control* (New York: Oxford University Press, 1987) 13–14.

sexually exploited for as long as the master wished); flogging was a "wide-spread" punishment for which little justification was required; agricultural and mining slaves, domestic slaves, and children were all subject to the same violence: "servile distinctions of status, function, age or sex gave no protection against arbitrary punishment."[25]

Second, even if some slaves in Greco-Roman society were treated with less severity than others, and could, indeed, become freedmen or freedwomen, psychosocial aspects of the institution itself were less than salutary. In his book *Slavery and Social Death,* Orlando Patterson analyzes the structure and dynamics of slavery based on a study of tribal, ancient, premodern, and modern slavery in sixty-six societies (including Greece, Rome, medieval Europe, China, Korea, the Islamic kingdoms, Africa, the Caribbean islands, and the American South).[26] He describes three constituent elements of slavery that typify master-slave relationships in all of these societies. Patterson argues that in anatomies of power in human relationships of inequality or domination, slavery is distinctive as a relation of domination in three ways.

1. Slavery is unusual in the extremity of power involved. That the master exercised total domination over the slave was normative, and a constituent feature of the relationship was the use of some forms of coercion. Force, violence, and might both maintained and perpetuated slavery. When slaves were manumitted or died, it became necessary to "repeat the original, violent act of transforming the free man into slave. . . . Whipping was not only a method of punishment. It was a conscious device to impress upon the slaves that they were slaves; it was a crucial form of social control particularly if we remember that it was very difficult for slaves to run away successfully."[27]

2. The slave relation is characterized by what Patterson calls the slave's "natal alienation." The slave, however recruited, is a socially dead person. "Alienated from all 'rights' or claims of birth, he ceased to belong in his own right to any legitimate social order. All slaves experienced, at the very least, secular excommunication."[28]

Slaves were "genealogical isolates." They had a past, but they were not allowed to freely integrate the experience of their ancestors into their lives, to inform their understanding of social reality with the inherited meanings of their natural forbears, or to anchor the living present in any conscious community memory. That they reached back for the past, as they reached

25. Ibid., 116–19, 123.

26. Orlando Patterson, *Slavery and Social Death: A Comparative Study* (Cambridge: Harvard University Press, 1982).

27. Ibid., 2–3.

28. Ibid., 5.

out for the related living, there can be no doubt. Unlike other persons, doing so meant struggling with and penetrating the iron curtain of the master, his community, his laws, his policemen or patrollers, and his heritage.[29]

The slave may have necessarily reached out to the "related living," but even the slave's own community and social relations were not usually recognized as legitimate and binding (marriages, removal of children, etc.).[30]

3. Slaves were persons who had been dishonored in a general way—their status held no honor; indignity, indebtedness, and the absence of all independent social existence reinforced the sense of dishonor. The slave was without power except through another; she or he had become "imprintable" and "disposable," the "ultimate human tool."[31]

But after admitting that slavery in Greco-Roman antiquity was more often attended by physical brutality, sexual exploitation, and emotional dehumanization than some care to think, the next question is: What are the implications of these data for our understanding of the New Testament (particularly references to slaves in such texts as Paul's letter to Philemon and allusions to slaves in the sayings of Jesus and in the *Haustafeln* [household codes])? I would argue that it is only as we move beyond euphemistic understandings of slavery in the lives of women and men in the Common Era that we can grasp some of the power of the biblical traditions that allude to slaves.

If Patterson is correct in his analysis of these three constitutive elements of slavery, then it is interesting to reread such passages as the christological hymn in Phil 2:7 and note the force of the comparison being made with the *doulos*:

> Have this in mind for yourselves which was also in Christ Jesus, who though he was in the form of God, did not count equality with God a thing to be grasp, but emptied himself, taking the form of a *doulou,* being born in the likeness of man.

The *morphen doulon* acquires its significance from the contrast with *morphe theou*, and it denotes Jesus' entry into humanity. But it is a particular "class" of humanity that sharpens the comparison here. The power and glory with which Jesus was invested is compared to that of one who was utterly powerless, for "there is no term which stands in greater contrast to *kyrios* or *theos* than *doulos*."[32]

29. Ibid.
30. Ibid., 6.
31. Ibid., 7.
32. Rengstorf, "doulos, douleuo, douleia," 278.

It is also interesting to note that the "slave" becomes a paradigm for discipleship elsewhere. Jesus himself washes the feet of the disciples—a task that was duty (John 13:1ff.).[33] Christians are often called the *douloi* of God and Christ (James 1:1; Titus 1:1; Col 4:12). The significance of the *doulos* symbol of powerlessness, bondage, and limitation on the one hand, and as paradigm for discipleship on the other, should not be trivialized.

The importance of the comparison of Jesus with the *doulos* in Phil 2:7 has also been noted by womanist theologian Shelia Briggs. Observing correctly that Phil 2:7b is neither *about* slavery, nor does it attribute cosmic or soteriological significance to the institution of slavery through its description of Christ taking on the condition of the slave, she avers, nonetheless, that the metaphor is significant. The significance of portraying Christ as a slave derives both from a loss of status and also from the degradation of being a slave.

> This sense of degradation if heightened by the assertion that it is a divine being who has become a slave, that the two opposites in the realm of being and worth have met in one person and one fate. . . . The Philippians hymn conveys the extremity of the self-abasement of Christ by placing it in the metaphor of the enslavement of God. Christ as divine was absolutely too worthy to be enslaved.[34]

Christ does not take on the so-called moral inferiority of the slave, nor does Phil 2:7b suggest Christ has a "morally defective" nature; rather, "Christ's obedience in his earthly existence makes him the anthropological model of the 'slaves of righteousness' (Rom 6:16–18) who are characterized through their obedience to God."[35]

A realistic understanding of the complexities of the conceptual universe of slavery in Greco-Roman antiquity, then, is of central importance in assessing the propriety of adopting a more euphemistic translation of *doulos* in biblical translation. An etymologically faithful reading of *doulos* is preferred to the more euphemistic reading, even if the motive for the euphemistic reading is purportedly conciliatory.

33. Ibid., 277.

34. Sheila Briggs, "Can an Enslaved God Liberate? Hermeneutical Reflections on Philippians 2:6–11," *Semeia* 47 (1989) 143.

35. Ibid., 148.

Amplifying Marginalized Voices

A survey of the aims and methodologies of feminist translation and interpretation in the last decade reveals their plurality and complexity. And yet, among the many overarching themes there is, as Elisabeth Schüsser Fiorenza has said, a commitment to a "search for the lost traditions and visions of liberation among its inheritance of androcentric texts and their interpretations."[36] To this end, a feminist critique and hermeneutic must engage in a multipronged investigative analysis:

> In order to unearth a "feminist coin" from the biblical tradition
> it [feminist critical interpretation] critically analyzes contemporary scholarly and popular interpretations, the tendencies of the
> biblical writers and traditioning processes themselves, and the
> theoretical models underlying contemporary biblical-historical
> and theological interpretations.[37]

Such critical analysis will help us achieve what Jane Schaberg considers a constitutive dimension of feminist translation: "Feminist translation . . . must amplify the whisper of women that can be heard in certain places in or under the biblical text, that 'steady undercurrent in the oral tradition' of anonymous voices."[38]

Womanist biblical interpreters share with their white feminist colleagues a concern for amplifying the voices of women in biblical narrative. A recent study of women's relationships in the Bible by womanist biblical scholar Renita Weems achieves precisely this aim.[39] But for the womanist biblical interpreter, fervid, if painstaking, searches for women's voices must proceed not only with reference to women in biblical narratives, but also with a concomitant concern for all of those who by virtue of *race, class,* or other *anthropological referents,* have been historically marginalized by the biblical traditions and/or writers themselves, and by interpreters of those traditions. *Not all of the suppressed voices and androcentric texts can be intoned in a feminist key.*

Definitions of "patriarchy" in white feminist literature usually emphasize the transactions of power between men and women. In her helpful discussion of strategies for "depatriarchalizing" biblical texts, Phyllis Trible's

36. Elisabeth Schüssler Florenza, *Bread Not Stone: The Challenge of Feminist Biblical Interpretation* (Boston: Beacon, 1984) 16.

37. Ibid.

38. Schaberg made this remark at the SBL section on Women in the Biblical World. The phrase "steady undercurrent in the oral tradition" is quoted from Gerda Lerner, *The Creation of Patriarchy* (New York: Oxford University Press, 1986) 226.

39. See Weems, *Just a Sister Away.*

discussion of patriarchy is concerned chiefly with that aspect of patriarchal domination centered on male-female relationships.[40] Mary Daly alludes to patriarchal institutions as institutions that "serve the interests of men at the expense of women."[41] Rosemary Reuther's analysis of patriarchy in *Women-Church: Theology and Practice of Feminist Liturgical Communities* explores male control and restrictions of women in the Hebrew Bible and the New Testament.[42] In secular feminist discourse, this preeminent focus on women's experience of domination under patriarchy is retained. Adrienne Rich conveys this sense in her discussion of patriarchy, where she describes it as

> the power of the fathers: a familiar-social, ideological, political system in which men—by force, direct pressure, or through ritual, tradition, law and language, customs, etiquette, education, and division of labor, determine what part women shall or shall not play, and in which the female is everywhere subsumed under the male.[43]

The critical exploration of predicaments posed by patriarchy in all human societies, ancient and modern, vis-à-vis *women*, is essential in any responsible feminist critique. But in fact, patriarchal domination did not—and does not—represent male domination of the female and the "feminine" only. Patriarchal oppression and degradation includes and transcends the category of gender. While many white, feminist biblical interpreters would affirm this fact, their critiques of patriarchy are concerned preeminently with the oppression and marginalization of women.

In the patriarchal hierarchies of biblical antiquity, the dominant male-master figure was supreme in rank, with wife, children, and slaves as subordinates.[44] Elisabeth Schüssler Fiorenza's definition of patriarchy incorporates all of these elements succinctly. "While androcentrism characterized a mindset, patriarchy represents a socio-cultural system in which a *few men have power over other men, women, children, slaves, and colonized people*"[45] (italics mine).

40. Phyllis Trible, "Depatriarchalizing in Biblical Interpretation," *Journal of the American Academy of Religion* 41 (1973) 30–48.

41. Mary Daly, *Beyond God the Father: Toward a Philosophy of Women's Liberation* (Boston: Beacon, 1985) 3. Cf. 13, 72, 162–63.

42. Rosemary Ruether, *Women-Church: Theology and Practice of Feminist Liturgical Communities* (New York: Harper & Row, 1985) 41–56.

43 Adrienne Rich, *Woman Born: Motherhood as Experience and Institution* (New York: Norton, 1976) 40.

44. William R. Herzog II, "The Household Duties' Passages," *Foundation* 24:3 (1981) 204–15.

45. Elisabeth Schüssler Fiorenza, *In Memory of Her: A Feminist Theological*

For the womanist theologian and biblical interpreter whose experience of oppression include the intrinsically linked aspects of gender, race, and class, critical analyses of patriarchal assumptions and paradigms in both the ancient and modern worlds must include a focus on *all* historically marginalized persons—women and men—who have been victimized by patriarchal dominance.[46] Womanist ethicist Toinette Eugene has noted that for the womanist and other non-white interpreters, it is not the issue of sexism alone that informs a critical womanist hermeneutics.[47] Thus, all ideologies of dominance and subordination in the biblical writers, the traditioning processes, and in the theoretical models underlying contemporary biblical historical and theological interpreters are *at once* invoked as constitutive of any womanist liberation hermeneutic.

Patriarchal oppression is not simply identical with androcentrism or sexism, and thus unconnected to other oppressive ideologies. Patriarchy defines not just women, but also subjugated peoples and races as "the others" to be dominated.[48]

Womanist concerns about translation and interpretation of the Bible necessarily include, then, a concomitant concern about the need to amplify the voices of *all* persons who are marginalized in the text. A more "holistic and inclusive" biblical translation requires such an emphasis.[49] A liberating anthropology is able to affirm that in Christ there is neither male nor female, but also that, "at the same time in Christ there is slave nor free, Jew nor Greek." Otherwise, as Justo Gonzalez notes, "The male will be quite con-

Reconstruction of Christian Origins (New York: Crossroad, 1985) 29.

46. Delores Williams is correct in her assessment, however, that a redefinition of patriarchy must be advanced by African American women. Patriarchy "loses its identity" for black women, because white women join with white men in oppressing black women. Williams observes that "patriarchy . . . is no longer just the power of fathers, or men, to oppress women. It is also the power of a certain group of females to oppress other groups of females. This inclusion of a group of women as oppressors—an assessment that speaks the truth of the Afro-American woman's history in North America—renders the feminist patriarchal critique of society less valid as a tool for assessing black women's oppression resulting from their relation to white-controlled American institutions. Therefore, one cannot claim that patriarchy, as it is understood by feminists, is the major source of all women's oppression." See Williams, "The Color of Feminism: Or Speaking the Black Woman's Tongue," *Journal of Religious Thought* 43:1 (Spring–Summer 1986) 48.

47. Toinette M. Eugene, "A Hermeneutical Challenge for Womanists: The Interrelation Between the Text and Our Experience," in *Perspectives on Feminist Hermeneutics,* ed. Gayle Gerber Koontz and Williard Swartley, Occasional Papers 10 (Elkhart, IN: Institute of Mennonite Studies, 1987) 21ff.

48. Ibid., 24.

49. Russell, *The Liberating Word,* 19.

tent with concentration on the fact that there is neither slave nor free; the free—and particularly the master—will piously agree that there is neither Jew nor Greek; and the Jew—the one who has the ethnic advantage—will gladly agree that there is neither slave nor free."[50]

There are traditions about men in the biblical narrative who have suffered not sexist marginality but classist or racist marginality in the traditioning processes and in the history of the interpretation of those traditions.[51] Because of the limits of this paper, I will examine only one instance of an individual in the Bible who, by virtue of his class, has suffered class bias in the history of biblical interpretation: Onesimus.[52]

I have always read with interest some biblical commentators' disparagement of Onesimus as the "n'er do well slave." This supposition is based on one interpretation of verse 18 in Paul's letter to Philemon, "if he has wronged you at all, or owes you anything, charge that to my account."

At least as early as the nineteenth century, commentators concluded that Onesimus must have been a "rascal" and a "thief." Two illustrations of this sentiment are represented in commentaries on Philemon.

J. B. Lightfoot, writing in 1875, observes the following of Onesimus:

> He had done what a chattel or an implement might be expected
> to do, if imbued with life and intelligence. . . . He had declined
> to entertain any responsibilities. There was absolutely nothing
> to recommend him . . . *he had confirmed the popular estate of his*
> *class and nation by his own conduct.*[53] (Italics mine.)

Similarly, G. B. Caird, writing in the mid-1970s, also assumes some culpability on the part of Onesimus, saying that

50. Justo L. Gonzalez, "Searching for a Liberating Anthropology," *Theology Today* 34 (1978) 387–88.

51. For a discussion of the racialist marginalization of a biblical character, consult my essay "A Chamberlain's Journey and the Challenge of Interpretation for Liberation," *Semeia* 47 (1989) 105–35. The essay explores the history of the interpretation of Acts 8:26–40, the story of the Ethiopian eunuch.

52. We cannot speak with certainty about Onesimus's race as that datum is not provided for the reader; however, since there is negligible evidence that slavery in Greco-Roman antiquity was ever based on race, we conclude that race is irrelevant here. For a discussion of the black presence in the Greco-Roman world and in biblical narrative, see Cain H. Felder, *Troubling Biblical Waters: Race, Class, and Family* (Maryknoll, NY: Orbis, 1989); and Frank M. Snowden, *Blacks in Antiquity: Ethiopia in the Greco-Roman Experience* (Cambridge: Harvard University Press, 1979).

53. J. B. Lightfoot, *St Paul's Epistles to the Colossians, and to Philemon: A Revised Text with Introduction and Notes* (New York: Macmillan, 1875) 377–78.

> he may have simply "packed up a thing or two" belonging to
> Philemon to provide for his journey. . . . *He certainly had not
> been a model servant,* but we have no reason to think that he had
> been a dishonest one before his flight.[54] (Italics mine.)

These commentaries (and others) assume that Onesimus was guilty of major and minor infractions because he was a slave. They assume that slaves are inherently morally bankrupt, though there could have been a number of reasons that Onesimus was "parted from" (v. 15) Philemon for a while. Philemon could have sent Onesimus to Paul for some particular reason, and Onesimus decided to remain with him; or, Onesimus could have run away from Philemon because of the conditions of slavery itself.[55] If the complexities of slavery in the American South should remind us of anything, it is that we should not assume *sine dubio* (without doubt) that a "Christian" slavemaster or slavemistress automatically treated slaves with "Christian" charity, kindness, and compassion.

For the womanist biblical interpreter, holistic and inclusive translations and interpretations of the Bible must avoid euphemistic renderings of biblical terminology; euphemistic translation risks "masking" socioeconomic or political verities that are of fundamental significance in assessing historical and symbolic meaning. The quest for holistic and inclusive translations and interpretations must also include strategies for "amplifying the whisper" of *all persons* who by virtue of race, class, or other anthropological referents, are assumed to be "morally bankrupt" or of negligible theological consequence within the narrative structure of biblical traditions. Alice Walker's words are instructive here. A womanist is "committed to survival and wholeness of entire people, male and female."[56]

Womanist Hermeneutics and the Function of the *Doulos* Paradigm in the History of Interpretation

As noted in the introductory paragraph of this essay, womanist biblical scholars bring *black women's* social, religious, and cultural experience and consciousness into the discourse of biblical studies, for all of these factors

---

54. G. B. Caird, *Paul's Letters From Prison: Ephesians, Philippians, Colossians, Philemon, in the Revised Standard Version, Introduction and Commentary* (Oxford: Oxford University Press, 1976) 214.

55. See Finley, *Ancient Slavery and Modern Ideology,* 95–97. Finley notes that awareness of the slave's unrestricted availability in sexual relation to their masters was commonplace in Greco-Roman literature from the time of Homer.

56. Walker, *In Search of Our Mothers' Gardens,* xi.

comprise constitutive elements in their conceptual and interpretive horizon and hermeneutics. Not surprisingly, then, womanist biblical interpreters are concerned with the critical assessment not only of the linguistic and socio-historical nuancing and interpretation of the *doulos* texts in the Common Era, but also with the critical assessment of the function of these texts in the history of the African American experience. The limits of this essay have made it necessary to focus primarily on some of the linguistic and sociohistorical issues at stake in the nuancing and interpretation of *doulos* in the New Testament. Questions remain, however, regarding the political implications of these data for post biblical—and particularly contemporary—interpreters.

How have the *doulos* texts functioned in the history of biblical interpretation in both pre and postmodern societies? Can, or should, biblical traditions that designate Christians as "slaves of God and Christ"[57] be appropriated complete as a whole? What concerns have been, and should be, registered in the face of attempts to appropriate and utilize the slave sayings in communities of faith?[58] While these questions deserve extensive comment and analysis, which is not possible here, the four following observations underscore the importance of assessing and critiquing the political impact of these texts in church and society in the Western world. These points should inform future formulations and investigations of the problem.

First, the question of how the *doulos* texts functioned to legitimate the enslavement of African Americans in North America remains an important subject of critical-historical study for biblical scholars and theologians, as well as historians, sociologists, and ethicists. That biblical traditions were so used is well attested. Describing slavery as "the most abominable institution ever to challenge Christian morality,"[59] sociologist and historian C. Eric Lincoln recounts the way in which the Bible was used to solicit the obedience of slaves to slavemasters and slavemistresses. The quotation of Scripture to

57. Rom 6:16–22; Eph 6:6. The recurrence of such terms as "slave," "freedman," and "redemption" in the New Testament all echo the sociopolitical reality and pervasiveness of slavery in the Common Era; the terms predominate in the New Testament Epistles. For a helpful introduction to the usage and function of these terms in the New Testament, see Francis Lyall, *Slaves, Citizens, Sons: Legal Metaphors in the New Testament* (Grand Rapids: Baker, 1984); and A. N. Sherwin-White, *Roman Society and Roman Law in the New Testament* (Oxford: Clarendon, 1963).

58. I am indebted to my womanist colleague Katie G. Cannon for sharing her reflections on this subject from the perspective of an ethicist-theologian.

59. C. Eric Lincoln, *Race, Religion, and the Continuing American Dilemma* (New York: Hill & Wang, 1984) 34. Lincoln is quoting Gilbert Osofsky, *The Burden of Race* (New York: Harper & Row, 1967) 40.

legitimate the slaves' subjugation—so it was believed—would provide the *coup de maître* (master stroke) in any apologetic for human bondage.

> Servants, be obedient to them that are your masters . . . with fear
> and trembling . . . as unto Christ. . . . Remember, God required
> this of you. . . . There is something so becoming and engaging
> in the modest, cheerful, good natured behavior that a little work
> done in that manner seems better done. . . . It also gains the
> goodwill and love of those you belong to. . . . Besides . . . your
> murmuring and grumbling is against God who hath placed you
> in their service.[60]

Not only was the Bible an important tool in proslavery ideology and rhetoric in general, H. Shelton Smith has noticed that in the eighteenth- and nineteenth-century South "the Southern churchmen's major argument in defense of human bondage was biblical in nature."[61] Both the Hebrew Bible and the New Testament served as the *summum jus* (the highest law) in the pronouncements of apologists for slavery. Authors of proslavery tracts appealed particularly to six New Testament texts to buttress their arguments: 1 Cor 7:20–21; Eph 6:5–9; Col 3:33, 4:1; 1 Tim 6:20–21; and Phlm 10–18. Stressing that since the biblical writers expected the dutiful obedience of slaves to masters, and that the slaveholders in the biblical texts were, after all, members of churches founded by Paul and other apostles, the defenders of human bondage contended that slaveholding was quite consistent with biblical teaching.[62] These six *doulos* texts were thus used in the service of a hermeneutics of dominion and sociopolitical hegemony for proslavery apologists.

An eclectic use of Scripture, a tendentious biblical literalism, and a wide range of hermeneutical distortions provided a steady stream of "grist" for the slave apologists' mill. In her helpful analysis of the ways in which Christian slave apologists employed hermeneutical distortions to keep racial slavery viable in the late eighteenth and early nineteenth centuries (to preserve economic benefits and sociopolitical power). Katie G. Cannon observes that the hermeneutical distortions were designed to achieve three aims:

> 1. Slave apologists argued that black people were either not
>   members of the human race, or that they were an "inferior

---

60. Ibid., 35. Echoes of Eph 5–6 and Col. are discernible in Lincoln's paraphrase.

61. H. Shelton Smith, *In His Images, But: Racism in Southern Religion, 1780–1791* (Durham, NC: Duke University Press, 1972) 129.

62. Ibid., 135.

species" of humanity at best. "The humanity of black people had to be denied, or the evil of the slave system would be evident."[63]

2. Sacred and secular history were reconstructed to perpetuate the view that Africans, "bestial savages" and "heathen," were by nature and providence destined for slavery.[64] Thus North American slavery became a divine and redemptive tool to expose Africans to Christianity.

Being enslaved in a Christian country was considered advantageous to Africans' physical, intellectual, and moral development. Slavery exposed Africans to Christianity which made them better servants of God and better servants of men.[65]

Most important for the present discussion, the law of God, with the law of the land, conferred upon Christian slave apologists the right to deprive black people of liberty,[66] with all of the attendant expressions of brutality and dehumanization which accompanied the sale and trafficking in the human lives of black women, men, and children. Christian theologians, biblical interpreters, and clergy regularly pressed the New Testament injunctions into service to legitimate slavery, even as others espoused juridical, economic, and political rationales.[67] Christian slave apologists in particular argued that since "neither Jesus of Nazareth, the apostles, nor the early church objected to the ownership of slaves," slavery was not a violation of God's law: "Physical slavery was spiritually meaningless under the all-embracing spiritualized hopes of salvation. This line of reasoning was of central importance in reconciling the masses of white Christians to the existing social order."[68]

The second observation concerns the nature of the hermeneutics employed by black women and men in the face of the overwhelming oppression that they (and their families) experienced during enslavement. Analysis of how the *doulos* text functioned to support a hermeneutics of domination and sociopolitical hegemony for proslavery apologists must be accompanied

63. Katie G. Cannon, "Slave Ideology and Biblical Interpretations," *Semeia* 47 (1989) 11.

64. Ibid., 13.

65. Ibid.

66. Ibid.

67. See, for example, the discussion of how legislative statutes and judicial decisions functioned to legitimate the subjugation of African Americans in A. Leon Higginbotham, Jr., *In The Matter of Color, Race and the American Legal Process: The Colonial Period* (New York: Oxford University Press, 1978).

68. Cannon, "Slave Ideology," 16.

by research that will further explore and identify the particular character of the black slaves' hermeneutics in the face of their oppression.

Black slaves were always distrustful of their masters' interpretations of the Bible, and preached the Christian gospel in terms of their own experience.[69] Understanding God to be a God of liberation who would make freedom a reality for all persons in Jesus Christ, they rejected a selectively enforced and enslaving biblical literalism[70] and brought a "hermeneutics of suspicion" to bear against prevailing arguments that the *doulos* verses should be a normative guide for their behavior. The slaves promulgated a gospel that averred that God is liberator of all oppressed peoples, and that God is opposed to all persons determined to maintain oppressive social systems. "Unlike any institutions in the larger white society, black churches have made a non-racist principle the center of their associational life."[71] Ongoing research on how a "hermeneutics of suspicion" was operative in the interpretation of the *doulos* texts will enlarge our understanding of the distinctive character, development, and contribution of African American biblical hermeneutics.

The third observation concerns the subject of the manumission of Christian slaves. Womanist exegetes (and others) must probe the layers of biblical traditions (and noncanonical writings) to determine whether anything in those traditions suggests that there were impulses at work in the earliest Christian communities that either ameliorated slavery and (or) advocated its abolition altogether. This amelioration and (or) abolition is suggested by such Hebrew Bible texts as the Exodus motif (Ex 1:1—16:36); and, by such New Testament texts as 1 Cor 7:23, "You were bought with a price; do not become slaves of human persons"; Rom 8:15, "For you did not receive the spirit of slavery to fall back into fear, but you received the spirit of sonship"; Phlm 15–17, where Paul says to Philemon regarding the slave Onesimus, "Perhaps this is why he was parted from you for a while, that you might have him back for ever, no longer as a slave but more than a slave, as a beloved brother, especially to me but how much more to you, *both in the flesh and in the Lord*" (italics mine).

There is evidence in both early Judaism and early Christianity that slaves may have been manumitted upon their conversion to the respective

69. Albert J. Raboteau, *Slave Religion: The "Invisible Institution" in the Antebellum South* (New York: Oxford University Press, 1978) 242–43.

70. James H. Cone, "The Sources and Norm of Black Theology," in *A Black Theology of Liberation* (New York: Lippincott, 1970) 50–81, esp. 66–67.

71. Peter J. Paris, "The Christian Way Through the Black Experience," *Word and World* 6:2 (1986) 129.

faiths.[72] The slave injunctions in the *Haustafeln* (household codes) that enjoin slaves and women to submission in the latter decades of the first century may suggest that the Christian vision of a more inclusive discipleship created tension and conflicts within the dominant cultural ethos of the patriarchal household.[73]

There is certainly evidence that black slaves discerned in the Bible those traditions that protect them in order to intensify their efforts to secure their freedom. Slavemasters often sought to prevent slaves from learning to read the Bible, for it was said that religious instruction made slaves "more intractable" and "rebellious," leading some to "entertain too high an opinion of themselves."[74] Slave narratives and spirituals betray the strong conviction and recurrent theme that Jesus Christ came to "lift the meek, the weak and the oppressed."[75]

The fourth and final observation concerns the need to engage in critical reflection about the biblical traditions and traditioning process. It is important to remember that simply creating taxonomic tables of biblical traditions that are either "proslavery" or "antislavery" will still not achieve all of the aims of a constructive womanist critical biblical hermeneutics. As noted above in the discussion of the need to amplify marginalized voices, womanist biblical interpreters also must engage in a multipronged investigative analysis and critique of the tendencies of the biblical writers and traditioning process. We should recognize, for example, that the biblical texts convey little information about the agency of slaves and manumission of slaves in the early Christian movement because these stories, like the stories of women, were considered to be either insignificant or a threat to the gradual patriarchalization of the Christian movement.[76] A womanist critical biblical hermeneutics, then, must not only critique the tendencies of the biblical writers and traditioning processes themselves, but must also analyze contemporary scholarly and popular interpretations and appropriations of those traditions, and the underlying theoretical models. But that is not the end of the story. A womanist biblical hermeneutic must clarify

---

72. Schüssler Fiorenza, *In Memory of Her*, 140–54; 214–36 (esp. 214–18).

73. Ibid., 251–79.

74. Raboteau, *Slave Religion*, 122–23.

75. Lewis V. Baldwin, "'Deliverance to the Captives': Images of Jesus Christ in the Minds of Afro-American Slaves," *Journal of Religious Studies* 12:2 (1986) 35; cf. James H. Cone, *The Spirituals and the Blues: An Interpretation* (New York: Seabury, 1972); Clifton Johnson, ed., *God Struck Me Dead: Religious Conversion Experiences and Autobiographies of Ex-Slaves* (Philadelphia: United Church, 1969); Felder, *Troubling Biblical Waters*, 53–117.

76. Schüssler Fiorenza, *In Memory of Her*, 52.

whether the *doulos* texts, potential "texts of terror" for black people, can in any way portend new possibilities for our understanding of what actually constitutes the radicality of the good news of the gospel:

> If art imitates life, Scripture likewise reflects it in both holiness and horror. Reflections themselves neither mandate nor manu-facture change; yet by enabling insight, they may inspire repen-tance. In other words, sad stories may yield new beginnings.[77]

In his discussion of the injunctions about women's subordination in the *Haustafeln* (the household codes, cf. Col 3:18–4:1; Eph 5:21–9; 1 Pet 2:18–37), Frank Stagg makes the following observation about the need to recognize that the historically conditioned regulations enjoining male domination of women should no longer be binding:

> The preoccupation for male authority over women is pagan, anti-Gospel. It cannot be redeemed; it can only be aborted. It is a negation of the Gospel of Jesus Christ.[78]

Stagg's statement has correspondence implications for the *doulos* texts, particularly since some of these texts are located in the household codes, where slaves as well as women are enjoined to be submissive to the patriar-chal head of the household. Can these *doulos* texts in the household codes and elsewhere be "redeemed" in any of their occurrences in the Pauline and non-Pauline writings? Should some of them be "aborted"? Can any of them enable new insight? Should they inspire repentance and personal and social transformation in some sense? These questions invite further critical analy-sis and investigation.[79]

Chipping away at oppressive structures, and identifying those texts that help black women to celebrate and rename incidents involving hu-man unpredictability in empowering ways, is at the heart of a womanist interpretive principle.[80] Similarly, the development, nurturance, and critical employment of the hermeneutics of suspicion, resistance, liberation, and hope in the interpretive process remain essential components of womanist

77. The phrase "texts of terror" is adopted from Phyllis Trible's penetrating book on the subject, *Texts of Terror: Literary-Feminist Readings of Biblical Narratives, Overtures to Biblical Theology* (Philadelphia: Fortress, 1984) 2.

78. Frank Stagg, "The Gospel, Haustafeln and Women: Mark 1:1; Col 3:18–4:1," *Faith Mission* 2:2 (1985) 63.

79. See my essay, "The *Haustafeln* in African American Biblical Translation: 'Free Slaves' and 'Subordinate Women,'" *African American Biblical Interpretation*, ed. Cain H. Felder (Philadelphia: Fortress, 1991).

80. Katie G. Cannon, "The Emergence of Black Feminist Consciousness," *Feminist Interpretation of the Bible*, ed. Letty Russell (Philadelphia: Westminster, 1985) 40.

biblical interpretation. This principle, and methodological tools from this hermeneutical cache, will make the possibility of holistic, inclusive, and kerygmatically empowering biblical translation and interpretation more real for all communities of faith.

CHAPTER TWO

Re-Reading for Liberation

African American Women and the Bible[1]

RENITA J. WEEMS

I am grateful to the planners of this conference[2] for the invitation to gather in the beautiful town of Ascona, Switzerland, to deliberate with women from around the globe on the ways in which our hermeneutics intersect with our social and political identities. Gathering with women from as far away as Australia and Palestine and as nearby (to the US) as Costa Rica and Canada has resulted in a heady week of exchanging stories, comparing journeys and learning to view the world through different eyes. Hearing stories about the brave and challenging work many of us are involved in as the first, only, or one of a handful of women in our countries, universities, religious traditions, and always in our families to reflect on the Bible with feminist eyes, to examine our faith and our culture through the experiences of other women has made all of us view our work differently. We return home feeling less lonely and more a part of a movement that is international in scope and certainly larger than ourselves. It was a week of mixed blessings.

Nestled away as we were in a remote, mountainous retreat, deliberating with women from various parts of the world and from vastly different backgrounds pushed all of us (and each of us) to a high level of self-reflection—more self-reflection than some of us were accustomed to, more self-reflection than some of us could stand. Tensions were strained at times. Our differences sometimes kept us from hearing and understanding each other.

1. Reprinted by permission of Continuum International Publishing Group.

2. The conference referred to was the Feminist Hermeneutic of Liberation conference in Ascona, Switzerland, July 2000.

But we never stopped trying. Even though it was clear to all very early in the week that five days would not be enough for us to shed all the assumptions and all the baggage that come with being women from colonizing countries and women from countries once colonized. But we tried.

That said, I believe many of us left the symposium more committed than ever to our work as interpreters and scholars of Scripture. As for myself, I left convinced of how important it is for African American women scholars to resist the myopisms of Western feminism by building bridges of dialogue with women from around the globe. Reading and interpreting the Bible with the help of those from other cultures reminds us of the extent to which one's context both limits and illumines interpretation. I knew this before as a biblical scholar and a North American African American woman, but I knew it differently after interfacing in Ascona with women from worlds different from my own. I discovered the truth of Kathleen O'Connor's observation, "we are drenched in our contexts."[3] By the close of the conference, we learned through much pain and effort how our contexts have both inspired and illumined our liberatory readings of the Bible and at the same time hindered and blinded us to the manner in which the Bible has been used to silence the marginalized and to justify centuries of oppressive activity.

Drenched in our contexts as we all proved to be that week in July 2000, most of us left Ascona committed to finding ways to continue the trans-cultural dialogue we started. Our future as women reading for liberation depends upon it. What do I mean? The only way most, if not all of us are apt to act and speak less arrogantly about our claims about the Bible, not to mention act and speak less arrogantly toward each other, is if we put ourselves in situations where we must spend days (preferably a lifetime) in diverse, multi-cultural, trans-cultural, heterogeneous contexts where, if we are to survive, *we must* learn to talk with and live peaceably and justly with people who think and see the world differently from ourselves.

Reflecting and Rethinking a Womanist Identity

One of the benefits of the Ascona symposium was that it forced me at least to bring to consciousness my own self-interests and to probe my assumptions—both the apparent and the hidden ones—in order to do what I could to make myself understood to those around me. I have always identified

3. Kathleen O'Connor, "Crossing Borders: Biblical Studies in a Trans-Cultural World," in *Teaching the Bible: The Discourse and Politics of Biblical Pedagogy* (Maryknoll, NY: Orbis, 1998) 324.

myself as a biblical scholar who not only traffics in the intellectual world-making enterprise of scholarship and academy. But I have also been eager to make my mark as a public intellectual, a woman in the academy who tries to make her work accessible and available to the non-specialists and grass-roots activists working for liberation in ecclesial and non-ecclesial contexts. The international context of our symposium brought home to me, as well as to others, the politics of our various identities and forced all of us to speak less smugly about the praxis of our work.

Reflecting on biblical interpretation within a multicultural context forced me throughout the week to be intentional about examining and explicating the context of my work. It also forced me to examine the ways in which, as a woman of African heritage born and reared in North America, I live a fractured existence as well as the ways in which my shifting identities stir conflicts within me and resist easy solutions. We women of color doing work in the Western academy are likely to find ourselves constantly dangling between two realities: the diasporic, postcolonial feminist discourse of our two-thirds world sisters and the privileged, hegemonic theorizing discourses of Western feminism. To proceed as though my North American context was self-evident, inconsequential, or, worst yet, universal, was to be guilty of what postcolonial feminists rightly criticize Western feminism of—namely, the universalist, essentialist, and globalizing tendency to presume a universal condition of oppression for all women.[4] I had to face the ways in which I belong both to a marginalized group of readers (African American women/womanists) and a privileged class of interpreters (Western/North American feminists) depending upon the context in which I find myself.

Reading the Bible in multicultural spaces makes (or ought to make) one acutely aware of the intellectual heritage, the political baggage, the social assumptions, and the economic worldview one brings to one's reading. It forces one to face and to declare explicitly on whose behalf one interprets. A constant hurdle for us to overcome as we tried throughout the week to create a safe space for critical dialogue was our inability, and sometimes flat out unwillingness, to acknowledge the ways we use language—especially biblical and theological language—to mask or reinforce differences among us. The politics of the symposium were such that we found ourselves having to work against others and our own cultural baggage in our struggle to understand and to be understood. There were moments in the discussion when

---

4. For a helpful discussion of postcolonial feminist theory in general, see Alexander M. Jacqui and Chandra Mohanty, eds., *Feminist Genealogies, Colonial Legacies: Democratic Futures* (New York: Routledge, 1996). Also, for a very helpful attempt to bring postcolonial feminist theory to bear upon reading biblical texts, see Musa W. Dube, *Postcolonial Feminist Interpretation of the Bible* (St. Louis: Chalice, 2000).

we succeeded, there were many more when we did not. We could not outwit cultural backgrounds and at difficult moments had to acknowledge the fact that we were first and two-thirds world women, Western and non-Western women, Anglo women and women of color, women from colonized parts of the world and women from colonizing nations, feminist, postcolonial, and womanist scholars, conservative readers and radical interpreters of Scripture trying to talk across a gulf of painful history. Nevertheless, we all walked away from the week acutely aware that even the risk of failure is no excuse for not trying to reach out to one another.

Reading with and reading across cultural borders is part of the ongoing work of women of color in the theological academy. We do not have the luxury of remaining content to analyze texts but must go the step further to analyze readings, readers, culture, and the worlds that frame each. Ultimately, reading the Bible for liberation is grounded in the acknowledgment and respect for the otherness of those whose otherness is silenced and marginalized by those in power. Thinking about my generation of African American female scholars working as academics in the field of religion, I can say that most of us do not view our work as *accountable* to the academy, even though we are involved in the discourse of the academy and are dependent upon the academy for a large part of our living. But we reserve the right to make our work accountable ultimately to grassroots African American women, women struggling for voice and representation in institutional circles, ecclesial circles especially.

Many of us who are African American women scholars in religion came into the academy as a second choice. We came to the academy of scholars of religions when we discovered as seminarians that despite our training there was no place for us thinking women of faith in the church. The church birthed us and then rejected us. We went on for our graduate degrees because it was the next best thing. And now we stand ambivalently before two audiences, belonging to neither but trying to carve out a space in the discourses of both. And why do we not walk away from the church? Why not reject the Bible? If it were an individual matter, then the choice would be a simple one, perhaps. There are many parts of myself, for example, that are post-Christian. But it is not just about our/my individual predilections. It is about our/my commitments. To leave the church would be to leave other African American women behind. To reject the Bible altogether would be to cut off my conversation with the women who birthed me and sent me off to seminary with their blessings.

Finally, on this point, I for one choose to remain within the black Christian tradition, despite my ambivalences toward it, because it keeps me in conversation with women I care deeply about. Despite the ways

American Christianity was forced on our ancestors, Africans brought to this country as slaves, and despite the ways in which patriarchal Christianity has wounded women over the centuries, I remain hopelessly Judeo-Christian in my orientation. I cannot escape its influence upon me. Indeed, as a scholar committed to scholarship that serves liberation purposes my very vision of what a just, equitable, humane, and righteous world order looks like is deeply influenced by the utopian imagination and impulses of my Judeo-Christian upbringing. The place where religion proves useful in multiracial, international discussions like the one in Ascona is when it forces us back to the table to reopen the discussion, to rethink our assumptions, to reread for our collective liberation, and to give dialogue another chance.

Reflections on Womanist Biblical Hermeneutics

Even after its introduction as a term more than fifteen years ago, "womanist scholarship" remains a nascent conversation in religious and theological studies. The reasons for this are many. Many of them have to do with our lack of a critical mass of scholars writing and reflecting on womanist research, as well as the demands and pressures on our attention as black women in the academy. The challenge over the years for us has been having to write, teach, theorize, and practice our hermeneutics amid obstacles designed to keep us women in the academy distracted, silent and forever beginning anew. We have only to observe how little attention is given to the traditions, religious worlds, epistemologies, and reading habits of non-Anglo, non-European women by mainstream feminist religious discourse to see how and why the work of womanists fills a crucial voice in gender and feminist studies.

Womanist biblical reflections arose out of feminist biblical hermeneutics and liberation theology. Womanist reflections upon the Bible underscore that the experiences of white feminists and those of black male liberationist thinkers are not "the universal experience" of all marginalized persons. While feminist biblical criticism and black liberation scholarship are inextricably linked, they are not the same. Sexism is one form of oppression black women confront. Racism is another. Classism is yet another. A womanist perspective underscores the fact that North American Anglo women's experience is not the "universal" experience of women in general. Nor is black male liberationist thinking the "universal" experience of people of color. The universalizing tendencies of North American feminists have obscured their Eurocentric biases, seeking to homogenize women in general and women of color especially without regard to our differences of race, religion, nationalities, sexual orientation, and socio-economic backgrounds.

Likewise, while black liberation thinking and womanist criticism are inextricably related, the experience of African American women has not always been fully appreciated by black male colleagues involved in liberation discourse. Black liberation work often focuses on race oppression in society, but fails to see oppression based on gender as equally unacceptable. Black theology emerged out of the black power movement. It was unifocal in its critique, focusing exclusively on white racism. It failed to address the sexism and the classism experienced by black women. Kelly Brown Douglas notes that "affected both by the feminist movement in church and society and their own experience of sexism, black women began to note the exclusion of black women's experience in black theology" as well as the feminist movement.[5] Womanist criticism within the theological academy emerged as a way to correct the myopism of both feminist and black liberation scholarship, believing that every marginalized group has a right and duty to name its own reality and to find a language for mapping out its own vision of liberation.

Like feminist biblical hermeneutics, womanist biblical hermeneutical reflections do not begin with the Bible. Rather, womanist hermeneutics of liberation begin with African American women's will to survive and thrive as human beings and as the female half of a race of people who live a threatened existence within North American borders. The interests of real flesh-and-blood black women are privileged over theory and over the interests of ancient texts, even "sacred" ancient texts. Even a cursory look at the literature and autobiographical writings of African American women will show that what is celebrated most in our writings is our determination to survive, to nourish, and to protect those things dear to us, and to assert our will to thrive in what often is a hostile and dangerous world. The Bible cannot go unchallenged in so far as the role it has played in legitimating the dehumanization of people of African ancestry in general and the sexual exploitation of women of African ancestry in particular. It cannot be understood as some universal, transcendent, timeless force to which world readers—in the name of being pious and faithful followers—must meekly submit. It must be understood as a politically and socially drenched text invested in ordering relations between people, legitimating some viewpoints, and delegitimizing other viewpoints.

Almost from the beginning of our engagement with the Bible as African Americans we have interpreted it differently from those who introduced this book to us. Instead of reading the passages our slaveholders

5. Kelly Brown Douglas, "Womanist Theology: What is its Relationship to Black Theology?" in *Black Theology: A Documentary History 1980-1992,* eds. James H. Cone and Gayraud Wilmore, vol. 2 (Maryknoll, NY: Orbis, 1993) 292.

drew our attention to as theologically rationalizing slavery and oppression, we insisted upon reading and interpreting the same passages differently or ignoring them altogether. That the Bible was not transmitted to American slaves as a fixed, written text that had to be accepted as is proved to be fortuitous. It freed us from rather rigid notions about the infallibility of its contents. As an aural text in the slave community, one passed down to black people through sermons, song, and public instructions, slaves were free to interact with its contents according to their own interests and cultural re-imaginings. For black women that meant we could elect either to reject totally those portions of the Bible we considered misogynistic, to elevate some portions over others depending upon one's interests, to offer alternative readings in order to counter the dominant discourse, or to supplant biblical teachings altogether with extra-biblical (i.e., cultural) traditions that (in their thinking) offered a fuller, more just vision of the way things ought to be. Because of their fundamental belief in their rights as human beings created in the image of God they rejected antagonistic readings that denied them any subjectivity.[6]

Any attempt, then, to describe African American women's relationship to the Bible and to adduce our strategies for reading the Bible has to take seriously the ways in which the Bible has been (and continues to be) used to rationalize the subjugation of African people of the diaspora living in North America in general and the sexual and gender subjugation of African women of the diaspora living in America in particular.[7] Placing our work in a stream of discussion with other women from different contexts as the Ascona conference did forces one to look at the ways in which our readings have been shaped by the unique circumstances of our North American context. It also reminds us of the ways in which our reading strategies both stand in solidarity with and differ from readings by other women from marginalized communities from around the globe.

A womanist hermeneutics of liberation shares with feminist hermeneutics of liberation the goal of changing consciousness and transforming

6. For a fuller treatment of the ways nineteenth-century African American women in particular rejected the dominant antagonistic readings of their day and held to their own "choice passages" as a way of defining their own subjectivity, see Chanta M. Haywood, "Prophesying Daughters: Nineteenth-Century Black Religious Women, the Bible and Black Literary History," in *African Americans and the Bible: Sacred Texts and Social Textures*, ed. Vincent L. Wimbush (New York: Continuum, 2000) 355–66.

7. For my fuller discussion of African American women's history of reading and interacting with the Bible, see Renita Weems, "Reading her Way through the Struggle: African American Women and the Bible," in *Stony the Road We Trod: African American Biblical Interpretation*, ed. Cain Hope Felder (Minneapolis: Fortress, 1991) 57–80.

reality. But the main point of our work as womanist scholars, I think, is to empower African American women as readers, as agents, and as shapers of discourse by uncovering the program and agenda of both biblical texts and dominant cultural readings. Real flesh-and-blood people with real vested interests were behind the production and transmission of the Bible's contents; and real flesh-and-blood readers are behind all modes of interpretation and readings with positions and agendas that prompt them to be more invested in one reading over another. The point here clearly is to decenter for marginalized readers the privileged status of dominant readings and the dominant community of readers. A womanist biblical hermeneutics takes as its starting point the fundamental notion that people have power, not texts. Meaning takes place in the charged encounter between the socially and politically conditioned text and the socially and politically conditioned real reader. Women have to reclaim their right to read and interpret sacred texts for themselves and should not have to be subject to the misogynistic, patriarchal interests of powerful male readers; and women of color have to insist upon their right to read and interpret sacred texts for themselves and should not have to defend or apologize for their interpretations to privileged women in the culture who remain ignorant to how class, race, and colonialism shape and divide us as women. It should come as no surprise, then, that in womanist criticism no one reading and no one methodology is privileged over another; instead, a creative use of multiple readings and the helpful insights offered by a variety of disciplinary approaches are employed to shed light on the question of how and why readers read as they do.

Because the Bible has been used here in North America not only as a source of liberation, but also paradoxically and curiously as a source of inspiration in African American women's struggle for survival, it remains a continuing task of liberation interpreters, as far as I am concerned, to shed light on one of the more intractable questions facing us in our ongoing efforts to rationalize the fact that it continues to occupy an important place in the hearts and minds of many African American women: despite all that we know about its antagonistic role in our oppression as women, how does reading admittedly sexually violent and misogynistic texts continue to have the power to fill many of us with passion and a vision for liberation?

Readers' Love Affair for Stories

To see African American protestant women's devotions to the stories of the Bible as a continuing example of a naïve attachment to the principle of *sola Scriptura* or as a slavish belief in these texts as the divinely revealed word of

God, the sole authority in all matters religious, is to traffic in partial truths and to be overly determined about a far more complex and subtle aspect of gender, reading, and culture. After all, women readers have been reading and identifying with secular texts written by men that romanticize their second class status for centuries.

My argument is that part of African American women's fascination with the Bible—despite all that they may come to know about the hopelessly patriarchal character of the world they inhabit—has to do in great part (though not exclusively, of course) with the insatiable appetite readers have for stories. Through stories grassroots African Americans communicated their understanding of life, love, suffering, and god(s) and their vision of freedom and liberation.

Let me state emphatically that I am not saying that our need or love for stories is the only or even the primary reason for women's devotion to the Bible. I am only asserting that it is one reason that has not been given sufficient (constructive) attention by feminist biblical interpreters. Of course, there are undeniably larger political, economic, historical, and ideological forces at work that help reinforce the illusion of biblical stories as truth/true, divinely inspired, sacred, and "the way things are and have been always."

People, when making moral choices and decisions in their lives, represent their choices and decisions by turning to stories. To facilitate those moral choices and decisions people look to stories to guide them. It is important to see readers' devotion to biblical stories in general and religious texts in particular as part of their broader fascination within society for narratives, stories, and testimonies. The possibility that the Bible alleges to offer its reader the earliest glimpses into human tragedy and triumph is immeasurably comforting to many of its readers. Gender studies may help shed light on how texts shape women's realities. Literary theory can help us understand how narratives are written and how they construct narrative universes for readers to inhabit. But the question of why readers choose this book over that book, why some books bear reading again and again, lies not in theory but in cultural history. As one writer put it, "It has to do with where we look when we try to understand our own lives, how we read texts and what largely unexamined cultural assumptions we bring to interpreting them."[8] This is particularly true for African American female readers who turn to the Bible to regain their hope of a world where the first is last and the last is first, where justice eventually dethrones injustice, and the despised are welcomed at the hospitality table and are given the seat of honor there

8. Jill Kerr Conway, *When Memory Speaks: Reflections on Autobiography* (New York: Knopf, 1998) 4.

at the table. Regardless of whether the protagonist is male or female, justice and liberation have to be (or perceived to be) at the heart of the story. That the protagonist is female, as in the case of the story of the woman caught in adultery in John 4 or the story of Esther, only sweetens the tale of political, economic, and social reversal at the hands of the divine.

There is no denying that a significant part of our work as womanist interpreters is to radically rethink what it means to continue to read certain kinds of obnoxious, oppressive stories in the Bible where rape, abuse, and marginalization are romanticized, subjugated, and excused for the sake of some alleged larger purpose in the story. Stories like those of the rape of Tamar in Gen 34, the butchering of the Levite's concubine in Judges 19, or the prostitute who anoints Jesus' feet with her tears and hair in Luke 7 are ones we cannot afford to continue reading without serious rethinking. Their story of women's abuse and subjugation may be too costly to hold on to and too hopelessly misogynistic to try saving. We have to find ways to break the hold that these and other androcentric biblical texts have on us as women by rereading these texts in ways they were not meant to be read. Part of rereading androcentric texts can entail choosing not to read them at all. Breaking the hold these texts have involves breaking the cycle of uncritically retelling and passing down from one generation to the next violent, androcentric, culturally chauvinistic texts and resisting where necessary the moral vision of such texts. We may find that we have to follow the path of black Christian women readers in the past who in their struggle for freedom and dignity ignored outright certain biblical passages altogether. I am reminded here of the story of the grandmother of theologian Howard Thurman who after slavery refused to hear passages written by the Apostle Paul because she had been made to hear sermons about slaves obeying their master all her life when she was a girl growing up in slavery. Only the Psalms and other parts of the New Testament qualified as worthy words of daily inspiration for Thurman's grandmother. The fact that women like Thurman's grandmother had "choice passages" demonstrates a perception on the part of even so-called uneducated readers of how the Bible can and has been used to promote a vision of a world that silences and further overlooks the oppressed. Its multiple ideological layers and the multiple roles it has played in both silencing and liberating generations of readers forces readers to read the Bible with different eyes, from multiple positions, and with a multi-layered approach. No one way of reading, thinking, and talking about biblical stories can be privileged over another.

Feminist scholars have noted for some time now that we have moved beyond the simple recovering and recounting of individual stories about exceptionally prominent or obscured women in the Bible. That was the work of first-wave biblical feminists and womanist scholarship. It was involved not only in exposing the strongly patriarchal environment from which the Bible arose (and hence its misogynistic biases) but also in exposing how women's presence has been further obscured by the biases of male scholars and interpreters. In addition to attempts to understand the social world of women by drawing on discussions from the social sciences, psychoanalysis, archaeology, and so on, works from this period aided us in trying to understand the social patterns, social roles, and how societies silence women, obscure the contributions of women, even how these societies seek to construct identity through narratives and legal materials.

The work of the second-wave of biblical feminist and womanist scholarship, namely, recovering and reclaiming women's contributions and presence in the bible, continues. It continues as long as there remain grassroots women who refuse to leave the churches that have both, they say, wounded them and blessed them. Recovering the contributions of women such as Hagar, Huldah, Judith, Deborah, Lydia, and the Canaanite woman is important for those desperate for role models, images, stories, and examples from the Bible to help them struggle and survive the hardships of gender oppression.

But we have witnessed a shift to what both feminists and womanists agree is a third phase of biblical liberation criticism, which involves rethinking the very act of reading biblical stories. Intrinsic to this movement is an interest in looking closely at stories and their construction, to see how identity is shaped and reinforced and how real readers negotiate identity and meaning when reading. That is: how do real readers read stories? How do stories shape identity? How do stories change identities? Why do some stories become more important to some readers than others? It is here in this third phase of biblical liberation criticism that womanist criticism situates itself best. Womanist biblical criticism is interested in the ways African Americans read the bible, the strategies they use in negotiating meaning and identity from stories, and those they use when resisting the meaning(s) and identities attached to certain stories. Part of what it means to break the hold that texts have over the imagination is for us as readers to be able to decide the strategies and conventions that went into making the texts in a way that sheds light on how texts mean and why they mean the way they mean.

I agree with Australian feminist historian Jill Kerr Conway when she argues that readers turn to stories, even biblical and religious stories, for a variety of reasons:

1. To learn about how the world looks from inside another person's experience.

2. Because stories satisfy our craving for coherence and our fear of chaos and unpredictability; they offer us the fictive illusion that life flows along a clear, logical line of causation, that it has a beginning, middle, and a tidy end.

3. Stories give readers an inner script by which they might live their lives, compare their lives, conform their lives, reshape their lives and test out their lives.[9]

Stories offer readers an inner script to live by, glimpses into the way things are and more importantly reason and a way to talk about how things ought not to be. Stories can lure readers into seeing the world in different ways, shock them into a critique of the world in which they live and help them imagine the ways things ought to be. In the symbolic, non-threatening way in which stories are passed down, they have the power to galvanize readers into reimagining the world in ways that were previously unthinkable and impossible. That the Bible purports to describe ancient peoples and ancient times is part of its seduction. For even if it does not in fact describe *the* beginning of human tragedy and human triumph, it does convey to the reader the possibility that *from* the beginning of time there has been human tragedy and human triumph. As a womanist biblical interpreter and teacher my role is to respect readers' needs to view the Bible as a collection of sacred stories while at the same time challenging them to understand their role as agents in the sacred act of preserving stories and passing them down to the next generation. As an agent in the task of preserving and transmitting stories from one generation of women to the next, readers must be empowered (1) to become a part of a story's audience and to feel free to raise questions of the author about his or her assumptions about the world and people's relationship to one another; (2) to use one's imagination to retell the story in ways it was never meant to be told in order to get at hidden truths and meanings embedded in stories; and (3) to take responsibility as a reader/interpreter/storyteller for the impact the stories we tell has on the lives of other women, men, and children who hear them and try to live up to them.

9. Conway, *When Memory Speaks*.

From Reading to Liberation

Finally, an important part of womanist biblical criticism involves empowering readers to judge biblical texts, to not hesitate to read against the grain of a text if needed, and to be ready to take a stand against those texts whose worldview runs counter to one's own vision of God's liberation activity in the world. For example, the woman reader who insists that the story of the butchered concubine in Judges is divinely inspired or that Ezekiel, Jeremiah, or Hosea's use of sexually violent imagery to connote divine judgment is holy must be made aware of her role and responsibility each time she literally, that is, unthinkingly/uncritically, passes these stories on to the next generation.[10] One of the most effective ways to introduce women students and interested male students to a hermeneutics of liberation is by turning their attention to stories of rape and violence in the Bible and asking them what kind of world would our world be if stories like these were normative, if we duplicated, reproduced, or transmitted them to the next generation without warning and comment? No wonder stories, whether religious or profane, ancient or contemporary, European or postcolonist, are potentially powerful tools for spreading liberation. After all, it is through the narrative, symbolic universe of stories that readers, ordinary readers, non-specialists—who rarely give their own lives a fraction of the same amount of attention—get to contemplate and talk indirectly about matters of culture, history, gender and identity, language, power relations, material conditions, all the things those of us in the bourgeoisie world of academy tackle in more rarified, highly theorized, but no less subjective ways.[11]

Finally, working as a womanist scholar committed to a hermeneutics of liberation entails opening my mind and those of others to radically new and different ways that different people read, tell stories, and testify to their understanding of God. Rereading for liberation is not done in a vacuum, nor is it a solitary enterprise. Liberation is the work of people reaching out to one another across the gulf of their real flesh-and-blood, painful gender, racial, national, religious, and geo-political differences like we tried to do in Ascona. It means hearing people out, respecting the way they read and interpret stories, making room for them at the table, and sharing power with them. For what is liberation without power? And what is power? Power is the ability to take one's place in whatever discourse is essential to change and having the right to have one's story matter regardless of how it is told, no

10. For my own discussion of sexual violent imagery and language in prophetic literature, see Renita Weems, *Battered Love: Love, Sex, and Violence in the Hebrew Prophets* (Minneapolis: Fortress, 1995).

11. Conway, *When Memory Speaks*, 17.

matter how rambling the story, no matter how unconventional the telling, no matter how irritating the inflections, and sometimes no matter how unthinkable the tale. Re-reading for liberation is risking failure and taking the plunge to divest yourself of some of your own power and privileges for the chance to enter another's world so as to understand and to make yourself understood to others.

CHAPTER THREE

Womanist Interpretation and Preaching in the Black Church[1]

KATIE GENEVA CANNON

A new and significant connection is beginning to exist between the new modes of critical inquiry created by African American women in the theological academy[2] and the central role that preaching plays as a cultural phenomenon in the black church community.[3] It is new because until recently black preaching has not asked questions about womanist interpretation and womanist theological studies have not included homiletics. It is

1. Katie Geneva Cannon, "Womanist Interpretation and Preaching in the Black Church," in *Katie's Canon: Womanism and the Soul of the Black Community* (Continuum, 1995).

2. The canon of womanist discourse is growing. Among many, see Toinette Eugene, "Moral Values and Black Womanist," *Journal of Religious Thought* 44 (Winter/Spring 1988) 23-34; "Roundtable Discussion: Christian Ethics and Theology in Womanist Perspective," *Journal of Feminist Studies in Religion* 5:2 (Fall 1989) 82–112 (lead essay by Cheryl J. Sanders; responses by Katie G. Cannon, Emilie M. Townes, M. Shawn Copeland, Cheryl Townsend Gilkes, and bell hooks); Delores S. Williams, "Women's Oppression and Lifeline Politics in Black Women's Religious Narratives," *Journal of Feminist Studies in Religion* 2 (Fall 1985) 59-71; Delores S. Williams, "The Color of Feminism: Or Speaking the Black Woman's Tongue," *Journal of Religious Thought* 43 (Spring/Summer 1986) 45-58; and Emilie M. Townes, ed., *A Troubling in My Soul: Womanist Perspectives on Evil and Suffering* (Maryknoll, NY: Orbis, 1993).

3. See Joseph A. Johnson, Jr., *The Soul of the Black Preacher* (Memphis: C.M.E., 1970); Charles V. Hamilton, *The Black Preacher in America* (New York: William Morrow, 1972); Henry H. Mitchell, *Black Preaching* (Philadelphia: J. B. Lippincott, 1970); Henry H. Mitchell, *Celebration and Experience in Preaching* (Nashville: Abingdon, 1991).

significant because the majority of the faithful who have heard and continue to hear black preaching are women.

While the majority of these churchgoers have little trouble testifying that a good sermon is a many-splendored art form, the articulation of an analysis by which we elucidate and delegitimize patriarchal teachings is not as easily arrived at. When sermons are written and presented in the interest of men, the categorical definitions of theoethical concepts lend an evidently weighty authority to androcentric conclusions about male preachers and masculine-centered culture.[4]

My own proposal for the form this womanist interpretation should take lies in the convergence of a feminist liberationist theoretical interpretation inspired by Elisabeth Schüssler Fiorenza's groundbreaking scholarship[5] and the seminal work of Isaac R. Clark. Sr., on black homiletics.[6] These two dynamic areas of interpretative discourse offer a challenging nexus for womanist scholars concerned with radically rethinking and revisioning "how duties and roles are advocated, how arguments are constructed and how power is inscribed"[7] in the black church community.

A womanist critique of homiletics challenges conventional biblical interpretations that characterize African American women as "sin-bringing Eve," "wilderness-whimpering Hagar," "henpecking Jezebel," "whoring Gomer," "prostituting Mary Magdalene," and "conspiring Sapphira." A womanist hermeneutic identifies the frame of sexist-racist social contradictions housed in sacred rhetoric that gives women a zero-image of ourselves. This analysis deconstructs biblically based sermons that portray female subjects as bleeding, crippled, disempowered, objectified, purified, or mad. It enables us to ask hard questions about the responsibility of black preachers to satisfy the *whole* congregation's spiritual hunger with their intellectual grasp, mastery of Scripture, social analysis, and constructive homiletical skill. Both areas of research, feminist liberation interpretation and preaching in the black church, reinforce each other by raising questions, clarifying

---

4. See Robyn R. Warhol and Diane Price Herndl, eds., *Feminisms: An Anthology of Literary Theory and Criticism* (New Brunswick, NJ: Rutgers University Press, 1991).

5. Elisabeth Schüssler Fiorenza, *In Memory of Her: A Feminist Theological Reconstruction of Christian Origins* (New York: Crossroad, 1983).

6. Isaac Rufus Clark Sr. was an extraordinary homiletician and master teacher for twenty-seven years at the Interdenominational Theological Center in Atlanta. Throughout this discussion I refer to his lectures and class notes.

7. Elisabeth Schüssler Fiorenza, *Revelation: Vision of a Just World* (Minneapolis: Fortress, 1991) 3.

problems, and amplifying issues that shape our collective consciousness about "the survival and wholeness of an entire people."[8]

Feminist Liberationist Interpretation

Following Schüssler Fiorenza's methodology, I would argue that the essential task of a womanist hermeneutic consists in analyzing black sermonic texts with regard to how they "participate in creating or sustaining oppressive or liberating theoethical values and sociopolitical practices."[9] Womanist analysis provides an interpretative framework that holds together the spiritual matrix of black religious culture while exposing the complex, baffling contradictions inherent in androcentric language. I am arguing for a critical evaluation of sermonic texts, including an analysis of when and how women are mentioned and whether these sermons adequately reflect African American reality.[10]

Schüssler Fiorenza's methodology can be likened to detective work, which does not rely solely on historical "facts" nor invent its evidence. Instead, it engages in an imaginative reconstruction that rests upon observation and inference; it employs a critical analysis of whether scriptural texts in sermons mention women only as problems or as exceptions. The task of womanist homiletics is to unearth what black preachers are saying about women and what we are saying about men.

A critical study of black sermons shows that African American church traditions and redactional processes follow certain androcentric interests and perspectives that do not reflect the historical contributions of African American women's leadership and participation in the life of the church. By showing the detailed and numerous androcentric injunctions about women's nature, place, and behavior in black preaching, we are able to identify and critique sermonic texts that express and maintain patriarchal historical conditioning. We are also able to highlight those sermons that

---

8. This is an essential component of Alice Walker's definition of "womanist" in her collection of essays *In Search of Our Mothers' Gardens: Womanist Prose* (New York: Harcourt Brace, 1983) xi.

9. Schüssler Fiorenza, *Revelation*, 9.

10. See, for example the sermons in the following anthologies: Walter B. Hoard, ed., *Outstanding Black Sermons*, vol. 2 (Valley Forge, PA: Judson, 1979); Robert T. Newbold, ed., *Black Preaching: Selected Sermons in the Presbyterian Tradition* (Philadelphia: Geneva, 1977); Milton E. Owens, Jr., ed., *Outstanding Black Sermons.*, vol. 3 (Valley Forge, PA: Judson, 1982); William M. Philpot, ed., *Best Black Sermons* (Valley Forge, PA: Judson, 1972); James Henry Young, ed., *Preaching the Gospel* (Philadelphia: Fortress, 1976).

reproduce and shape the liberative reality of all members of the worshiping community.

A womanist adaptation of Schüssler Fiorenza's integrative heuristic model seeks to provide a means of ethical assessment that can help the black church community look at the practices and habits, assumptions and problems, values, and hopes embedded in its Christian cultural mind-set. It does so with the hope of renewing and reforming the faith-justice praxis in the black preaching tradition. It is essential that womanist interpretive practices be employed not only in the critique of androcentric preaching with its references to patriarchal relationships of inequality. We must also use womanist methodology at the constructive stage of sermon preparation and delivery.

Preaching in the Black Church

The history of black preaching begins with the emergence of the black church as invisible institution in the slave community during the seventeenth century.[11] Utilizing West African religious concepts in a new and totally different context and blending them syncretistically with orthodox colonial Christianity, black women and men developed an extensive religious life of their own.[12] The black church was the only social institution in which African Americans could exercise leadership and power, and the preacher and preaching were held in the highest esteem in the black church community. Preaching was one of the principal instruments used by enslaved black leaders. They preached what they knew about the progression from patriarch to priest to prophet to Jesus to Paul and testified to what they had seen, exalting the word of God above all other authorities. The preacher sought close, empathetic, communal identification with the congregation. Holding forth in the pulpit on Sundays and throughout the week as one of God's earthly representatives, the preacher was the dominant, influential spokesperson for the community at large. The black preacher served as the

11. See Albert J. Raboteau, *Slave Religion: The "Invisible Institution" in the Antebellum South* (New York: Oxford University Press, 1978); and David Charles Dennard, "Religion in the Quarters: A Study of Slave Preachers in the Antebellum South, 1800–1860," PhD Dissertation, Northwestern University, 1983.

12. See Benjamin E. Mays, *The Negro's Church* (New York: Institute of Social and Religious Research, 1933); Harry V. Richardson, *Dark Glory: A Picture of the Church among Negroes in the Rural South* (New York: Friendship, 1947); Carter G. Woodson, *The History of the Negro Church* (Washington, DC: Associated, 1921).

arbiter of intellectual/moral life and the principal *interpreter* of canonized sacred writings.[13]

The continued self-inventiveness of black preaching is inescapably bound up with gifted orators gathering Bible stories, accounts of deeds, and sayings from their given theological contexts and transposing these words of faith into patterned episodes in clear, "gettable" language, i.e., language accessible to listeners. Black preaching is a running commentary on Scripture passages, showing how the Bible is an infinite thesaurus that provides hearers with resources in word and deed for overcoming oppressive situations.

Due to the oral proclivities of African American Christian culture, a written sermon cannot be understood apart from its delivery. The sermon is a combination of serious exegesis and imaginative elaboration of the stories in the Pentateuch, the sayings in Wisdom literature, the prophetic writings, and the New Testament. It is an unhampered play of theological fantasy and at the same time an acknowledgement of the cultural maturity and religious sophistication of traditional themes.

The homiletical explorations of Isaac R. Clark penetrate the soul of black preaching, providing us with insight into the way in which oral religious thought is organized and conceptualized. To be sure, Clark speaks of black preaching in the broadest sense, as a fundamentally creative, artistic cultural form of African American Christian speech that exhibits a distinct expressive style and flavor for communicating religious beliefs and theoethical considerations in an articulate oral pattern. According to Clark, preaching as the spoken representation of the dimensions of the holy is "*divine activity* wherein the *Word of God* is *proclaimed* or *announced* concerning *contemporary issues* with a view toward *ultimate response to God.*"

Black preaching is a narrative that exhibits all of the formal structures of rhetorical prose, such as a text, title, introduction, proposition, body, and conclusion. It is the major medium for making scriptural proclamation relevant to our times. By figuratively dramatizing biblical conflicts of dominance and submission, assertion and deference, the righted and the outlawed, the propertied and the dispossessed, the black preacher calls into question "the social network of power/knowledge relations."[14] In each preaching event, the religious practices and deep-seated theoethical beliefs of the black church are reinvented in and through specific scriptural in-

13. See Gayraud S. Wilmore, *Black Religion and Black Radicalism: An Examination of the Black Experience in Religion* (Garden City, NY: Doubleday, 1972); and Jualynne Dodson, "Nineteenth-Century A.M.E. Preaching Women," in *Woman in New Worlds,* ed. Hilah F. Thomas and Rosemary S. Keller (Nashville: Abingdon, 1981) 276–89.

14. Elisabeth Schüssler Fiorenza, *But She Said: Feminist Practice of Biblical Interpretation* (Boston: Beacon, 1992).

terpretation. Investigation of the integral connection between the preacher who creates the sermon, the sermon's internal design, the world that the sermon reveals, and the religious sensibilities of the congregation that are affected by the sermon invites us to a higher degree of critical consciousness about the invisible milieu in which we worship.

Divine activity refers to the customary three-tiered configuration that places the black preacher in the mediating position between God and the congregation. With one ear on the ground hearing the cries and longings of the people and the other ear at the mouth of God, the preacher has a special obligation to instruct the hearers in defining, interpreting, and solving problems related to the life we live, the life we dread, and the life we aspire to live. The preacher has the power and privilege to determine precisely what biblical text will be used and whose experiences are central and endowed with force and continuity in the encoding of norms and values for the black church community. Throughout the sermonic delivery the preacher must communicate that the authority for the sermon emanates from a guiding force beyond the preacher, from God.[15]

Word of God focuses on the word that becomes flesh and dwells with us as the living God; it does not simply apply to the "words" of canonized Scripture that we read and hear. The God-self is present as the content of the preached word. The Holy Spirit must work through the critically conscious preacher to present the person and work of Jesus Christ as recorded in the Bible to the body of believers.[16] Jesus, the kerygmatic Christ, pulsates with a quality of "isness," a particular contemporaneity that identifies the sacredness spoken of during the sermon with recognizable aspects of the congregation's everyday raw material of existence.[17] Preaching in the black church is a dynamic process that matches the scriptural texts with temporal sequences, provides etiological explanation for evil and suffering inflicted by human agency, and emphasizes the close union of heaven and earth, God and people.

---

15. See Gerald L. Davis, *I Got the Word in Me and I Can Sing It, You Know: A Study of the Performed African American Sermon* (Philadelphia: University of Pennsylvania Press, 1985); James H. Robinson, *Adventurous Preaching* (Great Neck, NY: Channel, 1956); and Bruce Rosenberg, *Can These Bones Live?* (Urbana, IL: University of Illinois Press, 1988).

16. James Forbes, *The Holy Spirit and Preaching* (Nashville: Abingdon, 1989).

17. See Jacquelyn Grant, "Womanist Theology: Black Women's Experience as a Source for Doing Theology, with Special Reference to Christology," *Journal of the Interdenominational Theological Center* 13:2 (1986) 195–212; and Kelly D. Brown, "God Is as Christ Does: Toward a Womanist Theology," in *Journal of Religious Thought* 46:1 (1989) 7–16.

Black preaching concentrates a lot of attention upon Jesus who acts decisively and speaks with pointedness.[18] The gospel stories about Jesus are linked back to quite definite events of the Greco-Roman world and to the life of the present-day community. However, in the final analysis it is not the historical Jesus who occupies the central place, but the divine power that holds sway over him as the Word incarnate.

Proclaimed or *announced* is the preacher's indicative mode for declaring the biblical ideas, beliefs, and systems of thought in the vernacular of the hearers. To be most effective and efficient the preacher artfully amplifies sacred referencing in a language that includes the idiomatic and colloquial forms most recognizable to black churchgoers. The exposition of the scriptural text must be delivered with vigor and vitality in order to bear witness to the preacher's enthusiasm for being called to this sacred task. Parishioners participate in a call-and-response dialogue with the preacher that subjects biblical preaching to dynamic, in-the-moment expressions of resurrection.

The narrative strategies of black religious lore recapitulate the lives and decisive action of biblical ancestors who are not thought to belong merely to the past, but are considered also to be living, in, with, and beyond their faith descendants. Black preaching takes great liberty in tapping into the inexhaustible treasurers of wisdom and spiritual power lodged in the biblical canon.[19] Black preaching encourages proclamation of the "good news" Bible stories in ways that are interactive, memorable, and commonly public.[20] Anthropomorphism in the black preaching tradition transforms biblical characters, adventures, and behavior into a larger context of experience so that the finite mind can grapple with the eternal creative act.

Contemporary issues are determined by gifted communicators transforming and reinterpreting their divine call as it interfaces with Scripture and the existential circumstances of the hearers. Clark's study of sacred rhetoric suggests a number of intriguing approaches that open up windows to the biblical concepts structured into the imaginative core of the black worship experience. By communicating with gestures, facial expressions, and chanted deliveries, the black preacher builds a compelling sermon

18. E. L. McCall et al., *Seven Black Preachers Tell: What Jesus Means to Me* (Nashville: Broadman, 1971).

19. Cain Hope Felder, ed., *Stony the Road We Trod: African American Biblical Interpretation* (Minneapolis: Fortress, 1991).

20. C. L. Franklin, *Give Me This Mountain: Life History and Selected Sermons*, ed. Jeff Todd Titon, foreword by Jesse Jackson (Urbana, IL: University of Illinois Press, 1989); Samuel Gandy, ed., *Human Possibilities: A Vernon John Reader* (Washington, DC: Hoffman, 1977); William Lloyd Imes, *The Black Pastures* (Nashville: Hemphill, 1957); Sandy Ray, *Journeying through the Jungle* (Nashville: Broadman, 1979); Gardner Taylor, *The Scarlet Thread: Nineteen Sermons* (Elgin, IL: Progressive Baptist, 1981).

by preserving and "making plain" the stories of the Bible that have been handed down through the years.[21] Equilibrium is maintained by sloughing off memories that no longer have relevance while proclaiming the religious inheritance of ancestral mothers and fathers that enhances narrative variation for audience responses in new situations.

The black sermon is more than a mere tangent to social history.[22] It has a special affinity with contextual reality insofar as it connects the experience of finitude with the transcendent dimensions expressed with the biblical culture of bygone days. It encompasses vivid descriptions, colloquial diction, and concrete imagery drawn from both the Bible and daily life that symbolizes liberating possibilities between actuality and hope, real and ideal, earth and heaven. In other words, Bible stories are relived, not merely heard; the preacher gives enough details and embellishes the actions with metaphors to keep the story moving so that the hearers stay abreast of their present-day identification with the biblically based narratives.

Given the complexity of and ambiguity of the black church community, preachers verbalize their homilies with more or less close reference to the African American lifeworld, assimilating the abstract world of theology to the more immediate, familiar world of everyday life and struggle. Homiletical proclamation is enmeshed with historical and social events in the African American community, engaging knowledge in the arena where human beings struggle with one another.

The overall objective and purpose of preaching is to call the worshiping congregation to an *ultimate response to God*. According to Clark, the black preacher's primary activity is to inform, engage, and point out contradictions within situations of complacent security in order to invite the congregation to make a decision for or against emancipatory praxis. Preaching not only helps us to know what we believe and why, but it is the medium through which events of transformative understanding shake up creeds, question social power, and transform traditions. The preacher thinks through complex problems and articulates solutions by verbalizing a "why crisis" that motivates the listeners to contemplate the complicated series of theoethical assertions. The constant exposure to the abounding iniquity in the world opens the congregation to a gracious message of deliverance.

Clark's rhetorical methodology shows why black preaching has acquired a particular and unique physiognomy, why certain theoethical

21. See Williams E. Hatcher, *John Jasper* (New York: Revell, 1908); and Ralph H. Jones, *Albert Tindley: Prince of Black Preachers* (Nashville: Abingdon, 1982).

22. See Samuel D. Proctor, *Preaching about Crisis in the Community* (Philadelphia: Westminster, 1988); and Kelly Miller Smith, *Social Crisis Preaching* (Macon, GA: Mercer University Press, 1984).

themes and motifs are present and others absent, why certain stylistic treatments are accepted and others rejected. In other words, this signifying process enables us to see how theoethical canons, standards, and conventions are produced and maintained in African American homiletical texts. Black sermons are characterized by the combination of biblical retrospect and exhortation in which the worshiping community is called forth to be among the chosen, fully grasping and proclaiming the character of Yahweh as the liberating God of history. Black sermons have a great deal to teach us concerning the congregation's call to redemption through the fullest imaginative response.

Clark effectively solves the problem of intellectually organizing the data of text and context by developing a rhetorical methodology of *definition, elaboration, exemplification,* and *justification,* thus establishing a line of continuity inside the mind. The syntax, rhythm, and balanced patterns in repetition of these four formulary essentials help implement rhythmic discourse that act as retention and ready recall aids in their own right. Also, they form the substance of thought itself. Clark's coordinated homiletical structure, through which the syntactic and theological ideas are generated, expands the aesthetic dimensions of black preaching, achieving the most effective, consistent, innovative "telling of the old, old story."

Womanist Queries

My particular concern is how a womanist critical evaluative process, understood in its contextual framework, can suggest possibilities for eliminating the negative and derogatory female portraiture in black preaching. An intensive examination of sermonic texts shows how preachers follow certain androcentric interests in objectifying and commodifying black women. Even in "text-led" biblical preaching, where the representation of women may occupy a central place in the expository structure, women are often occluded. By unmasking those detailed and numerous androcentric injunctions, womanist hermeneutics attempts to expose the impact of "phallocentric" concepts that are present within black sacred rhetoric.

For instance, when we turn to the experience of black churchwomen to establish criteria for interpreting and determining the value of sermonic texts we need to ask what difference it makes that African American Christians hear sermons full of linguistic sexism, in which images of and references to women are seldom positive. As womanist theologians, what can we do to counter the negative, real-world consequences of sexist wording that brothers and sisters propagate in the guise of Christian piety and virtue? How disruptive are such gender-biased androcentric sermons for social relations within the African American family? What is the correlation between what is preached in church on Sunday and what Abbey Lincoln describes as the African American woman's social predicament?

> Her head is more regularly beaten than any other woman's, and by her own man; she's the scapegoat for Mr. Charles, she is forced to stark realism and chided if caught dreaming; her aspirations for her and hers are, for sanity sake, stunted; her physical image has been criminally maligned, assaulted, and negated; she is the first to be called ugly, and never yet beautiful.[23]

As clergywomen committed to the well-being of the African American community, how are we refuting gender stereotypes that are dehumanizing, debilitating, and prejudicial to African American women?[24] Can we change male supremacist attitudes by prescribing alternatives to discriminatory word usage? What happens to African American female children when black preachers use the Bible to attribute marvelous happenings and unusual circumstances to an all-male cast of characters? The privilege, power, and prerogative in developing such sermons are in themselves significant. The marginalization of women from the cast of characters constitutes a significant choice within these larger patterns of decision.

What are the essential liberating strategies that African American clergywomen use in our own sacred rhetoric that will continue to encourage an ethic of resistance? What are we doing that will allow a womanist interpretation to emerge, an analysis that shows how black women underneath patriarchal teachings and relations of domination are complex, life-affirming moral agents? I maintain that a womanist analysis provides the internal analytical categories of the valuation system for this genre of sacred rhetoric.

The sensibilities of a womanist interpretation of preaching in the black church require sacred orators to be responsive to the emotional, political, psychic, and intellectual implications of our message. We anticipate and

23. Abbey Lincoln, "Who Will Revere the Black Woman?" *Negro Digest*, September 1966, 18.

24. See, for example, sermons written and published by African American women in the following anthologies: Ella Pearson Mitchell, ed., *Those Preaching Women: Sermons by Black Women Preachers* (Valley Forge, PA: Judson, 1985); Ella Pearson Mitchell, ed., *Those Preaching Women: More Sermons by Black Women Preachers*, vol. 2 (Valley Forge, PA: Judson, 1988); Helen Gray Crotwell, ed., *Women and the Word: Sermons* (Philadelphia: Fortress, 1977); Justo L. Gonzalez, ed., *Proclaiming the Acceptable Year: Sermons from the Perspective of Liberation Theology* (Valley Forge, PA: Judson, 1982); David A. Farmer and Edwina Hunter, eds., *And Blessed Is She: Sermons By Women* (San Francisco: Harper & Row, 1990); Annie L. Milhaven, ed., *Sermons Seldom Heard: Women Proclaim Their Lives* (New York: Crossroad, 1991).

embrace both power and subsequent actions in the creation and in the delivery of our sermons. Therefore, we must identify the qualities of an "ideal" black churchwoman and a "realized" Christian woman. In appreciating the complexity of the genius of black preaching, we must be able to analyze how this genre is both sacred and profane, active and passive, life-giving and death-dealing. Womanist interpretation calls for a balanced tension between the accuracy of the spoken word—organization, language, fluidity, and style—and the expressed political aim of our sermonic content. In order to present co-equal discipleship, the preacher must reflect upon the sacred words that underrepresent and truncate women in the creation of African American women's image, voice, and agency.

A womanist hermeneutics seeks to place sermonic texts in the real-life context of the culture that produced them. The basic premises of sermonic development aim to operate inside the boundaries both of canonized Scripture and the circumstances in which the sermon is written and delivered. Images used throughout the sermon can invite the congregation to share in dismantling patriarchy by artfully and deftly guiding the congregation through the rigors of resisting the abjection and marginalization of women. A womanist interpretation requires each component of black homiletics to adhere to the emancipatory practice of a faith community. The preacher is obliged and expected to show the listeners how to "trace out the logic of liberation that can transform patriarchal oppression."[25]

Womanist hermeneutics regards sociocultural context as an important component of the sermon. The preacher's testimonial function is necessarily looked at within a personal-existential framework. The utterances of the preacher must be examined in the situation in which they are produced and delivered to the hearers, that is, in terms of the preacher's and congregation's own experiences. Nothing prohibits us from asking questions about the role of social factors in shaping sermonic texts and what part the preacher's gender plays in selecting the kinds of biblical stories and sayings that she or he uses in preaching. Womanist analysis of sermons inquires into the depictions of women's experiences, missionary circles, mothers and female saints of the church, and the women officers and leaders in the ecclesiastical community. This practice removes men from the "normative" center and women from the margins. It leads to the alteration of prevailing masculine models of influence. To avoid perpetuating traditional, binary assumptions, womanist theory offers a helpful strategy for focusing on the oppression of women while simultaneously providing visions of liberation. Using Clark's tools and methods on preaching in the black church and relating them to

25. Schüssler Fiorenza, *But She Said*, 9.

Schüssler Fiorenza's writings on feminist liberationist criticism, we can provide precise answers to the questions of (1) how meaning is constructed, (2) whose interests are served, and (3) what kind of worlds are envisioned in black sacred rhetoric. Every choice that a preacher makes in constructing a sermon will have certain connotations, inherited from its forebears among the sermons that preceded it. Preaching in the black church is as much affected by issues of misogyny, androcentricity, and patriarchy as by homiletical form. Within this complex discursive construction of sacred rhetoric, women and men who cast their lot with us must make an intervention, no matter how slight, in the dominant religious discourse of our time.

CHAPTER FOUR

An African Methodology for South African Biblical Sciences

Revisiting the *Bosadi* (Womanhood) Approach[1]

MADIPOANE J. MASENYA (NGWAN̄A' MPHAHLELE) (UNISA)

Introduction

Any place for "Africa" in South African biblical studies?

Let us imagine a cow that has grappled for some time with the appearance of her horns and the mockery she has endured from other animals about the alleged ugliness of her horns. Ultimately the cow succumbs to the pressure to have reconstructive surgery performed on her horns. In her view she had decided that the horns that would best suit her head would be those of the merino sheep.

I invite you to picture the sight of this cow after such "cosmetic" surgery! The horns might be beautiful in her view and in the view of her mockers, but "beautiful" as they might be they are not her original horns. They are artificial horns that will fail to serve the exact function of the original ones.

The Northern Sotho proverb says, *dinaka tsa go rweswa ga di gomarele hlogo* ("counterfeit horns cannot stick permanently on a different head"). The proverb's meaning is that attempts at imitating others, however,

---

1. Madipoane Masenya, "An African Methodology for South African Biblical Sciences: Revisiting the Bosadi (Womanhood) Approach," *Old Testament Essays* 18:3 (2005). Reprinted with permission.

excellent they might be, will prove inefficient on account of their simulated nature.

Elsewhere, I have used this proverb in conjunction with the folk tale of a hare that pretended unsuccessfully to be a lion(ess) to demonstrate the state of biblical studies/Old Testament studies in present day South Africa.[2] I have argued that the theological curricula as well as those of Old Testament studies in South Africa, still rely heavily, if not totally, on the West rather than on Africa itself. I have shown that as a result of this dependence, a legacy inherited from colonial and apartheid South Africa, Old Testament scholars have produced graduates who, after completion of their studies, remain irrelevant to their Africa-South African[3] contexts: a situation that is alarmingly similar to what used to be the case in apartheid theology during apartheid South Africa. In the latter context, the powerless were trained to read the Bible as though they were in power. For example, an African person generally ends up being trained to read the Bible as though she or he is white, and a poor person could be steeped in elitist hermeneutics.[4]

I have shown the dilemma of an African scholar who chooses to be faithful to the context of many grassroots African Bible readers who do not have the luxury to carry out biblical hermeneutics distant from the harsh realities of life on the ground. Such a commitment is bound to earn one an insider-outsider status:

> ours is a theological education characterized by one assuming the role of an insider in one context and that of an outsider in another context. One becomes an insider as one is being trained as a student, an insider to the theologies which are foreign to oneself, an insider as one trains African students in Western-oriented studies of the Bible, an insider as one does research. If the research conducted is not played according to the rules

2. Madipoane Masenya, "Teaching Western-Oriented Old Testament Studies to African Students: An Exercise in Wisdom or in Folly?" *Old Testament Essays* 17:3 (2004) 455–69, 457–58. Cf. my article "Is White South African Scholarship African?" *Bulletin for Old Testament Studies in Africa* (2002) 12, 3–8. In that article, I lament the basic absence of African-oriented biblical studies or Old Testament studies in South Africa, irrespective of the latter's geographical position on the African continent. For responses to this article, cf. I. Himbaza, "La recherchè scientifique et la contextualization de la Bible," *Bulletin for Old Testament Studies in Africa* 13 (2002) 1–11; and K. Holter, "Is it Necessary to be Black?" *Bulletin for Old Testament Studies in Africa* 13 (2002) 7–8.

3. The apparently repetitive phrase "African-South African" is used in this paper, as I usually do in my writings, to designate the indigenous peoples of South Africa. One finds in this category the Pedis, Tswanas, Vendas, Xhosas, etc.

4. See Madipoane Masenya, "The Bible, HIV/AIDS and African/South African Women," paper read at Interdenominational Theological Center, Atlanta, GA, USA, 2004, 5.

inside the game, it will not earn this "insider/outsider" accreditation to the Western academic status quo, which itself remains basically an outsider to the African status quo.[5]

I have further argued that:

Even as one interacts with one's colleagues, one is still confronted with these "insider/outsider" dynamics. In an attempt to take off the lion(ess)'s skin/artificial horns, and to become an outsider to the academic status quo, one runs the risk of not making sense to one's peers and of one's methodologies being dubbed by some as being unscientific. In such circumstances, one cannot but suffer academic suffocation. It is no wonder that one usually finds African (out-of-South Africa) academic encounters quite refreshing and affirming, though we must acknowledge that there are other Western contexts which are willing to listen to African voices.[6]

The above analysis is meant to inform the reader about the struggle that one still encounters in finding "Africa" in South Africa despite the observation that we are already ten years into a democracy. The latter has enabled South Africa to come up with one of the most beautiful constitutions in the world, the beauty of which consists in its supposedly inherently liberatory nature.

The "othering" of "Africa" in South Africa is evidenced in the following examples:

It is commonplace to hear academics commenting as follows, "There are applications of students who come from Africa" or "I have been attending a conference in Africa." Coupled with this is the observation that even in continental and global circles, South Africa is usually viewed with esteem and appreciation. Almost everybody seems to wish to visit South Africa at some point in time. Why? Is it because of the alienation that South Africa has suffered through the years on account of the apartheid policy? Is it because of the resources easily tapped in terms of the lower exchange rates, particularly between the South Africa and and the currencies of the North?

What is even more disturbing is that this "othering" of Africa and African peoples is more glaring among fellow African persons. The negative appellation *makwere-kwere*[7] to refer to fellow African persons from other

5. Masenya, "Teaching Western-Oriented Old Testament Studies," 460.

6. Ibid., 460–61.

7. This demeaning appellation stems from the "inability" of African persons from other African countries on the continent to express themselves perfectly in the accent of the indigenous peoples of South Africa. This "imprecision" is very natural in that if

parts of Africa has said it all. It denotes the hate and denigration of African-South African peoples for fellow African peoples. This is an unfortunate xenophobic situation indeed, particularly given the important role that some of them played for many African-South African exiles during the apartheid era.

An important question for the present text is, if the African context is still "othered" in South Africa, particularly in our theological and biblical hermeneutical endeavors, can we claim full liberation in the "non-sexist," "non-racist" post-apartheid South Africa?

In my quest to claim Africa for South African biblical hermeneutics and to affirm the African-ness of African-South African wo(men) I have developed what I call a *bosadi* approach to biblical texts.[8] The *bosadi* approach is the resolve of a process engaged in removing the artificial horns of other women gender discourses.

Given the diversity of women's experiences covered by the women theologians in the Circle of Concerned African Women Theologians,[9] a herstory of my initiation into women liberationist discourses[10] will reveal that I underwent two major horn surgeries.

Initially, after becoming attracted to women's liberationist theologies through reading feminist resources, with no mentor by my side, I underwent my first surgery and came out sporting feminist horns. As I continued to read and teach myself about issues pertaining to women (*bosadi*) I came to realize that African American women (womanists) also articulate their own experiences in their search for affirming definitions of what it means to be a woman. I did not have to read many sources to understand that, probably sooner rather than later, I would need to undergo another surgical operation. Why? I found the situation of my African American sisters to be closer to that of African-South African women in terms of going beyond the gender category to address issues of class and race in their discourse.

African-South Africans were to settle permanently in one of the African countries and venture to speak in the local indigenous languages, the same "imprecision" would be heard from them!

8. Madipoane Masenya, "Proverbs 31:10–31 in a South African Context: A Bosadi (Womanhood) Approach," DLitt et Phil Thesis, University of South Africa, Pretoria, 1996.

9. See T. Okure, "Invitation to African Women's Hermeneutical Concerns," *African Journal of Biblical Studies* 19:2, 71–95. See also P. N. Mwaura, "Gender Mainstreaming in African Theology: A Woman's Perspective," in *Global Voices for Gender Justice*, ed. R. T. H. Dolamo et al. (Cleveland: Pilgrim, 2001) 165–79.

10. Madipoane Masenya, "Proverbs 31:10–31"; and Madipoane Masenya, *How Worthy is the Woman of Worth? Rereading Proverbs 31:10–31 in African-South Africa* (New York: Peter Lang, 2004).

Indeed, I went into surgery again. I had to. All these surgical procedures were prompted by my desire to name myself appropriately. I noticed that given our racial history, a history in which African peoples were named and their culture defined, I needed—even at the cost of being misunderstood—to name myself appropriately. I already knew then that it was going to be artificial if not impossible to share the same gender biblical discourse with my white counterpart.

It was only when I was a visiting scholar in Garrett-Evangelical Theological Seminary in Evanston, Illinois in the United States that I came to be aware that though an African American womanist had close points of resemblance with what might be an African-South African biblical hermeneutical discourse, it was still uniquely African American. On account of this discovery, as well as my commitment to make "Africa" a hermeneutical focus,[11] I have decided to name my framework a *bosadi* (womanhood) approach to the reading of biblical texts. I, therefore, underwent one more session of surgery, which has enabled me to put on horns that will for the first time hopefully stick!

The *Bosadi* Biblical Hermeneutics

Since my employment of the concept *bosadi* in several published works,[12] readers have drawn their own perceptions about this hermeneutics. Some have found close similarities between the *bosadi* approach and African enculturation hermeneutics. Plaatjie holds:

> Masenya's approach is somewhat akin to African enculturation hermeneutics, which compares biblical and African cultures. A

11. In the light of this preoccupation with Africa and its concerns, it becomes a misunderstanding to regard the *bosadi* approach as a local approach, restricted only to the Northern Sotho (cf. S. Nadar, "A South African Indian Womanist Reading of the Character of Ruth," in *Other Ways of Reading: African Women and the Bible*, ed. Musa W. Dube [Atlanta: SBL, 2001] 159; and T. S. Maluleke, "African 'Ruths,' Ruthless Africas: Reflections of an African Mordecai," in *Others Ways of Reading*, 243). Although the approach uses the Northern Sotho African-South African context as a point of departure, the goal was to develop, not only an African-South African woman-friendly biblical hermeneutic but an African one.

12. Madipoane Masenya, "Redefining Ourselves: A *Bosadi* (Womanhood) Approach," *Old Testament Essays* 10:3 (1997) 439–48; "Reading the Bible the *Bosadi* (Womanhood) Way," *Bulletin for Contextual Theology in Southern Africa and Africa* 4:2 (1997) 15–16; "Proverbs 31:10–31 in a South African Context: A Reading for the Liberation of African (Northern Sotho) Women," *Semeia* 78 (1997) 55–68; and "A *Bosadi* (Womanhood) Reading of Genesis 16," *Old Testament Essays* 11:2 (1998) 271–87.

feature that distinguishes Masenya's approach from enculturation is that she foregrounds gender concerns.[13]

She devotes almost four pages to what one might, to a large extent,
call an unfounded critique of the *bosadi* approach.[14] In this critique, Plaatjie
makes definite conclusive, yet erroneous assumptions regarding the *bosadi*
concept. Her arguments were based on an article that was submitted to *Semeia* in 1995,[15] while research on this same concept was still in process.
Some such erroneous readings are in order from the above quotation:
"Masenya's approach is somewhat akin to African enculturation hermeneutics, which compares biblical and African cultures."[16]

The *bosadi* approach is not simply a comparative analysis between the
biblical text and the African culture. It critiques both cultures and texts not
only in terms of gender concerns. It also includes issues of class, "woman-
as-strange" and "Africans-as-strange" in their own territory. Unlike in many
past black South African male theological discourses and those discourses
that foreground enculturation hermeneutics, in the *bosadi* concept, the idea
of the Bible as Word of God is not accepted uncritically.[17] In this approach,
there is acknowledgement of how the notion of Israel's election has been
used in apartheid theology to justify the exploitation of black peoples.[18] At
the same time, though the *bosadi* concept is an attempt to resuscitate the
African culture from the ashes, it does not idolize the culture as some have
argued.[19]

Perhaps the use of the word *bosadi* itself has misled readers quickly to
judge it as being culturally oriented, preoccupied only with "ethnic" concerns. Maluleke remarks:

> It is my reticence that Masenya's proposal, although not always
> argued well and often misunderstood, blazes a new trail and

13. G. K. Plaatjie, "Toward a Post-Apartheid Black Feminist Reading of the Bible:
A Case of Luke 2:36–38," in *Other Ways of Reading: African Women and the Bible*, ed.
Musa W. Dube (Atlanta: SBL, 2001) 121.

14. Ibid., 124–28.

15. This article ("Proverbs 31:10–31 in a South African Context," [55–68]) was later
published. A close reading of this article through the lens of Plaatjie's critique will also
reveal her misunderstanding of the *bosadi* concept.

16. Plaatjie, "Toward a Post-apartheid Black Feminist Reading of the Bible," 121.

17. Madipoane Masenya, *How Worthy is the Woman of Worth? Rereading Proverbs
31:10–31 in African-South Africa* (New York: Peter Lang, 2004) 24; Cf. I. J. Mosala, "The
Use of the Bible in Black Theology," in *Voices from the Margin: Interpreting the Bible in
the Third World*, ed. R. S. Sugirtharajah (Maryknoll, NY: Orbis, 1991) 50–60.

18. Masenya, *How Worthy is the Woman of Worth?*, 54–66.

19. Nadar, "A South African Indian Womanist."

holds great potential for future African hermeneutics. Unlike many critiques of Masenya, my reticence about *bosadi* has little to do with its ethnic tenor. *Bosadi* is no more "ethnic" than Alice Walker's womanism or Oduyoye's bold and otherwise preposterous declaration that all African women are "daughters of Anowa," an Akan woman. It is inadequate and ineffectual to engage Masenya at this level.[20]

Indeed, to those readers who choose to read this approach through Western eyes, the *bosadi* concept might appear ethnic and local. However, given the brief background on the need to foreground Africa given earlier on, it should be stated that the coinage of the *bosadi* concept was done not only with national and continental concerns in mind, but also with global concerns! To do this effectively, one had to start at home, from the African-South African setting. As I have stated elsewhere, the word *mosadi* does not only occur in the Northern Sotho setting, it also occurs, though in different words, in other African-South African languages: *wansati* (Xitsonga); *umfazi* (Zulu); *musadzi* (Tshivenda); *mosadi* (Tswana and Southern Sotho).[21] I have deliberately made the African-South African women's context the main hermeneutical focus by using a familiar word, a male construct.[22] I have therefore desired, first and foremost, to be committed to my own context. The words of Okure concerning the desirability of a relationship between grassroots African women and professionally trained theologians seem to endorse my convictions:

> Our greatest, but not yet fully tapped resources, are these so-called ordinary women. They are close to life at the grassroots; they see themselves in the texts of Scripture and respect them as God's abiding word, sometimes too literally and in ways that oppress than liberate them. The professionally trained African women theologians, on the other hand, can be tempted to subscribe to abstract ways of theologizing in order to find acceptance in the field. Thus they can lose focus on life, or seek answers to hermeneutical questions put by others, instead of

20. Maluleke, "African 'Ruths,' Ruthless Africas," 243.

21. Masenya, *How Worthy is the Woman of Worth?*, 122.

22. Cf. Maluleke, "African 'Ruths,' Ruthless Africas," 243–44. Although Maluleke is right in arguing that the *bosadi* concept is a male-construct, I find this to be an unfortunate criticism given the patriarchal history that has shaped the languages of the world. I am not aware of any words used to designate women for example, "woman," "feminine," and "female," which were originally coined by women. In the light of such a history, I have employed this male-constructed terminology, and redefined it, to affirm those who have not only been named, but those whose roles have been defined and prescribed by outsiders to their gender. Cf. ibid., 122–58.

identifying and addressing their own questions. The sisterhood
in reading is needed by all.[23]

The *bosadi* concept cannot, therefore, afford to be an elitist concept
read and practiced from the comfort of academic halls as Plaatjie argues:
"Masenya neither reads with nor from non-academic Northern Sotho
women. . . . She chooses to speak for them, and places them in the role of
sub-alterns who cannot speak. Rather she theorizes about the *bosadi* approach and applies it from the comfort of academic halls."[24]

As I have already argued that reclaiming the use of the very African-
South African indigenous word *mosadi/bosadi* is, in my view, one demonstration of my commitment to African-South African women, particularly
those at the grassroots. As these are women with whom I interact constantly
in a more natural and spontaneous way, I do not need to conduct a Bible
study in order to "read with" them. I pray with them, rejoice and weep with
them. I sit at their feet to hear them share from the Bible even as they also
do likewise to me.

The *bosadi* approach also succeeds in enabling these women to read
the Bible in a way that affirms them. My choice of this particular "elite" text
was motivated by my observation of how this same text is abused by the
powerful to the detriment of the powerless grassroots woman "others."

From the discussion in the above paragraphs, it can be argued that the
major hermeneutical focus of the *bosadi* biblical hermeneutics is the unique
experiences of an African-South African woman, with her view to her liberation. It is first and foremost, an African woman's liberation hermeneutic.
African women, facing such multiple, life-denying forces as sexism in the
broader South African society, inherited from the legacies of colonialism
and apartheid, sexism in the African culture, post-apartheid racism, classism, HIV/AIDS, and xenophobia are made the main hermeneutical focus.
As in liberation theologies,[25] the experiences of the marginalized, in this
case African-South African women and not the contexts that produced the
Bible, serve as the starting point for one's encounter with the biblical text.
The words of Renita Weems concerning African American women make
sense in this regard:

> Real flesh-and-blood people with real vested interests were be-
> hind the production and transmission of the Bible's contents;

23. T. Okure, "Invitation to African Women's Hermeneutical Concerns," *African
Journal of Biblical Studies* 19:2 (2003) 74.

24. Plaatjie, "Toward a Post-Apartheid Black Feminist Reading of the Bible," 127.

25. See Sugirtharajah, *Voices from the Margin*, 436–37. G. O. West, *The Academy of
the Poor* (Pietermaritzburg: Cluster, 2003) xvii–xviii.

and real flesh-and-blood readers are behind all modes of interpretations and readings with positions and agendas that prompt
them to be more invested in one reading over another. The
point here clearly is to decenter for marginalized readers the
privileged status of the dominant readings and the dominant
community of readers. A womanist biblical hermeneutics takes
as its starting point the fundamental notion that people have
power, not texts…women of color have to insist upon their right
to read and interpret sacred texts for themselves and should not
have to defend or apologize for their interpretations to privileged women in the (dominant) culture who remain ignorant to
how race, class and colonialism shape and divide us as women.[26]

What is the place of the Christian Bible in the *bosadi* methodology?
We now turn to this question.

The Bible in the *Bosadi* Biblical Hermeneutics

Underlying the use of the *bosadi* methodology is the presupposition of
the powerful role that the Bible continues to play in African-South African women's struggle for liberation and survival. As a matter of fact, the
Bible as an important resource in African women's lives is not only uniquely
African-South African, it is also a key feature in the lives of African women
on the continent. Oduyoye captures this central role of the Bible in Africa
succinctly:

> The Bible empowers us to proclaim God's will in the name of
> Jesus and in the power of the Holy Spirit. . . . The Spirit that
> came mightily at Pentecost is alive and well and powerful in
> African Christianity. . . . The Bible has brought the message of
> hope to Africa and African Christians; therefore we hail and
> love the Bible. If one finds the bible in a cot in Africa, one should
> know that it is a symbolic expression of God's continued care of
> the whole of creation, especially of those too weak to fend for
> themselves.[27]

In the *bosadi* approach, the positive role that the Christian Bible continues to play in the lives of African-South African women believers is acknowledged. African-South African women continue in faith to experience

26. Renita J. Weems, "Re-Reading for Liberation: African American Women and
the Bible," in *Feminist Interpretation of the Bible*, ed. Sylvia Schroer and Sophia Bietenhard (London: T. & T. Clark, 2003) 26.

27. Oduyoye, *Reading from This Place*, 38.

the power of the risen Christ confirmed in their everyday lives. It is this power that enables them to cast out demons, to heal the sick, and to proclaim liberation to those who are in bondage. These women are humbled by the belief in the Christ who identifies with those at the margins of society; the poor, women, Gentiles, etc.—hence the important emphasis put on the Bible as the word of God in this African-South African setting.

However, given the harsh reality of the use of the Bible to endorse patriarchal domination in South Africa, the *bosadi* concept is somewhat cautious about the notion of the Bible as "Word of God." Elsewhere I have argued the following:

> This rosy picture I have given about the Bible does not, however, imply that the Bible is an innocent book. It does have the elements that alienate some people including women, the poor and dwellers in rural areas. Such areas reveal its ideological nature because the Bible is a human book. As I have argued, it is the responsibility of the interpreter to spot such elements and reject them for they will not be in line with the words of life which the Bible proclaims. . . . The Bible is both oppressive and liberative. What would be beneficial, would be to look for relevant ways by which to render the Bible message relevant to Bible readers in 21st century post-apartheid South Africa.[28]

In my interpretive context, as in other such contexts on the African continent, the Bible is approached with hope, with a view to transformation by its liberative power.[29]

The *bosadi* approach's foregrounding of the element of a believer's faith makes sense in such a context.[30] The Bible is not viewed first and foremost as a book for scholarly arguments and mental gymnastics. As word of God, it is believed to have the power to change women's situations positively.[31] It is no wonder that the authority of the Bible as the word of God is taken for granted in such situations. Okure contends that

> Such a reading implies that the reader is one who believes that he or she can discover life from the Bible. In other words, I am

28. Masenya, *How Worthy is the Woman of Worth?*, 24.

29. See P. N. Mwaura, "Gender Mainstreaming in African Theology: A Woman's Perspective," in *Global Voices for Gender Justice*, ed. R. T. H. Dolamo, A. M. Tependino, and D. N. Hopkins (Cleveland: Pilgrim, 2001) 176; Okure, "Reading from This Place," 55–56; and A. I. Phiri, "Doing Theology as an African Woman," in *A Reader in Christian Theology* (London: SPCK, 1997) 55.

30. Masenya, *How Worthy is the Woman of Worth?*, 11.

31. Ibid., 24.

interested here, not in any scientific or literary reading of the Bible that leaves the believer's life untouched by the exercise. I am concerned rather with a person who believes that the Bible is fundamentally the word of God, even though it is being expressed in human language with all its sociological and historical moorings. In this respect, the question whether or not the bible can be regarded as word of God does not really arise. . . . Readers who approach the bible from this standpoint of faith . . . seek in it the message of God that can challenge, liberate, and energize their lives in their own social locations.[32]

An important question at this stage is how may socially engaged biblical scholars who use the critical tools of biblical scholarship interact in a more balanced way with readers who have such a strong commitment to the Bible as the word of God?

If we are particularly concerned with making marginalized persons the main focus of our hermeneutical endeavors, then we will also be open to engage their views in a more balanced way.

Conclusion

As a methodology for the biblical sciences, the *bosadi* approach will prove helpful in the following ways, just to name a few:

[1] The curricula for the biblical sciences in South Africa still rely heavily on the West. The *bosadi* approach with its commitment to the African context can bring a balance to this situation. This balance will be achieved as the subject matter of these sciences is allowed to address issues of concern in the areas of poverty, unemployment, landlessness, and HIV/AIDS to name but four.

As we foreground "Africa" in our hermeneutical efforts, "Africa" will be enabled to have an "active" share in the global village.

What makes the *bosadi* methodology even more compelling in this regard, is its commitment to the context of African women in South Africa. The latter issue has received little attention from previous African, black, and liberation theologies. Issues pertaining to patriarchy, particularly in its multi-faceted forms in differing women's contexts need to be treated as a matter of urgency in our biblical hermeneutical endeavors. However, it

32. Okure, "Reading from this Place," 56.

must be acknowledged that there are South African institutions that have made significant progress in this regard.

[2]In fields such as the biblical sciences, whose methodologies have for so long been preoccupied with the "biblical past," an approach that is committed to the context of the modern Bible reader, particularly if the latter has close affinities with the Bible, will prove to be beneficial. Approaches such as the *bosadi* one is likely to attract many of these readers to scientific studies of the Bible.

[3]Related to the preceding point is the gap between an academic in the biblical sciences and a grassroots Bible reader. Through the employment of the *bosadi* methodology, with its recognition of the important role played by the Christian Bible among South African communities of faith as well as its critical approach towards the Bible, such a gap can be bridged.

The words of the former president of the Republic of South Africa, President Nelson Mandela on the African renaissance come to mind as I conclude this article:

> As we dream and work for the regeneration of our continent, we remain conscious that the African renaissance can only succeed as part of the development of a new and equitable world order in which *all the formerly colonized and marginalized take their rightful place, makers of history rather than the possessions of the other.*[33]

In our attempt to create a new landscape for the biblical sciences in South Africa, prompted by our commitment to the African renaissance, let us develop methodologies that will do justice to "Africa" and its various contexts.

---

33. J. Crewys-Williams, *In the Words of Nelson Mandela: A Little Pocketbook* (London: Penguin, 2004) 7.

CHAPTER FIVE

Marginalized People, Liberating Perspectives

A Womanist Approach to Biblical Interpretation[1]

KELLY BROWN DOUGLAS

Before addressing this issue of biblical interpretation in our multicultural and ever-changing world, the first thing I must say is perhaps that which many of you already know: I am a theologian and not a biblical scholar. While Scripture is typically a significant source for much of our Christian theologies, and while our biblical interpretations inevitably have theological implications, the language, the tools, and the overall nature of the disciplines are quite different. While I have a profound respect for the delicate and intricate hermeneutical skills required in the field of biblical scholarship, it is important for me to approach this timely issue as a theologian and not a biblical scholar. That said, however, there are some methodological concerns that I believe are germane to both theological and biblical interpretation and certainly significant to our discussion.

Just as our theologies reflect as much, if not more, about the persons doing them as they do about God, so too do our perspectives on the Bible. No theology emerges in a social, historical, or cultural vacuum, and neither does any particular interpretation or approach to Scripture. Both theological and biblical discourse are shaped by the complicated historical realities of the persons conducting them. Just as our theologies reflect the particular, complex reality into which God has entered and out of which God's

1. Kelly Brown Douglas "Marginalized People, Liberating Perspectives: A Womanist Approach to Biblical Interpretation," *Anglican Theological Review* 83:1 (2001) 41–47. Reprinted by permission of the *Anglican Theological Review* and of Kelly Brown Douglas.

revelation is perceived and understood, so too do our approaches to the Bible. The texts we go to, the way we read those texts, and the authority we give the Bible itself are inevitably informed by who we are as embodied beings, how we experience life socially and culturally, as well as what we perceive as the meaning and value of life. It is for this reason that as we contemplate this issue of biblical interpretation we must remember that we cannot talk about any singular or universal approach to the biblical witness. Instead, we must recognize that just as there are various angles of vision from which to perceive God's revelation, there are various ways in which to view the biblical witness to that revelation.

Yet, with that said, I am not suggesting a kind of vulgar relativism in which anything goes. Such a vulgar relativism is found in various pronouncements often made to me in an attempt to end conversation over some controversial issue, such as homosexuality or women's roles in the church. "Oh, well, you can find whatever you want in the Bible so my view is just as valid as yours," is an example of such a pronouncement. To accept this type of declaration is an acceptance of a kind of vulgar relativism. Such acceptance suggests that slaveholders who used the Bible to place a "sacred canopy" over chattel slavery were just as justified in their use of the Bible as were the enslaved who used the Bible to support their quest for freedom. In essence, an "anything goes" approach to the Bible implies that it is just as appropriate to use the Bible as a weapon of terror and dehumanization as it is to use it as a source for empowerment and liberation.

How is it then that we can adjudicate between these different claims upon the Bible? Does the biblical witness accommodate both tyranny and justice? Or does the biblical witness suggest a preferred perspective on God's revelation and hence a rendering and use of the sacred texts that would invalidate a biblical tradition of tyranny or terror? The answers to these questions bring me to the topic at hand: "Marginalized People, Liberating Perspectives: A Womanist Approach to Biblical Interpretation."

A womanist approach to biblical interpretation, like womanist perspectives in general, begins with the recognition that our society and many of our churches are marred by interlocking and interactive structures of domination. These structures are characterized by white patriarchal privilege and undergirded by white supremacist ideologies. This means that a people's sovereignty is diminished inasmuch as that people lack any one valued human characteristic, namely whiteness or maleness. For instance, to be both white and male affords one the highest level of political, social, economic, and ecclesiastical privilege and dominance. To be white and female eliminates the claim to gender (i.e., male) privilege but preserves the fight to race (i.e., white) privilege. To be black and male portends a "racialized" male privilege. Specifically, black men are able to exercise sovereignty only in relation to black women. To be black and female is to have virtually no claim to the privileges accorded in a white patriarchal society and/or church. The black female reality is a marginalized reality. Yet, to be marginalized is not to be powerless. Marginality does not signify powerlessness. Rather, it signals a certain liberating agency that has several implications for biblical interpretation in our complicated world. In order to fully appreciate these implications let us look more closely at the liberating agency associated with marginal realities.

The Power of Marginal Realities

Existing on the margins of society and church provides a people with a special epistemological advantage, a certain way of knowing, that is fundamental to creating a just society and church. There are at least two interrelated aspects of the epistemological advantage inherent to marginal realities. Sociologist Patricia Hill Collins points to one aspect of this advantage in her discussion of "outsider/within locations."[2]

Outsider/within locations represent one of two marginal perspectives. These locations, as Collins correctly argues, provide a distinctive angle of vision on the contradictions and nuances of domination. For while those on the margins may be on the outside of actual dominating privilege, their "within" location gives them a singular view of how such privilege actually functions and sustains itself. This is, for instance, the view/location of the black female scholar in the academy, the black female secretary in relation to the president, and/or the black female bishop in the church. Such outsider/within marginal locations provide one with the unique opportunity to demystify and demythologize the conundrums of domination. They allow for a realistic perspective on the "powerful"—the outsider inevitably recognizes that dominating power is predicated on "unjust" privilege, not on innate superiority. The outsider who is within also has the opportunity to witness the machinations and insidious manifold discourse required to appropriate and secure unjust privilege. Essentially, outsider/within marginal realities enable one to see that "life in the big house is not actually what it is cracked up to be," or as hip-hop culture would put it, "it ain't all that."

Knowledge concerning the fragility of dominating power subsequently provides the outsider who is within access to a certain moral agency. This agency compels the critique of the corruptions endemic to domination.

2. See Patricia Hill Collins, *Black Feminist Thought: Knowledge, Consciousness, and the Politics of Empowerment* (New York: Routledge, 1991) 11–13.

Such agency also holds the outsider who is within accountable not to the powerful, but to those who are absolutely on the outside of power, those who incur the unmitigated penalty of white patriarchal systems and structures of dominance—the "least of these." The perspective of the least of these reflects the second dimension of marginal locations and hence the second form of epistemological advantage associated with these locations.

The "least of these" are the underside of marginal realities. They experience unjust systems of privilege in their rawest, vilest forms. They rarely experience even a modicum of circumscribed privilege, that accorded to outsiders/within. As the underside, their view on the inhumanities of domination is unqualified. They have a preferred perspective. This is, for example, the perspective of the black female who is unable to find an adequately paying job to support her family and is thus forced to suffer the indignities of the welfare system. It is also the perspective of the black woman unable to get humane healthcare for her family, or the perspective of the black woman with children deprived of their father by structures and systems that, in order to survive, demand and ensure black male "social" dysfunction. Those on the underside of marginal realities experience the desperate evil of white patriarchal structures and systems of domination. Such an experience gives those on the underside access to a preferential moral agency.

Preferential moral agency is characterized by efforts to dismantle any systems or structures based on such unjust privilege. Preferential agency is accorded to those on the underside because they are the ones most unlikely to be deceived into thinking that certain systems and structures of domination are not inherently evil but can be mended to be more just. In other words, those on the underside are not vulnerable to the temptations available to outsiders/within—the temptation to protect the modicum of privilege that they have somehow managed to secure. The underside are better situated to see the radical and revolutionary change required to ensure that all human beings have access to what is needed to live and to fulfill our full human potential.

In this regard, preferential moral agency essentially compels a transformation in our notions of power. It makes clear that true power lies outside of and on the underside of places of privilege, i.e., white patriarchal privilege. Indeed, to secure a position in a system of unjust privilege is to have no power at all. For true power is the moral agency found in marginal underside locations. It is the power that perhaps Paul was referring to when he said that the weak will confound the strong. It is the power of a God who came into the world through a manger. It is the power to change the world so that all people are free. The epistemological advantage of the underside in fact provides the moral agency necessary to define the true meaning of freedom. In order to clarify the meaning of freedom it is necessary to explore the theological advantage of marginal realities.

Theological Advantage of the Marginalized

As Gustavo Gutiérrez suggested, there is a "preferential option for the poor."[3] That is to say, the revelation of God is best understood from the vantage point of the marginalized, the oppressed, the least of these in society. This is the significance of God's election of the enslaved Israelites and not the enslaving Egyptians. This is also the meaning of the incarnate God entering human history through a manger and not Herod's palace. The "least of these," those less encumbered by the corruptions and temptations of privilege and domination, are better able to perceive the radicality of God's vision for God's people.

God's vision is characterized by the absence of unjust hierarchies of privilege and domination. Jesus describes it as a world where "the last are first and the first are last" (Mark 10:31). These words do not portend a reversal of fortunes. Rather, they foretell a time when the first are last, the last are first, because they are literally indistinguishable. In other words, there are no rich, there are no poor, and there are no unjust hierarchical orders of privilege and domination. Such a "divine" vision necessitates an absolutely new arrangement of human relationships. The nature of these relationships is suggested by the Christian witness to a trinitarian God.

To claim that God is trinitarian is to profess a God that is internally and externally relational. Such a God is a God that does a "perfect dance" with God's self, as implied by the Greek word *periochoresis* used by the Cappadocians during the fourth-century debates to describe the trinitarian nature of God. Theologian Christopher Morse explains, "The fullness of God's being . . . is to be thought of as dancing equally throughout the three inseparable distinctive ways that the one God is God."[4] God's perfect dance is one where the three aspects of God as creator, redeemer, and sustainer exist or dance in a relationship of mutuality and reciprocity. It is this trinitarian view of relationship that provides the foundation for the way human beings are called to relate to one another. And again, it is those who are on the underside of unjust hierarchical relationships of privilege who are most inclined to grasp the need for this radical new "trinitarian" way of relating. Those on the un-

---

3. See for instance Gustavo Gutiérrez, *A Theology of Liberation* (Maryknoll, NY: Orbis, 1973) and *The Power of the Poor in History* (Maryknoll, NY: Orbis, 1984).

4. Christopher Morse, *Not Every Spirit: A Dogmatics of Christian Disbelief* (Valley Forge, PA: Trinity, 1994) 131.

derside are better able to know the true measure of freedom—a freedom defined by the vision of a trinitarian God for God's people.

The question now becomes, what does this have to do with biblical interpretation? More specifically, what does this suggest for adjudicating between interpretative traditions of tyranny and interpretative traditions of liberation?

If indeed, as suggested by nothing less than the fact of God's entrance into the world through a manger, there is a certain moral agency and hence preferential option intrinsic to marginal realities, then we are called as theologians, as biblical scholars, and as church people to listen to and learn from those on the underside of church and society. We must learn from them as they bear witness to and engage the biblical witness to God's revelation. We are to value the perspectives of the "least of these," the underside. To do so implies that we do several things in our approach to the Bible.

Foremost, it requires that we name our own points of privilege in order to recognize that our vantage point may indeed not be the best vantage point from which to engage the biblical witness to God. Such a naming then frees us to appreciate the perspectives of those on the underside.

An appreciation for these perspectives means that as we enter the biblical world and encounter various biblical stories, we must do so from the view of those who represent the most marginalized, the least of these in the stories. Womanist theologian Delores Williams does this in her reading of the Abraham, Sarah, and Hagar story (Gen 16:1–16 and 21:9–21). She approaches this story through the eyes of Hagar. In so doing, she discerns that the God whom Hagar encounters in the wilderness is not necessarily a "liberator," since that God sends Hagar back to the household of Abraham and Sarah. Entering the story through Hagar thus calls into question any simple, static descriptions of God as a liberator.

Essentially, when we view God from the vantage point of the most marginalized in the Bible, we are likely to be reminded that the God of our theologies is not necessarily the God of our lives. God is, in fact, transcendent. God, therefore, cannot be reduced to or contained by any theological rhetoric or exegetical attempt to make simplistic the complexity and mystery of a transcendent God. Moreover, entering the Bible from the underside always prompts us to check our understandings of what it means for God to be a liberator with those who are most oppressed, even as they are represented in the Bible. If our theological or exegetical claims about God are not liberating for them, then we must reevaluate those claims. This leads us to a further implication involved in recognizing the preferred perspective of the underside.

Given the fact that various biblical texts do indeed lend themselves to oppressive interpretations, and thus can set in motion a biblical tradition of terror, we are compelled to adopt a certain "hermeneutic of suspicion" in the way we use and interpret the Bible. This hermeneutic should reflect the preferred perspective and preferential moral agency of the underside. Inasmuch as any text or interpretation of a text diminishes the life and freedom of any people, then those texts and/or interpretations must be held under "suspicion," critically reevaluated and perhaps lose authority. We must fundamentally denounce any attempts to use the Bible in ways that terrorize others, such as women or gay and lesbian persons. Moreover, the perspective of "the least of these," those who feel the "terror" of a particular text or interpretation, is the adjudicating perspective in this regard.

In the final analysis, to affirm the moral agency of the underside means recognizing the impact that our use of the Bible can have on people's lives. It can be used as a weapon of oppression or a source of liberation. We should therefore do biblical interpretation not only with a certain humility, but also with the commitment to nurture a liberating, not terrorizing, biblical tradition. This means engaging the Bible not as a means to gain certain privileges, or to protect unjust systems or structures, but rather to promote a church and world where all persons—regardless of race, gender, or sexual expression—are valued. Such an approach to the Bible indeed reflects a womanist approach.

CHAPTER SIX

Our Mothers' Gardens

Discrete Sources of Reflection on the Cross in Womanist Christology[1]

JOANNE MARIE TERRELL

What might have been? He's never far from my mind. I was reading in Scriptures where the Lord Jesus Christ was scarred. His visage, his face was marred beyond that of any other man, and Emmett came to me. I said, "Oh my God, what a comparison." The spirit spoke to me as plainly as I'm talking to you now. And the spirit said, "Emmett was race hatred personified. That is how ugly race hatred is." I said, "Oh." I had to sit down. It struck me really hard. If Jesus Christ died for our sins, Emmett Till bore our prejudices, so…

—Mamie Mobley, Mother of Emmett Till

Why I'm not good enough? Harpo ast Mr.____.

Mr.____ say, Your mammy.

Harpo say, What wrong with my mammy?

Mr.____ say, Somebody kill her…

[Harpo]: It not her fault somebody kill her. It not! It not!

—Alice Walker, *The Color Purple*

1. JoAnne Marie Terrell, *Power in the Blood? The Cross in the African American Experience* (Eugene, OR: Wipf & Stock, 2005) 126–43. Reprinted by permission of the author who holds the copyright.

In analytical psychology, liberation from alienation entails anamnesis, or retrieval of experience that is painful yet necessary for the healing/ wholeness of the psyche. Borrowing from this insight, womanist theology recognizes reflection upon personal and collective experience as discrete sources in the construction of theological statements. Although it is varietal, womanist theology is fundamentally a theology of liberation; its discipline requires commitment to the wholeness of entire peoples, male and female. Collective anamnesis requires thoroughgoing honesty about the ways in which black women and their families have been disempowered by the social sins of racism, sexism, heterosexism/homophobia, and classism. Womanists affirm the didactic value of "intergenerational dialogue"[2] with their predecessors—the slave women who first articulated the meaning of African American women's struggle to come to faith—as well as the families and constituencies to which womanists belong and from which they derive theological insight.

My penchant for theological reflection began at an early age, as I tried to understand the circumscription of black families in the southern work force. My family was embroiled in a complex of issues that often resolved in domestic violence, some of which stemmed from the economic and social stress we were experiencing, some of which stemmed from both my parents' profound self-alienation and social alienation. My mother's story, in particular, is that of a woman who, for the better part of her short life and for all of my life with her, lived in deep grief over personal losses too numerous and painful to recount. Lost in a fog of addiction, after several failed marriages, miscarriages and broken relationships, she, too, was shot and killed by her lover. Her murder attests to the insidiousness of sexism within the African American community and to the truth of the radical critique of the hermeneutics of sacrifice put forth in the little ditty that some Black Power advocates sang in opposition to the Civil Rights movement, which I take liberty to paraphrase here: "Too much love . . . nothing kills a [woman] like too much love."

Building on Abelard's insight that Christ's example teaches and saves us, I believe that anyone's death has salvific significance if we learn continuously from the life that preceded it. I often resort to my mother's garden— her life story—which, for many years I regarded as a tragic tale that had moralistic theological import, at best. Whenever I have failed to heed the lessons I have learned, it reflects the fact that I had neglected to tend her garden. Sometimes, I have to admit, I very nearly forget the "rose" that she

2. Cf. Jacquelyn Grant, "Womanist Theology: Black Women's Experience as a Source for Doing Theology, with Special Reference to Christianity," *Journal of the Interdenominational Theological Center* 13:2 (Spring 1986) 195–212.

was—sweet, fragile, beautiful, funny, boisterous, quiet, complicated—much like Margaret Avery in her depiction of Shug Avery in the movie *The Color Purple*. Although her self-alienation was evident long before I was born, in light of her considerable gifts of music, poetry, intellect and humor, upon my mother's demise, I was compelled to ask Mobley's question, "What might have been?" as a grieving child. As a consequence of my own alienation, I have been compelled many times to ask Harpo's questions. As a religious person and as a scholar in the tradition of "faith in search of understanding," I search wholeheartedly for answers to them all. The personal crosses I have borne form the basis of my engagement in proto-womanist and woman-ist reflection on the cross in the African American experience. As a black/ woman/person with roots in the poor and working classes, I bring all of my experiences and insights to bear on my womanist theological reflection, in hope of *sacramentally* witnessing to who and what God is in me.

A Womanist Musing/Womanist Prose

What might have been? Why I'm not good enough? What's wrong with my mammy? The above citations instance the experiences of African American males Emmett Till, a mid-twentieth century lynching victim and martyr (d. 1955) and Harpo, a fictional character in Alice Walker's controversial novel. Till was a fourteen-year-old boy accused of whistling at a white woman. When his body was discovered, he had been shot and beaten, his neck rigged with a gin-mill fan around it. Harpo's mother, Annie Julia, had been shot and killed, like my own mother, by a jealous lover. Each crime disclosed demonstrates how inextricably linked are the sufferings of African American women and men and their children. The narrator relating each fatality nods to the world of spirit: Mobley, to the Holy spirit, out of her Christian conceptualization; Walker, to the world of dreams (Harpo has just awakened from a nightmare) out of her nonpersonalistic theism and humanistic commitments. Each in her own way, for better and worse, con-firms the creedal postulation of a "communion of saints." In their accounts, death destroyed neither the love that bound each family nor the causes for the lament that went up to the Spirit-world in consequences of each victim's falleness. Mobley's question implicates the brutality of white racism in the interdiction of a well-intended life. Drawing the comparison with Christ's suffering, she also implicates (or absolves) God, invoking the hermeneu-tics of sacrifice. Harpo's questions evoke legal stipulation that would have affected chattel slavery for life: *partus sequitur ventrem*, that is, "the child follows the condition of the mother." Stigmatized by his mother's fate, he was powerless to overcome his own social alienation and win the approval of his beloved Sofia's father.

Walker's humanistic leanings and nonpersonalistic doctrine of God can be discerned in the words of Shug Avery, singer, lover and priest of sorts to Celie, the protagonist, whom Shug leads to a powerful, new understanding of who, or rather, *what* God is, apart from the silent, obdurate, white, male authority figure to whom Celie has been writing letters,[3] the medium through which the entire story unfolds. In the exchange Shug celebrates neither human agency nor God alone but a dimension of the human-Divine encounter that is not traditionally emphasized in Christian thought. Through Shug's witness to the character, creativity, and oneness of God Walker affirms the ability to delight oneself/Godself in the things and people of the created realm:

> [Celie:] Shug a beautiful something, let me tell you. She frown a little, look out across the yard, lean back in her chair, look like a big rose. She say, My first step from old white man was trees. Then air. Then birds. Then other people. But one day when I was sitting quiet and feeling like a motherless child, which I was, it come to me: that feeling of being part of everything, not separate at all. I knew that if I cut a tree, my arm would bleed. And I laughed and I cried and I run all around the house. I knew just what it was. In fact, when it happen, you can't miss it. It sort of like you know what, she say, grinning and rubbing high up on my thigh.
>
> *Shug!* I say.
>
> Oh, she say. God love all them feelings. That's some of the best stuff God did. And when you know God loves 'em you enjoys 'em a lot more. You can just relax, go with everything that's going, and praise God by liking what you like.
>
> God don't think it dirty? I ast.
>
> Naw, she say. God made it. Listen, God love everything you love—and a mess of stuff you don't. But more than anything, God love admiration.[4]

The exchange between Celie and Shug is reminiscent of the nonpersonalistic theism of Hinduism, in which devotees worship the impersonal God Brahma yet also worship the incarnating God Krishna. As the Supreme Personality of the Godhead, Krishna is the Supreme *Enjoyer* of everything that is.[5] According to the Lord Krishna, "If one offers Me with love and

3. Alice Walker, *The Color Purple* (New York: Washington Square, 1982) 175–79.

4. Ibid., 178.

5. *Bhagavad-Gita As It Is,* trans. His Divine Grace A. C. Bhaktivedanta Swami

devotion a leaf, a flower, fruit or water, I will accept it" (9:26).[6] Although one of Western Christianity's major interpreters, St. Augustine, posited God's *dilectio* (delight) in creation and ours in God as the basis for communion with God, this dimension was overshadowed by his preoccupation with sin. A certain cherishable, devotional aspect of Christianity has been nearly lost in the Western church's continued focus on sin and its remedy, putatively revealed in Christ's death on the cross and in one's embodiment of the hermeneutics of sacrifice, which is described as the sine qua non of Christian witness and is echoed in Mobley's understanding of the theological significance of her son's brutal death.

Mobley cites the fourth song of Deutero-Isaiah's Suffering Servant songs (Isa 42:1–2; 49:1–6; 50:4–11; 52:13—53:12). Although the Servant is identified in none of them, according to Rabbi Stephen Geller of the Jewish Theological Seminary (New York City) the text possibly refers to (a) a prophet, (b) a priest or (c) a king because prophetic, priestly and royal motifs abound in the Servant songs and because all are noted "servants of God" in the Hebrew Bible.[7] The specific verse Mobley quoted simulates royal imagery by drawing its antithesis: the king is supposed to be good-looking; for example, Saul is lifted up because of his singular handsomeness (1 Sam 9:2); the Servant has no attractive features. The king has the authority of speech; the Servant does not open his mouth. Whereas the king is divinely chosen and anointed, the Servant is "inhumanly disfigured," perhaps with leprosy, a condition that suggested divine disfavor in that context. If a royal figure is involved, the passage may intentionally refer to the ritual humiliation of kings in other ancient Near Eastern cultures.[8] Some legal injustice may also be indicated (Isa 53:8). The anti-royal, righteous sufferer motif runs throughout the passage. As Gellar noted, the idea that the Servant suffers vicariously and performs an atoning work for the sins of the people through his death (Isa 53:4–10) is a new theological development of the late-Exilic era. This climaxes in a statement that issues forth in a promise of resurrection, another new theme: "Yet it was the will of the Lord to bruise him; he has put him to grief; when he makes himself an offering for sin, he shall see his offspring, he shall prolong his days; the will of the Lord shall prosper

Prabhupada (New York: Collier, 1972 [1974]) 300. CF. Barbara Stoler Miller, ed., trans., *Love Song of the Dark Lord: Jayadeva's Gitagovinda* (New York: Columbia University Press, 1977).

6. *Bhagavad-Gita As It Is*, 478.

7. Lecture, 28 April 1992.

8. Cf. James B. Pritchard, ed., *The Ancient Near East*, vol. 1 of *An Anthology of Texts and Pictures* (Princeton: Princeton University Press, 1958 [1973]); and vol. 2 of *A New Anthology of Texts and Pictures* (Princeton: Princeton University Press, 1975 [1992]).

in his hand" (v. 10). Together, the righteous sufferer motif, atoning work, death, and resurrection of the Servant account for the Christian appropriation of the songs to describe the career and significance of Jesus. In Jewish interpretive tradition the Servant is usually identified as the Jewish people or a "remnant" thereof; nevertheless, the songs provided a blueprint for the *imitatio Christi* for the church in persecution and slavery, and they still guide African Americans' apprehension of Christian kerygma and doctrine.

Like the Servant, Jesus, and the Jewish people, African Americans have been devalued, marred, and killed by the violence of oppressors. Given their experiences of massive collective suffering, the notion that divine disfavor is operative contributes to the ambiguity with which persons in both communities understand their relationship to God. Although the love ethic in the black church is predicated on the theme of righteous suffering and is sustained by the compensatory mechanisms of promise, it is unclear if Mobley appeals to it prescriptively and thereby absolves God concerning Emmett's death. Yet it is abundantly clear that she recognizes the destructiveness in the human agency of those responsible. Thus, her comparison of Emmett's suffering with that of Christ's strikes me as having been made not as an inflated or sanctimonious claim but descriptively, in consequence of genuinely living in the theodical question. As one standing within the interpretive tradition of the black church, Mobley's willingness to be taught by the Spirit is likely an affirmation of the goodness and sovereignty of God in opposition to white supremacy. Nonetheless, the ambiguity of her statement is instructive because it is self-enjoining to a higher code of conduct.

Mobley's image of God, reflected in the face of her mutilated son, as well as Walker's conceptualization of God, recall the lattice-work whatnot that graced my early home (with its dual images of Jesus crucified and Christ glorified) and my family's experience of plantation farming. Just as the cross and the croker sack evoked in me the same reaction of resentment of suffering, when I looked again on the cotton fields of North Carolina, a more attractive picture emerged from a second, skewed image of *that* crucifixion through circumscription. Like the triumphalist God, plantation labor also fascinated me, for two reasons: (1) because the element of surprise was always great among the mass of folks working together, and (2) because the opportunities to marvel at nature were simply rife. Like the juxtaposed images of Jesus crucified and Christ glorified, like croker sacks/white overseers/aching backs and sun/sky/singing voices/variegated insects/smells of earth, Mobley's and Walker's images of God present me with something fascinating to behold and ponder in the light of my black, womanist and Christian commitments. Perhaps in contemplating this mandala I can affect some relief from my sense of alienation, and find in it, as I did in the first and second mandalas, spiritual principles that bring meaning, purpose, and direction to my life.

The appeal of the term "womanist" among black women scholars of religion cannot be gainsaid. One only has to note the growing number of book titles that convey a womanist perspective. Nevertheless, some scholars do not accept it. bell hooks, for example, fears that the designation detracts from feminist unity and power.[9] Other black women accept the womanist label in a limited way; not all components of the term Walker coined are embraced by all the black women who use it to describe themselves. Womanist ethicist Katie Cannon has argued that one cannot make the claim of being a womanist or of advocating womanism without embracing its whole meaning. Unfortunately, racism and classism, the profundity of unexplored misogynistic, heterosexist, self-abnegating tendencies, and the fear of vulnerability and transformation militate against the cultivation of womanist principles that enhance black women's ability to survive, be free, and creatively express themselves. Sometimes black women stumble under the weight of so much domination.

The proper naming of things or persons calls them into existence or brings them to light so they may be seen in their proper relationship to other things or persons. White feminists for example, term male domination of women "patriarchy." Black women do not deny the bonds of oppression that unite women. Williams, however, identifies a "substantial difference between [white women's] patriarchally-deprived-privileged-oppression" and black women's "demonically-derived-annihilistic-oppression," which she termed "demonarchy."[10] In recent writings Williams has backed away from this usage, perhaps because it is essentialist, characterizes relations between black people and whites as always adversarial (which belies the courage of conviction shown by some white abolitionists and co-workers in the Civil Rights movement) and undercuts white accountability for racist thought and actions. Nonetheless, naming black women's oppression "demonarcy" sheds light on the differences between the womanist and feminist experiences and mandates.

In light of these difficulties, I offer some reflection on what it means to be a womanist theologian, with reference to each of the four instances of

9. bell hooks, *Feminist Theory from Margin to Center* (Boston: South End, 1984) 26. A cursory reading of hooks's writings reveals that she never employs the definite article when referring to *feminist movement* (*not* the feminist movement). For hooks, this rhetorical technique refutes monolithic conceptions of the nature of women's involvement in feminism, which she describes as a "movement to end sexist oppression."

10. Delores S. Williams, "The Color of Feminism," *Christianity and Crisis*, April 29, 1985, 164–65.

the definition articulated by Walker, and with the view in mind that each can become a source for helping African American women articulate critical perspective on their own experiences of the crosses of racism, sexism, heterosexism/homophobia, and classism.

To Be a Womanist

Womanist theology is being developed by black women, who are *feminists of color*. Walker proffered the term "womanist" as an alternative to "feminist" because feminism is usually associated with white women's critique of sexism or patriarchy. Key issues in feminist theologies such as rape and domestic violence, women's work, female bonding, inclusive language and the gender of God, economic autonomy for women, and heterosexism affect all women.[11] Still, most black women agree that white feminists do not adequately address the issues of black women.

To be black in America is to have suffered a collective history of chattel slavery and to have that history purportedly justified by divine sanction. White catechists told the slaves that they must endure servitude and its attendant miseries as a result of the "Hamitic curse" (Gen 9:18–29) deploying the hermeneutics of sacrifice. While it is true that white women were similarly circumscribed on the basis of their sex, they do not share in the exponentially charged experience of interstructured[12] oppression with black women, and in fact, are signal contributories, along with white children and men, in the oppression of black children, women, and men. Although sexism is a constant in the oppression of all women and poverty *may* be part of white women's experience, the cultural value of white femininity/white skin and white women's relative wealth inure them from the kind of totalistic ontological assault black women/black people face. Linda Burnham, a member of the National Council of the Alliance Against Women's Oppression, warns African Americans not to adopt uncritically the view that poverty is becoming a phenomenon that is based solely or primarily on gender. This view, which some feminists advocate, "presents a highly distorted picture of the general dynamics that are at the source of poverty in

11. Karen Ludwig, "Womanists Theology/Feminist Theology: A Dialogue," *Daughters of Sarah* 15:2 (March/April 1989) 6–7. The article reports on what several black women think is distinctive about womanist theology, citing a lecture on womanist and feminist theologies given by ethicist Cheryl Sanders.

12. See Marcia Riggs, "The Logic of Interstructured Oppression: A Black Womanist Perspective," in *Redefining Sexual Ethics*, Susan Davies and Eleanor Haney, eds., (Cleveland: Pilgrim, 1991).

the U.S. These distortions are the inevitable result of a point that abstracts women as a group out of the overall socioeconomic trends in U.S. capitalist development."[13]

Burnham has written that the "feminization of poverty" theory obscures factors relevant to the impoverishment of black women, overstates white women's vulnerability to impoverishment, ignores or underestimates the impoverishment of black men and does not deal effectively with working class exploitation as a constitutive element of late capitalism. As Burnham pointedly states, "The emiseration of black women has not been accompanied by a rise to affluence of black men.[14]

Despite hegemonic interpretations of the Bible that continue to relegate their lives to subservience and contentment therewith, African Americans in and since slavery counted their own experience as that through which the truth of the Bible was to be mediated. Reflecting on biblical ties that bound black families together in their suffering and that make collective, and in some ways, *exclusionary* reflection an ongoing, necessary condition of their theological project, Cannon states that, in slavery:

> Ideas and practices that favored equal rights of all people were classified as invalid and sinful because they conflicted with the divinely ordained structure that posited inequality between Whites and Blacks. The doctrine of biblical infallibility reinforced and was reinforced by the need for social legitimization of slavery. Thus, racial slavery was accepted as the necessary fulfillment of the curse of Ham. This had the effect of placing the truthfulness of God's self-revelation on the same level of Black slavery and white supremacy. The institutional framework that required Black men, women and children to be treated as chattel, as possessions rather than as human beings, was understood as being consistent with the spirit, genius and precepts of the Christian faith.[15]

Because of this eurocentric history of interpretation, womanist theological reflection is not wed to notions of biblical authority that support black peoples' and women's subservience. Womanist biblical scholar Clarice Martin agrees with feminist theologians on the need to use inclusive language, for example, in order to project alternative feminine images of God

13. Linda Burnham, "Has Poverty Been Feminized in Black America?" *The Black Scholar*, March/April 1985, 14.

14. Ibid., 17.

15. Kate Geneva Cannon, "Slave Ideology and Biblical Interpretation," in *Katie's Canon: Womanism and the Soul of the Black Community* (New York: Continuum, 1995) 41.

and paradigms for humankind.[16] She proposes that womanist theologians increasingly adopt and promote the use of inclusive language in ways that go beyond the concerns of feminists to include the particularities of race and that demonstrate how biblical language is used to reinforce racial oppression. Martin postulates that faithfully rendering biblical terminology in appropriate English can yield a "quadrúocentric" hermeneutics that addresses issues of gender, class, language, and race. She denounces the way in which the Greek terms for slave/slavery (*doulos/douleia*) have been euphemistically rendered in English translations of the Bible in the rhetoric of servant/servanthood, as does womanist theologian Jacquelyn Grant. In the American context the effect of this has been to preclude substantive dialogue about slavery in theological, ethical, political, and social discourse.

Although womanists have criticized Eurocentric biblical interpretation, most have not rejected Christianity or the Bible wholesale but accept them as valid expressions of African Americans' striving toward an understanding of both God and the moral and ethical obligations of the community. Womanist ethicist Cheryl Sanders cites the liberation of women and valuing *families* (namely, *heterosexual* families) as primary obligations of black people.[17]

Notwithstanding her emphasis, most womanists resist making the family the central paradigm of oppression, since doing so can obscure the interrelatedness of structural sins and lead to further privatization of the meaning of oppression by (1) obstructing meaningful class analysis and (2) obfuscating the need for white people to address (a) the presumption of privilege that upper and middle class whites hold on the basis of whiteness, (b) the tenacity with which they defend the privileges accorded themselves and (c) the rapacity with which they deny the same to poor and non-white persons. The Personal Responsibility Act of 1995, for example, debated in the US Congress on March 23 and 24, concerned the issue of "entitlements." Opposing extensions in welfare benefits and the continuation of federally funded meals for Head Start programs, the representative from Florida held up a sign that read, "Do not feed the alligators." Several African American members of Congress objected strenuously to the bestialization of poor and working-class people, and to the inhumane implications of taking meals from the mouths of their children, many of whom are black and who benefit tremendously from the Head Start program. Williams implicates the

16. Clarice Martin, "Womanist Interpretations of the New Testament: The Quest for Holistic and Inclusive Translation and Interpretation," *Journal of Feminist Studies in Religion* 6:2 (1990) 41–61.

17. Cheryl Sanders, *Empowerment Ethics for a Liberated People: A Path to African American Social Transformation* (Minneapolis: Fortress, 1995).

genocidal intent of whites in the need of African Americans to stand together against "white racial narcissism":

> White racial narcissism indicates a malfunction in the Ameri-
> can national psyche that can ultimately lead the culture to self-
> destruct or can lead the powerful racially narcissistic group to
> genocide members of a less powerful racial group. One way of
> dealing with white racial narcissism in the culture is for the vic-
> timized group to stand against the powerful, racially narcissistic
> group in a permanent posture of self-defense.[18]

Sanders identified the priority issues of black women that arose in
consequence of slavery and that seek to thwart the genocidal intent of white
supremacists. They include physical survival and spiritual salvation of the
family (with equality between males and females); the redistribution of
goods and services; encountering God as family; and ending white, gender,
and class supremacy.[19]

Despite the communal nature and locus of black oppression and black
responses thereto, womanists are compelled to articulate their own understandings of their faith. Although black men are targeted, censured, and
victimized by the American criminal justice system and constitute the majority of homeless people—significant factors in feminists' minimization of
black impoverishment—many of them are still enslaved to the ideology of
male superiority characteristic of patriarchy from primordial times. Black
men, as well as white men and white women, dehumanize black women,
exploiting them in the work place and in the home.

Celie's and my mother's stories testify to the stranglehold of sexism in
the African American community in each of its incarnations. Her image of
God and my mandala also reveal one mechanism by which black people
internalize racism and sexism: by imbibing cultural projections of whiteness
and maleness as the standard of the holy. Influenced by the cultural revolution engendered in early nationalist sentiment and reprised in the Black
Power movement underway in the late 1960s, black theologians reacted
enthusiastically to the hypocrisy of white culture and of white theologians,
who basically ignored the plight of African Americans as if it were a matter
of no consequence in the theological enterprise. Dovetailing Bishop Turner's
bold declaration that "God is a *Negro*," they posited the liberating intent of
the "Black Christ,"[20] consistent with the christocentrism of the black church,
radicalizing the black creative imagination concerning the Divine. None-

---

18. Williams, *Sisters in the Wilderness* (Maryknoll, NY: Orbis, 1993) 88.

19. Ludwig, "Womanist Theology/Feminist Theology: A Dialogue," 7.

20. Cf. Alex Poinsett, "The Quest for a Black Christ," *Ebony*, March 1969.

theless, black theologians did not pose a self-critique concerning sexism within their ranks until summarily challenged by womanist theologians.[21] Jacqueline Grant's seminal essay "Black Theology and the Black Woman" incriminated the African American community's historical "focus on manhood" in the silencing of black women in the emergent discipline of black theology:

> By self-appointment, or by the sinecure of a male-dominated society, Black men have deemed it proper to speak for the entire Black community, male and female. In a sense, Black men's acceptance of the patriarchal model is logical and to be expected. Black male slaves were unable to reap the benefits of patriarchy. Before emancipation they were not given the opportunity to serve as protector and provider for Black women and children, as White men were able to do for their women and children. Much of what was considered "manhood" had to do with how well one could perform these functions. It seems only natural that the post-emancipation black men would view as primary importance the reclaiming of their property—their women and children. Moreover, it is natural that Black men would claim their "natural" right to the "man's world." But it should be emphasized that this is logical and natural only if one has accepted without question the terms and values of patriarchy—the concept of male control and supremacy.[22]

To be a womanist is to be *outrageous, audacious, courageous, willful, responsible, in charge, serious, and curious* (that is, wanting to know more and in greater depth than is considered good for one). These qualities comport with black women's historic roles. Proto-womanists Phyllis Wheatley, Sojourner Truth, and Harriett Tubman evinced these qualities, which helped them endure, survive, and resist forced breeding, separation from their children and spouses, and death. Accordingly, early womanists Grant, Williams, Cannon, and others gave evidence of these qualities and proved themselves capable of developing their own theological perspectives and adjudicating their own moral responses to sexism, racism, and classism.

21. I applaud the work of Cone and other black theologians who have attempted to make the womanist critique integral to their work because I am challenged in turn to understand the peculiar plight of black men in the American context. See his preface to the revised edition of *A Black Theology of Liberation* (Maryknoll, NY: Orbis, 1990 [1986, 1970]).

22. Jacquelyn Grant, "Black Theology and the Black Woman," in *Black Theology: A Documentary History*, James H. Cone and Gayraud S. Wilmore, eds., vol. 1 (Maryknoll, NY: Orbis, 1993) 325–26.

Williams has stated that womanist theological methodology utilizes black women's history, literature, religious experience, and other elements of African American culture in a diagnostic capacity and is informed by a multi-dialogical, liturgical, and didactic intent.[23] Thus, womanist theory resists meta-narrative views of *his*tory, insisting upon a dialogical approach and emphasizing the importance of sharing *her*stories in order to provide context to theological speculations. For some black women, womanism means coming to voice, finding their voice, growing up. For these women, it is not so much a case of duplicity that impedes their total embrace of womanism but the need to discover themselves. In my case I entered the womanist enterprise with much trepidation. This was, in part, because I was accustomed to being silent and invisible; in part, because of my captivity to the Bible *vis-à-vis* the hermeneutics of sacrifice. I had to learn to watch, fight, and pray and to tell my stories in order to find healing. Becoming an advocate of womanism and empowering others to do so is a task for the audacious, courageous, and forbearing.

To be a womanist is to love *women and individual men, sexually and/ or nonsexually.* Sanders challenged warrants for the use of womanist no-menclature on this point, expressing concern to make clear the distinction between what is consistent "Christian" doctrine (and therefore the proper task of the Christian theologian or ethicist) and what is not. In this instance of the definition of womanist Walker raises the issue of sexual preference by affirming lesbian and bisexual relationships, lifestyles the practice of which Sanders questioned as liberative praxes for the physical survival of the African American community and for which she questioned the endorsement of Christianity.[24] Walker evinces here a didactic and multi-dialogical intent. In a society that devalues blackness *and* femaleness and that exploits and denigrates women's bodies, that a womanist "loves women" and "*individual* men" is instructive. Womanist grounding enables black women to assert the

23. Delores S. Williams, "Womanist Theology: Black Women's Voices," *Christianity and Crisis*, March 2, 1987, 69.

24. Cheryl Sanders et al., "Roundtable Discussion: Christian Ethics and Theology in Womanist Perspective," *Journal of Feminist Studies in Religion* 5:2 (Fall 1989). Although almost no one disputes the apparent heterosexism and/or homophobia of Sander's query, Sander's criticisms are also methodological. A major question that arose from her inquiry is, without clear Christian commitments, is Womanist Theology a proper discipline in which Christian scholars should engage? Although Walker's definition of womanism is not exclusive of Christianity, it is not particularly inclusive of it either, especially not conceptions of Christianity that derive from a literalist biblical perspective. Although this proclivity is apparent in Sander's early essay, as of this writing she employs the womanist label and focuses on the development of Afrocentric ethics within the discipline.

worth of their lives apart from those men who engage with black women in ways that mimic dominant power dynamics. Moreover, it enables women who love women sexually to counter monolithic conceptions of the African American community by building on the same claims to freedom that black liberationists and heterosexual womanists make for themselves. Renee Hill, a self-identified lesbian, challenges womanist and black theologians to make the issues of heterosexism and homophobia within the African American community integral to their work:

> The lesbian voice is silenced in Christian womanist theology. Heterosexism and homophobia are nonissues in the Christian womanist paradigm for liberation. There is no widespread discussion of sexuality in African American Christian theology in general. Christian womanists, like their male counterparts, focus for the most part on the impact of racism on the Black community. The Christian womanist focus on gender is to a great degree a focus on the retrieval of black women's stories, words and perspectives. There is no great emphasis on the impact of sexism on the Black community. This may be a key to the lack of discourse on sexuality.[25]

By acknowledging same-sex relationships womanism also counters antiquated biological and axiological assumptions concerning human sexuality that help maintain all women in subordinate positions. Through its open embrace this womanist principle has the power to bring the silenced voices and experiences of lesbians, gay men, and bisexuals to conversations about the shape and means of black redemption. As Hill states:

> Sexuality is an issue for Christian womanist theologians. It is not any less or any more important than community or survival. It simply is a part of community and survival. Sexuality (and male dominance) must be discussed in the Black community. Only then will we be able to address subjects like rape, the AIDS epidemic, as well as sexual orientation in the Black community.[26]

The freedom to love whomever one wills is a cherished tenet in liberal thinking. Still, the whims of love are not above critique. In the womanist view affirmation provided in love relationships should be met in accordance with a praxis that enhances prospects for survival, liberation, and creative self-expression. For me, the critical principle is self-love, irrespective of one's

25. Renee L. Hill, "Who Are We for Each Other? Sexism, Sexuality and Womanist Theology," in *Black Theology: A Documentary History, 1980–1992*, ed. Cone and Wilmore, vol. 2 (Maryknoll, NY: Orbis, 1993) 346.

26. Ibid., 347.

mate, as part of one's responsibility to oneself and God. For women to "love women," whether sexually or nonsexually, is to reject the misogynistic and heterosexist norms of patriarchy and demonstrate the inviolability of self-acceptance and self-love that are reflected in acceptance and love of one's own kind. It is to affirm the beauty of women and to celebrate the fecundity of women's gifts. To be a womanist is to be, traditionally, *capable.*

Womanists agree that black men and women can ill afford sectarianism in the struggle against the common experience of race oppression, but they rigorously advocate/agitate for the end of sexist oppression, not as a subordinate but as a concomitant ethical and moral necessity for the survival and liberation of the entire African American community. Dominant ideologies tend to portray power as a zero-sum game in which more power for some means less for others, thus dividing oppressed communities into factions competing for the crumbs of empowerment. Nevertheless, because womanists are linked to black men by familial ties and the common experience of race oppression, they are committed to the survival and wholeness of entire people, male and female. To be womanist is to be, traditionally, *universalist.* Hence, womanists are *non-separatist.* (Except in matters of health. Because matters of health matter most, womanists refrain from emotionally or physically abusive relationships.) The womanist paradigm challenges those in the lived-world to model healthy intimate relations between women and women, and women and men, and remains true to its multi-dialogical and, I think, *sacramental,* intent.

To be a womanist is to love *music, dance, the moon, the Spirit, love, food, roundness, struggle, the folk, herself. Regardless.* It is to be both creation-affirming and God-affirming. It is to celebrate who black women are and who they can be in community and in God. In the religious experience of African Americans the ability to transcend and endure, while enjoying life, has proven essential for maintaining spiritual and emotional health in a context of oppression. The freedom to love *what* one loves (that is, to have *fun*) and to love *whom* one is, is fundamental to the worship of God in Walker's paradigm. Williams identifies self-love (*regardless*) as the sine qua non of womanist thought,[27] evincing, again, a didactic intent. If self-love is the critical principle in effecting liberation, a proper exegesis of the nature of love is required. Consistent with the biblical injunction to love the neighbor as one loves oneself, black women need to love themselves so they can genuinely love others. Nevertheless, their historical roles as sustainers of their communities implicate them in their refusal to embrace fully their

27. Delores S. Williams, "The Color Purple," *Christianity and Crisis,* July 14, 1986, 230–32.

own liberation as women. Frequently black women do not assert their right to mutuality and respect in relationships. Yet without these basic elements a relationship cannot thrive.

Womanist is to feminist as purple is to lavender. This suggests heightened experience of the many possible negative ramifications of sexism. For example, black women are three times as likely to be raped as white women. By analogy the color purple evokes the impact of multiple oppressions together on their bodies and psyches. The analogy also recognizes that language developed at cost to black people and women. Womanist methodology thus is committed "both to reason and to the validity of female imagery and metaphorical *language* in the construction of theological statements."[28]

Transforming the Language of Sacrifice

As I have tried to indicate, I am aware of the problematic nature of the language of sacrifice, the potential and actual abuses thereof; nevertheless, I have cited from my mother's story in order to posit a transformed, *sacramental* notion of sacrifice that has saving significance for the African American community and for black women in particular. Hence, I agree with other womanists that I have the right and responsibility to challenge Christian language and tradition.

As a womanist liberationist I do not believe that oppressed people are obliged to love their oppressors categorically. Although I do not preclude this motivation as a response of a true devotee, my position is at odds with the hermeneutics of sacrifice, which exhorts enemy-love[29] and is recapitulated in the popular but unbiblical proposition to "love everybody." Although I wish to dispute neither the scriptural warrants nor the psychological benefit to be derived from this position, I take cues from the Johannine communities' stress on loving "one another"[30] and the biblical command to "love the

---

28. Ibid.

29. Cf. Walter Wink, *Violence and Nonviolence in South Africa: Jesus' Third Way* (Philadelphia: New Society, 1987).

30. See especially, 1 John 4:7–12: "Beloved, let us love one another; for love is of God, and he who loves is born of God and knows God. He who does not love does not know God; for God is love. In this the love of God was made manifest among us, that God sent his only Son into the world, so that we might live through him. In this is love, not that we loved God but that he loved us and sent his Son to be the expiation for our sins. Beloved, if God so loved us, we also ought to love one another. No one has ever seen God; if we love one another God abides in us and God's love is perfected in us." Cf. John 15:12–17.

neighbor" (Matt 22:39 and parallels)[31] whomever one is obliged to respond with the milk of human kindness, whoever needs you. Mobley, for example, channeled the pain of her son's death into community service, lecturing for the NAACP, eventually becoming a schoolteacher. When asked, she professed not to harbor bitterness toward Roy Bryant and Big Jim, W. J. Milam (the men who killed Emmett) or toward whites generally: it certainly would be unnatural not to, yet I'd have to say I'm unnatural. From the very beginning that's the question that has always been raised: "What would you do to Milam and Bryant if you had the opportunity?" I came to the realization that I would do nothing. What they had done was not for me to punish and it was not for me to go around hugging hate to myself, because hate would destroy me. It wouldn't hurt them.[32]

While Mobley did not *profess* love for Milam and Bryant, she *confessed* that her son's death did not nullify the biblical command to love the neighbor and testified that it was God's empowerment that enabled her to keep it:

> The Lord gave me a shield, I don't know how to describe it myself. It was as if he put me in a neutral zone where I had no feeling whatsoever toward Milam and Bryant. I did not wish them dead. I did not wish them in jail. If I had to, I could take their four little children—they each had two—and I could raise those children as if they were my own and I could have loved them.[33]

Although Mobley grounds her love ethic in her evangelical faith,[34] she *struggles* to affirm God and the Spirit assists her efforts. Moreover, she does not make her claims uncritically, without recognition of white brutality. Everyday she lives with the fact of her loss. It carries with it the kind of pain that passing of time does not diminish. In my view Mobley is under no moral compulsion to love the men who murdered her son nor their children, yet she does not allow them to circumvent her freedom to love mercy and work for justice in the venues where she was called. This is what I think it means to witness *sacramentally* to the character of God: loving one's own, *not* loving others uncritically and, most important, *not* being defined by one's victimization but by one's commitments.[35]

31. See also Matt 5:43, 19:19; Rom 13:9; Gal 5:14; Jas 2:8.

32. Studs Terkel, *Race: How Blacks and Whites Think and Feel about the American Obsession* (New York: New Press, 1992) 21.

33. Ibid.

34. Ibid., 21–22. Mobley is a member of the Church of God in Christ, the largest Pentecostal denomination in the United States.

35. Thus, as a black liberation theologian, I would restate the womanist principle in this way: a black liberationist loves black people and *individual* whites. This affirms

In developing a *sacramental* understanding of sacrifice as a dimension of holistic spirituality I also take cues from the slave community, which proposed in song, "Lord, I *want* to love everybody [be a Christian] in my heart." I will to love all of creation, in accordance with the womanist sensibilities Walker describes in her image of God. Although I situate myself within the radical tradition of black theology, my personal praxis is pacifist activist, not merely because I believe it is sound strategy enhancing my prospects for survival, liberation and creative self-expression, but because I believe that there are some things that are worse than dying—namely, *killing*—for one's cause. Worse yet is killing without cause, a most horrible transgression of the Oneness in which I delight.

Nevertheless, I cannot in good conscience proscribe the liberative options of any people engaged in protracted struggle because I believe in self-defense as a human right that in no way reflects on the capacity to love another. In the imposition of sacrifice, protracted struggle is not seen under the rubric of self-defense but as a violation of the ethical codes of Vedic religion and Christianity. Despite the way the hermeneutics of sacrifice functions in Christian moral theory to misconstrue self-defense as violence, my interpretive model[36] in conversation with my particularities informs me that, since God is love, love cannot be prescribed, circumscribed, or even defined. It can, however, be mediated through human instrumentality, a means by which God can do whatever God wills, whether God wills to forgive or "smite" the wicked. In my *sacramental* model my aim is to foster human freedom and to garner holistic spirituality from whatever sources are revealed. Thus, I do not seek to enjoin one image of God. Rather, God is, as revealed in Christ, loving and challenging, humane and sovereign, culturally engaged yet countercultural, personal, a healer and a mystic, a co-sufferer and a liberator. *Sacramentally* witnessing to the character of God as a black person, as a woman and as a Christian, I maintain, abrogates none of my duties or any of my human rights. The *Bhagavad Gita* also ascribes to this *sacramental* understanding of human agency on the part of its devotees.[37]

African Americans' worth apart from whites *and* their right to love whomever they will, or must.

36. In my interpretive model Scripture *becomes* the word of God when it mediates a word that *witnesses* to creativity, goodness, oneness, and power of God in a person or a community. It is predicated upon my belief that the point of theology is in its *doing*, both in what it does to people and in what it makes people do. This makes theology, including Scripture-making, a divine and a human project.

37. Gandhi advocated the critical principle of *ahimsa* or *non-injury*, along with *satyagraha* or *truth-force* in Hinduism as the basis for his call to nonviolence. Many Western interpreters conveniently overlook the exegetical consideration that the *Bhagavad Gita,* from whence these principles derive, is an exhortation by the Lord Krishna

This has dramatic implications for women who are embroiled in abusive relationships, who remain in them for economic reasons and/or because their own self-concept is debased by the misogynistic norms of the church and the culture; who are themselves vulnerable to the murderous impulses of patriarchally driven persons; and who may be conflicted about defending themselves physically and/or emotionally.[38] Yet, in the imposition of sacrifice, the first word of Jesus (in the gospel of Mark)—*repent*—is appropriated privatistically, so that the sinfulness of oppressors is never construed as a major issue.[39] I would argue that this is another conventionally missed exegetical consideration, along with Jesus' own profound militancy in his oppressive context. Nonetheless, I agree with the wisdom of this ancient testimony:

> Weapons are tools of bad omen,
> By gentlemen not to be used;
> But when it cannot be avoided,
> They use them with calm and restraint.
> Even in victory's hour
> These tools are unlovely to see;
> For those who admire them truly
> Are men who in murder delight.[40]

In the early church's appropriation of the language of sacrifice, Jesus' death on the cross was said to have been the pouring out of God's own life, ending sanction for sacred violence, *once for all*. This claim could only be made in the light of the whole story about Jesus, including the incarnation,

---

to the warrior Arjuna to be the instrument of God and to fight, *literally*, in the cause of righteousness. Thus, a liberation impulse in Vedic Scripture specifically enjoins humanity to be instruments of God's love and justice as warriors in the cause of righteousness, having, therefore, the authority of God to affect their liberation as exigencies arise. In the purports of the *Gita, ahimsa* is described as "not arresting the progressive life of any living entity." A positive way of stating this might be that the principle seeks to further the spiritual happiness of the people in general, so that their full purpose might be realized. This Vedic witness is consistent with the principle, "There can be no reconciliation without liberation." The fact that many oppressed people have had to kill—and many more have died—for these congruent principles is mitigated by the fact that the non-realization of *ahimsa* carries with it the understanding that one kills with authority.

38. Cf. Angela Browne, *When Battered Women Kill* (New York: Free Press, 1989).

39. Yet in Israelite sacrifice, sin was regarded with such odiousness that the moral onus was placed on the subsequent actions of the one/ones for whom the sacrifice was performed.

40. Lao Tzu, *Tao Te Ching (Way of Life)* trans. R. B. Blakney (New York: Mentor, 1955) poem 31, 83.

ministry, suffering and death, resurrection and continuous intercession of the Holy Spirit. However, the martyrdom ethos in which Christianity was baptized virtually guaranteed that its central image would become the cross. This reality lent ultimacy to their claims concerning sacrifice. In truth, the martyrs evinced a *sacramental witness*; they sought to demonstrate bodily the utter feasibility of life in love and honor, as their association with Jesus had taught them.

Perhaps the cross is central to black Christian identity because black Christians suffer, like Jesus and the martyrs, unjustly. The cross in the African American experience *is* theodicy. Moreover, the death it points to is the way of all flesh. As theologians, it is tempting to forget that religious persons are concerned with what is beyond the grave and have constructed comforting myths that we will overcome its terror. Hence, some are "empty cross" Christians. I do not think that the problem is with the imagery per se; the cross, in its original sense, embodied a *scandal,* that something, anything good could come out of such an event. Seen in this light Jesus' sacrificial act was not the objective. Rather, it was the tragic, if foreseeable, result of his confrontation with evil. This bespeaks a view of Jesus and the martyrs as empowered, *sacramental* witnesses, not as victims who passively acquiesced to evil.

As I stated before, anyone's death has saving significance inasmuch as we learn continuously from the life that preceded it. My baptism into the ethos of sacrifice compels me to reflect on it as a vital component of my self-understanding as a religious person and as a person in community. Although I may never be required to give of my life for the sake of my ultimate claims, the peculiar efficacy of my mother's sacrifice as well as the Christian story prevent me from discarding the idea altogether, particularly the notion of sacrifice as the surrender or destruction of something prized or desirable for the sake of something with higher claim, a potentially salvific notion with communal dimensions that got lost in the rhetorical impetus of the language of surrogacy. Yet I believe that in the final hours of her life, I became a higher and more pressing claim to my mother—more important than her addiction, more important than her companion, more important, even, than her life, which he had threatened on more than one occasion. I speculate that this prevented her from challenging my abusive father-figure sooner.

I believe that continuous learning will be facilitated for oppressed Christians by always situating the call to sacrifice in historical context—by employing liberative hermeneutics, taking note of dissonances within the text, the experiences of the community, and the community's understandings of God. My mother's ultimate sacrifice and those of countless other black women who suffer abuse and die at the hands of patriarchal, violence-driven persons—whose deaths go unreported and under-reported, unprosecuted and under-prosecuted—are potentially liberating for women if we learn from their experiences, if we see how they exercised or did not exercise their moral and creative agency. This seems a much more relevant view of the atoning worth of women's blood. Although it is true, as some feminists assert, that women's blood loss has been devalued in Christian sacrificial tradition, Jesus' own life and *sacramental* example of affirming the intrinsic worth of women enable humankind to see women's blood as sacred.

Conclusion

The distinction between demonarchy and patriarchy recalls again the mandala of my youth. Although I unequivocally rejected the first, suffering image, I was never quite comfortable with the second, triumphalist image, because this God was in the image of my oppressors. Although he was clean, the visceral impact of watching him was subtly oppressive, like the sensation of being gently smothered. It took me a long time to articulate my discomfort, but once I was able to discern the wisdom of William's insight on patriarchy/demonarchy, I recognized that shifting my focus from the view of the suffering God to the view of the triumphalist God can, and often does, result in merely exchanging paradigms of oppression. The alternative, spiritualized image seemed to imply that I would find the complete relief I sought in the afterlife, which left my suffering mitigated but unremitted. Yet I cannot gainsay the value of the Christian story for understanding and ordering the early phases of my life and vesting me with power to withstand the storms therein. Although I despised the melodrama captured in the depiction of Jesus crucified, I could not avoid contemplating the suffering God because here was a mirror to my world. Viewing his pathos, I saw my mother's and my own. Secretly I despised Jesus, my mother, and myself because I resented what seemed to be needless suffering. And yet I loved above all because I willed it, and because somehow I knew I *was* loved. It was evident in the Providence I encountered in nature, whom I could not believe sanctioned the suffering brought on by evil human choices. As a child of six or seven, having very little to go on doctrinally but having had devastating experiences of physical and emotional abuse on which to reflect, I reformulated the classical theodical statement in this God-affirming way: *since* God is so good, why are people so evil? When I was eight years old, I "baptized" myself in a solemn ceremony so God would know that I chose not to be evil.

Like Mamie Mobley, like the early church, as a teenager I sought to find meaning in the suffering I encountered in the violent death of someone I loved and still love (I *believe* in the communion of saints). When I entered seminary in 1987, I brought the questions of my youth with me and learned that structures of oppression exist that generate not only a world of sin but also a worldview of sin that reflects on the moral characteristics of individuals or on the presumed shortcomings of God. I learned to reformulate the question, "What wrong with my mammy?" into, What were the social and economic factors that led to her alienation and ultimately to her demise? To the question, "Why I'm not good enough?," that is, for those who rejected me personally; for the racists who refused me employment, for the black church that sought to delimit the expression of my gifts, I came back with questions like, What benefits accrue to men/whites/male hierarchy from the circumscription of women/blacks? What notions of power are operative? On whose authority? No longer stigmatized, I began then to discern, resent, implicate and name the hermeneutics of sacrifice in the suffering that has pervaded my experience as a poor, African American woman who has also been called into ministry. One does not get to be a womanist by virtue of her blackness and femininity. Nor does one become a womanist simply because one reads, understands, and makes the appropriate adjustments in her life. The lived-world struggle to appropriate self-love as the operative principle is formidable. Black women entering the womanist enterprise commit to exploring further the contradictions that shape their collective and personal lives in the spirit of critical inquiry and in the spirit of hope. I have pursued this project in quest of holistic spirituality, which entails communion with God and all of my neighbors, and freedom to work, to love, and to enjoy life. I have tried to show, through an exploration of the etiological moorings of my faith, that the received story—while rife with difficulty—can bring value to black women's lives. As I have matured as a woman, as a scholar, and as a Christian, it has become increasingly necessary for me to learn more, more about Jesus and the redemption he putatively brings about for us, for all the particular communities of which I am a part. Hence, my book on the cross in the African American experience.

CHAPTER SEVEN

"This Little Light of Mine"

The Womanist Biblical Scholar as Prophetess, Iconoclast, and Activist

MITZI J. SMITH

Womanist biblical scholars follow in the footsteps of nineteenth-century proto-womanists interpreters of sacred Scripture like Old Elizabeth, Jarena Lee, Zilpha Elaw, Sojourner Truth, Maria Stewart, Julia Foote, Amanda Berry Smith, and others.[1] Such audacious luminaries privileged God's revelation in and to them over Pauline texts that ostensibly mandated and were used to justify the public silencing of women and the enslavement of black peoples. The Spirit of God consecrated, compelled, enlightened, and fortified these and other nineteenth-century black women enabling them to challenge and rise above attempts to deny, circumscribe, and mute their calls to public intellectual, prophetic preaching ministry.[2] Julia Foote argued that the Joel 2:28–29 prophecy included women and men and if, as some claim, "the power to preach the gospel is short-lived and spasmodic in the case of women, it must be equally so in that of men; and

---

1. William L. Andrews, ed., *Sisters of the Spirit* (Bloomington, IN: Indiana University Press, 1986); and Maria W. Stewart, *America's First Black Woman Political Writer: Essays and Speeches*, ed. Marilyn Richardson (Bloomington, IN: Indiana University, Press, 1987); Mitzi J. Smith, "'Unbossed and Unbought': Zilpha Elaw and Old Elizabeth and a Political Discourse of Origins," *Black Theology* 9:3 (2011) 287–311.

2. See Smith, "Unbossed and Unbought"; Katherine Clay Bassard, *Transforming Scriptures: African American Women Writers and the Bible* (Athens: University of Georgia Press, 2010).

if women have lost the gift of prophecy, so have men."[3] Zilpha Elaw, Old Elizabeth, Jarena Lee, and others expressed an existential, metaphorical, and metaphysical relationship between their own prophetic calls and those of the biblical prophets.[4]

Womanist biblical scholars attempt to walk in the proverbial shoes of proto-womanists who broke with iconic interpretations, reading and critiquing texts and their interpreters for themselves while conscious of their own unique contexts. Sojourner Truth argued that while she was subjected to the same hard labor as men and was not the object of the courtesies lavished on white women, she maintained a sense of her own womanhood. In response to the theological view of Eve as the first sinner, Truth declared that if Eve was strong enough to flip the world upside down all alone, God could use women collectively to reverse what Eve did. In answer to the supposed superiority of man because of the manhood of Jesus, Truth retorted that Christ was born of God and a woman and not of a man and a woman.[5] Amanda Berry Smith did not consider equality with God something to which the Scriptures could attain, stating that "Nothing is absolutely perfect but God. Let Him be your standard."[6] Smith further argued that if there is a time for women to keep silent in the church, the same applies to men in the church.[7] Howard Thurman's grandmother cast her lot with Jesus over against Paul (unlike some first-century Corinthian believers, 1 Cor 1:12–13) and acting as an iconoclast she refused to participate in the exaltation of the

3. Julia A. J. Foote, "A Brand Plucked from the Fire: An Autobiographical Sketch," in *Sisters of the Spirit: Three Black Women's Autobiographies of the Nineteenth Century* (Bloomington, IN: Indiana University Press, 1986) 208. Foote likened herself to the prophet Zechariah—she was a "brand plucked from the fire" (Zech 3:2)—and Elijah (1 Kgs 19:4).

4. Judy Fentress-Williams, "Lee, Jarena," in *Handbook of Women Biblical Interpreters: A Historical and Biographical Guide*, eds. Marion Ann Taylor and Agnes Choi (Grand Rapids: Baker Academic, 2012) 324–26. Lee identified with the prophet Jonah because like him she delayed responding to God's call. But Zilpha Elaw and Old Elizabeth identified with the Apostle Paul who expressed continuity between his call and those of the ancient prophets whom God called while they were in their mothers' wombs (Gal 1–2). See Smith, "Unbossed and Unbought."

5. Sojourner Truth, "Ain't I a Woman," Sojourner Truth's Speech to the Akron Convention, 1851, http://www.suffragist.com/docs.htm (accessed May 12, 2014). Carla L. Peterson, *"Doers of the Word": African American Women Speakers & Writers in the North (1930–1880)* (New Brunswick, NJ: Rutgers University Press, 1995) 52.

6. Adrienne M. Israel, *Amanda Berry Smith: From Washerwoman to Evangelist* (Lanham, MD: Scarecrow, 1998) 161. See also Eric Brandt, "Smith, Amanda Berry," in *Handbook of Women Biblical Interpreters: A Historical and Biographical Guide*, ed. Marion Ann Taylor and Agnes Choi (Grand Rapids: Baker Academic, 2012) 450–52.

7. Amanda Smith, *An Autobiography: The Story of the Lord's Dealings with Mrs. Amanda Smith, the Colored Evangelist* (Chicago: Meyer & Brother, 1893) 321.

Apostle Paul and his household codes; Grandmother Thurman, if I may, de-canonized Pauline texts that were so often used to encourage the voluntary submission of African slaves to their masters.[8] Proto-womanists rhetorically challenged and physically transgressed oppressive scriptural mandates, in-terpreters, and interpretations. But they also actively sought to transform society; many were activists engaged in the struggle to dismantle oppres-sive systems. As black feminist Patricia Hill Collins avers, "Black feminist thought is *for* Black women in that it empowers Black women for political activism" (emphasis author's).[9] Nineteenth-century proto-womanist em-bodied black feminist thought and/or womanism.[10]

Like proto-womanist Grandmother Thurman, womanist biblical scholars selectively use and engage texts and contexts that resonate with God's revelation in and to black women, with black women's desire and need for liberation, survival, and wholeness, and with black women's lived realities. Civil Rights activist Ella Baker deduced that "the very god who gave us life, gave us liberty. And if we don't have liberty, it is because some-body else stood between us and that which God has granted us."[11] Black women's (and other women of color) lives have been and are confronted, interrupted, diminished, terrorized, and annihilated by racism, classism, sexism, (neo)colonialism, and heterosexism, which they experience as interlocking structures of oppression.[12] Thus, womanist biblical scholars cannot, for example, analyze texts, contexts, and readers through the frame-work of gender and ignore issues of race or through the lens of race and overlook concerns of class. Yet black women have sometimes been lulled into prioritizing the gender concerns of white women at the expense of the health and wholeness of minority women and our communities. Too many

---

8. Howard Thurman, *Jesus and the Disinherited* (Boston: Beacon, 1996) 30. Thur-man's grandmother permitted him to read to her 1 Cor 13, the love chapter, from the Pauline corpus.

9. Patricia Hill Collins, *Black Feminist Thought: Knowledge, Consciousness, and the Politics of Empowerment* (New York: Routledge, 1991) 32.

10. Following, Layli Phillips (*The Womanist Reader* [New York: Routledge, 2006], xx–xxi) I do not consider black feminism (and feminism) and womanism as identical. While womanism and black feminism are linked in their critique of sexism, classism, and racism as interlocking systems of oppressions, womanism is also related to other critical theories and liberation movements. Further, womanism is not limited to black American contexts. Womanism has been expressed and advanced globally both intui-tively and analytically.

11. Rosetta E. Ross, *Witnessing & Testifying. Black Women, Religion, and Civil Rights* (Minneapolis: Fortress, 2003) 49.

12. Collins, *Black Feminist Thought*, 33–34.

times we have   been silenced and sometimes bamboozled.[13] As bell hooks asserts, all too often the silencing of women of color by white feminists has occurred in semi-public or private spaces like classrooms or in living-room gatherings; and it is seldom written about.[14] I recall, as a doctoral student, an incident of silencing in a feminist biblical interpretation classroom. The professor had broken us up into small groups, and one small group as their project created a chant with a refrain that stated, "Never again!" The small group of white, female, master's students had prepared a litany of global atrocities that had been historically committed against peoples. Yet they omitted American slavery from their litany. I questioned how they could fail to mention, here on American soil, the atrocity of American slavery. My white sisters responded without a moment of reflection that they did not have enough time to mention it. And I responded, "I can say it in less than a second—'American slavery.'" What was also disturbing was the initial silence and lack of critical awareness displayed by my sisters of color in the classroom who were initially oblivious to the omission and its implications. Womanist biblical scholars patently acknowledge our social location and the lenses with which we read the Bible, realizing that every interpreter's "context both limits and illumines interpretation,"[15] regardless of whether one is conscious of (and admits) such contextual impact or not. All readers, readings, and texts are contextual and subjective.

The Womanist Biblical Scholar as Prophetess

As womanist Hebrew Bible scholar Renita J. Weems argues we cannot limit ourselves to analyzing texts, "but must go the step further to analyze readings, readers, culture, and the worlds that frame each."[16] Infused with and guided by the Spirit of God, the womanist biblical scholar as prophetess

---

13. "Bamboozled" refers to the deceiving of people by covert, less obvious means such as flattery or trickery. Bamboozled is also the title of a 2000 satirical film written and directed by Spike Lee about a modern televised minstrel show featuring black actors donning blackface makeup and the violent fall-out from its success. Lee explores the history of racist entertainment in the US, and suggests that the same forces that made, for example, *Birth of a Nation* so popular are still very much present, in a more covert way.

14. hooks, *Feminist Theory*, 12.

15. Renita Weems, "Re-Reading for Liberation: African American Women and the Bible," in *Womanist Theological Ethics: A Reader*, ed. Katie Geneva Cannon, Emilie M. Townes, and Angela D. Sims (Louisville: Westminster John Knox, 2011) 52. This essay is also included in part 1 of this volume.

16. Weems, "Re-Reading for Liberation," 54.

confronts and names oppressions in texts, contexts, readers, readings, and cultures.

Womanist prophetic work is sacred and polymorphous in continuity with the prophetic tradition of the biblical text. Women prophets in the Hebrew Bible "proclaimed and/or performed the divine word [as] . . . predictive and interpretive oracles, which could be sung and accompanied by percussion, exercise of statecraft, poetic composition, political dissent, and literal, physical embodiment of the message proclaimed."[17] Similarly, womanist biblical scholars, like proto-womanists and Civil Rights activist Mrs. Fannie Lou Hamer, do not limit their work to the written page, but they prophetically lower their pens to paper and fingers to keyboards, raise their voices, and lift their feet to write and right, to teach and to preach, and to sing "truth to power" with a goal toward transformation and the dismantling of oppressions and oppressive structures, toward revolutionary change. Proto-womanist Fannie Lou Hamer' theme song, "This Little Light of Mine" was sung as a counter narrative confronting the racist ideology that there was nothing good in black people, nothing but darkness. "There was a mission behind [Hamer's voice] and in it . . . [she] always sang with a mission," recalls Harry Belafonte.[18] Hamer sang in order to keep going; she sang when she was locked up in jail and hadn't done anything wrong to anybody, except to dare to be a black woman confronting unjust systems. She explains the origins or etymology of "This Little Light of Mine" as follows:

> This same song goes back to the fifth chapter of Matthew, which is the Beatitudes of the Bible, when he says a city that sets on a hill cannot be hid. Let your light so shine that men would see your good works and glorify the father which is in heaven. I think singing is very important. It brings out the soul.[19]

Like Hamer, womanist biblical scholars understand the light of God and the goodness of God to be situated in black female bodies. And we are determined to shine a light on injustice even when it is found in the black ink of the sacred text and to declare truths that can lighten and enlighten the paths of the most marginalized.

17. Wil Gafney, *Daughters of Miriam: Women Prophets in Ancient Israel* (Minneapolis: Fortress, 2008) 117.

18. Kay Mills, *This Little Light of Mine: The Life of Fannie Lou Hamer* (New York: Plume, 1994) 19, 20. Mrs. Hamer (1917–1977) was a civil and voting rights activist from Ruleville, Mississippi. She survived poverty, sharecropping, being jailed unjustly, and a savage beating while in jail. In 1961 she was sterilized without her knowledge. She served as chairperson of the Student Nonviolence Coordinating Committee (SNCC) and as a Mississippi delegate to the 1972 Democratic National Convention.

19. Ibid., 21.

Womanist biblical scholars declare that black women and other women of color experience and produce truth and light; they are repositories and creators of legitimate epistemologies. All knowledge production is subjective. Womanist biblical scholars acknowledge the existence of more than one truth, especially with regard to biblical texts, contexts, readings, and readers; truths and potential truths exist;[20] malestream biblical scholars have no monopoly on truths.

Womanist biblical scholars prophetically assert that truth and light can be found in those who are doubly marginalized residing in the periphery of the margins. Uncomfortable with the emotional display of rural black worship, W. E. B. Du Bois likened the frenzied way black people in the South worshipped God to a "pythian madness, a demonic possession that lent terrible reality to song and word."[21] For the womanist biblical scholar, the Pythia slave girl in Acts 16, whom Paul demonized because of her annoying prophetic oracles, is an example of truth-telling to power, despite the discomfort of some with the experiences of women who exist in the fringes of the margins. Like the Pythian slave girl with her truth-telling oracles, the womanist biblical scholar must engage in prophetic truth-telling at the risk of annoying the powerbrokers, at the risk of being demonized. There are times when we ought not so easily, or at all, read from the position of the Apostle Paul and other biblical characters and authors. For to do so may marginalize our own experiences and truths as black women.

Prophetic womanist biblical scholars challenge the prescriptive use of descriptive, subjective testimonial texts as pronouncements of objective divine truth that negates or demonizes the truths and experiences of black women and other marginalized peoples. For example, the Psalmist testifies that he has never seen the righteous forsaken nor his seed begging for bread (Ps 37:25). But for African slaves, African Americans, and other poor and marginalized peoples who have had to beg and have experienced abandonment, that is not their testimony.[22] Nevertheless, God loves and was/is with them, even while human-made capitalistic systems and their beneficiaries maintain poverty and employ biblical texts such as "the poor you have with you always" (Matt 26:11) to justify capitalistic greed. Capitalism survives and thrives on the backs of a constructed, perpetual underclass of undered-

20. See Brian K. Blount, *Cultural Interpretation. Reorienting New Testament Criticism,* reprint edition (Eugene, OR: Wipf & Stock, 2004).

21. W. E. B. Du Bois, "Of the Faith of the Fathers," in *The Souls of Black Folk* (New York: Bantam, 1989) 134.

22. See Mitzi J. Smith, "'Give Them What You Have': A Womanist Reading of the Matthean Feeding Miracle (Matt 14:13–21)" *Journal of the Bible and Human Transformation* 3:1 (2013) 1–22.

ucated, underpaid, and underemployed laborers. Womanist biblical scholars might recognize in the parable of the laborers (Matt 20:1–6) a devaluing of human labor within a proto-capitalistic system that exploits laborers and their labor. The parable supports the idea that no matter how hard or long a laborer works, all are equally devalued (not valued). The denarius for a normal day's work that each received regardless of how long they worked would scarcely "maintain a family at the subsistence level."[23]

Because the biblical text is sacred to black women and their communities, they authoritatively mine and recover texts and characters that have been white-washed, demonized, silenced, and obfuscated by patriarchal, imperial or colonial, androcentric, misogynistic, and elitist male authors and contexts. Such acts of retrieval uncover an embedded, constructed elevation of males, such as the Apostles Peter and Paul,[24] and the silencing and marginalization of women (e.g., Mary Magdalene, Luke 24; Philip's four prophesying daughters, Acts 21:9–11). This act of biblical excavation helps womanist biblical scholars to speak about, to, and out of black women's lived realities in dialogue with the biblical text while maintaining a sacred relationship with the text.

But black women's relationship with the sacred biblical text does not trump her relationship with the God about whom the text testifies. In singing, teaching, and preaching "truths to powers," womanist biblical scholars prophesy that power and powers are relative in relation to God as the Power. God is the ultimate Power transcending and trumping all powers. And God can be found in black women and other marginalized women and peoples and their contexts. The Bible as sacred text can be a source of power, a powerful tool, and vehicle of God's transformative, redemptive, prophetic revelation. But the Bible is not *the* Power. God and the Bible are not synonymous.

23. M. Eugene Boring, "Matthew" in *The New Interpreter's Bible*, ed. Leander E. Keck, vol. 3 (Nashville: Abingdon, 1995) 393. While the point of the parable might be to demonstrate equality within the kingdom of God (the last receives the same remuneration as the first who begin working in the vineyard) it does so within the framework of a day labor system somewhat similar to the sharecropping system in the American south. In ancient society, day laborers were among the poorest people. Each laborer received a "usual daily wage" regardless of when he started work or how hard he worked (20:2, NRSV). The landowner is free to treat his laborers as he wills without restraint, regardless of whether it is unjust to some.

24. In her book *Mary Magdalene, the First Apostle: The Struggle for Authority*, HTS 51 (Cambridge: Harvard University Press, 2003) Ann Graham Brock argues that when the Apostle Peter is elevated, Mary Magdalene is diminished in the gospels.

The God of the Bible is the God of the oppressed, the God of libera-tion.[25] In the tradition of our African slave ancestors who "brought to their reading of biblical Scripture an ongoing quest for freedom and thus took from it a hermeneutic of freedom that recognized the abolition of slav-ery and the exercise of individual liberty as central to Christian faith and worship,"[26] womanist scholars exegete Scripture within the overarching her-meneutic of liberty and justice for the oppressed and most marginalized. Yet as Delores Williams argues in her reading of the Hagar narrative, God is not always a liberation God; Hagar remained a slave (just as many African slaves died as slaves) but God is sometimes a God of survival and quality of life.[27]

Just as the biblical prophets are fallible or flawed human beings, the womanist biblical scholar recognizes and admits her fallibility as interpreter of Scriptures, texts, and contexts. She maintains humility toward the text, God, her communities, and her humanity. She will attempt to avoid sitting and sulking under the bush like the prophet Jonah, asking God to take his life because he thought his prophetic utterances, though inspired or given by God, constituted God's final word. As Abraham Heschel argues "the pro-phetic utterance has . . . no finality. It does not set forth a comprehensive law, but a single perspective. It is expressed *ad hoc*, and often *ad hominem*, and must not be generalized."[28] The womanist biblical scholar will try to steer clear of over-generalizations and universal interpretations, even with regard to women of color and their communities.

At the same time, womanist biblical scholars reject and challenge a theology of exceptionalism. A theology of exceptionalism lifts up the excep-tions as a standard for the masses and is often blind to the need to dismantle systems of oppression. The exception becomes the rule. A theology of ex-ceptionalism says that if Senator Barack Obama, as the child of a single par-ent, can become the first African American President of the United States, every black child of a single parent should be able to succeed, regardless, or there is something pathologically wrong with him or his mother. While we can recognize the hope that can be found in the lives of people like President Barack Obama, we also recognize that other factors have a bearing, such as the presence of significant others in a child's life, emotional wounds, as

25. See James H. Cone, *The God of the Oppressed* (Maryknoll, NY: Orbis, 1999).

26. Derek Q. Reeves, "Beyond the River Jordan: An Essay on the Continuity of the black Prophetic Tradition," *Journal of Religious Thought* 37:2 (1980–81) 43.

27. Williams, *Sisters in the Wilderness*, 20–21. Williams argues that "the issue is an understanding of biblical accounts about God that allows various communities of poor, oppressed black women and men to hear and see the *doing* of the good news in a way that is meaningful for their lives," (author's emphasis) 199.

28. Abraham J. Heschel, *The Prophets* (New York: HarperCollins, 1955) 28.

well as systems of oppression that too often envelope and overwhelm the poor and minorities (e.g., systemic police profiling and the biased so-called war on drugs).[29] A theology of exceptionalism claims that God heals those who have enough faith; that those who are healed must have had an exceptional mustard seed faith. The biblical stories of persons whom God, Jesus, or the prophets commended for their faith, those lifted up as exceptions or exceptional, are taken as universal narratives and are mapped onto all healing stories and strapped onto the backs of all Christians. This despite the fact that Jesus often performs miracles out of compassion and not because of someone's faith (see e.g., Matt 12:9–14 [Mark 3:1–6; Luke 6:6–11]; Matt 15:32–39 [Mark 9:1–10; John 6:1–13]). Some nineteenth-century preaching women like Zilpha Elaw felt that their calls to ministry were exceptional and claimed that Paul was correct in teaching women to be silent; he just was not talking to them because their calls were special. Womanist biblical scholars reject a theology of exceptionalism because it liberates the few and imprisons the masses. A theology of exceptionalism supports a Thomasonian pull-yourself-up-by-your-boot-straps philosophy that denigrates the masses of poor and most marginalized peoples.[30]

Womanist biblical scholars read against the grain and between the lines of the biblical text, calling attention to how certain interpretations and theologies such as the prosperity gospel is oppressive and misrepresents the life and ministry of Jesus; that it is built upon the sands of flimsy, self-interested, egocentric hermeneutics. The prosperity gospel falsely contends that Jesus of Nazareth was wealthy and not poor and that tithing will eliminate poverty. Many preachers and parishioners simultaneously argue for a literal reading of the Bible while displaying an ignorance of the text and its context.

Like the ancient biblical prophets, womanist biblical scholars are concerned for the liberation of the entire community but not at the expense of black women's health and wholeness. Individuals who are oppressed, especially those who are unaware of their own oppression, do not or cannot fight for the liberation of communities, at least not in helpful and healthful ways. We recognize that in order to transform the world or to concern ourselves with transformation of the world into a just place for black women and other marginalized peoples, we must concern ourselves with what Cornel

29. See Michelle Alexander, *The New Jim Crow: Mass Incarceration in an Age of Colorblindness* (New York: New Press, 2012).

30. Supreme Court Justice Clarence Thomas claimed in about 1991 that he pulled himself up by his bootstraps during the hearings regarding his alleged sexual harassment of law professor Anita Hill. Justice Thomas's statement is known by many as the "bootstrap myth." http://www.pbs.org/newshour/bb/law-jan-june07-thomas_05-23/ (accessed May 16, 2015).

West calls "existential freedom," since a people are not likely to fight for "social freedom" without the "self-realization of human individuality in community."[31] West writes that "existential freedom empowers people to fight for social freedom, realizing its political dimension. Existential freedom anticipates history and is ultimately transhistorical, whereas social freedom is thoroughly a matter of this-worldly human liberation."[32] Christianity that is prophetic will realize that individual freedom and communal or "social freedom" are "two inseparable notions of freedom. . . . Existential freedom empowers people to fight for social freedom."[33] God's divine revelation in and to proto-womanist biblical interpreter Zilpha Elaw that legitimized her call, liberating her from oppressive, constricting social and biblical constructions also empowered her to preach an anti-slavery message among the slaves in the South, risking her own life and liberty in the process.[34] The womanist prophetess submits herself to God as a text to be read, indicted, and transformed so that she in turn can be a revolutionary, transformative force in the world.

The Womanist Biblical Scholar as Iconoclast

Womanist biblical scholars do not take for granted that knowledge produced, petrified, and sacralized[35] by malestream (white men and other men) and white feminist scholars addresses the needs of black women, is non-oppressive, and/or should be accepted as putative iconic truths. The sacred prophetic work of womanist biblical scholars is necessarily sometimes iconoclastic. Womanists must sometimes be iconoclasts for the sake of the health and wholeness of black women and other marginalized peoples and communities. The womanist biblical scholar like the ancient prophets

---

31. Cornel West, *Prophesy Deliverance! An Afro-American Revolutionary Christianity* (Philadelphia: Westminster, 1982) 18–19. For an analysis of gender inclusivity of women as part of the social activism of the black church see Sandra L. Barnes, "Whosoever Will Let *Her* Come: Social Activism and Gender Inclusivity in the Black Church," *Journal for the Scientific Student of Religion* 45:3 (2006) 371–87.

32. West, *Prophesy Deliverance!*, 18.

33. Ibid., 16, 18.

34. Andrews, "Zilpha Elaw." See also Mitzi J. Smith, "'Unbossed and Unbought': Zilpha Elaw and Old Elizabeth and a Political Discourse of Origins," *Black Theology* 9:3 (2011) 287–11.

35. Sacralization is the process where secular ideas are made sacred or transposed into a tenet of religious faith. See Cain Hope Felder, *Troubling Biblical Waters* (Maryknoll, NY: Orbis, 1989) 38.

is an iconoclast, challenging the apparently, holy, revered, and awesome. Beliefs cherished as certainties, institutions endowed with supreme sanctity, [s]he exposes as scandalous pretensions . . . the prophet knew that religion would distort what the Lord demanded of [wo]man, that priests themselves had committed perjury by bearing false witness, condoning violence, tolerating hatred, calling for ceremonies instead of bursting forth with wrath and indignation at cruelty, deceit, idolatry, and violence.[36]

In confronting biblical texts, contexts, and interpretive traditions, including long-held theological constructions and commentaries that fail to consider the implications of race, gender, class, and empire womanist biblical scholars must sometimes break down and discard traditional, putative interpretive icons or images and paradigms that are oppressive of women of color and our communities and dismissive of our struggles and concerns. Like the biblical prophets, we must destroy the golden calves such as the iconic image of the black male preacher as the sole theologian and intellectual interpreter in the black church. Proto-womanists like Zilpha Elaw itinerated even to the antebellum South to preach about the evils of slavery and to advocate for freedom. Thus, with their bodily presence, their audacity, and their hermeneutics of liberation they penetrated the iconic domain of the male slave preacher and inflicted a crack in the southern idolatrous master-slave relationship. As prophetic iconoclasts, womanist biblical scholars must be, as Delores Williams argues

> guided more by black Christian women's voices, faith and experience than by anything that was decided centuries ago at Chalcedon. . . . Our black communities are engaged in a terrible struggle for life and well-being. All of our talk about God must translate into action that can help our people live. Womanist theology [and biblical interpretation] is significant *only* if it contributes to this struggle.[37]

Womanist biblical scholars must sometimes challenge and dismantle or deconstruct "constructed, oppressive epistemic iconography," including nomenclature, categories, traditions, and theological constructions that are treated as "universal, objective, putative, and iconic knowledge . . . that circumscribes how we ought to read"[38] and be in the church, in the world,

36. Abraham J. Heschel, *The Prophets* (New York: HarperCollins, 1955) 12–13.

37. Delores Williams, *Sisters in the Wilderness. The Challenge of Womanist God-Talk* (Maryknoll, NY: Orbis, 1998) 203.

38. Mitzi J. Smith, "'Knowing More than is Good for One': A Womanist Interrogation of the Matthean Great Commission," in *Teaching All Nations: Interrogating the*

and/or in relationship to each other. (See my essay in this volume entitled "'Knowing More than is Good for One': A Womanist Interrogation of the Great Commission.") Many pastors and lay leaders (and some scholars) still teach and preach that iconic hermeneutical claim that God changed Saul's name to Paul when it was not Saul's name that needed changing but his vision and willingness to do violence to others; God honors the names our parents give us. The Acts of the Apostles clearly states that Paul was also known as Saul, and in the chronology of the narrative he is called Saul after his Damascus road experience; in fact, Ananias invokes his Jewish name when he anoints him (Acts 9:17–22; 13:1, 9). Why would God prefer Saul's Roman name above his Jewish name? And why would some biblical interpreters continue to make such anti-Jewish claims about Saul and God? Paul is thoroughly Jewish and never forsakes his Jewish heritage or culture.[39] It is the colonizers and oppressors who like to change the names of those whom they conquer and subdue erasing vestiges of any culture and socio-historical past. God is not a (neo)colonizer; God is not a slave master nor is the slave/master binary an appropriate metaphor for God. (For example see Matt 18:23–35.) Why is it acceptable for God to be referred to as a slave master and not as a black woman?

Womanist scholars will resist the exaltation of the Apostle Paul as an icon that sometimes trumps liberating images and portrayals of Jesus in the Gospels. Paul, like the Apostle Peter, has become a sacred institution that is conveniently used to justify the silencing of prophetic preaching women, the maintenance of master-slave relations and their progeny (i.e., Jim Crow, systemic racism) and the submission of women to men.

The Womanist Biblical Scholar as Activist

Civil Rights activist Mrs. Fannie Lou Hamer proclaimed that "Christ was a revolutionary person, out there where it was happening. That's what God is all about, and that's where I get my strength."[40] As prophetic activist, the womanist biblical scholar knows her power is derived from her relationship with the God who created the universe and everything in it, and who cre-

---

Matthean Great Commission (Minneapolis: Fortress, 2014) 137–38, reprinted in this volume.

39. For a thorough treatment of the Apostle Paul and his Jewish context, see Pamela Eisenbaum, *Paul Was Not a Christian: The Original Message of a Misunderstood Apostle* (HarperCollins, 2009).

40. Kay Mills, *This Little Light of Mine: The Life of Fannie Lou Hamer* (New York: Plume, 1994) 18.

ated all human beings equal. She knows that all flesh is grass (Isa 40:6). We are accountable to God and the justice, love, and peace that God calls us to. As African American Congresswoman Shirley Chisholm asserted when she ran as an US presidential candidate, the womanist biblical scholar is called to be "unbought and unbossed."[41] As prophetic, political activists, womanist biblical scholars do not speak solely or primarily to or for the academy, the professional guild, or its institutions, but she actively reaches beyond the academy, through her scholarship, preaching, teaching, stomping, petition-signing, and social media presence to confront racism, sexism, classism, heterosexism, and other isms. The womanist biblical scholar will attempt to speak for, when necessary, and give voice to oppressed African American women, and other marginalized persons, who occupy the church pews and the homeless shelters, who survive under highways and in byways and those who subsist between the two. As Weems has argued "we reserve the right to make our work accountable ultimately to grass-roots African American women, women struggling for voice and representation."[42]

The experiences of grass-roots African American women inform black womanist biblical scholars' work as activists. Activist Charles McLaurin learned much from Fannie Lou Hamer who was always looking for an opportunity to help her people. McLaurin learned how to be an activist from Mrs. Hamer and other women who confronted the racist white people who had victimized them all their lives, demanding their rights:

> It told me something. It was like a voice speaking to me, as I stood there alone, in a strange place and an unknown land. This voice told me that although these old ladies knew the risk involved in their being there [at the Indianola Courthouse], they were still willing to try. It said you are the light, let it shine and the people will know you, and they will follow you, if you show the way, they will go, with or without you.[43]

The black church has from its inception been involved in political activism—for equal access in terms of housing, employment, and the political process; for voting rights, social uplift generally, and judicial justice —and it has been through the black church's political activism, in partnership with likeminded people, that black people have seen the arm of God move the needle of injustice a little more in the direction of justice. The black church has sat in, stood up, marched, spoken out for Civil Rights and voting rights.

41. That phrase is the title of Shirley Chisholm's autobiography, *Unbought and Unbossed* (New York: Houghton Mifflin, 1970).

42. Weems, "Re-Reading for Liberation," 54.

43. Mills, *This Little Light of Mine*, 42.

Yet even as women are the majority in most black churches and even though black women's oppressions, especially with regard to sexual assault, have been the impetus for the Civil Rights movement,[44] the black church has failed on any significant scale to be an activist for gender inclusivity and sexual orientation. As womanist biblical scholar Raquel St. Clair argues, a womanist hermeneutic characterized as a hermeneutic of wholeness cannot be complicit in or support the oppression of African American women or any other person or group.[45] Womanist biblical scholars through their hermeneutical work will expose the sexism in the Bible, in the church, and in the world; will call the church into account for its failure to be a truly inclusive and non-oppressive institution that has instead chosen to imitate the ways of their oppressors; and will refuse to support institutions that oppress black women and others. As Emilie Townes argues black women are called to be "unapologetically confrontive," never apologizing "for naming injustice for what it is or for challenging the Black Church and the church universal to live into more of what it is called to be."[46]

For womanist biblical scholars the prophetic as political has a this-worldly gaze, even as it maintains a hope in God who both inhabits and transcends this world; it maintains a healthy tension between living in, caring for this world and anticipation of "the sweet by and by." Heaven is an ideal image of what life can be in this world and not an ideal only to be realized by death, resurrection, or rapture. Womanist biblical interpretation is concerned with the mundane, this-worldly lives of black people and their access to necessary resources, the recognition of their civil rights, and the exercise of agency and the negotiation of power as it relates to the health and wholeness of every member of the community and in the world. Black womanist scholars will concern themselves with human sex trafficking in Detroit, Nigeria, and Cambodia; with voter suppression in North Carolina and in

44. For an exhaustive treatment of the struggle to protect black women from rape and sexual assault by white men as the impetus and origins for the Civil Rights Movement see Danielle L. McGuire, *At the Dark End of the Street* (New York: Vintage, 2010). Sexual violence against black women "enacted and enforced rules of racial and economic hierarchy," (35). Even though for years the courts refused to hold white men accountable for the rape of black women, black women continued in "a tradition of testimony and truth telling that stretched back to slavery"; they spoke out long before the women's movement began, (ibid.).

45. Raquel St. Clair, "Womanist Biblical Interpretation," in *True To Our Native Land: An African American New Testament Commentary*, ed. Brian K. Blount (Minneapolis: Fortress, 2007) 59.

46. Emilie M. Townes, "Ethics as an Art of Doing the Work Our Souls Must Have," in *Womanist Theological Ethics: A Reader*, ed. Katie Geneva Cannon, Emilie M. Townes, and Angela D. Sims (Louisville: Westminster John Knox, 2011) 46.

Afghanistan; with for-profit prisons that target poor and minority children from cradle to the grave; with the tendency of black and other churches to act as hostile squatters in inner city poor neighborhoods on Sundays; with unjust Stand your Ground laws that primarily benefit white males but that fail to protect battered black women such as Marissa Alexander and black men who defend themselves from violent crowds, like Michael Giles; with war crimes; and with other contemporary injustices. These issues and others will frame the prophetic hermeneutical task and guide the interpretative agenda. As Lincoln and Mamiya have asserted "prophetic functions refer to involvement in political concerns and activities in the wider community."[47] We read, exegete, and write as agents of social change in the church, in the community, and in the world.

Womanist biblical scholars will also challenge and attempt to change through dialogue unjust interpretations, theologies, and pedagogies of our sisters. As stated above, a womanist biblical scholar, as human text, will allow God to read, indicted or convict, and transform her soul so that she will speak the truths to powers wherever injustice is found. She must constantly make available to God her fallible humanity so that God might continually encourage, transform, and regenerate her for the work she is called to do for herself and her community. We must hold ourselves accountable before God and before one another. For example, bell hooks challenges black feminists activists to hold accountable and hopefully change the perspectives of contemporary feminists and womanists who continue to support imperialism and militarism. Additionally, we cannot make the assumption that women are inherently nonviolent,[48] either in the biblical text or in our communities. We and our sisters cannot confront and attempt to eradicate sexual and domestic violence and remain silent about nuclear weapons, genocide, drones, gun violence, and other domestic and global atrocities that may be the byproduct of a colonialist past, a neo-colonial present, and/or foreign or domestic terrorism.

The womanist biblical scholar as activist will not only give voice to the marginalized and oppressed through her prophetic hermeneutical endeavors, but she will also, when possible, disrupt, interrupt, or create space for marginalized and oppressed women, non-scholars, black "women more commonly,"[49] to speak for themselves and others, by freeing up and seiz-

47. C. Eric Lincoln and Lawrence H. Mamiya, *The Black Church in the African American Experience* (Durham: Duke University Press, 1990) 12.

48. bell hooks, *Feminist Theory: From Margin to Center* (Boston: South End, 1984) 128–29.

49. Alice Walker, "Coming Apart (1979)" in *The Womanist Reader*, ed. Layli Phillips (New York: Routledge, 2006) 7.

ing space for their concerns in the classroom, in social media, and in our scholarship. As when womanist biblical scholar Dr. Wil Gafney was asked to interrupt her introductory Hebrew Bible class to discuss issues of race, and she seized the opportunity. Gafney posted the following on Facebook: "If your seminary education is not relevant, it is worthless. Context is more than a buzz word."[50] In such spaces oppressions can be named and in the process of naming, we put flesh on the bones of the thing or phenomenon we name, making it visible. By naming the world, we begin the process of changing it. As Paulo Freire says, "once named, the world in its turn reappears to the namers as a problem and requires of them a new *naming*. Human beings are not built in silence, but in word, in work, in action-reflection"[51] (emphasis author's).

There is a difference, however, between naming that furthers oppression and naming that transforms oppressors and oppressive structures. Othering is a type of naming that furthers injustices by constructing others over against ourselves and as simultaneously subordinate to ourselves. As womanist biblical scholars we must become conscious of projects of othering in the texts, behind the texts, and in front of the texts or in the world in which we live. And as prophetic activists we recognize, address, and challenge reinscriptions of othering of characters and groups located in biblical texts. Such othering projects in the Bible have a reach beyond the text in that they get reinscribed in our teaching, preaching, and social interactions. For example, Jews are characterized too often by Christians as legalistic and either beyond or in need of salvation because of the way "the Jews" are portrayed in, for example, the Gospel of John and in the Acts of the Apostles. As Carolyn Sharp argues "it is an ethical imperative for us to interrupt scriptural discourse that coerces [through definitive perspectives and universal claims that disregard the particular] in a way that is destructive to the experience of others."[52] For the "other," the one who is like us but for whom we choose to magnify her differences because she is too proximate (resembles us too closely in various ways that we perceive as threatening to us or not advantageous to our agendas) we construct an identity that highlights our differences and supports our suppression of the other. As J. Z. Smith argues, othering is a political project and has more to do with proximity or similarity than with absolute difference.[53]

50. Wil Gafney, https://www.facebook.com/wil.gafney (accessed April 30, 2014).

51. Paulo Freire, *The Pedagogy of the Oppressed* (New York: Continuum, 1997) 69.

52. Carolyn Sharp, *Wrestling the Word: The Hebrew Scriptures and the Christian Believer* (Louisville: Westminster John Knox, 2010) 39. Sharp is interpreting Emmanuel Lévinas's philosophical program with regard to the Other.

53. Jonathan Z. Smith, "What a Difference a Difference Makes," in *"To See Ourselves*

In many ways the once oppressed can allow themselves to become the oppressors, and one sure way is to ignore, reinscribe, or become complicit with projects of othering. As womanist Hebrew Bible scholar Cheryl Anderson has shown the construction and representation of groups as the Other "makes physical violence against that group as more palatable."[54] Both black feminism and womanism are political movements to end oppression[55] and not to supplant it. Womanist biblical scholars will not stifle the voice of the other, even if they represent dissenting voices.[56] It is not the practice of liberation to ignore and silence the voices of our sisters and brothers when they disagree with us. Such a response to dissenting or other voices constitutes a deployment of the master's tools,[57] and will never dismantle the master's house, but merely constitutes a renovation of old structures. Another primary tool the master deploys is to "keep the oppressed occupied with the master's concerns."[58] We addressed this issue somewhat above. Too many black women have been persuaded that they should be more concerned with the anti-abortion issue than with poverty, inner-city violence, and the de facto segregated and substandard education serving mainly poor and minority children. Too many black women and marginalized communities have been duped into being more concerned with prohibiting gay civil rights than with stopping the erosion of the voting and civil rights for minorities. Many minority and poor people voted for George Bush for a second term as president of the US simply because he was anti-abortion and anti-gay marriage. At the same time, President Bush was busy fortifying the Supreme Court with conservative Chief Justice John Roberts and Justice Samuel Alito. This strongly conservative court recently ruled in Schuette v. BAMN that a Michigan university can consider admission preferences for applicants whose ancestors (favoring of course white applicants) had attended the school while decreeing that any such allowances on the basis of race are unconstitutional. Justice Sotomayor wrote a fifty-something-page dissenting opinion:

---

as Others See Us": Christians, Jews and "Others" in Late Antiquity, ed. Jacob Neusner and Ernest S. Frerichs (Chico, CA: Scholars, 1985) 3–48; See Mitzi J. Smith, The Literary Construction of the Other in the Acts of the Apostles: Charismatics, the Jews, and Women (Eugene, OR: Pickwick, 2011).

54. Cheryl B. Anderson, Women, Ideology, and Violence. Critical Theory and the Construction of Gender in the Book of the Covenant and the Deuteronomic Law (New York: T. & T. Clark, 2004) 96.

55. hooks, Feminist Theory, 17.

56. Ibid., 9.

57. Audre Lorde, Sister Outsider (Freedom, CA: Crossing, 1984) 112.

58. Ibid., 113.

The effect of Section 26 is that a white graduate of a public Michigan university who wishes to pass his historical privilege on to his children may freely lobby the board of that university in favor of an expanded legacy admissions policy, whereas a black Michigander who was denied the opportunity to attend that very University cannot lobby the board in favor of a policy that might give his children a chance that he never had and that they might never have absent that policy.[59]

The prophetic womanist biblical scholar as activist confronting and challenging unjust systems and oppressions, takes a stand on issues that arise so as to impact the present and the future. As prophetic activists we seek to confront and transform present unjust realities to improve the freedoms and quality of life for current *and* future generations. Angela Davis writes, "The work of the political activist inevitably involves a certain tension between the requirement that positions be taken on current issues as they arise and the desire that one's contributions will somehow survive the ravages of time. In this sense the most difficult challenge facing the activist is to respond fully to the needs of the moment and to do so in such a way that the light one attempts to shine on the present will simultaneously illuminate the future."[60]

In Alice Walker's definition of womanist, she alludes to the activism of Harriet Tubman when she writes that a womanist is "traditionally capable, as in: 'Mama, I'm walking to Canada and I'm taking you and a bunch of other slaves with me.' Reply: It wouldn't be the first time."[61] Although along the way Tubman was assisted by the underground railroad, she made nineteen solo trips into the antebellum South, risking her newly seized liberty, returning north with a shotgun and her sometimes reluctant passengers.[62] Since historically black women and other women of color have not delayed addressing a pressing problem or issue due to lack of official acknowledgment or assistance, "the womanist activist mantra might be, 'We can do it

---

59. Justice Sotomayor, Dissenting, Schuette v. BAMN, 572 US at 21, April 22, 2014. http://www.supremecourt.gov/opinions/13pdf/12-682_j4ek.pdf (accessed April 25, 2014).

60. Angela Y. Davis, *Women, Culture, and Politics* (New York: Vintage, 1990) xiii.

61. Alice Walker, *In Our Mothers' Gardens: Womanist Prose* (New York: Harcourt Brace, 1983) xi–xii. The term "womanist" is first defined in Walker's 1979 short story, "Coming Apart" in Phillips, *A Womanist Reader*, 3–11.

62. Jessie Carney Smith, *Epic Lives: One Hundred Black Women Who Made a Difference* (Detroit: Visible Ink, 1993) 529–30.

with or without you.'"[63] Or as my mother would to say to me, "one monkey don't stop the show." We press on, regardless!

Conclusion

I have attempted to demonstrate how the womanist biblical scholar, like their proto-womanists luminaries, can function as prophetess, iconoclast, and activist. Through those interlocking sacred vocations black women address and attempt to dismantle racism, sexism, classism, neocolonialism, and heterosexism as interconnected oppressions and systems that invade and infiltrate the lived realities of black women and marginalized communities. Womanist biblical scholars often see themselves are "peripheral prophets" that exist and work in "subcommunities that stand in tension with the dominant community."[64] As female prophets who live in the margins, womanist biblical scholars must not be blinded by the center and its entrapments, but must maintain a peripheral vision focused on the struggles, concerns, and needs of black women and the masses of marginalized peoples. We recognize that God dwells in us as peripheral prophetesses, that God resides in the margins with the oppressed, and that from the margins we can and are called to speak truths to powers, to shatter oppressive strongholds, iconic traditions and beliefs, and to actively participate in the revolution to transform this world into the likeness of God's incarnate justice, peace, and love. We too are lights in the academy, in the church, in our communities, and in the world. "We are gifted gifts."[65] This little light of mine, I am going to let it shine.

63. Phillips, *The Womanist Reader*, xl.

64. Walter Brueggemann, *The Prophetic Imagination: Second Edition* (Minneapolis: Fortress, 2001) xvi.

65. Speaking at an Association of Theological Schools Mid-Career meeting for racial ethnic minorities in March 2014, keynote speaker Dr. Lee Butler reminded us of our giftedness.

Part Two

Reading the Bible as a Womanist Biblical Scholar

CHAPTER EIGHT

A Womanist Midrash on Zipporah

WIL GAFNEY

Zipporah (Hebrew: *Tzipporah*, songbird) is a motherless daughter, a sister, a shepherd, a survivor, a wife, a clergy spouse, a mother, a woman who struggles with God, a woman with her own spiritual knowledge and power, abandoned by that same (ungrateful!) man, divorced, a single mother, and a biblical matriarch. Zipporah transcends and transforms stereotypes that are often applied to black women, and she has her own black identity as an Afro-Asiatic Semite. She is a Midianite, kin to Israel and Nubia, descended from Keturah and Abraham.

Zipporah was the daughter Reuel/Jethro, the priest of Midian; she was Moses' woman, wife, and the mother of his children. Her name is preserved in the narrative, while her father's name is given as three or four different possibilities.[1] The confusion is particularly interesting given the status of Zipporah's father, priest of his people and more significantly, a priest of God-of-the-Holy-Name whom Moses will encounter in the burning bush on the sacred mountain.[2] The name of the mountain is also confused, sometimes Sinai, sometimes Horeb.

---

1. Zipporah's father is Reuel in the first text in which he appears, Ex 2:16–22. He is Jethro (*Yitro*) in the bulk of Ex (but in Ex 4:18a he is called *Yether*, a variant of *Yitro*) and he is Hobab in Numbers and Judges. In Num 10:29 Hobab is the son of Reuel.

2. The text does not name Jethro's God. Some scholars limit knowledge/worship of YHVH to the Israelites. I do not. Zipporah's knowledge and performance of circumcision to appease YHVH demonstrate knowledge and worship of their shared deity. In addition, Midianites were descended from Abraham. There is no reason to exclude them from the worship practiced by their shared ancestor.

While Moses is a great leader in the text and subsequent tradition, it is through Zipporah and her family that Moses is (re)introduced to the God of his ancestors. Her father is a priest of YHVH, when Moses does not even know that name. When Jethro visits Moses and the Israelites on their journey, he, not Moses, presides over the sacrifice, indicating his seniority in the tradition to which Zipporah was born and in which she was raised.[3] Zipporah is an initiate of the family religion, as she will demonstrate when God begins killing Moses and she knows how to save his life.

Zipporah's torah—here, "revelation" and "teaching"—is submerged in *torat Moshe* (the laws, teaching, revelation and more through Moses) her estranged husband.[4] Womanist midrash offers a way to listen more closely for her voice between the lines attributed to her spouse by his canonizers and to hear a word that resonates with the experiences of black women, particularly in the Americas.

Torat Tzipporah (The Torah of Zipporah)[5]

Ex 2:16: Now the priest of Midian had seven daughters. They came to draw-water, and they filled the troughs to water their father's flock. 17 Then some shepherds came and drove them away so Moshe (Moses) rose and saved them and he watered their flock. 18 They came to their father Reuel, and he said, "Why have you all rushed back today?" 19 They said, "A man, an Egyptian, delivered us from the hand of the shepherds; he even drew-water for us and he watered the flock." 20 He said to his daughters, "Where is he? Why did you all leave the man? Call him [daughters] and let him eat bread." 21 Moshe was willing to dwell with the man, and he gave his daughter Tzipporah (Zipporah) to Moshe as his wife. 22 She gave birth to a son, and he named him Gershom (Sojourner There); for he said, "I am a sojourner in a strange land."[6]

Ex 4:18: Moshe went and returned to Yitro (Jethro) his father-in-law and said to him, "Please let me go and let me return to my kin

3. See Gene Rice, "Africans and the Origin of the Worship of Yahw*h," *Journal of Religious Thought* 50:1/2 (1993) 27. While this theory, also called the "Kenite Hypothesis" is not universally accepted, I find it convincing.

4. The semantic range of torah is so broad that reducing it to "law" is often a mistranslation. Torah regularly functions as instruction, revelation, teaching, individual laws, legal collections, and Scripture (the first five books, and generically).

5. These verses represent the entirety of the explicit Zipporah tradition in the Bible. These and all subsequent translations are mine.

6. I preserve the Hebrew names of the biblical characters with traditional phonetic spelling and indicate the subject of the feminine plural imperative "call" with the bracketed "daughters."

in Egypt and see if they are still living." And Yitro said to Moshe, "Go in peace." 19 The Holy One said to Moshe in Midian, "Go, return to Egypt; for all the men who were seeking your life are dead." 20 So Moshe took his woman and his sons, mounted them on a donkey and went back to the land of Egypt.[7]

4:24: And it was on the way (back to Egypt) at the inn, the Holy One met Moshe and sought to kill him. 25 So Tzipporah took a flint and she cut off the foreskin of her son, and touched it to Moshe's thighs, and said, "This-is-because you are a bridegroom of blood to me!" 26 So God let Moshe alone. Then Tzipporah said, "A bridegroom of blood" to the circumcision-pieces.

Ex 18:1: Yitro (Jethro) the priest of Midian, Moshe's father-in-law, heard of all that God had done for Moshe and for Israel his people, how the Holy One had brought Israel out of Egypt. 2 Yitro Moshe's father-in-law took Tzipporah Moshe's wife after Moshe had divorced her, 3 and her two sons. The name of the one was Gershom, (for he said, "I am a sojourner in a strange land."). 4 And the name of the other, Eliezer (for he said, "The God of my father is my help, and delivered me from the Pharaoh's sword"). 5 Yitro, Moshe's father-in-law, came bringing Moshe's sons and wife to him into the wilderness where Moshe was encamped at the mountain of God. 6 He said to Moshe, "I am your father-in-law Yitro, coming to you with your wife and her two sons." 7 So Moshe went out to meet his father-in-law. He bowed down and kissed him; each-man asked after his companion's wellbeing. Then they went into the tent.

Here ends the Torah of Zipporah. She is never seen, heard from, or spoken of again in the Scriptures.

Womanist Midrash

The word "midrash" stems from the root *d-r-sh*. In biblical Hebrew to *drash* is to seek, often to seek God as in Amos 5:4 and 6: *seek God and live*. In addition, when an individual seeks God using that stem, the expression

7. "Lord" is a pious circumlocution for YHVH read (*Qere*) instead of the written (*Ketiv*) Hebrew text; there are many other options for articulation in classical and contemporary texts. My choices are inspired in part by the Reconstructionist siddur (prayer book) *Kol HaNeshamah*, (Federation of Reconstructionist Congregations and Havurot [Wyncote, PA: Reconstructionist, 1994]). My preferential choice is "the Holy One," using large and small caps to indicate the Tetragrammaton.

serves as a euphemism articulating seeking God through a prophet.[8] In later Hebrew usage, the root comes to mean biblical exegesis and interpretation almost exclusively. In classical and contemporary Judaism the interpretation of Torah or another part of Scripture is midrash. Midrash is an ancient, venerable scholarly approach to the text of the Hebrew Bible. As such, I find it to be compatible with contemporary historical-critical and cultural hermeneutic approaches to the biblical text; none offer a singular nor complete path to some attainable singular truth.[9] Hence *womanist midrash*, an exegetical approach to the Hebrew Scriptures is grounded in my womanist, black feminist identity and experience, and my knowledge and love of classical midrash.

Some characteristics of classical midrash that I employ as a womanist biblical scholar include: close reading and analysis of the text in Hebrew, translating the text myself, asking questions of the text and answering them, filling in spaces in the text, and providing names for characters for whom the text provides no name.[10] Doing midrash as a womanist means using the cultural knowledge and experience of black women, often but not exclusively in the Americas, as normative, attending to marginalized and missing women in the text, attending to other submerged and marginalized characters in the text, naming violence against women and children in the text, advocating for the wellbeing of the community in and beyond the text, questioning, talking back to and challenging the text when it fails to advocate for women, children and other minoritized persons, and rebuking those who use the text to subordinate women and other targeted classes.

A womanist midrash of *Torat Tzipporah* or Zipporah's Torah offers the following revelations:

Zipporah is a black woman.
Zipporah is a daughter of Keturah, a daughter of Abraham.
Zipporah is a motherless daughter.

8. See Wil Gafney, *Daughters of Miriam: Women Prophets in Ancient Israel* (Minneapolis: Fortress, 2007).

9. Classical midrash has formal rules attributed to Rabbis Ishmael and Akiva, both second century CE (though there are earlier claims and later traditions). Rabbinic literature including the Mishnah and Talmuds in addition to self-titled volumes of midrash are the primary examples of classical Jewish midrash. Contemporarily, midrash includes the broad work of interpreting the Hebrew Bible and is not necessarily limited to Jewish (religious or secular) scholars.

10. My initial contact with midrash was as a graduate student studying Rabbinic literature. Now as a biblical scholar who *drashes*—gives the sermon, interpreting and teaching Torah—in a Reconstructionist *minyan* (prayer congregation) midrash is an explicit part of my exegetical methodology.

Zipporah is a sister.
Zipporah is a shepherd.
Zipporah is a survivor.
Zipporah is a wife.
Zipporah is a clergy spouse.
Zipporah is a mother.
Zipporah is a God-wrestler.
Zipporah is a church mother.
Zipporah is a divorcée.
Zipporah is a single mother.
Zipporah is a biblical matriarch.

Zipporah is a black woman. As a womanist biblical scholar, I identify Zipporah as a black woman descended from African peoples, recognizing that the construct of race did not exist in the biblical world. My identification is based on the categorization of the peoples of North, East, and Central Africa, West Asia, and the Arabian Peninsula and their languages as Afro-Asiatic.[11] This is not simply an interpretive reading in which Zipporah *represents* black women. Rather, I affirm her blackness in the face of the erasure and cooption of black- and brown-skinned biblical characters and their world by dominant culture biblical scholarship and popular culture.[12]

Zipporah's blackness does not distinguish her from Moses or his people into whom she married; they too are Afro-Asiatic. As a Midianite, Zipporah and her people are the ancestors of Arabic speaking people according to the biblical narrative. In addition to their identification with Arabia, Midianites are identified with Nubia (biblical Kush) in southern Egypt and northern Sudan.[13] That association led Zipporah to be misidentified as the Nubian woman who replaced Zipporah as Moses' wife in Num 12—thereby avoiding the problem of his divorce. That misidentification and its proponents' tendency to acknowledge the blackness of the Nubians (Kushites) as distinct from the whiteness they project onto the biblical characters and

11. See Rodney Sadler, *Can a Cushite Change His Skin? An Examination of Race, Ethnicity, and Othering in the Hebrew Bible* (New York: T. & T. Clark, 2005); and Roger Woodward, *The Cambridge Encyclopedia of the World's Ancient Languages* (Cambridge: Cambridge University Press, 2004).

12. I have blogged extensively at www.wilgafney.com on the issue of physical and visual representation of biblical characters by white actors in projects like the History Channel's *The Bible* mini-series and Dan Aronofsky's *Noah* motion picture, staring white, European and Australian actors. Doing the work of biblical scholarship in the public square is an important womanist value, *making it plain*.

13. G. Mendenhall, "Midian (Person) Midianites," in *Anchor Yale Bible Dictionary*, ed. David N. Freedman (New York: Doubleday, 1992) 4:815.

inhabitants of the ancient world has meant Zipporah has been identified as black when confused with the Nubian woman who replaced her. Liberating biblical characters and their ancient counterparts from the clutches of white supremacist scholarship is womanist work, enabling hearers and readers of the biblical text to see the ancient world in its context, see diversity in the biblical and contemporary worlds as normative and God-designed, and to see themselves as the image of God represented in their Scriptures. For me, renowned biblical scholar Martin Noth writing at the height of the Civil Rights Movement in the United States represents the normative scholarship of the post-Enlightenment biblical guild that makes this work necessary:

> Exclusive of Negroes, who play a role only on the border of the Near East as neighbors of Egypt, we meet with members of the long-headed, dark-coloured, short-statured, Mediterranean race and specifically with its African sub-type in North Africa, including Egypt, and with its Oriental sub-type in southwest Asia. The latter sub-type is usually simply called the Oriental race. We also meet a dark-coloured race with round head and with flattened occipital region, which race von Luschan calls Armenoid and which could be designated simply as Southwest Asian. It seems to have appeared first of all in the northern part of the ancient Near East, in North Syria and in the northern and northeastern front ranges. Finally, the Aryan race also had a part in the population of the ancient Near East.[14]

Of the Egyptians, Noth offers scathing criticism that they should portray their own neighbors—whom they have seen in the flesh and he has not—as "Negroes." For him and generations influenced by him, none of the African peoples of Scripture are black, not the Egyptians, not the Nubians nor their Midianite kin; none are black, or in his language, Negro:

> Egyptians also portrayed the people living along the Nile south of Egypt in a generalized and certainly incorrect manner, with typical Negro faces, beardless, and with large earrings, especially in the stereotyped lists of conquests in foreign lands . . . by incorrectly classifying the Nubians as Negroes. The Nubians were at most very slightly related to the Negroes bordering them on the south.[15]

The Enlightenment's (or perhaps better, the *Enwhitenment*) use of modern scholarly tools to whitewash the ancient world, particularly the

---

14. Martin Noth, *The Old Testament World* (Philadelphia: Fortress, 1966) 234–35.
15. Ibid., 236.

Scriptures, while peoples of color were throwing off colonial rule and insisting on human and civil rights is not the sorrowful past of biblical studies
and other disciplines. Consider the 2009 claim of R. Dennis Cole, that "[t]
he term Cushite may refer to a distinguishable physiological trait, such as
that of the deeply tanned Midianites from northwest Arabia."[16] For Cole
not even the Nubian woman is black, she is "tanned," i.e., she has browned
her presumptively white skin. In other words, she and her people may look
black, but they are really white underneath their Arabian tans. This womanist midrash reclaims Zipporah's African heritage while not negating her
Asian heritage and asserts that Zipporah is a black woman. The value of this
assertion for girls and women of African descent looking for themselves in
their Scriptures cannot be overstated. Zipporah is a black woman.[17]

As a Midianite, Zipporah descends from Keturah, *Qeturah*, the
woman Abraham took in Gen 25:1–5 after Sarah's death in Gen 23:2, Hagar
having been liberated from slavery and death in the wilderness long ago
(Gen 21:8–21). Because family and family history is important in womanist
discourse, Zipporah's ancestors are part of the cloud of witnesses who accompany and shape her and my interpretation of her. Since Abraham's first
wife Sarah was his half-sister and his family practiced internal, incestuous
unions, it may not have been his choice to wed her.[18] Neither was it his
choice to wed Hagar, so Abraham's union with Keturah may have been his
only truly consensual union. Yet for some reason Abraham enters into a
secondary or low-status union with Keturah unlike the primary unions he
enters with Sarah and Hagar (however reluctantly) signaled by the use of the
Hebrew terms *pilegesh* (*secondary wife*, for Keturah) and *isshah*, (*woman*, for
Sarah and Hagar).[19] As a result, he does not give his children with Keturah

16. R. Dennis Cole, "Numbers," in *Genesis, Ex, Leviticus, Numbers, Deuteronomy*,
Zondervan Illustrated Bible Backgrounds Commentary: Old Testament 1, ed. John H.
Walton (Grand Rapids: Zondervan, 2009) 357.

17. I am editing this essay while Nevada rancher Cliven Bundy is lecturing on the
Negro being better off in slavery and the (perhaps soon-to-be-former) owner of a professional basketball team has been suspended indefinitely for saying that his girlfriend
should not take pictures with or bring black people to his games, making the discussion
about race in relation to sacred text all the more urgent.

18. Abraham's uncle Nahor married his niece (Abraham's cousin) Milcah, Gen
11:26–29. The tradition continues in the unions of Rebekah and Isaac, cousins, and
the insistence that his bride be a blood relative, Gen 24:4. The family tradition may also
underlie the story of Lot's incestuous relationships with his daughters in Gen 19:30–38;
Lot is Abraham's nephew.

19. While there is no biblical Hebrew word for "wife," conjugal relationships in the
Hebrew Scriptures are analogous to marriage as modern readers understand it. In biblical Hebrew, all adult female humans are women but only some women are what we
would call wives. The same word is used for both, *isshah*, singular, *nashim*, plural. A

a full inheritance and sends them away. Keturah and her six sons including Midian settled, survived, and thrived without him in the Arabian sands. As a Midianite, Keturah was neither Israelite nor Ishmaelite, though she would marry into Israel.

Contemporarily when we think about children of Abraham, we focus nearly exclusively on Isaac and Ishmael, neglecting the six sons Keturah gave birth to for Abraham: Zimran, Jokshan, Medan, Midian, Ishbak, and Shuah. When we talk about Abrahamic religions, we name Judaism, Christianity and Islam; Judaism and Christianity descend from Isaac, Islam through Ishmael. But what about the children of Keturah? Where do they fit in the Abrahamic religious world? Where Judaism and Christianity largely neglect Keturah and her descendants, Islam embraces and reveres Keturah and her descendants. While not mentioned in the Quran, Keturah and Zipporah are both mentioned by name in the Hadith (unattested but still influential teachings of the Prophet Mohammed).

The account of Zipporah first meeting Moses in the Hadith has a charming story. After Moses rescued her and her sister Liya (she only has the one there who is named unlike the circle of six sisters in the Torah) Zipporah walked in front of him and the wind blew allowing him to see the outline of her buttocks through her clothing. Moses then instructed her to walk behind him demonstrating that he was trustworthy, a prerequisite for marriage.[20] A womanist midrash cannot overlook the significance of Zipporah in Islam because womanism transcends religion and culture. And Muslim womanists are a crucial conversation partner for Christian womanists and Jewish feminists in biblical studies, holding us accountable to our biases reminding us that we do not own these characters and their stories.[21]

---

pilegesh is a secondary wife or wife of low status. In addition, contemporary marriage and biblical marriage are so different that it is not always useful to use the same terminology: there are multiple forms of biblical marriage including rape and abduction. Equally common was plural and hierarchical marriage with multiple female spouses including enslaved women, some designated as primary wives other as secondary or lesser wives. A man could also enter into a secondary marriage with his first and only wife. The text designates both Zipporah and the unnamed Nubian woman who follows her in Num 12 as Moses' primary wives. First Chr 1:32 identifies Keturah as Abraham's secondary or low-status wife, a *pilegesh*. In Gen 16:1–6 Sarai, Abram's *isshah*, primary wife, gives her slave Hagar to him as an *isshah*, v. 3, so that the child will be his fully legitimate heir. In Judg 19:1, 2 Sam 15:16 and 2 Sam 20:3, second-order, *pilegesh*, modifies wife, *isshah*. The traditional translation, "concubine" is not useful because it does not confer legitimacy.

20. Tabarī Muhammad Ibn-Garīr and William M. Brinner, *The History of Al-Tabari: The Children of Israel*, vol. 3 (Albany, NY: State University of New York Press, 1991) 43–48.

21. See Debra Mubashshir Majeed, "Womanism Encounters Islam: A Muslim Scholar Considers the Efficacy of a Method Rooted in the Academy and the Church,"

Zipporah is a daughter of Keturah, a daughter of Abraham, a matriarch to Muslims, Christians, and Jews.

Zipporah is the daughter of a woman who does not appear in the story (in the Bible or in the Quran); neither is her name preserved. Names confer dignity and concretize personhood. The overwhelming namelessness of women characters in biblical narratives demeans and marginalizes women in the Bible and contributes to our marginalization in traditions that look to them as Scripture. Following the practice of the rabbis and previous feminist biblical scholars I name Zipporah's mother *Poriyah*, "fruitful," like the fruitful vines of Isa 32:12 and Ps 123:8, for she is the mother of seven daughters. There is no mention of sons, neither lack of nor longing for sons, which is rare in the Scriptures.

Zipporah's mother is dead, missing and/or simply erased as irrelevant from the narrative. The presence and absence of mothers in our lives and the nature of those relationships has been a primary source of exegesis for womanists.[22] A simple reading of the text sees Zipporah's mother birthing and raising her seven daughters, nursing them for at least two years before conceiving the next. Adding however long it took her to first become pregnant and however long after her last birth she survived (or stayed) provides at least a fifteen-year window for Zipporah's overlooked mothering. She may have been there the whole time, behind the scenes, like David's mother at his anointing. (She at least is written of later in the biblical text and named by the rabbis.)

The mother-shaped hole in the text may well correspond to a mother-shaped hole in Zipporah's life. Where is her mother when Zipporah marries and gives birth? It is easy, too easy to say that her mother has died. But her mother is not the only woman missing from the story. Yes, there are seven daughters. But there are no other women, no women servants or slaves, or even other wives. Did all seven daughters have the same mother? Was Jethro

in *Deeper Shades of Purple* (New York: New York University Press, 2006) 38–53; Phyllis Trible and Letty M. Russell, *Hagar, Sarah, and Their Children: Jewish, Christian, and Muslim Perspectives* (Louisville: Westminster John Knox, 2006). While she self-identifies as a feminist Islamic scholar, Amina Wadud's feminism is black feminism and analogous to womanism, see her *Inside the Gender Jihad: Women's Reform in Islam* (Oxford: Oneworld, 2006).

22. Renita J. Weems starts with the biblical canon as the sanctioned locus of exegesis in *Just a Sister Away* and expands her canon to her own experience in *I Asked for Intimacy*; in some cases she used Scripture secondarily, in others she exegetes her own past, offering exegesis of her relationships with her unborn child, her mother, her father, and girlfriends with those on the crucifixion from Mary's perspective, Leah's relationship with Jacob and Gomer's relationship with Hosea, *Just a Sister Away: A Womanist Vision of Women's Relationships in the Bible* (San Diego: LuraMedia, 1988); and *I Asked for Intimacy: Stories of Blessings, Betrayals, and Birthings* (San Diego: LuraMedia, 1993).

the rare monogamous biblical patriarch? Or is her mother's invisibility a sign that Zipporah too would be invisible if she had not married "well"? In turn Zipporah disappears into the text that has never acknowledged her mother or the mothering she received or lacked.

If we read Zipporah as a motherless daughter who has lost her mother through death by the time she appears in the narrative, then we might read each aspect of her story tinged with grief that she has no mother to counsel and comfort her, to celebrate with her. If her mother was truly missing from her life as well as from the story, then certain aspects of the text take on new meaning. She goes to her marriage without her mother's preparations for sex, marriage, and childbirth. She goes through two pregnancies without her mother's experiences to guide her. She and her new family have a terrifying encounter with God and she cannot talk it over with her mother. Her husband leaves her, rather sends her back to her father, and her mother is not there to receive her. Reading Zipporah as a motherless daughter may also make her more accessible to motherless daughters, women who have lost their own mothers to death, abandonment, or fractured relationships.

There are some women and girls in Zipporah's life; she has six sisters. I am focusing on Zipporah, but with the exception of her marriage to Moses and those things that stemmed directly from it, the bulk of this womanist midrash applies equally to Zipporah's sisters. The names of her six sisters join that of her mother in the void of the biblical text, condemned to namelessness. Having named Zipporah's mother Poriyah, "fruitful," I offer names for the six sisters whose identities are submerged in the text in a new genealogy to be added to Ex 2:16:

Now the priest of Midian had seven daughters *who Poriyah of Midian gave birth to for him. The name of the first was Tzipporah, the second Liya, Aminah the third, Minnah the fourth, Taima the fifth, Yarah the sixth, Zizah the seventh.* They came to draw-water, and they filled the troughs to water their father's flock.[23]

In the absence of a mother figure, the text portrays Zipporah possibly assuming responsibility for nurturing her sisters (they spend their days with her not their father).[24] Zipporah and her sisters share the work of

---

23. The portion between the asterisks is the addition. I've drawn the names from Hebrew and Arabic names that share forms and meanings, since Semitic languages Hebrew, Arabic, and Midianite are closely related, preserving the Arabic name for the one sister from the Hadith. Poriyah=fruitful, Tzipporah=songbird, Liya=distant water (her only sister from the Hadith) Aminah=true, Minnah=kind (from Arabic) Taima=an Arabian oasis, Yarah= revelation (same root as *torah*) and Zizah=flower.

24. It is reasonable to imagine that Tzipporah was the eldest, making her the first eligible for marriage.

shepherding, doing the work that feeds them and their father—he owns the flocks, the women herd them. They are hardworking women. Shepherding is hard work, often dirty, sometimes bloody. They are not confined to their tent-home or segregated from the world at large or men in particular. They are not waiting for a mysterious stranger or prince of Egypt to come to the rescue, (though that will happen for one of them). They are making a life for themselves, with their own hands and the resources that have been entrusted to them. There are no male servants or shepherds in the narrative. The sisters do the work alone. Yet they cannot be certain that they will inherit any of the wealth their hands have built; there is no way to know if their father will allow them to inherit or what, if any, dowry he will give them.

There is a space in the text after Moses' encounter with the seven sister-shepherds, between the reporting of his aid and the offer of hospitality in return in verse 20. It appears that Zipporah and/or her sisters have to go, find him, and bring him home. That the women do not run home to tell their father that they were rescued by a man nicely subverts the damsel in distress narrative. They were, no doubt, appreciative for his aid. But they, and they imagine he, has moved on.

When she leaves with Moses, Zipporah leaves her sisters behind. If they are truly motherless daughters, then Zipporah's leave-taking could have been extraordinarily sorrowful. Zipporah's sisters are the women's community the text provides for her, a biblical precursor to the sista-circle that has become an important locus of womanist work in congregational and other community settings. As the only one among them named in the biblical text and the first one of them to marry, Zipporah may be the elder. But while she is singled out by the use of her name and her future, the women function as a group. The verbs are feminine plural, they speak and act together: v. 16, "they (the women) came," "they (the women) drew-water," "they (the women) filled." In v. 17 they all (a gender-inclusive plural object) were driven away by male shepherds. Moses comes to their (feminine plural) defense and waters their (inclusive plural) flock. In v. 18 "they (the women) go" to their father; he asks why "they (the women) have rushed (back)." In v. 19 the women speak as one. In v. 20 Reuel addresses his daughters as a group. Only in v. 21, in the marriage announcement is Zipporah identified. Only here does she do something without her sisters. She marries Moses.

Zipporah and Moses reside with her father and her sisters for sometime after their union. It is the call to liberate the Israelites that disrupts their family. Without that call Zipporah may well have remained with her extended family. It is not clear whether that would have happened if Moses was not a fugitive and had an ancestral home to take his new family to. It is possible that the conjugal practice of Zipporah's people was such that

Zipporah and her sisters expected their spouses to reside with them and their father, perhaps due to his status.[25] In that reading the sisters may well have expected to raise their children together. In that case, Zipporah's leaving would have been a breaking of that tight-knit circle. And when Moses sent her packing with her children, her sisters would have welcomed her home even if they had to travel from the places where they made their own lives.

Zipporah and her sisters are shepherds. They join Israelite matriarch Rachel and the beloved woman of the Song as *pastor*, the Latin term for shepherd that has taken on new meaning in the history of the church. It strikes me that the insistence of some that women are not called to pastoring, shepherding, in the church is particularly insensible given the origin of the vocation as egalitarian. The image of Zipporah and her sisters as shepherd is perhaps the most powerful for me. While contemporary readers and hearers of the Scriptures are likely to hear the term "shepherd" as masculine, the early hearers and readers of the stories that became Scripture knew it to be an inclusive term. It might be a useful exercise then for Christian readers to articulate the shepherd texts of the New Testament as explicitly feminine in order to experience them as truly inclusive. For example: *As a shepherd, she separated the sheep from the goats. At times she would sleep in the fields, keeping her flock by night. She who enters by the gate is the shepherd of the sheep. Her sheep know her and know her voice. Her sheep were not harassed and helpless because she, their shepherd, was with them.*

The brief description of the shepherding encounter in Ex 2:16–17 raises a number of questions. How large were the family herds? Did Reuel ever herd his own flock? Were there other, hired shepherds or servants to protect the flock and ensure access to the well? It does not appear that there were other shepherds in Reuel's employ. His expectation that his daughters would successfully shepherd their flocks and secure the life-giving water suggests that the sisters were in the habit of taking on their competitors and gaining access to the water, however long it took, on a regular basis. Moses' welcomed assistance sped up the process, but they were no helpless damsels in distress. They would have been a small army of armed women, practiced in wielding their rods and their staffs to the comfort of their flock—and their investment.

In Ps 23 an imaginary sheep reflects on its shepherding by God. In other passages, the shepherds are mortal, pasturing God's flock (2 Sam 5:2; Isa 44:28). It is not uncommon for a psalm to shift back and forth between

---

25. The Israelites would practice both matrilocation and patrilocation. It may well have been the same for the Midianites.

God and a male shepherd (for example, Ps 45:6–7) with some confusion resulting from the superfluity of male pronouns. Borrowing from and combining those genres (and the Ps of Deborah) in my sanctified imagination, I can hear a shepherding-psalm in praise of God for providing the sister-shepherds to tend the flock as a metaphor for God's own care of God's people.

The God of the mountain shepherds the clouds
as a shepherdess shepherds her flock.
She guides them to green pastures
and refreshes their souls with living waters.
My shepherd is the Mighty One of Midian,
the rock of Reuel,
the stronghold of seven sister shepherds.
The God of the mountain shepherds fire
as a shepherdess shepherds her flock.
She tends the nursing she-sheep
and carries the little lambs in her bosom.
The Shepherd of Midian has blessed God's servant Reuel with seven daughters.
The Shepherd of Midian has blessed Tzipporah and her sisters forever.
Blessed be the herd-women.
Blessed be Tzipporah above all herd-women.

Zipporah is a survivor. I read the struggle over access to water as a physical one; the water source wasn't just blocked, denying the women access. The other shepherds actively drove, forced, the women away from the water. That action includes physical force in addition to the threat of physical force. God uses the same Hebrew verb, *g-r-sh*, to describe driving nations from their land in Ex 34:11, also connoting force. And I understand the conflict to have been an ongoing one. When Zipporah and her sisters return home sooner than expected, their father's question, "how is it they are back so soon," indicates he knew they regularly fought to water their sheep. (Which makes the lack of male servants or even his presence with the sheep all the more interesting.) When they explain that a stranger has helped them, they refer to their adversaries as "the shepherds," with no further explanation, also suggesting that they and their regular attacks were well-known.

Water is life. In fighting to water their sheep, Zipporah and her sisters are fighting for all of their lives including their father's. Surviving repeated and even regular physical attacks is a deeply resonant tone in womanist discourse. It evokes the womanist sacred text, "All my life I had to fight."[26] Zipporah returned to that fight day after day, determined to do whatever it took to provide for her household, in order that they all might survive, together. Zipporah will take that fighting, protective spirit into her marriage. Moses will live to deliver his people because she will deliver him. It may be that Moses' male ego could not come to terms with having his wife save his life.

Zipporah is a Midianite. By marrying outside of Israel, Moses joins worthy ancestors like Judah, Joseph, and Simeon, all of whom either married or fathered children with non-Israelite women. While Moses' union with the Midianites will become problematic later in the Torah, in Ex it is presented as providential: Moses happened to settle in the land of Midian and happened to settle by a certain well. He happened to be near that certain well when seven shepherding sisters brought the family flocks to be watered at the well. When he herds (some of?) those sheep he will stumble upon a miraculous sight, encounter the living God as the Fire of Sinai, be introduced to the Most Holy Name of God and commissioned to deliver his people.

Zipporah is suppressed in the narrative as Moses becomes acquainted with the ancestral God of her people and his, a God who Zipporah's family is on record as serving while Moses' religious education in Egypt is suspect. Zipporah and her sisters are nowhere to be seen while Moses herds her family flocks when he encounters the burning bush. It is important in the narrative that Moses and only Moses encounters God-in-the-bush. But are we to imagine that Moses takes over the shepherding work of all seven women, or have they divided the herds? How would he know where to graze them without Zipporah and her sisters? Has he wandered off from where she directed him? (It's clear he doesn't know enough about the holy ground on which he walks *not* to herd sheep there.)

The text presents Moses as a nearly solitary deliverer of Israel. Aaron attends him but not as a peer. Miriam is put in her place when she states the truth, she is every bit as much a prophet as he. Zipporah is simply erased. She is there, between the lines of the familiar drama. Moses leaves their bed to tell Pharaoh the word of the God that Zipporah's family served before Moses was ever taught the sacred name. After each frustrating encounter he returned to their temporary home, supped at her table, and took refuge

---

26. In *The Color Purple*, the novel by Alice Walker and (1985) film adaptation, Sophia says, "All my life I had to fight. I had to fight my daddy. I had to fight my brothers. I had to fight my cousins and my uncles. A girl child ain't safe in a family of men. But I never thought I'd have to fight in my own house." *The Color Purple: A Novel* (New York: Harcourt Brace Jovanovich, 1982).

in her arms and between her thighs. In due time Zipporah will fulfill her culturally cued wifely obligation to bear Moses a heir and a spare.

Though Moses will be excluded from the Israelite priesthood along with his descendants, he functions as clergy, as intermediary between God and God's people, and as the most significant conversation partner for the divine in the canon. A womanist reading of Zipporah as Moses' wife sees her as a clergy spouse, pastor's wife, and First Lady. Like many women married to clergymen in traditions that do not ordain women—there are no priestesses of YHVH in the Bible—Zipporah has her own knowledge of God, longer and deeper than that of her spouse, which may point to her own suppressed vocation. Also like many clergy wives, Zipporah is the daughter of a clergyman. Yet she is secondary and ultimately expendable in Moses' bed as well as in the narrative. But before they part ways, Zipporah accompanies her husband in his calling.

Specifically Zipporah evokes that woman who, knowing the life of a clergy wife well and having observed her mother, chooses a layman for her spouse and later finds herself married to a clergyman despite her best efforts when he answers a late-in-life call into the ministry. Zipporah and Moses live with her father long enough for her to have given birth to at least one son, suggesting a period of some years when he worked in her family herds with no thought of a religious vocation. That changes when Moses wanders on to the mountain where the God of Zipporah and his ancestors meets him.

Zipporah disappears from the story in Ex 3 when Moses encounters God on God's mountain in a fire that burns but does not consume and learns the Most Holy Name of God. In Ex 4:18–20 Moses returns from the mountain with his vision and commission. The text would have us believe he only speaks of these things to his father-in-law. But my womanist sensibilities tell me that he also discuss them with Zipporah. I can only imagine that the first telling of that story, which would eventually be recorded and canonized as Scripture, began with her family who have become his family; after all, they had some experience with the God of the mountain. (Zipporah will shortly use her knowledge and experience to save Moses' life when he has no idea what to do to satisfy God-of-the-Holy-Name.)

The biblical text is not interested in whether Zipporah supported her husband or how. Since the text will not credit her with disloyalty, which would be a useful charge to explain away the impending divorce, I choose to read that she supported him fully. Like many pastors' wives she gives up her whole life, leaving her home and family to stand by her man as he goes to his first congregation. They face and overcome danger, together. And then she disappears from the text again. Let me write her back in:

When the sun begins to set and Moshe and his flock have not yet returned Tzipporah mounts a donkey and goes looking for him. Checking with her sisters who did not see him in any of their regular pasture sites, she heads towards the mountain of God. Even though she explained to him that no animal or human was to touch the mountain of the Holy God, she knew he was likely to ignore her counsel and that of her father. Her rebuke died on her lips when she saw his face. Something had happened to him. He was a changed man. Her God had spoken to him. She sent him to confer with her father while she organized their household for the journey, she knew what lay ahead. Tzipporah said her goodbyes to her sisters, not knowing if she would ever see them again. Lastly she bid her father farewell. Yitro promised his beloved daughter that he would come see about her as soon as he could.

While Moses is declaring unto Pharaoh to let God's people go—to use the King James inspired idiom of the black church—where is Zipporah? She starts the journey with Moses but disappears into the wilderness and the text after she saves his life in 4:24–25. But using my sanctified imagination, the source of indigenous African American midrash in the black church, I pick up her story. Where the Bible has Aaron alone coming to meet Moses who is also mysteriously alone in the wilderness, I envision a larger reunion:

On the outskirts of Egypt Tzipporah and Moshe and their son Gershom were met and welcomed by his sister Miriam and their brother Aaron and his wife Elisheba and their children. Moshe's reunion with the sister who kept the memory of his people alive in his heart long after his mother's wet nursing days were over was especially tender. The woman-prophet and the priest's daughter had much to discuss, their God-talk kept them up into the night. They all returned to Egypt together and began laying the groundwork for liberation. The elders would meet and hear Moshe out, then return to homes where womenfolk had already heard and shared the news and had made up their minds to be free. There would be no wavering. And should their menfolk doubt, the women would urge them on. It was decided, whether the men knew it or not. As Moshe and Aaron spoke to Pharaoh, Tzipporah and Miriam spoke to the people.

I choose to read Zipporah as accompanying Moses and Israel across the bitter dangerous water to freedom after observing the first Passover. She would have danced with Miriam and the Israelite women in the vanguard of her adopted people during the sea crossing. She would have seen the mighty way the God of her father, her God, used her husband. But at some point her marriage ended.

Before she left home to partner in the liberation of Israel, Zipporah became a mother. Motherhood is an extremely important trope in womanist interpretation. Mother is for many a more useful image of God than father.

Mothering also represents a communal love ethic that extends far beyond womanists who have given birth or legally adopted. Foster mother, other mother, godmother, and play mother are important roles in many African diasporic communities, particularly in the Americas. Zipporah is a mother who will be abandoned, divorced, and replaced, becoming a single mother. Mothering as a single parent is one of many familial paradigms and the one that is most often identified with black families, often framed as pathology. It appears that for the bulk of her life Zipporah was a single mother.

The brevity of her marriage suggests that Zipporah will be a single mother longer than she was a wife and mother. Zipporah was surrounded by family when she delivered her first child, Gershom (Sojourner) whom Moses named reflecting on his experience sojourning in Midian with her family. At that point there is no thought of returning to Egypt. Moses has found a new family; after losing the family of his birth and the family of his nurture Moses was fortunate to find yet another family to welcome and embrace him. Zipporah and Moses and their child formed an intergenerational household with her father and possibly her sisters and their families if any were married. Any unmarried sisters were virtually certainly present.

The absence of Zipporah's mother—if occasioned by death and not neglect of the biblical authors—is particularly poignant as she nurtures life in her womb, gives birth, nurses, and embarks on family life. The lack of women in the story apart from Zipporah and her sisters surely obscures midwives and neighbor women and woman-kin. In spite of her textual isolation it is not reasonable to believe that Zipporah journeyed into motherhood unaccompanied.

In spite of its diminished portrait of her, the Torah presents Zipporah as undertaking two significant actions for the wellbeing of her family, arguably rooted in her identity as a mother: she accompanies Moses back to Egypt to do the work of liberation and saves Moses' life (I discuss the episode subsequently). The text denies her agency in the journey. She is the object of Moses' verbs. He "took" her and "mounted (her on)" a donkey. Even so, I read her as his partner, not subordinate. Going with Moses to demand the freedom of the Israelites meant an uncertain future, trusting in God and her husband to provide for all of them.

At some point, it is not clear when, Zipporah gives birth to a second son, Eliezer (God-is-my-help). Ex 4:20 has that "sons" are loaded on to the single donkey with her when they leave for Egypt, but in the circumcision narrative that follows in the next few verses there is only one son. He is not named until chapter 18, suggesting the reference in 4:20 is asynchronous. It is impossible to know how old Gershom is when Zipporah and Moses take him to Egypt. It is impossible to know when Zipporah gave birth to Eliezer and how much space is between the boys. For the sake of the narrative, the second birth comes somewhere between chapters 4 and 18.

There is only a single episode in which Zipporah can be said to be mothering. In a midnight encounter with a God intent on killing her husband and perhaps her son, Zipporah demonstrates that she is the kind of mother who will even stand up in the face of God if that is what is called for to save the life of her child. Exodus 4:24–25 records an encounter between Zipporah, Moses, and God that I find comparable in some ways to Jacob's encounter with the divine being at the Jabbok. On their way back to Egypt, God-of-the-Holy-Name met them and sought to kill Moses. At least that's how I read the text. The truth is, it is inscrutable. Specifically, the text says YHVH met "him," either Zipporah's uncircumcised son or Moses. And God sought to kill "him." It could be: God met and tried to kill Moses, God met and tried to kill Zipporah's son, God met Moses and tried to kill the child or God met the child and tried to kill Moses. All are grammatically possible.

Reading "God met Moses" makes sense relationally. But whom is God looking to kill? I believe Moses is the divine target, but it is not unheard of for the character of God in the Bible to strike a child for the failings of his parents. (Moses is, after all, going to prophesy the death of the firstborn children along with firstborn animals in Egypt to punish the Pharaoh.) God's "killing" is modified by the Hebrew verb b-q-sh, "to seek." I have often thought of this as God "starting to" or "trying to" kill Moses in this episode; this is supported by the semantic range according to *HALOT*.[27] But it is more than that. There is a nuance of God seeking opportunity or perhaps even permission to kill Moses according to the range in the *Dictionary of Classical Hebrew*, "seek, ask, request, require, entreat." And that is where Zipporah comes in.

Zipporah prevents God from killing Moses. She intervenes. She saves his life. There is no activity or agency ascribed to Moses here. He may well be unconscious or thrashing about on the ground unable to help himself. He is near death, whether the process of his dying has begun or been accelerated or not. In this passage, God is Death. I see God standing invisibly in the way as the divine messenger stood in Balaam's way in Num 22:22. Zipporah springs into action, likely risking her own life by intervening— teaching Moshe a valuable lesson that he will repeat often by intervening with God for the Israelites when God begins killing them off for various and sundry infractions in the wilderness.

But why is God trying to kill Moses when thwarted by Zipporah? The text does not explain any of this explicitly. The reader/hearer/interpreter

---

27. *Hebrew and Aramaic Lexicon of the Old Testament.*

must assemble these few cryptic words into a coherent narrative with much less textual support than is regularly available when engaging the text for the regular task of biblical interpretation. Zipporah cut off her unnamed son's foreskin and touched it to Moses' penis—wait, what?—and God left him alone. Zipporah is the only woman in the Scripture credited with performing a circumcision. The practice was widespread in the ancient Near East, including Egypt but had particular religious significance for the Israelites and arguably for the Midianites, ably demonstrated by Zipporah.

Zipporah touches the foreskin to Moses' *raglayim*, most literally "feet"; however in Hebrew idiom, feet are not the portion of the body from the ankles to toes, but rather the portion of the body from thighs to toes.[28] More than mere "touching," Zipporah strikes, *n-g-*, "deals a blow" or even "plagues" Moses' genitalia with the bloody foreskin. And, God "withdrew," "ceased," or in anthropological idiom "dropped [the divine] hands." This fascinating snippet of what must have been a longer account has spawned a significant amount of classical midrash offering a variety of solutions to the interpretive questions:

Moses only failed to circumcise the child so he wouldn't suffer on the journey but was planning to do it later.[29] The attacker is Satan (or the angel of God) the child is the victim (arguing "bridegroom" means "child-to-be-circumcised" but apparently only here). Anger and Wrath (who might be one or two angels) swallow the child from head to thighs as a sign to Zipporah.[30] Rashi identifies the child as Eliezer. In other conversations the text will be amended to reject Zipporah performing the circumcision, having her find some man conveniently wandering in the wilderness to do it, or starting it but yielding to Moses.[31] Alternatively, an angel swallowed Moses

---

28. See Deut 28:57 where a woman's afterbirth emerges from between her *raglayim*, obviously thighs. The expression for male urination is to cover the *raglayim* (with the hands) in which case *raglayim* is genitalia, see Judg 3:24; 1 Sam 24:3 (v. 4 in Hebrew). Similarly, urine is water of the *raglayim* in 2 Kgs 18:27 and Isa 36:12; genitalia fits here as well. So when in Isa 7:20 God threatens to shave the *raglayim* of the King of Assyria, the threat is not to shave his legs, but his genitalia. As I have observed in "Mother Knows Best: Messianic Surrogacy and Sexploitation in Ruth," this makes Naomi's instruction to Ruth to place herself at Boaz's *raglayim* and wait for him to instruct her explicitly sexual (in *Mother Goose, Mother Jones, Mommie Dearest* [Leiden: Brill, 2009], 23–36). That sort of male sexual humiliation is not unprecedented, in 2 Sam 4:10 when some of David's envoys are forcibly shaved and have their garments cut off in the middle exposing their buttocks; I understand the shaved "beard" to have been pubic hair, eventually known as the "lower beard" distinguished from the "upper" (facial) beard.

29. *Talmud Bavli, Nedarim*, 31b.

30. *Talmud Bavli, Nedarim*, 32a.

31. *Talmud Bavli, Avodah Zarah*, 27a. The Rabbis wrestle with the requirement that the person who circumcises must himself [sic] be circumcised in light of Zipporah's

up to his circumcised penis whereupon Zipporah recognized the protective benefit of circumcision, so she then circumcised her unprotected child.[32] In one account the angel is Gabriel taking the form of a serpent.[33] As for what she does with the foreskin, Rashi follows the Jerusalem Talmud in reading that she throws the flesh to the ground at his feet, exchanging "touch" for "throw" and limiting "feet" to its most narrow reading.[34] This passage has also been scrutinized by feminists and other scholarly voices adding to the voices of the rabbis.[35] Ilana Pardes draws fascinating connections between Zipporah (songbird) and winged Isis in the Osiris resurrection account, which also involves a penis. [36]

Rereading and retranslating the text and wrestling with some of the ensuing scholarship on this fascinating vignette, I conclude Zipporah to be a God-wrestler, even though she did not grapple with God in physical form. Drawing on the narrative tradition of the African American church, I locate the struggle at the midnight hour, a cultural "thin place" when the supernatural and natural worlds overlap most extensively. Zipporah has been raised in the faith and fear of the God of Sinai. She knows that her son, who I understand to be Gershom, should have been circumcised on the eighth day. I have no doubt that she and her father told Moses, but he clearly didn't listen.[37]

Unlike Balaam who did not know his path was blocked by a divine being and Moses who does not know who the God of Sinai/Horeb is, Zipporah knows exactly what and who she is dealing with. She circumcises her son while God is killing Moses and then she touches someone's genitals with the bloody foreskin. It does not make sense for her to touch her son with his foreskin since what was called for was its removal. It does make sense that

actions in *Devarim Rabbah* 6:1.

32. *Shemoth Rabbah* 5:8.

33. *Zohar A*, 93b.

34. *Talmud Yerushalmi, Nedarim*, 3:9.

35. Ellen Frankel's *The Five Books of Miriam: A Woman's Commentary on the Torah* (New York: Putnam's, 1996) is a contemporary feminist rabbinic text that supplements classical rabbinic midrash with contemporary feminist midrash and was particularly formative for me. A list of feminist conversation partners on this text would be prohibitively long. I cite those that have been most generative in my own thinking, adding Karen Winslow's article to those mentioned previously: Karen Strand Winslow, "Ethnicity, Exogamy, and Zipporah," *Women in Judaism* 4:1 (2006).

36. Ilana Pardes, *Countertraditions in the Bible: A Feminist Approach* (Cambridge: Harvard University Press, 1992).

37. Since there is no birth narrative and his name has not yet been mentioned I do not understand Eliezer to have been born. It does not appear that the text knows when he was born either.

if Moses was already circumcised and could not in fact be re-circumcised to dedicate his circumcision to her God of the mountain, to whom Moses had so recently been introduced.[38] In this unique episode Zipporah wrestles with God for the life of Moses and for that of her son who may have been the next target, and she prevails. The text does not record her naming God as Hagar did, though that could be what is meant by the cryptic exclamation, "bridegroom of blood." Perhaps God or the divine messenger named *her* after withdrawing from Moses: *You have (vattisarneh) striven with God and prevailed. No longer shall your name be called Tzipporah but you shall be called Tisrael.*[39] Now, wouldn't that be something.

In the black church, church mothers are known for their rich prayer lives, often praying through the night. Many can be found on their knees at the midnight hour. In that light Zipporah is a church mother. Zipporah's preparation to do what the circumstance called for evokes for me as a womanist reader, women whose lives are bathed in prayer. I think of the church mothers in African diasporic Christianity, some wise with age and experience, others intimate partners of and with God in prayer. Church mothers can be First Ladies but the status of Mother is not automatically conferred on a pastor's wife. A mother in the church is a woman who has labored—in both senses: work and birth—in prayer. The language of prayer warriors also comes to mind; Zipporah goes into battle for her family. There is no guarantee that she will survive her encounter with a God bent on death.

How Zipporah comes by her religious knowledge is not worthy of elaboration by the narrator. That Zipporah is *bat kohen* (the daughter of a priest) may be more relevant here than a wider cultural practice of circumcision. Did Zipporah *only* circumcise her son because Moses failed to do it? Does her standing as priest-daughter, priest-woman, have particular implications here? The rabbis will come to call women like Zipporah priestwomen, *kohenoth* (plural of *kohenet*). Like their male priestly kin, women born to priestly families (but not those who have married in) have access to holy food from the divine offerings in the Torah.[40]

38. Susan Ackerman's article ("Why Is Miriam Also Among the Prophets? [And Is Zipporah Among the Priests?]," *Journal of Biblical Literature* 121:1 [2002] 74) shaped my thinking while I was still finding my womanist voice.

39. By tradition in Gen 32:28, the name *Yisrael*, Israel, is derived from the root *s-r-h*, "to strive." Jacob is told, "*sarita*, you have striven." The *yud* prefix would be the third person masculine pronoun in the imperfect. The corresponding feminine pronoun would be *tav*, hence "Tisrael."

40. Lev 10:14: "Now the breast of the wave-offering and the thigh of the gift-offering, you and your daughters and your sons as well may eat in any ritually-appropriate place; for they are your portion and the portion of your descendants from the sacrifices of the offerings-of-wellbeing of the daughters and sons of Israel." I highlight the inclusion of

Zipporah speaks what may be ritual words to accompany her ritual act in verse 25, "*This-is-because you are a bridegroom of blood to me!*" These words have no peer in the text or tradition and may point to the ritual practice of Zipporah and her people or even a particular role for Midianite women in priestly families. Women and men offer, donate, sacrificial animals but only men are described as actually killing, sacrificing them. Before the establishment of the Israelite priesthood a number of male figures sacrifice the animals they offer to God. No women are portrayed as wielding the sacrificial knife in the Scriptures. Circumcision is a covenantal act and can be read as a form of blood sacrifice. That this marriage will be sealed in a blood covenant makes its dissolution all the more problematic.

Is Moses Zipporah's bloody bridegroom? The use of pronouns, once again, muddies the issue. She and Moses have been married for long enough to have produced a child. He is no longer her bridegroom; he is her husband. God? That would be extraordinary. But it is grammatically possible. Also possible and even less likely is her son. God accepts Zipporah's ritual and withdraws from Moses after her words. Then perhaps because Moses is dazed and does not understand, she repeats for him in v. 26, "a bridegroom of blood through circumcision." Grammatically, it appears she addresses the circumcision pieces: *lamuloth*, "to the circumcisions." That doesn't make a lot of sense, but I have retained it. As a church mother Zipporah wields her knowledge without the formal power of authority, then, and fades from the story again, for a while.

Even though Moses has become who he is because of her, both her saving his life and his connection to her father through her, Moses will leave her (and their children) and turn up with another woman (in Num 12). Ex 18:2 begins with the acknowledgement that Moses has divorced Zipporah

women in this passage, placing them first in the sequence and making their presence among the "children" of Israel explicit.

Some of the material in Leviticus pertains to the exercise of priestly function and therefore to male descendants of Aaron, but as a whole Leviticus pertains to *all* of the people of Israel and in places *all* of the descendants of Aaron, without regard to gender. Some material speaks to women directly as in Lev 10:14. And in some places women are hidden in expressions like "Israelites" at the end of v. 14 and "sons" in v. 15, (lacking daughters this time). In each case daughters are present among the people of Israel and in the intended audience for Leviticus, *any human person who brings an offering*. In addition, there were restrictions on where the offerings could be eaten which has gender implications: there were some spaces in the sanctuary that were reserved for priests, therefore women were not permitted. This is the case with the sacred meals that are designated solely for Aaron's male descendants, see 6:18ff; 24:9. However, in Lev 10:14, the daughter-descendants of Aaron may eat the sacred food in any ritually appropriate (*b'maqom tahor*) place. Whether any of these practices are borrowed or adapted from the Midianite priesthood is unclear.

sometime in the past. Divorce here is *shillucheyha*, "her divorce," yet one is hard pressed to find a translation that translates Moses' divorce as divorce: She is "sent away,"[41] "sent home,"[42] or "sent back."[43] However, NRSV.translates the root *sh-l-ch* as divorce in Deut 22:19, 29; 24:1, 3; Isa 50:1; Jer 3:8 and notably in Mal 2:16 where God says that "God hates divorce." Some translations use "put her away," in the Deut texts, but there is no doubt that a "bill of divorce" is not a "bill of being sent away/home/back." Some scholars argue that the expression simply refers to Zipporah taking her dowry with her when she returned to her father, (see Carol Meyer's 2005 commentary) however this does not account for the consistent translation of the term as "divorce" in other cases.[44] Included in the notion of divorce is sending away, but sending away without explicitly naming divorce is such an insufficient translation as to be misleading.

Like many male clergy, Moses has been held beyond reproach with many biblical translators conspiring to preserve his image by obscuring his divorce. The notion of great men getting (or taking) an ethical pass because of their charisma and status is not new and not relegated to religious leadership. It does thrive with a pernicious persistence in religious circles facilitated by claims of divine favor. If power is an aphrodisiac, there is perhaps no greater power than that of one's God and his (sic) male surrogate. Configuring God as male in human terms makes it easy to imagine God's male prophet or pastor as an extension of the divine. As a feminist and as a womanist, I see male clergy elevated to all-but-divine status while their misconduct is systematically overlooked and institutionally enabled. In some cases male clergy misconduct is intentionally based on the Bible's patriarchal discourse.

The text does not explain why or even when Moses divorces Zipporah. Given the status of Moses in the Bible, it is not surprising that the text glosses over his embarrassing familial circumstances. At some point between the night Zipporah saved his life (ch. 4) and the Exodus (chs. 14–15) and its aftermath, specifically the war against Amalek at Rephidim (ch. 17) Moses divorces Zipporah and sends her and their children back to her father. She traveled with him back to the lethal danger of Egypt with their child, having another with him at some point. Given how much of his time he spent with Pharaoh, when did Moses have the time to determine that his marriage

41. Wycliffe, Geneva Bible, Revised Standard Version, Dead Sea Scrolls Bible.

42. Jewish Publication Society, English Standard Version.

43. Tyndale, King James Version, Bishop's Bible, Douay-Rheims (LXX/Vulgate).

44 Carol L. Meyers, *Exodus* (Cambridge: Cambridge University Press, 2005). The New English Translation of the Septuagint uses "dismissal" translating *aphesin*, "release," while the Vulgate has *remiserat*, "send back."

wasn't working for him?[45] Was it after the power and passion of the escape from Egypt and the parting of the Sea of Reeds? Perhaps it was in chapter 16 when the Israelites complained so bitterly to and about Moses for the first time:

Husband, after all you've done for them, after all you've sacrificed for them, I can't believe they would look you in the face and say they would be better off in Egypt. We would be better off with my father than fooling with these ungrateful people. Why are you angry with me? When you said you heard voices in the wilderness, I believed you. When you said God spoke to you in a bush that burned and wasn't consumed I believed you. I believed you so much I left my family and came with you and supported you when everyone else said you were crazy. A fugitive, going to tell the Pharaoh to let his slaves go because a God he has never heard of said so. No matter what anyone said about you—and trust me they said plenty—I stood with you. I put my life on the line to save yours when God whose name is HOLY was killing you in that desert. I could have died and left my child motherless because I chose to stand between you and God. Your anger is not with me, don't bring it home to our tent.

I am reminded of the high-profile divorce of Winnie and Nelson Mandela, after Mandela was released from prison. Their marriage survived the life-threatening times but could not survive that which came afterwards. Whatever it is that has happened has happened in the recent past. Perhaps in response to the divorce or for reasons of his own, Jethro goes to see Moses and brings Zipporah and their children with him. In Ex 18:6 when Jethro tells Moses he is bringing his wife and children back to him, Jethro only refers to them as "her two sons." Moses does not acknowledge Zipporah or his sons. Instead, he embraces his father-in-law and only his father-in-law, and they inquire after each other's wellbeing. Moses does not inquire after Zipporah's wellbeing or that of their children. He does not speak to their sons.

Their marriage is over. Moses has divorced his wife and their children. Jethro accepts this state of affairs and inexplicably remains close to Moses, serving as an advisor. I'd like to think he hoped they would reconcile. But there is no evidence of that in the text, and it is not likely it would be there. Zipporah disappears from the text. In Num 12 Moses appears with a new wife and is rebuked by Miriam (for which rebuke God punishes her severely). Zipporah is a divorced woman, left with two sons whose famous father goes on to great things without them. The aftermath of the divorce will be violent beyond the pale: another Midianite bride will be savaged on

45. Drawing on the *Mekhilta* Rashi cites a tradition that Aaron told Moses to send his family back as soon as they all arrived so as not to add to the numbers of the suffering in Egypt.

her wedding day and her killer rewarded in Num 25:6–15; and Moses and
God will call for the annihilation of his wife's people with no exceptions in
Num 31. That Moses once married into Midian will not be mentioned.

As a single mother perhaps Zipporah drew on the memory and example of her foremother Keturah after widowhood. The text does not track her
journey home with her children when Moses sends her away as recorded
in Ex 18:2. Unlike the womanist icon Hagar, Zipporah is not attended by
angels. There is no story of God meeting her on her way, neither divine
promise nor provision. In going home she returns to her father and possibly
her sisters and their families; there she will be able to provide for her children. Even if there were shame (and false blame) attached to her because of
her failed marriage, Zipporah was willing to endure the shame, gossip, and
whatever might be waiting for her, in part I believe to ensure her children
would have a future. What may have been waiting for her in light of the call
to exterminate her whole people was a bloody death making her words over
Moses a prophecy. If she and her father and her sisters and their families
fell to the Israelites, then those words would have been proved true. Moses
was a bridegroom of blood. (In the grammar of the text with its masculine
pronouns, the words would also apply to God.)

Zipporah is a biblical matriarch. But her matriarchy is invisible. Zipporah's children have been relegated to the margins of the Scriptures despite
the fact that her children are Moses' children. The text is surprisingly vague
on lineage of perhaps the greatest character in all of the Hebrew Bible, certainly in the Torah. In Judg 18:30–21 Gershom's son Jonathan and his sons
served as priests to an idol in the tribal lands occupied by Dan. First Chr
23:14–18 recounts a paltry genealogy listing Gershom's son Shebuel, some
sort of chief with no offspring credited, but not the disgraced Jonathan or
his kin. The genealogy also names Eliezer's only son Rehabiah who is also a
chief and his many (nameless) offspring. So ends the lineage of Moses the
Lawgiver.[46]

Moses' propensity for non-Israelite women is clearly a problem in
and for the Torah. If successful, the genocide he calls for against Zipporah's family will eliminate the evidence of his exogamy; in the text it is God
who calls for the genocide, absolving Moses of culpability.[47] That he calls
for that genocide after his divorce and remarriage is significant, as is the
sexual violence he authorizes—without a divine command this time. They

46. The text does not acknowledge any children for him with his Nubian bride of
Num 12.

47. Num 25:16: "YHVH said to Moshe 'Attack the Midianite women, men and
children, and strike them.'" Num 31:1: "YHVH spoke to Moshe, saying, 'Avenge the
Israelites on the Midianites; afterward you shall be gathered to your people.'"

will be slaughtered and through their daughters, raped out of existence.[48] The actions will be justified based on a lie, that the Midianites, particularly their women led Israel astray at Peor. They weren't even there. Rather than hold Israelite men accountable for their own choices, "foreign" women are blamed for being sexually irresistible. The hostility of Deuteronomists or other editorial hands towards the Midianites cannot be read without considering it a comment on Zipporah and her sisters, her father Jethro and Moses' intermarriage.

Zipporah: Sainted Mother

A womanist midrashic reading of Zipporah reveals that she is a black woman, a daughter of Keturah, an outsider to Israel transcending the binary of Israel and Ishmael. She is a motherless daughter, a sister, a shepherd, and a survivor all before she is a wife. She is a mother, a God-wrestler, and a divorcée. Then Zipporah became a single mother. Zipporah is a biblical matriarch whose matriarchy has been all but erased. Zipporah can be read as a clergy spouse and a church mother; she could be the patron saint of black church women married to preachers.

There was a largely successful attempt to eradicate the people and priestly family of Midian who worshiped the God of the holy mountain when Moshe did not even know God's name. It seems that there is no place for a priestly woman who knows how to offer an acceptable blood sacrifice, appease the God of Sinai/Horeb and perpetuate the covenant of blood made with the descendants of Hagar, Sarah and Keturah—for all of Abraham's descendants inherited the promise and its covenant. Zipporah, her mother, her sisters and her people have been dismissed, sent packing, by the Torah, yet they remain.

Zipporah remains for me as a biblical ancestress of the single mother whose contemporary image is tarnished and used to denigrate peoples of color in particular. She is the long-suffering clergy spouse who has spent her married life in support of her partner's clergy vocation and suppressed her own. Zipporah is a witness that even the marriages of religious folk, and religious folk in leadership fail. Zipporah lives on through her memory preserved in the Scriptures and through her children and their children,

48. Numbers 31:15, 18, and 35: "Moshe said to them, 'You all have let-live all the females! . . . Now then, kill every male among the little ones; and every woman who has known a man by lying with a male, you all shall kill. And all the little ones among the women who have not known a man by lying with a male, keep alive for yourselves . . . thirty-two thousand human souls in all, from women who had not known a man by sleeping with him.'"

some of whom survived Israel. Her grandson Jonathan, became a priest even though he was not a descendent of Elisheba and Aaron, the mother and father of acceptable biblical priests. It may be that he perpetuated the priestly lineage passed to him by his mother Zipporah from her father the priest of the God of the holy mountain that would come to be known as Sinai.

I grew up hearing black folk describe themselves as Hagar's children. We would be well served to claim Zipporah as our mother as well. Tzipporah bat Yitro, I call your name. Ashé.

CHAPTER NINE

Fashioning Our Own Souls

A Womanist Reading of the Virgin-Whore Binary in Matthew and Revelation

MITZI J. SMITH

Introduction

The construction of women as virgins and whores is neither of divine origin nor natural, in the sense of being biologically determined. God did not create women as virgins or whores, but as females made in the image of God. Yet women who are viewed as whores (sometimes called tramps, prostitutes, sluts, hoes, etc.) are constructed over against a supposed biological and social understanding of women as virgins. Virgins are primarily females and virginity is generally expected of females. Virgin/virginity, in popular imagination, refers to females that have not experienced sexual intercourse with a man and/or whose hymen is consequently intact. Of course, a woman's hymen can be broken when engaging in sports or some other vigorous physical activity aside from sexual intercourse. No contemporary medical definition for virginity exists.[1] According to the Torah whether or not a young girl or woman was a virgin definitely could be demonstrated by vaginal bleeding on her wedding night when the hymen is ruptured. A woman who did not bleed, for whom the sheets were not spotted with blood, was judged not to be a virgin, defiled (impure) despite her and her

1. Jessica Valenti, *The Purity Myth. How America's Obsession with Virginity is Hurting Young Women* (Berkeley, CA: Seal, 2010). Of course, America is not the only country obsessed with the virginity of young girls and women.

family's protests to the contrary; the young bride would be considered a whore or prostitute and would be stoned to death (Deut 22:13–21).[2] I could only imagine that a number of animals were sacrificed and their blood sprinkled on bed sheets in order to verify the virginity of a daughter, given that not all virginal women will bleed.

This binary construction of women as virgins or whores is a social construct inscribed in the sacred narratives of the Bible. The social and literary construction of women as virgins and whores (and synonyms like lady, tramp, or prostitute, hoe) has served as a means of patriarchal control of women's sexuality, reproduction, and self-understanding or identity in relation to men. Associated with such social and literary constructions are various forms of violence committed against women by men and women who, wittingly or unwittingly, benefit from and/or support that system of control. Violence against women and children, both in ancient literary and in contemporary texts and contexts, is connected with the binary construction of women as virgins and whores. Such labels betray the sexual objectification of females, functioning primarily, if not only, for the benefit of men and male sexual desire. Persons viewed as objects are not understood to be or expected to exercise agency; they are acted upon and not the actors. Men act upon female sexuality, as men see fit. And when women decide to act, to act independently as other than the object of male sexual desire, they can be verbally, physically, spiritually, and emotionally punished or assaulted by men and women. And men sense a loss of control and/or identity when women reject their own sexual objectification.

In this essay I argue that black women (and women in general) should reject altogether the labeling and construction of women as virgins and whores (and their synonyms) which is tied to ideas of manhood. This gendered sexual dichotomy, its construction and its arbitrary fluidity, which is controlled by men (and by women as men's surrogates in upholding the social construction to the detriment of themselves and their sisters) is inscribed and reinforced in ancient texts that many African American women deem sacred and authoritative for their lives. In this essay I shall discuss the intersection of race, sex, and religion in black women's history in the colonies and in America and the labeling of black women as the perpetual mistress or whore. Second, I shall explore the virgin/whore binary inscribed in the New Testament, particularly in first and last books of the New Testament, the Gospel of Matthew and chapters 17 and 18 of Revelation (the Apocalypse). As I analyze this virgin/whore binary of difference, I shall

2. Of course, the Levitical priests could only marry virgins; they could not marry widows, divorced or defiled women, or prostitutes (Lev 22:13–14).

discuss the violence against women in the texts and contemporary violence against black women. Black women, for the sake of health and wholeness, must take charge of their own sexuality, including naming and defining themselves in ways that promote healthy self-esteem and self-love, as well as love of others and that represent God's graciousness, wholeness, and holiness. According to Alice Walker's definition a womanist is "in charge" and like proto-womanist Harriet Tubman who defied the master/slave binary seizing her own freedom and helping others to do the same,[3] womanists encourage black women to take charge of their own lives, their souls. Tubman serves as paradigmatic precedent for womanists to critique and dismantle oppressive binary systems even when inscribed in sacred texts and contexts, codified as unjust laws, and expressed as unhealthy, unhelpful, and biased norms.

Black Women and the Politics of Race, Sex, Class, Empire, and Religion

Historically, the nexus of racism, sexism, classism, and Christian or religious ideology have colluded to construct black women as inferior beings and sexual deviants; black women collectively have been labeled as wrenches, whores, sexually corrupt, immodest, or as simply filthy. Prior to the legal enslavement of black peoples as perpetual property, blacks arrived in America as indentured servants, working alongside white and native Indian servants; this does not preclude that many Africans were forcibly transported to the colonies by kidnappings and other means. The need for a permanent, inexpensive, and reliable work force coupled with disdained miscegenation, resulted in white colonists denigrating black women while elevating white women and gradually committing black people, de facto and de jure, to perpetual slavery. Christians and/or colonists were determined to distinguish between black women and free white women.[4] In "this early multinational corporation, later called America" acquisition of land and human beings for profit became central to expansion.[5] As the numbers of Africans, who represented both sources of wealth and means to satisfy the sensual needs of the English, increased in the colonies, the African became the other over against whom white men would construct an ideal virtue for themselves

3. Alice Walker, *In Search of Our Mothers' Gardens: Womanist Prose* (New York: Harcourt Brace, 1983) xi.

4. Paula Giddings, *Where and When I Enter: The Impact of Black Women on Race and Sex in America* (New York: Bantam, 1984) 35.

5. Ibid.

and white women. Africans were degraded as black savages who lacked self-control.[6] A race/sex dialectic emerged in which English slave traders constructed black women as both hypersexual and possessing vulgar, immoral sexual proclivities and an inclination for white men. This dialectic was codified by colonial administrators first in the 1630 *Re: Davis* decision that stated as follows: "Hugh Davis to be soundly whipt [sic] before an assembly of negroes & others for abusing himself to the dishonor of God and the shame of Christianity by defiling his body in lying with a negro which fault he is to actk [sic] Next Sabbath day."[7]

The increase of Africans in the Virginia colony from twenty-three in 1625 to three hundred in 1640 became problematic. Any African entering the colony after 1640 could be sentenced to lifelong servanthood.[8] In 1641 when Massachusetts, a Puritan stronghold, became the first among the colonies to enact a law formally legalizing slavery, the first to be sentenced was a white servant who hit his master. In the same year a white man who impregnated a black woman was sentenced to do penance before the church, but the black woman was to be whipped for her indiscretion.[9] The white man had committed a sin against God and church by having sexual relations with a black woman. The black woman was not considered subject to the church but was incorrigible in the eyes of the church and God—she was inherently incapable of morality, she had no soul, and could be treated like an animal in need of discipline.

As Michel Foucault argues, power over the sexuality of persons is manifested and exercised in the enactment of laws and the effects of the laws are determined by obedience rendered to said laws; confronted by law those subject to such laws submit.[10] In 1629 Virginia labeled black women, together with all adult male servants, as "tithable persons"; this meant that black women could be forced to work in the fields. This exception to the usual gendered division of labor confirmed the view of some that black women were "wenches," "nasty," and "beastly" and therefore unsuitable to be domestic servants, as opposed to white indentured servants.[11] By 1643

6. Ibid.

7. Ibid. The man in question is most likely a white man, since black men were referred to generally only by their surnames. And the "negro" is a female as court records tended to specify surnames of black men.

8. Ibid., 36.

9. Ibid. And Virginia, in the seventeenth century, would enact and enforce laws that codify and solidify white colonists' control over black bodies.

10. Michel Foucault, *The History of Sexuality: An Introduction*, vol. 1 (New York: Random House, 1978) 85.

11. Giddings, *Where and When I Enter*, 36.

the status of blacks had become that of property in Virginia. In 1662 Virginia legally recognized slavery as a lifelong, *hereditary* condition. And by 1668, Virginia considered all black women, free and enslaved, as "tithable."[12] Shortly thereafter Virginia passed legislation that said any mulatto children born of an English man and a black woman would assume the social status of the mother and that "if any Christian shall commit fornication with a Negro man or woman, he shall pay double the fines of the former act."[13] Paula Giddings states that with the enactment of this law that connected "racism, sexism, greed, and piety" the denigration of black people, and black women particularly, was complete. It was un-Christian to have sexual relations with a black woman or man, and therefore the fine for such offense was greater than if persons within the same racialized group had committed fornication. This law sets the stage for all children born to black women under slavery to be slaves, and for black women to become breeders for white slave masters as an economical means to replenish and to increase his human property holdings. Even before the full enslavement of Africans, white men holding Africans as indentured, lifelong servants would prefer to pay the fines for impregnating black women since through black women's wombs they could inexpensively increase their labor force.[14]

By the early eighteenth century the necessary (social and juridical) structure was in place to stratify women as wives, mistresses, and whores, as Plato conceived. Black people were human property and a permanent labor force, white men could sexually abuse and impregnate black women with impunity, and black women alone birthed slaves.[15] All of this was achieved "within the context of the Church, the operating laws of capitalism, and the psychological needs of White males. Subsequent history would be a variation on the same theme."[16] The repression and hegemonic control of other bodies and sexualities, reaching a culmination by the end of the nineteenth century, constitutes a self-affirmation of white bodies,[17] but also, the degradation of black bodies.

Enslaved black women in America were labeled and treated as hypersexualized Jezebels, as nonhumans with biological female organs to which slave owners had unbridled access, either by rape or by coercion. Black

12. Ibid., 36–37.

13. Ibid., 37.

14. Ibid. White women as indentured servants were not exempt but they could be sentenced to pay penance with the church (ibid., 37–38).

15. Ibid., 38–39.

16. Ibid., 39.

17. Foucault, *The History of Sexuality*, 122–23.

women, according to the dominant ideology, deserved to be raped, needed to be raped. The black slave woman was never considered a virgin, lady, or even a woman. Former slaves Harriet Jacobs (aka Linda Brent) Henry Bibb, Elizabeth Keckley, Olaudah Equiano, and others[18] discuss in their narratives how black women were violently and persistently coerced to enter into illicit sexual relations or assaulted and raped by white slave masters and overseers. Mary McLeod Bethune's grandmother Sophie carried the scars from the whippings her slave master inflicted upon her for resisting his and the overseerer's sexual advances; Bethune's mother Patsy's breasts were scalded with hot soap for resisting.[19] Black women had no virtue and no right to resist being treated as sexual objects devoid of feelings. In this context, black women struggled to maintain a sense of their own womanhood, purity, and virtue, and also bore the guilt and shame of being raped and assaulted with impunity.[20]

In the late nineteenth century to the early twentieth, Ida B. Wells launched her one-woman anti-lynching campaign, recognizing that lynching of black men had as much to do with gender as with race. Black men were thought to perpetrate rape against white women because of the lustful and lewd sexual nature of black women and at a time when a peoples' morality was said to be determined by the moral character of their women.[21] Giddings quotes a white southern woman's view of black women's lack of

18. See William L. Andrews and Henry Louis Gates, Jr., eds., *Slaves Narratives* (New York: Library of America, 2000); and Elizabeth Keckley, *Thirty Years a Slave, and Four Years in the White House or Behind the Scenes* (New York: Carleton, 1868).

19. Joyce A. Hanson, *Mary McLeod Bethune and Black Women's Political Activism* (Columbia, MO: University of Missouri Press, 2003) 25, 27.

20. White men were not charged and convicted for raping black girls and women until 1965. In that year in Mississippi Norman Cannon, a white man, raped Rosa lee Coates, a fifteen-year-old black female claiming the sex was consensual, but he was found guilty of rape and sentenced to life in prison (black men were sentenced to death for rape). It would not be until 1975 that a white man was successfully tried and convicted of raping or sexually assaulting a black woman with a less than stellar sexual past. Joan Little, a small twenty-year-old black woman, was forced to strip naked by Clarence Alligood, a sixty-two-year-old white jailer. Alligood attempted to force Little to perform oral sex on him and she killed him with an ice pick and escaped. Whites in general could not believe a black woman could be raped and therefore defaulted to the Jezebel stereotype. The prosecuting attorney depicted Little as a seductress and calculating killer. With the support of the black community, ultimately Joan Little was found not guilty and freed. See Danielle L. McGuire, *At the Dark End of the Street: Black Women, Rape, and Resistance—A New History of the Civil Rights Movement from Rosa Parks to the Rise of Black Power* (New York: Vintage, 2010) 233–78.

21. Paula Giddings, "The Last Taboo," in *Words of Fire: An Anthology of African American Feminist Thought*, ed. Beverly Guy-Sheftall (New York: The New York Press, 1995) 415.

virtue, in accordance with popular imagination, as published in the *Independent* in March 17, 1904:

> Degeneracy is apt to show most in the weaker individuals of any race; so negro women evidence more nearly the popular idea of total depravity than the men do. They are so nearly lacking in virtue that the color of a negro woman's skin is generally taken (and quite correctly) as a guarantee of her immorality. . . . I sometimes read of a virtuous negro woman, hear of them, but the idea is absolutely inconceivable to me.[22]

Since women generally are considered the weaker sex and black people are considered the most morally depraved race of all peoples, then it follows that black women were considered as totally lacking in virtue. Any black women said to be virtuous constituted the rare exception and not the rule.

Post-slavery, black women with their new found freedom attempted to take control of their own bodies, but found that even beyond slavery, they could still become the victims of both white and black men's sexual objectification too often manifested in sexual violence. Black women continued to be the object of white men's sexual lust and rape in the streets and alleys of the post-Civil War, Jim Crow South and as domestic workers in urban northern cities during the great migration. Still they struggled to measure up to the dominant society's ideals of womanhood and virtue.[23]

Addressing the economic situation of black men and women after slavery and the poverty into which they were plunged, W. E. B. Du Bois remembered the lives of four women: his widowed mother; his married cousin Inez; Emma a young, single, not-yet-married girl who struggled and managed "to crush her natural, fierce joy of love" and "became a cold, calculating mockery"; and Ide Fuller the "outcast" who it was said "embodied filth and wrong,—but whose filth, whose wrong?"[24] These women existed for and were named after the men to whom they were married or connected to "and not after the fashion of their own souls."[25] Women labeled as virgins and whores exist and are named in relation to men and by men. Du Bois continues that "[a]ll womanhood is hampered today because the world on which it is emerging is a world that tries to worship both virgins and mothers

---

22. Ibid., 416.

23. See for example Anna Julia Cooper, *A Voice from the South* (New York: Oxford University Press, 1988).

24. W. E. B. Du Bois, "The Damnation of Women," in *Darkwater: Voices from within the Veil* (Hazleton, PA: Electronic Classics Series, 2007–2014) 110.

25. Ibid.

and in the end despises motherhood and despoils virgins."[26] Slavery and racism denied that black women had any virginity that white men should honor and respect while elevating the motherhood and virginity of white women, and honoring the children of white women while enslaving those of black women. Du Bois, however, lifts up black women, who through all of the degradation heaped upon them remain pure in body and soul; because contrary to the claims of the dominant society, the control and defilement of black women's bodies does not render them impure. Du Bois writes:

> I honor the women of my race. Their beauty,—their dark and mysterious beauty of midnight eyes, crumpled hair, and soft, full featured faces—is perhaps more to me than to you, because I was born to its warm subtle spell; but their worth is yours as well as mine. No other women on earth could have emerged from the hell of force and temptation which once engulfed and still surrounds black women in America with half the modesty and womanliness that they retain. I have always felt like bowing myself before them in all abasement, searching to bring some tribute to these long-suffering victims, these burdened sisters of mine, whom the world, the wise, white world, loves to affront and ridicule and wantonly to insult. I have known the women of many lands and nations,—I have known and seen and lived beside them, but none have I known more sweetly feminine, more unswervingly loyal, more desperately earnest, and more instinctively pure in body and in soul than the daughters of my black mothers.[27]

Even as white womanhood is worshipped, Du Bois argues, black women are forgotten. African mothers were celebrated in Africa, but American slavery crushed the black woman with its prohibitions against slave marriages, family, and control over their children.[28] Du Bois rejects the opinion of some who say that "nothing decent in womanhood" came from black slavery but "adultery and uncleanness."[29] Instead he argues that the "Negro" women are responsible for millions of daughters and granddaughters who "continue to grow in wealth and character."[30] Du Bois "doubts if any other

26. Ibid., 111.
27. Ibid., 125.
28. Ibid., 114.
29. Ibid., 115.
30. Ibid. "The evil and desecration committed against black women should not be viewed as a stain on black women's bodies and souls."

race of women could have brought its fineness up through so devilish a fire."[31]

By the last half of the nineteenth century ideas about difference were expressed as binary opposition, in terms of gender, class, race and sexuality and such dualities of difference would function as social control in times of radical technological change.[32] Black people's and black women's continued efforts to live into the patriarchal category of virgin and to label those who fail to as whores or hoes puts black women's bodies at the mercy and control of male patriarchy. Instead of maintaining and reifying this gendered sexual dichotomy and mapping it onto the lives and psyches of black women, black woman should critique and reject the social construction of women as virgins and whores and the violence associated with such images, especially in texts and contexts considered sacred and/or authoritative in the black community. But black religious women (and men) continue to appropriate this dichotomous classification of women as virgin and whores despite our history and contemporary assaults (which I will discuss below) on black women based on such classifications. Black religious women (and men) continue to submit to and/or to be complicit in, at least rhetorically or apologetically, the construction of women as virgins and whores because of the authority they give to the biblical text. But such constructions, even though found in the Scriptures, are biased social constructions aimed at controlling women's bodies so that they remain at the service and availability of men, rather than recognizing women's God-given agency—the right to fashion their own souls in relation to God.

The Virgin/Whore Binary in the Gospel of Matthew and Rev 17–18

The virgin/whore binary of difference found in the New Testament is at least informed by the Old Testament. Sometimes Old Testment Scriptures and characters are inserted into New Testament texts to create an intertextuality and continuity. In both testaments the virgin/whore binary is about control of female bodies. Cheryl Anderson in her analysis of gender and violence in the Old Testament law codes argues that "the most striking characteristic in the BC [Book of the Covenant, Ex 20:23–23:19] and DL [Deuteronomic Law, Deut. 12–26] is that female sexuality is to be controlled by a male."[33]

31. Ibid.

32. Giddings, "The Last Taboo," 417–18.

33. Cheryl B. Anderson, *Women, Ideology, and Violence: Critical Theory and the Construction of Gender in the Book of the Covenant and the Deuteronomic Law* (London:

This control of female sexuality by males systemically within patriarchal societies promotes and justifies violence against women; and when it is inscribed in sacred texts that we read uncritically, it negatively impacts our social realities. Thus, I shall analyze the virgin/whore binary in the Gospel of Matthew and in chapters 17 and 18 of Revelation.

The Virgin/Whore Binary in Matthew's Genealogy (Matt 1:1–17)

In Matthew's genealogy, Joseph is identified as the husband of Mary (1:16); whereas in Luke's Gospel Joseph is the son of Heli (Luke 3:23). By inserting Mary at the end of his genealogy, Matthew provides a contrast between Mary who is later identified as a virgin and the other women in the genealogy who would be known by Matthew's Jewish readers as prostitutes and/or women who participated in illicit sexual relations in opposition to Mary as the virgin par excellence. Thus, this virgin/whore dichotomy is reinscribed within the story of Jesus' life, as God with us.

Many readers consider the inclusion of four women in Jesus' genealogy as a positive revisioning (1:1–16) especially given that all four women are outsiders, non-Israelite women (Tamar, Rahab, Ruth, and Bathsheba). They are also women who have engaged in improper or illicit sexual relations with men, involuntarily and voluntarily. Two of the women, Tamar and Rahab, were Canaanites who either "played the prostitute" or was a prostitute by profession (Gen 38; Josh 2:1–21; 6:22–25). After Tamar's husband died (and one of his brothers who was expected to have sex with her to provide an heir for his dead brother) she tired of waiting for Judah's (her father-in-law) young son to grow up to fulfill his duty. So Tamar ditched her widow's outfit, veiled her face, and positioned herself on the roadside where she might hook up with Judah. Judah assumes Tamar is a prostitute, but she seems to know him; and she allows him to have sexual intercourse with her without revealing her identity (Gen 38:14–19); Rahab, the prostitute (*zonah*) (identified first in the text by her profession) concealed two Israelite spies who had been sent to survey Jericho, and they spent the night in her home (Josh 2:1–24); Ruth seduced Boaz in order to obtain a next-of-kin redeemer for Naomi, her mother-in-law and for herself; and Bathsheba, the wife of Uriah, was summoned by King David so that he might have sexual relations with her (taking what he had the power to take) and afterward returned home (2 Sam 11:1–5). Virgins become wives; nonvirginal others may give birth to legitimate heirs of patriarchs, but their social condition

T. & T. Clark, 2004) 75.

remains unchanged. And all are controlled by men. Muse Dube asserts that "the use of the figure of Rahab, a woman, to articulate domination [in Joshua], however, also comes to serve, reinforce, and naturalize the subjugation of women in societies in which these narratives are used."[34] And the weaving of Rahab along with the other three women into the genealogy reinforces the categorization and subjugation of women trapped in a virgin/whore binary of difference. In the book of Hebrews, written about the same time as Matthew's Gospel, Rahab is also identified as a prostitute (11:31).

The inclusion of Tamar, Rahab, Ruth, and Bathsheba in Matthew's genealogy did not change their social status among the Israelites. In this volume Yolanda Norton argues that the book of Ruth functions to reinforce normative power structures, enforcing white, male norms to the detriment of black women; Ruth assimilates and pledges unwavering loyalty to Israel but never fully achieves the status she urgently seeks. Indeed, Norton points out that even the son that Ruth gives birth to as a result of her relationship with Boaz is said to be Naomi's son (Ruth 4:17). Reading Ruth's character as representative of her people, the Moabites, who were known as sexually perverse peoples, Norton argues that it is Ruth's sexuality that is used to find a restorer and nourisher for Naomi in her old age. No pain is given to Ruth's experience of trying to fit into a religio-cultural framework in which she is doubly oppressed, as an outsider and a woman. She, like Hagar, is merely a surrogate.[35]

Lynne St. Clair Darden argues that the women included in the prologue of Matthew's Gospel are outsiders who as "extremely strong supporters of the Israelite nation . . . each in her own way, denied her own people."[36]

34. Musa W. Dube, *Postcolonial Feminist Interpretation of the Bible* (St. Louis: Chalice, 2000) 144.

35. Yolanda Norton, "Silenced Struggles for Survival: Finding Life in Death in the Book of Ruth," in *I Found God in Me: A Womanist Biblical Hermeneutics Reader*, ed. Mitzi J. Smith (Eugene, OR: Cascade, 2015). Contra, Elaine Wainwright ("The Gospel of Matthew," in *Searching the Scriptures: A Feminist Commentary* [New York: Crossroad, 1998], 643) argues that "the women's presence functions . . . as a critique of patriarchy and introduces a point of tension into the narrative that must guide the reader." Amy-Jill Levine ("Gospel of Matthew," in *Women's Bible Commentary*, revised and updated, ed. Carol A. Newsom, Sharon H. Ringe, Jacqueline E. Lapsley [Louisville: Westminster John Knox, 2012], 467) argues that the women in the prologue "model Matthew's concern for 'higher righteousness,'" and they "represent the socially vulnerable." Musa Dube (*Postcolonial Feminist Interpretation of the Bible* [St. Louis: Chalice, 2000], 143) on the other hand argues that the term "higher" or "greater righteousness" "reflects colonized people's competition for power among themselves, where they no longer have it, as well as their fight for the favor of the colonizer." Dube also reminds readers that Rahab's story is not her own; it is told from the perspective of her subjugators.

36. Lynne St. Clair Darden, "Privilege but No Power: Women in the Gospel of

Such assimilation is attributed to a hybridity that occurs among colonized peoples. Darden argues that inclusion of Rahab, Tamar, Ruth, and Bathsheba must be read within the framework of nation building[37] among a religious people. That context resembles the historical framework within which black women as indentured servants and then as slaves were rendered a permanent underclass of sexually immoral outsiders. As black women struggled for liberation, they also consciously and not so consciously reinscribed in their own lives the virgin/whore binary, giving up some of their own freedom in order to fit into the established hegemonic order.

Each of the four women, as outsiders, is identified in relation to the children she bore and not in relation to the man for whom she bore them. Conversely, when Mary's name is introduced in the genealogy, she is identified implicitly as Joseph's wife ("Jacob the father of Joseph the husband of Mary of whom Jesus was born," 1:16). It is clear that Mary's child was born into a legitimate marital relationship. The four other women in the genealogy are linked to their sons by a prepositional phrase "out of/from" (Greek, *ek tēs*) attached to each woman's name, as if to merely acknowledge her for her womb. But Bathsheba is not even mentioned by name; she is identified as the "wife of Uriah" (in contrast to Mary) highlighting the illicit relationship between Bathsheba and King David (1:6). Solomon, according to the genealogy is born out of wedlock, out of (*ek tēs tou Ouriou*) an adulterous relationship. Although there is no biblical or extrabiblical support for Rahab as the mother of Boaz,[38] she is included as one of the foreign women in whose womb the child of an Israelite was born. The inclusion of the women by way of the grammatical preposition highlights them as other and less than virginal wives, as surrogate mothers. Many African slaves have been surrogates bearing the master's mulatto children, and as asexual, loyal "Mammy" caring for the master's white children and hopefully their own. Delores Williams has raised questions about the usefulness of the terms "virgin" and "virginity" in light of black women's history of surrogacy.[39]

The Messiah of God could only be born from a virgin, and proof of Mary's virginity—despite her pregnancy—is given in Joseph's refusal to expose her and his willingness to still marry her. Also the angel of the Lord verifies in a dream to Joseph that it is safe to take Mary as his wife and

---

Matthew and Nineteenth-Century African American Women Missionaries through a Postcolonial Lens," in *Teaching All Nations: Interrogating the Matthean Great Commission*, ed. Mitzi J. Smith and Lalitha Jayachitra (Minneapolis: Fortress, 2014) 117.

37. Ibid., 121.

38. Jane Schaberg, *The Illegitimacy of Jesus: A Feminist Theological Interpretation of the Infancy Narratives* (San Francisco: Harper and Row, 1987) 25.

39. Williams, *Sisters in the Wilderness*, 180–81.

that she is indeed a virgin. Virgins are marriage material and virgins are not exposed or stripped, like whores are, in the literary tradition of the Hebrew Bible (e.g., Hosea). To ensure that the baby was conceived of the Holy Spirit, Joseph does not consummate the marriage until after the child is born (1:25). In the Christian apocryphal text *The Protoevangelium of James* (The first Gospel of James [the brother of Jesus]) Salome, using her finger, performs a virginity test on Mary after the birth of Jesus to see if she is indeed a virgin.[40] If people had doubts about Mary's virginity after the birth, they certainly had them beforehand. In some contemporary societies and/or regimes, women and girls are forced to submit to virginity tests.[41] One wonders if this was not the case of the three hundred Nigerian school girls who were kidnapped from a Christian school by the militant, extremist anti-education Muslim group Boko Haram. One young girl who managed to escape testified that because she was a virgin she was given to one of the terror leaders as a wife; one man raped her. But other girls, she claims, who were not virgins were gang raped up to fifteen times a day, forced to convert to Islam, and killed if they refused. Both virgins and those considered to be "whores" or who have had a sexual experience with a man are sexually takable or rapable; both can be raped.[42]

Wise and Foolish Virgins (Matt 25:1–13)

Not all virgins are created equal. Fundamentalist and some evangelical Christians have made allowances for women and girls who have "lost" their virginity to be redeemed by repentance and conversion and thus to become honorary or "secondary virgins."[43] So there are real virgins, since virginity

---

40. Wilhelm Schneemelcher, ed., "The Protoevangelium of James," in *New Testament Apocrypha* (Louisville: Westminster John Knox, 1991) 434.

41. For example, women who protested in Tahrir Square in Cairo, Egypt were detained a month after Mubarak's overthrow and subjected to "virginity tests." The tests were ordered by the supreme council of armed forces (SCAF) that replaced Hosni Mubarak. They hoped to shame women away from demonstrating. Virginity tests take place regularly in Egypt, but it is different when it is the state forcing women's legs open to appeal to "the god of virginity." Mona Eltahawy, "These 'virginity tests' will spark Egypt's next revolution," *The Guardian*, June 2, 2011, http://www.theguardian.com/commentisfree/2011/jun/02/egypt-next-revolution-virginity-tests (accessed November 5, 2013).

42. Rod McPhee, "The School Girls Stolen as Sex Slaves by Nigeria's Anti-Education Jihadists Boko Haram," *Mirror*, May 03, 2014, www.mirror.co.uk/news/uk-news/boko-haram-329-schoolgirls-stolen-3489356 (accessed May 5, 2014).

43. Valenti, *Purity Myth*, 34. Secondary virginity requires both abstinence from partner-sex, masturbation, and lust (thinking about and desiring sex).

is something one can never retrieve once it is "lost," and pseudo-virgins. But most discussions about women's purity center around white women. "Because the sexuality of young women of color—especially African Americans and Latinas—is never framed as 'good girls gone bad'; rather they're depicted as having some degree of pathologized sexuality from the get-go, no matter what their virginity status."[44]

Not all virgins are constructed equally in the sacred biblical text, as in the parable of the Ten Virgins (*parthenoi*) (Matt 25:1–13). The virgins are divided into the categories of wise and foolish. The wise virgins, like the wise slaves (24:45–51; 25:14–30) are expected to know and anticipate the master or bridegroom's every whim so as to properly cater to his desires. Wise virgins are constructed in relationship to and by the men for whom they are constructed; and they can be deconstructed by the same men. And foolish virgins are those who fall short and do not anticipate the needs of the bridegroom; thus, they fail by omission to allow themselves and their identities to be fully constructed by the men in their lives. It does not matter that they could not know that the bridegroom would be late; it matters that they were not prepared for his tardiness, regardless of the reason. In order to stay in the good graces of the master/bridegroom and to maintain their position in relation to him, the wise virgins will not share their oil with the foolish virgins. The foolish virgins still expect to have access to the bridegroom by reason of their virginity, but they are rejected for failure to expect the unexpected—to allow for men's capricious and total control over them. The language of rejection that the bridegroom uses, "I do not know you" is the language of sexual intercourse (25:12) of consummation denied. This is the ultimate rejection for a virgin whose entire identity is constructed in relationship to men and their in/ability to sexually satisfy them, particularly as potential bridegrooms or husbands.

I wonder where the bride is in this wedding party. Is it possible that this is a wealthy, powerful man or king who had planned to marry ten virgins? What is the socio-historical reality behind the parable or to which it points? Would Matthew's readers see the virgins as conquered prisoners of war, slaves, given to the victors as wives (see Judg 21:12; Esther 2:2)? The declaration of not knowing the five foolish virgins represents the bridegroom reneging on a promise to marry simply because they failed to be totally submissive as expected of slaves and women. The parable is positioned between two other parables about slaves and slave masters (24:45–51; 25:14–30). In any case the parable highlights the capricious manner in which males in patriarchal societies have control of and can change that status of women even

44. Ibid., 47.

within sexual categories to which women submit themselves or into which society forces them. Virgins are as subject to male rejection and abuse as are women who are labeled as whores. And to protect men and their manhood, both virgins and whores will be sacrificed (Judg 19:24).

The Virgin/Whore Binary in Rev 17–18

The use of the whore metaphor in Rev 17 and 18 reinforces the virgin/whore binary of difference and its application to all things female.[45] The whore of Rev 17 and 18 is the antithesis of the virginal bride in Rev 19:7; 21:1–22; 22:17, and the woman clothed with the sun in Rev 12:1–6, 13–17. As Surekha Nelavala argues, the "whore" (as well as the virgin I would argue) in Revelation must be seen as more than metaphorical "because of its parallels to the lives of real women."[46] Both the literary and social construction of individuals and/or groups as whores or virgins is almost exclusively linked to the feminine gender both in sacred texts and in real contemporary life. As Nelavala also argues, Revelation's political use of the gendered whore metaphor has implications for real women's lives by reflecting and reinscribing gendered relations.[47] One can ignore the implications of the gendered whore construction from a place of racial or class privilege.[48] Poor and minority women are more likely to be consistently and systemically conceptualized, labeled, and treated like whores. Elisabeth Schüssler Fiorenza states that a rhetorical critique of Revelation must not be limited to gender, but the "personifications of mother, virgin, and whore" should also be problematized "in terms of the systemic structures of race, class, and imperialist oppression."[49] The use of the label "whore" implies its binary opposite, virgin, and both have implications for mothers and the children they birth.

45. Although as an exception, the virgins in chapter 14 of Revelation are males who have not defiled themselves with women (14:4).

46. Nelavala, "Babylon the Great Mother of Whores," 60, 62. Contra, Fiorenza (*The Book of Revelation*, 218) further argues that Revelation's metaphorical use of gendered terms such as "mother," "virgin," and "whore" function "as a politics of meaning that does not speak about actual wo/men but inculcates the kyriarchal gender ideology of femininity, i.e., that of the 'white lady.'"

47. Nelavala, "Babylon the Great mother of Whores," 62.

48. Brian K. Blount (*Can I Get A Witness? Reading Revelation through African American Culture* [Louisville: Westminster John Knox, 2005]) reads revelation through the lens of African American's resistance to slavery and subjugation, but he neglects to read or analyze the gendered political metaphorical constructions of Revelation 17–18 and elsewhere in the text.

49. Elisabeth Schüssler Fiorenza, *The Book of Revelation: Justice and Judgment* (Minneapolis: Fortress, 1998) 218.

Black women as enslaved, taken-for-granted whores could only give birth to enslaved whores.

Marion Carson is correct that the whore in Revelation must be understood within the framework of such images in Jewish prophetic literature of the Hebrew Bible/Old Testament.[50] Considering the image of the whore in Jewish prophetic literature, Caroline Vander Stichele convincingly argues that the woman as great whore identified as Babylon in Revelation 17 refers to a real woman, namely Jezebel who is described as a whore (she teaches and seduces God's servants to practice fornication and is thrown into a bed where men commit adultery with her) and whose body Elijah predicted the dogs would devour (1 Kgs 21:23; 2 Kgs 9:36–37; Rev 2:20–22); Jezebel is the woman who is called a whore in Rev 17. And as the paradigmatic whore, Jezebel becomes a metaphor for Babylon (symbolically the Roman Empire) in Rev 18.[51] Jezebel, like the woman in Rev 17, was as "high class call girl" as the wife and daughter of kings (1 Kgs 16:31; 2 Kgs 9:34). As Brian Blount argues this image of the whore in Rev 17–18 is "no ordinary street harlot; this is an expensive call girl, an alluring courtesan of the highest order."[52] Although the whore is represented as an expensive call girl, she shares the accoutrements or "trappings of a street hooker; she sports her name tattooed across her forehead."[53] The elitist or upper class position of the whore in Rev 17–18 is also demonstrated by her clothing—purple is the color of royalty, and scarlet is associated with prostitutes (cf. Rahab, Josh 2:1–18). But the woman in Rev 12, the one clothed with the sun, is reminiscent of Eve before her fall; she is not clothed with human made clothes. Since she has no shame, she needs no clothing. And she, unlike the whore, gives birth to a child, a God-honored child (12:5). If it were not for the whore's social status, she would have been violated daily rather than in some eschatological future judgment.

50. Marion Carson, "The Harlot, the Beast, and the Sex Trafficker: Reflections on some Recent Feminist Interpretations of Revelation 17–18," *Expository Times* 122:5 (2011) 218–27.

51. Caroline Vander Stichele, "Re-membering the Whore: The Fate of Babylon According to Revelation 17:16," in *A Feminist Companion to the Apocalypse of John*, ed. Amy-Jill Levine with Maria Mayo Robbins (New York: T. & T. Clark, 2009) 106–20.

52. Brian K. Blount, *Revelation. A Commentary* (Louisville: Westminster John Knox, 2009) 314.

53. Blount, *Revelation*, 315.

Whores Can Be Violated with Impunity

Women who are socially constructed as whores can be subjected to violence—verbal, emotional, spiritual, and physical abuse. Decadence in society has been attributed to the so-called immorality of its women; therefore women considered immoral can be subjected to violence in order to stop the contagion and moral decline (17:6). The whore can be stripped of her clothing—made naked, isolated, raped by those who had sexual relations with her, cannibalized, and consumed with fire (17:16; cf. Hosea 2:1–4). And such violence is sanctioned by God or even said to be executed by God (17:17). She deserves double for her seductions (18:6). The whore can be tortured with plagues, pestilence, mourning, and famine before she is finally destroyed (18:8).

Whores can be subjected to violence because they are whores. And almost any woman can be labeled a whore. Any female who does not respond to the unsolicited and unwanted catcalls of men can be labeled a whore and subjected to verbal and possibly physical abuse. The labeling of women as whores, tramps, or prostitutes also results when women break their silence about male sexual abuse and the misuse of authority. In 2012 Lieutenant Monique Patterson came forward to lend legitimacy to the claims of another woman, Mrs. Robinson, that Detroit Police Chief Ralph Godbee had an inappropriate sexual relationship with her. Both women were "underlings" in the police department and had been sexually harassed. In a FOX 2 News interview Lieutenant Patterson stated that she was promised a promotion in exchange for sex. Fox 2 News reporter Charlie LeDuff, a white male, interviewed Lt. Patterson, an African American female, and towards the end of the interview Mr. LeDuff blatantly asked Lt. Patterson, "Are you a tramp?" There was no push back to this outrageous question from the two African American anchors who spoke with LeDuff on air after the taped interview aired. Patterson responded to LeDuff in the interview by stating that "people can call me whatever . . . it's fine, you know, if my behavior then two years ago earned me that title, then okay. I have a new life and the department needs a new chief."[54] Because she submitted to the police chief's abuse of power she could be labeled as a tramp with impunity. She was publicly and verbally abused. No one suggested that the officer who abused his

54. "Will Godbee Resign? Bing to Hold Monday News Conference," MyFoxNews-Detroit.com, October 5, 2012, http://www.myfoxdetroit.com/story/19750499/will-godbee-resign-bing-expected-to-hold-monday-news-conference?autoStart=true&top VideoCatNo=default&clipId=7808240 (accessed May 20, 2014). "Chief Ralph Godbee Sex Scandal: Mystery Woman Reveals Herself to Charlie LeDuff," MyFoxNewsDetroit. com. http://www.myfoxdetroit.com/story/19708341/chief-ralph-godbee-sex-scandal-mystery-woman-reveals-herself-to-charlie-leduff (accessed October 12, 2012).

authority and harassed the women in the police department was a whore or tramp. Even readers who responded in the comments section under the video blamed the woman and labeled her as a "whore" and a "tramp." The implication is that women who can be labeled a tramp, whore, or prostitute are never victims but deserving of violence. Art imitates life: In an April 10, 2013 episode of *Law and Order*, a detective stated the following about a woman's rape: "she is not a victim. She is a prostitute." But, of course the same labels and concomitant abuse and violence seldom apply to men in general.[55]

The Whore is a Mystery, and Men are Seldom Culpable

The whore in Rev 17:5 is given a name that removes all culpability from the men who consorted with her: "and on her forehead was written a name, mystery: 'Babylon, the great, mother of whores and of earth's abominations'" (NRSV). That a woman should have such power over a man is a mystery. At the same time, by naming her "Babylon" (a metaphor for the Roman Empire) her condemnation as a whore is justified. A woman who is so seductive as to have many and powerful suitors must be immoral and must be a whore. If the seductive powers of the whore remain a mystery, then there is no need to examine male culpability. To solve the constructed mythical mystery of black women's sexuality, of the stereotype of black women as hypersexual Jezebels is highlighted by the early-nineteenth-century exhibition of Sara Bartmann's naked body. Because of her unusually large and shapely buttocks, Sara Bartmann's (a South African woman also known as the "Hottentot Venus") naked body was displayed for five years in London and then in Paris where she died. The degrading, so-called "scientific" display of Ms. Bartmann's body continued with the placement of her sexual organs in the Musée de l'Homme in Paris. Paula Giddings asserts that "it was no coincidence that Sara Bartmann became a spectacle in a period when the British were debating the prohibition of slavery. . . . By the nineteenth century,

55. If a woman is perceived of or is labeled a whore/tramp/prostitute, violence against her is justified. John Quinonez, the star of ABC's *What Would You Do?*, showed a group of male and female actors posing as hazing victims of fraternity/sororities. More people stepped up and earlier for the young men who were being hazed. But for the young women, one guy pulled up a chair to watch; another guy stood watching, as they thought it was entertaining to see girls call other girls names like whores, fat, disgusting, not worthy of breathing the same air, pouring alcohol down their throats, and stripping off their clothes. A couple of women even stopped and participated in the hazing of the women by joining the name calling. With both groups persons were willing to either video tape or take pictures at the request of the girls who were hazing other girls.

then, race had become an ideology, and a basis of that ideology had become sexual difference."[56]

The whore of Babylon is quite active in contradistinction to the bride who Tina Pippin argues "is the most passive of female characters in the Apocalypse."[57] The whore has seduced the kings. She provided the wine, and they drank it (18:3). The kings have committed fornication with her because she is a whore; not because of their own lust and lack of control. Similarly, black women were historically to blame when white men entered into sexual relationships with them. The whore's sexual partners have drunk of the wine of her fornication, 17:2. She holds a cup full of abominations, 17:4. She is impure, 17:17. Other nations who fornicate with the whore are identified as male and not female. By lumping the nations together and not naming them the paradigm of the whore who seduces men remains intact. As in contemporary society, the Johns of prostitutes (many of whom are underage girls and a high proportion are poor African American teens who have been lured into prostitution) are seldom targeted and prosecuted by law enforcement. Without the participation of Johns in prostitution and sex trafficking it could not be such a lucrative business. Those who indulge in the whore's sexual favors remain redeemable while she is a perpetual and irredeemable whore. To say the nations are to "come out of her" and to cease partaking of her sins is another way of reinforcing the idea that the whore is responsible for the downfall of nations/men, 18:4. The statement in which the whore identifies herself, saying "I rule as queen," furthers the point that a whorish woman is to blame for the downfall of men, for they are kings and she is queen, like Jezebel, (18:7). The merchants of the earth can perhaps be equated as those who pimped the woman benefitting from her as a whore; they too are spared violence despite the luxurious life they built as a result of the relationship between the queen whore and the kings (18:3c, 15). Like the white men who impregnated black women in the seventeenth-century English colonies, the nations will do penance before God while the woman will be treated violently and annihilated (18:8, 19, 21).

Whores Give Birth to Whores

Revelation 17:5 reinforces the idea that whores give birth to whores. Enslaved black women's children inherited the legal, social, and moral status of their mothers, just as the whore of Revelation is considered a "mother of whores" (17:5). The recognition of black women as mothers did not

56. Giddings, "The Last Taboo," 416–17. Slavery was abolished in Britain in 1833.
57. Tina Pippin, "Revelation/Apocalypse of John," 631.

constitute a recognition of them as human beings—even animals gave birth. Black women could be "Jezebels" and/or "mammies". The movie the *Imitation of Life* is the story of the tragic mulatto who could pass for white and who repeatedly tries to pass in order to escape her "blackness," which is most visible and epitomized in the blackness of her mother. Passing as a white woman she has access to a certain quality of life that she cannot have as a black woman; she can fit in with the dominant white society. Peola,[58] the tragic mulatto, detests when her mother refers to herself as "mammie." If her mother is a mammie, then she is a mammie's child. Historically, mammies served in white households, taking care of white babies and children and their own children as well, as did Delilah, Peola's mother. Kelly Brown Douglas argues that "the Jezebel and mammy images crafted in White culture allowed White people to cruelly exploit black female bodies with relative impunity."[59] The construction of black females as mammies enabled slave owners to continue to treat black women as Jezebels while creating a subclass or division among slaves whom they could convince to be loyal to white households, trusted custodians of their children, maternal and asexual; but mammy did not always conform and sometimes used her position subversively and to help other slaves. Still mammies were sometimes attractive and pursued by white males in the household and thus seen as a sexual threat to the white slave mistress.[60] These images of black women as Jezebel and Mammy can be seen in more contemporary images imposed on black women, such as the "domineering matriarch" (and/or the single parent head of household). The Jezebel figure also remains intact in for example the naming of black women as welfare mothers/queens.[61]

Any Woman is a Potential a Whore

Women who achieve social status may still be labeled and treated as whores, no matter how high they rise. They may be considered outsiders based on racial/ethnic or religious difference. Jezebel is constructed as a whore because Jezebel and her people worshipped Baal and she dared to be a shrewd and ruthless businesswoman. She dared to call herself a prophet, and according to her haters she taught God's servants to practice fornication and to eat

58. In the 1934 version Peola is played by actress Fredi Washington (an African American mulatto in real life) and Louise Beavers plays her mother, Delilah.

59. Kelly Brown Douglas, *Sexuality and the Black Church: A Womanist Perspective* (Maryknoll, NY: Orbis, 1999) 44.

60. Douglas, *Sexuality and the Black Church*, 41.

61. Ibid., 50.

foods sacrificed to idols (2:20). For this transgressive independent behavior she would be made sexually available to men who are not her husband—thrown on a bed and pimped. Those men who engage in sexual intercourse with her can repent (like white men who had sex with black women); but her time for repentance has expired (2:21, her patrons still have time). And Jezebel's children will be murdered (2:22, 23) because whores give birth to little whores. Jezebel was a mother, but her role as mother was not valued, because of who she was determined to be. Jezebel was her own person, even as a wife, who refused to be controlled by men. Women who are not submissive to the men in their lives, especially to their fathers and then to their husbands, are not considered virtuous and therefore do not fit into the category of virgin; they are whores. Jezebel reminds us that all women are viewed as potential whores by not conforming to patriarchal religious expectations or by belonging to a despised racial/ethnic group; they are viewed as capable of exchanging their sexual favors, even within marriage, for money or material gifts. Their behavior is contagious; other women will follow suit and men will acquiesce (cf. Esther 1:17–20). Nelavala states that in Indian mythology all women are viewed as potential adulterers or whores "having an adulterous nature."[62]

The Fine Line between Love and Hate

Despite the binary opposition set up in the virgin-whore dichotomy, because men control the nomenclature and can transgress the categories fairly easily, there is a slim and sometimes fluid line between virgins and whores as social constructs. Women can be labeled as whores by rejecting men's unbridled control over them and for choosing not to submit to patriarchal rule in home, church, and the larger society. Virgins and whores are rapable; even wives are rapable and can be blamed for their own rapes. A woman who has never engaged in sexual intercourse can be labeled a slut, prostitute, whore, or any other term in binary opposition to the construction of women as virgins (or ladies) simply by not conforming to certain behavioral expectations. For example, a woman can be labeled a whore, slut, tramp, or prostitute if she dares to wear her dress too short by certain standards, allows herself to become inebriated in the company of males, refuses to respond positively to male attention, or if she is lured into sexual intercourse

62. Surekha Nelavala, "'Babylon the Great Mother of Whores' (Rev. 17:5): A Postcolonial Feminist Perspective" *Expository Times* 121:2 (2009) 61. Women in Indian patriarchal culture, argues Nelavala, must continually struggle to be good women since they are perceived as having a natural propensity for playing the whore.

through a date rape drug or the excessive drinking of alcohol. Virginity is a fluid construct even in the Old Testament and other ancient texts. As noted earlier, a woman could be dissolved of her status as a virgin if she fails to bleed on her wedding night, but also if she is raped or if persons of authority should spread rumors about her that she is unable to prove false (2 Sam 13:1–14; Susanna).

Both whores and virgins can be subject to violence, depending on the needs of men. In some African countries, there is a myth that having sex with a virgin will cure HIV/AIDS, for instance in South Africa where sixty children are raped daily; there may nor may not be a direct correlation.[63] This same myth exists in parts of the Caribbean.[64] In April 2011 the then Jamaican Minister of Health Rudyard Spencer cited the following as challenges to reducing the incidence of HIV/AIDS in Jamaica:

> These include a widely held belief that sex with a virgin can cure HIV/AIDS, the high level of sexual relations between older men and young girls and a persistently hostile anti-gay environment which all contribute to the stigmatisation and discrimination of infected and affected persons. A strong religious culture also inhibits open discussion on matters of sexuality. . . . We too need to begin the process of unlearning those beliefs that endanger the health lives of others and rethinking the tendency to be obscene and degrading in rejecting values that conflict with our own.[65]

The construction of women as virgins and whores renders them powerless; they are hated and loved at the pleasure of men and their surrogates. Like Hagar and the Virgin Mary, whores and virgins, Delores Williams argues, are "always powerless and never able to take care of their own business or set their own agenda for their lives."[66]

---

63. Mike Earl-Taylor, "HIV/AIDS, the Stats, the Virgin Cure and Infant Rape," Science in Africa, April 2002, http://www.scienceinafrica.com/old/index.php?q=2002/april/virgin.htm (accessed May 24, 2014).

64. I learned this from a local pastor and his wife while visiting Montego Bay, Jamaica in December, 2009.

65. Jamaica Observer, "Jamaicans Making it Impossible for Gays to Stay with One Partner," April 23, 2011, http://www.jamaicaobserver.com/news/Jamaicans-making-it-difficult-for-gays-to-stay-with-one-partner-_8567822 (accessed May 24, 2014).

66. Williams, Sisters in the Wilderness, 182.

Conclusion—Fashioning Our Own Souls

I am not proposing that black women become promiscuous (however women might define it for themselves despite racism, classism, sexism, and oppressive religious ideologies) but simply that we critique and reject the imposition of binary differences that promote the control and violence of women by men and other women; that black women take charge of our own sexuality, naming our own experience and refusing to be placed into boxes that do not work, do not work in terms of developing healthy self-images or self-esteem. In a racialized society in which black women, and black people in general, are viewed as inferior in every respect, any attempt to conform or assimilate to a binary system controlled by the dominant majority—male, particularly white males—will only guarantee that black women's sexuality will continue to be under assault and devalued. In addition, black women, and women in general, must not allow all of their human value or self-worth to be deposited in or based on their sexuality. Our sexuality should not define or devalue our humanity. We cannot allow our sexuality to continue to be used against us arbitrarily, and to in turn use it arbitrarily as a weapon against our sisters, as when women slut-shame other women. In addition, black women, and women in general, should not be made to or voluntarily assume the burden of affirming social constructions of manhood that are based on the submission and sexual objectification of women.

Du Bois has argued that men must cease to be horrified by the thought of women having full control over their own sexuality if men will be free: "The present mincing horror at free womanhood must pass if we are ever to be rid of the bestiality of free manhood; not by guarding the weak in weakness do we gain strength, but by making weakness free and strong. . . . The world must choose the free woman or the white wraith of the prostitute. Today it wavers between the prostitute and the nun."[67] The world would rather not set women free from the control of men, but to keep them trapped in the binary of "the prostitute and the nun." But women are not powerless to free themselves.

We must read critically contexts and texts that inscribe the virgin/whore binary. As womanist biblical scholar Wil Gafney argues with regard to gender, for example: "responsible exegesis requires intentionality in text selection, translation, and interpretation. Those interpretive communities and individuals who use biblical portrayals of gender roles to construct contemporary gender roles must and do choose among liberative, egalitarian,

---

67. Du Bois, "The Damnation of Women," 111.

and oppressive paradigms."[68] It is imperative that we employ a critical consciousness and intentionality to guard against reinscribing oppression and oppressive structures (e.g., racism, sexism, classism, colonialism, capitalism, religious dogmatism) through our readings and theological constructions. The impact of unjust readings and teachings produced by academy and church have a reach—an often violent reach—beyond the church and the academy. Jacquelyn Grant poses the question "How much of what happens to women inside and outside of the church is related to what the church teaches about women?"[69] This and other questions cause Grant to focus on the "lies, sex, and violence" that occur in the church and that we must confront.[70] If we do not confront the "lies, sex, and violence" in the biblical text that we regard as sacred and authoritative, we are less likely to challenge them in the church and in the wider society. The black church has either refused to engage in open and honest discourse about sexuality except within the framework of submission and abstinence, despite the problems that churches face with regard to sexual abuse by clergy, in our churches, families, and in the wider society. Douglas argues that "the tacit refusal of the Black church and the Black community to engage in sexual discourse signals Black people's complicity in the sin of White culture."[71]

As bell hooks states "sexism has never rendered women powerless. It has either suppressed their strength or exploited it. Recognition of that strength, that power, is a step women together can take towards liberation."[72] We as black women, as women in general, have the ability and power to read for ourselves and to define and name ourselves. As females created in the image of God, we are creative agents of God. We can find God in us, in our yellow, beige, brown, and ebony skin. We can celebrate the God in us and fashion our souls in the likeness of the God who is no respecter of persons and has given us all the power to shape our lives and destinies in partnership with God's Spirit. As nineteenth-century proto-womanist, activist, and educator Anna Julia Cooper wrote in her book *A Voice from the South* "only

68. Wil Gafney, "Reading the Hebrew Bible Responsibly," in *The Africana Bible. Reading Israel's Scriptures from Africa and the African Diaspora,* ed. Hugh R. Page, Jr. (Minneapolis: Fortress, 2010) 50.

69. Jacquelyn Grant, "Freeing the Captives: The Imperative of Womanist Theology," in *Blow the Trumpet in Zion! Global Vision and Action for the 21st Century Black Church,* eds. Iva E. Carruthers, Frederick D. Haynes III, and Jeremiah A. Wright, Jr. (Minneapolis: Fortress, 2005) 86–87.

70. Ibid., 87.

71. Douglas, *Sexuality and the Black Church,* 124.

72. bell hooks, *Feminist Theory: From Margins to Center* (Boston: South End, 1984) 93.

the BLACK WOMAN can say 'when and where I enter, in the quiet, undisputed dignity of my womanhood, without violence.'"[73]

73. Anna Julia Cooper, *A Voice from the South* (New York: Oxford University Press, 1988) 31.

CHAPTER TEN

A Womanist-Postcolonial Reading of the Samaritan Woman at the Well and Mary Magdalene at the Tomb

LYNNE ST. CLAIR DARDEN

At first glance, the events in two important narratives in the gospel of John that feature women—the Samaritan Woman at the Well (4:1–42) and Mary at the Tomb (20:1–18)—appear to signify that the women in the Johannine community fully participated in leadership positions with the men. It has been suggested by several scholars that early in the Johannine communal development women were allowed to be leaders because leadership was based on a charismatic and prophetic tradition.[1] However, by paying close attention to the actions/events narrated immediately after the textual units that seemingly support, promote, and affirm the role of women in the Johannine world, it is obvious that the text also denies the role of women in public society. This paper proposes that the ambiguity that lies within these two narratives may reflect a major paradigmatic shift regarding women's roles as the Johannine community developed over time.

Through the interplay of inclusion and exclusion articulated in each of the narratives (which illustrate the persistent theme of dualisim throughout the text) I suggest that the Johannine community, a community that has been doubly marginalized by the Roman Empire and by the members of the Jewish synagogue, constructed a radical alternative "otherworldliness" that, at one point in the community's stage of development, countered or mocked the oppressive ethos of the "this world," yet eventually, at some point, slips

1. See for example, Mary Rose D'Angelo, "(Re)Presentations of Women in the Gospels: John and Mark," in *Women and Christian Origins*, eds. Ross Shepard Kraemer and Mary Rose D'Angelo (New York: Oxford University Press, 1999) 129.

to mimicking the ethos of the "this world" in their social interactions with each other.

I further suggest that the Johannine community's cultural hybridity resulted in the production of a radical alternative otherworld that was a mirror of the sociopolitical schema of the existing religio-political system. This is evident in the construction of an otherworldliness heavily dependent on an ideology based on absolute opposition and absolute authority. I propose that those who neglect the ambivalent nature of marginalized hybridity—the desire *as well as* the resistance, the mockery *and* the mimicry (versus the dualism of desire *or* resistance, the mockery *or* the mimicry)—become susceptible in failing to sustain and maintain a radical alternative worldview because they fail to take into account the complex dimensions of the dominant ethos in the construction of identity. I argue that this is the inherent danger that lies within the Johannine community's radical otherworldliness, a world that was dualistically constructed by a strict absolute opposition that eventually marginalized and oppressed the women within their own community.

Womanist Biblical Hermeneutics

Womanist biblical hermeneutics is an area in biblical studies in which African American female scholars explore issues and concerns that are important to women of African descent.[2] As Clarice Martin states, "African American women's struggles comprise the constitutive elements in their conceptual and interpretive horizon and hermeneutics for experiences of oppression, like all human experience, affect the way in which women code and decode sacred and secular reality."[3] The work of womanist bibli-

2. The term "womanist" was coined by Alice Walker, particularly in her book, *In Search of Our Mother's Gardens: Womanist Prose* (New York: Harcourt Brace, 1983). The term is meant to connote the audacious behavior of African American women. Womanist theology as conceived by Kate Cannon, Jacqueline Grant, and Delores S. Williams has played an extremely influential role for womanist biblical scholars. See Kate Cannon, "The Emergence of Black Feminist Consciousness," in *Feminist Interpretation of the Bible*, ed. Letty Russell (Philadelphia: Westminster, 1985) 30–40; Jacquelyn Grant, *White Women's Christ and Black Women's Jesus: Feminist Theology and Womanist Response* (Atlanta: Scholars, 1989); Delores S. Williams, "Womanist Theology: Black Women's Voices," *Christianity and Crisis*, 47 (1987) 66–70. Williams's seminal work, *Sisters in the Wilderness: The Challenge of God-Talk* (Maryknoll, NY: Orbis, 1993) focuses on the Hebrew Bible characterization of Hagar as a typology of the experience of African American women. See also Emilie M. Townes, *Womanist Justice, Womanist Hope*, American Academy of Religion Series 79 (Atlanta: Scholars, 1993).

3. Clarice Martin, "Womanist Interpretations of the New Testament: The Quest

cal scholars, therefore, includes unmasking the specific agendas, cultural biases, ideological motivations, and political influences that produced the texts in their final form, as well as the history of interpretation that accompanies these texts by the modern reader.

Howard Thurman's grandmother, an ex-slave, serves as a good illustration of womanist biblical interpretation:

> "During the days of slavery," she said, "the master's minister would occasionally hold services for the slaves. Also, the white minister used as his text something from Paul. 'Slaves be obedient to them that are your masters . . . as unto Christ.' Then he would go on to show how, if we were good and happy slaves, Christ would bless us. I promised my Maker that if I ever learned to read, and if freedom ever came, I would not read that part of the Bible."[4]

Just like Mrs. Thurman, womanist scholars deny biblical interpretations that bind rather than liberate. However, instead of avoiding problematic texts as Mrs. Thurman's strategy proposed, womanist biblical scholars engage the biblical texts in a hermeneutical key that is, to use a term first made popular by Edward Said, contrapuntal[5] to the Euro-American ideological framework, and they are committed to exposing and challenging a system that promotes the social inequality of African American women in particular, and the African American community, in general as the prevailing norm. In approaching this vital task, womanist scholars have mainly adhered to a hermeneutic of liberation, striving to revive a diasporan community that has been burdened by displacement, slavery, disenfranchisement, marginalization, and persistent racism.

Womanist scholars have made important contributions to the scholarly guild based on the use of this emancipatory framework. This is particularly the case when liberation hermeneutics is fused with complementary theoretical and methodological approaches that effectively reflect new forms of relevant and constructive praxis. The complementation of other approaches is possible because womanist biblical hermeneutics is extremely "interdisciplinary friendly," which allows for the cultivation of a

for Holistic and Inclusive Translation and Interpretation," *Journal of Feminist Studies in Religion* 6:2 (1990) 42.

4. Howard Thurman, *Jesus and the Disinherited* (Nashville: Abingdon, 1949) 30–31.

5. "Contrapuntal" is a phrase that Said used to convey a manner of reading that aims to "give emphasis and voice to what is silent or marginally present or ideologically represented." Edward Said, *Culture and Imperialism* (New York: Vintage, 1993) ii. Further discussion and the limitations of this term are discussed in chapter 3.

vast analytical repertoire. In addition to the resources of black liberation theology and womanist theology, ideological criticism, narrative criticism, African American literary criticism, gender theories, and postcolonial theory are just a few of the methodological tools that complement this scribal activity.

Since the analysis of race, gender, and class is the work of the womanist scholar, the thought of African American sociologist Patricia Hill Collins continues to frame a womanist reading of texts.[6] Collins's work is valuable because she understands these three social issues not merely as distinctive systems of oppression, but as part of an overarching, dominant structure. Following the thought of Kimberle Crenshaw, Collins positions the categories of race, class, and gender as interwoven systems of oppression. By investigating the intersectionality of this "trinity of oppression," the focus of analysis shifts from simply describing the similarities and differences between these oppressive systems to a greater attention on how they interlace. This is a radical paradigmatic shift that allows for the domination of African American women to be understood as being structured by a system in any given socio-historical context.[7]

While a major task of womanist scholars is to challenge and advocate for a just society, it is equally important to extend that challenge to their own communities by cautioning the communal appropriation and adherence to the oppressive elements of a capitalistic, patriarchal society that is structured on a Western epistemology based on hierarchical binary opposition.

This is illustrated quite clearly in Cheryl Kirk-Duggan's essay "Let My People Go! Threads of Exodus in African American Narratives."[8] In her essay, Kirk-Duggan challenges the African American ideological view of the exodus narrative as a quest for liberation, arguing that the oppression-

6. See Patricia Hill Collins, *Black Feminist Thought: Knowledge, Consciousness, and the Politics of Empowerment* (London: HarperCollins, 1990). Her work is often more implicit than explicit in womanist scholarship.

7. I agree with the claims that Randall Bailey, Tat-siong Benny Liew, and Fernando Segovia assert in the introduction of *They Were All Together in One Place: Toward a Minority Biblical Criticism* that Patricia Hill Collins's rejection of binary thinking corresponds to the situation of racial-ethnic minorities. They propose that her theoretical concepts are useful in articulating a minority criticism. They write, "racial-ethnic minorities in the US—going back to Du Bois's 'double consciousness'—are also amenable to accepting 'the both/and conceptual stance' that Collins highlights in Black feminist thought." See Randall C. Bailey, Tat-siong Benny Liew, and Fernando F. Segovia, eds. *They Were All Together in One Place? Toward a Minority Criticism* (Leiden: Brill, 2009) 14.

8. Cheryl Kirk-Duggan, "Let My People Go! Threads of Exodus in African American Narratives," in *Yet With a Steady Beat: U.S. Afrocentric Biblical Interpretation*, ed. Randall C. Bailey (Atlanta: Society of Biblical Literature, 2003) 123–44.

liberation paradigm does not adequately inform the African American community. She claims that it is much easier to deal with the concept of a chosen people and to cheerfully disregard matters of manifest destiny than how the vast complexities of class and diversity plays out within the biblical narratives. She urges liberationists to be mindful not only of the two-edged nature of the texts, but also, I would suggest, of their own double-conscious identity when examining the ambiguities and paradoxes within the Bible, for there will always be the potential for the adoption/adaptation of the oppressive elements of Western society. She states that "many womanist scholars question the move to use the biblical experience as a normative model for validating God's liberative acts for all oppressed peoples of the world." And, that "although the warrior-God tradition inspired social movements of liberation and freedom they are themselves violent and antithetical to peace and social justice."[9]

Thus, a womanist scholar is a moral compass of the community regarding the cultural negotiation that transpires within her community and also outside of her community. I posit that this role of the womanist is particularly vital since there is a growing number of African Americans that are moving into the center of American life and therefore are more susceptible to (consciously or unconsciously) embracing the oppressiveness of the status quo.

Kirk-Duggan's essay highlights that African American cultural identity is split "between an urge toward blackness—conceived in cultural terms—and the continued presence of European cultural ideas."[10] Therefore, I suggest that a main objective of the womanist scholar is to present the full complexity of the double-conscious ethos of the twenty-first-century African American community. Or, in postcolonial theoretical lingo, the *cultural hybridity* of African American identity must be taken into account by womanist biblical scholars when reading for liberation.

Postcolonial Criticism

The term "post-colonial" was first used after World War II to demarcate a historical period following the dismantling of European colonies in Africa, Asia, the Caribbean, and Latin America and the ensuing re-configuration of the various leaderships, parties, and governments that had gained their

9. Kirk-Duggan, "Let My People Go!," 129.

10. Anthony Pinn, "In the Raw: African American Cultural Memory and Theological Reflection," in *Converging on Culture: Theologians in Dialogue with Cultural Analysis and Criticism*, ed. Delwin Brown (New York: Oxford University Press, 2003) 106–23.

independence from colonial rule. [11] As the result of this global re-configuration, an enormous degree of creative scholarship was produced that focused on multiple issues including political, sociological, psychological, and religious concerns of the decolonized or "third world" countries.

These social dynamics that erupted in the aftermath of European colonialism were, of course, reflected in the literary works of Franz Fanon, C. L. R. James, Albert Memmi, Aimé Césaire, V. P. Naipaul, J. M. Coetzee, Chinua Achebe, Buchi Emecheta, Bessie Head, and Ngugi wa Thiong'o, to name just a few that were produced within the post-colonial nations.[12] Each in their own way articulated the multilevel sociopolitical damage that colonialism had inflicted on millions of people. However, it was not until the late 1970s that the term "postcolonial" denoted a critical practice. Led by the literary critic Edward Said at Columbia University, the re-conceptualization came about when Third World literary scholars and cultural critics re-focused their lens, zooming in on the practices, experiences, and peculiarities of European colonialism. This intensity resulted in the formulation of a theoretical discipline that produced new insights and inquiries regarding the interrelationships of literature, power, and empire with a political commitment toward those who were formerly colonized. Post-1970s, postcolonial now refers to a critical system of thought aimed at revealing and disrupting

11. The knotty position of the United States attests to the fluidity in colonial power dynamics. This can be illustrated by tracing US history from its British colonial roots and its simultaneous role as an "internal colonizer" to its present status as *the* world's super (neo)colonizer. The United States surely occupies an extremely ambiguous position in relation to postcolonial discourse. See Lawrence Buell, "American Literary Emergence as a Post-Colonial Phenomenon," *American Literary History* 4:3 (1992) 411–13; Amritjit Singh and Peter Schmidt, "On the Borders Between U.S. Studies and Postcolonial Theory," in *Postcolonial Theory and the United States: Race, Ethnicity and Literature*, ed. Amritjit Singh and Peter Schmidt (Jackson: University of Mississippi, 2000) 3–72; C. Richard King, "Dislocating Postcoloniality, Relocating American Empire," in *Postcolonial America*, ed. C. Richard King (Champaign, IL: University of Illinois Press, 2000) 1–20.

12. After some initial hesitation by postcolonial critics, the work of W. E. B. Du Bois, Marcus Garvey, and the work of the Harlem Renaissance literary writers—Langston Hughes, Claude McKay, Eric Walrond, Zora Neale Hurston, and Nella Larsen, just to name a few—are now included in the list of postcolonial studies. The expansion of the canon signifies that the general emphasis of the discourse allows for a wider range of cultural investigation in the commonality of power dynamics and how those similar dynamics are negotiated differently in various cultural contexts. In particular, Du Bois's entrance as an early contributor to postcolonial studies is a further indication of the complexity and fluidity of the discourse, since his concept of double-consciousness is actually a pre-"postcolonial" construct articulated in 1903, and thus, long before European decolonization, a process that did not begin to occur in earnest until after World War 2. See Robert Philipson, "The Harlem Renaissance as Postcolonial Phenomenon," *African American Review* 40:1 (Spring 2006) 145–60.

the manipulative political and cultural strategies of colonial occupation, as well as establishing the diverse ways the colonized articulate their identity, self-worth, and political empowerment.[13] By the 1990s, postcolonial studies had become fully steeped in the discursive waters of literary studies, history, anthropology, sociology, psychology, classics, medieval studies, cultural studies, religion, and biblical and theological studies.

Presently, the critical engagement concentrates on: 1) favoring a focus on the boundaries that exist on the cusp of imagined determinate categories; 2) the provocation of a Western epistemology that is established on binary thinking; 3) the disavowal of homogeneity and totality; and 4) theorizing the complex dynamics of empire, nation, transnationalism, migrancy, and hybridity with modes of cultural production across a global field of political circumstances, including the circumstances of those on the margins in the United States.

Therefore, the term "postcolonial" has morphed from a purely histori-cal designation and transformed into a theoretical/methodological weapon wielded as protection against certain political and philosophical construc-tions that presumes continuity between the colonial and the postcolonial periods. "Postcolonial" is now defined as a catalyst that instigates and cre-ates opportunities for critical forces to converge together to assert their denied rights and to upset the center.[14]

For many, the term remains a very slippery designation since it not only signifies that which succeeds the colonial, but also refers to the neo-colonized. In addition, it has been suggested that the discipline's primary focus on the British Empire fails to locate itself within a larger historical framework. This failure has often led to the perception of colonization as a modern phenomenon. However, postcolonial scholars argue that post-colonial analysis transcends time, maintaining that the "placing of ancient history alongside the present, is not asking for a reduction of disparate geopolitical experiences to one generic framework, but is rather seeking a sensitivity to the relationships between the two so as to understand both in ways that relate to the here and now."[15]

In addition, while African American biblical scholars may concede that the term "postcolonial" may be inadequate when the approach is used to speak to the African American experience of neocolonialism and that

13. Ato Quayson, *Postcolonialism: Theory, Practice or Process?* (Cambridge: Polity, 2000) 25.

14. R. S. Sugirtharajah, *The Postcolonial Bible* (Sheffield, UK: Sheffield Academic, 1998, 23).

15. Deepika Bahri, "Once More with Feeling: What is Postcolonialism," *Ariel* 26:1 (1995) 61.

W. E. B. Du Bois's concept of double consciousness pre-dates the postcolonial concept of cultural hybridity, scholars, myself included, who are interested in revealing the intersections of cultural domination both in the ancient and contemporary worlds, acknowledge that approaching the text via a postcolonial lens with its emphasis on empire, nation, ethnicity, and migration provides a very provocative reading strategy.

I see the fusion of postcolonial studies to womanist biblical hermeneutics as particularly fruitful for illustrating the complexity of identity construction that is produced by the double-movement of denying the Western constructions of the "Other" while simultaneously (and ironically) shifting towards appropriating the ideological, theological, linguistic, and textual forms of Western power. The blending of a womanist-postcolonial perspective proves effective because both approaches: 1) focus on the devastating aspects of neocolonialism and the lingering forms of discrimination and inequality that the system perpetuates; 2) critique Western epistemology that is based on hierarchical binary formation; and 3) utilize the concept of cultural memory in articulating the experience of officially sanctioned domination and oppression. Thus, both disciplines are compatible and enhance one another. Whereas, postcolonial theory contributes to womanist biblical hermeneutics by resituating it out of its local context and placing it into a broader global conversation, womanist biblical hermeneutics is ideally situated to reveal the (neo)imperial/patriarchal practices within and outside their own community. Therefore, the supplementation of postcolonial theoretical concepts to the framework of womanist biblical hermeneutics aids in producing a reading strategy that better reflects the often complicated cultural negotiations of a post-enslaved community.

The blending of womanist biblical hermeneutics and postcolonial theory, therefore, fulfills a lacuna in postcolonial biblical hermeneutics. The synthesis reveals that the emphasis on cultural specificity exposes the unique ways in which a particular group within a particular community negotiates domination and subjugation and that the end result need not be universal, although contain common practices and processes. And, when postcolonial theory is supplemented to womanist biblical hermeneutics, there is the opportunity for an enhanced understanding of the work Scripture does in the construction of a specific hybrid cultural identity.

The Gospel of John

There are two scholarly opinions about the Gospel that are important to my reading of the Samaritan Woman and Mary at the Tomb through a womanist lens that is informed by postcolonial analysis. The first is the prevailing scholarly consensus that the text is so loosely sewn together that, scholars argue, it is possible to peak through the textual seams and historically reconstruct the life of a Christian community. It has been hypothesized that the gospel is as much about the life and death of Jesus as it is about the Johannine community.[16] By taking note of the multiple inconsistencies in the text that contradict geographical movement, the numerous repetitions, and by noticing how certain episodes and characters in the Johannine text seem to mirror the life of a specific community, it is suggested that the gospel reveals a three-stage development of the Johannine community.[17]

The first stage is when the community was part of the Jewish synagogue. This is evident by sections of the text that present a "low Christology" (1:29–51). Scholars posit that the low Christology signifies when the Johannine community was a part of the Jewish synagogue. It is proposed that the majority of the Jewish population would not be opposed to the Johannine Christians understanding of Jesus, for example, as the Messiah, the lamb of God, or as Rabbi, all of which are examples of a "low Christology." The second stage of development occurred when the Johannine community welcomed the Samaritans (cf. 4:1–42) and Gentiles (cf. 4:46–54) into their sub-community. This inclusion instigated conflict and tension between the Johannine community and members of the Jewish synagogue. And, the third and final stage of development occurred when the Johannine community was expelled and ostracized from the majority because of their increasingly determined stance against those they considered to be nonbelievers: those who were accommodating to the "this-world" of the Roman Empire, "the Jews," and "cryptic Christians" who believed in Jesus Christ as Lord and Savior but refused to publicly confess him as such because they wanted to remain within the social security of the Jewish synagogue. The story of the blind man in chapter 9 tells of the Johannine community's expulsion. Scholars propose that the expulsion from the wider Jewish community resulted in the development of a "higher Christology" eventually leading to the use of the *Ego Eimi* (I am) and the idea of the preexistence of Jesus as the Logos (1:1–18). It is in the working of this community development hypothesis,

16. J. Louis Martyn's *History and Theology in the Fourth Gospel* (1968) and Raymond Brown's *The Community of the Beloved Disciple* (1978) have been the leading works in developing a theory for the historical and literary understanding of the Gospel of John. Both attempted to provide a rationale for the obvious redactions, repetitions and multiple inconsistencies in the text. While not always explicitly referred to in most recent Johannine scholarship, the work of these scholars continues to undergird contemporary Johannine scholarship.

17. The differences between the synoptics and the fourth gospel is one way in which scholars discern that the Johannine text reflects the needs of a specific community.

that scholars present the idea that the actual experiences of the formation of the Johannine community are embodied in the text.

Community exclusion or disenfranchisement from the majority left its mark throughout the Gospel. For instance, it is possible to discern that, in their own self-estimation, the Johannine community believed they made a great sacrifice in welcoming in the "Other," even when they knew that inclusion would result in conflict and jeopardize their own social stability. Consequently they developed a sense of contempt for those who believed in Jesus, but did so secretly in order to avoid punishment.[18] No other Gospel is so judgmental about the inadequate faith of other followers of Jesus.[19] According to Raymond Brown, in the eyes of the people, the ostracized Johannine community was thought to be unnecessarily brash, rude, and totalitarian.[20]

Adele Reinhartz echoes Brown's sentiments when she says, "most discussions of the community imply that it was self-contained, tightly knit, and concentrated in a particular location, such as Ephesus, where it existed in a hostile relationship to the larger Jewish community."[21] Wayne Meeks, in his classic essay, "The Man from Heaven in Johannine Sectarianism" also views the Johannine community as a group that had to defend and define itself over against other groups. At the same time, those who do believe are drawn into intense intimacy with him and become similarly detached from the world. This pattern signals the insularity of the Johannine community and its alienation from the prevailing community.[22]

The second issue this paper considers in terms of Johannine scholarship is its emphasis on dualism or hierarchical binary opposition. As noted above, one of the main tasks of a womanist-postcolonial analysis is to critically examine the Western way of knowing that is based on a hierarchical binary formation. The Johannine text clearly presents a hierarchical binary opposition throughout the narrative: light versus darkness, ascend versus

18. Raymond E. Brown, *An Introduction to the Gospel of John*, ed. Francis J. Moloney (New Haven, CT: Yale University Press, 2003) 76.

19. Ibid.

20. Raymond Brown's hypothesis rests entirely on the relationship between the Johannine community and the Jewish synagogue. I suggest that the community also maintains the same absolutism towards those who accommodate to the Roman Empire, as well.

21. Adele Reinhartz, "Women in the Johannine Community: An Exercise in Historical Imagination," in *A Feminist Companion to John*, eds. Amy-Jill Levine with Marianne Bickenstaff, vol. 2 (Sheffield, UK: Sheffield University Press, 2003) 30–31.

22. Wayne Meeks, "The Man from Heaven in Johannine Sectarianism," *Journal of Biblical Literature* 91:1 (March 1991) 44–72. See also David Rensberger, *Johannine Faith and Liberating Community* (Philadephia: Westminster, 1988) 135.

descend, good versus evil, otherworldly versus worldly, us versus them. While liberation scholars might argue that the gospel presents a radical alternative vision of society in which God is on the side of the oppressed, the dualistic nature of the text actually functions to demarcate the Johannine community from all others who do not accept their brand of Christianity. In other words, it is the Johannine community and not the Roman Empire nor the Judeans who determine between the privileged and the unprivileged; "the elect," and "the world," "the saved" and "the lost." This exclusivist stance presents to us the opinion that only a "Johannine Christianity" is the "light" and that all other religious traditions, including other forms of Christianity are "dark."

As one might imagine, the persistent theme of dualism in the Gospel of John is extremely problematic for womanist-postcolonial biblical scholars because it forms the basis for the justification of exclusion, marginalization, oppression, and absolute opposition.

The Johannine Prologue as Postcolonial Alternative

According to Fernando Segovia, the power of John's Gospel to bring down "all established dominions and substituting an alternative dominion in the midst of a firmly entrenched and powerful imperial-colonial formation is truly a postcolonial proposal."[23]

It is in the prologue of John (1:1–18) that the understanding of a radical alternative otherworld is first presented in dualistic formation in contrast to a world constructed by imperial Rome and colonial Judea. This binary set out from the opening verses of the gospel is a "grounding imaginary for John's vision of reality" and frames the reading of the entire narrative.[24] Segovia claims that "1:1–18 raises the question of geopolitics and sets forth the fundamentals of an alternative path—a substitute reality and experience to be acknowledged, embraced and executed."[25] He goes on to state that politically the prologue sets out,

> a variety of interrelated and interdependent central tenets: 1) a vertical chain of command operative between both worlds and within each world resulting in a set ethos of hierarchy and obedience, 2) a stance of extreme othering toward the outside

23. Fernando F. Segovia, "John," in *A Postcolonial Commentary on the New Testament Writings*, ed. Fernando F. Segovia and R. S. Sugirtharajah (New York: T. & T. Clark, 2009) 168.

24. Ibid.

25. Ibid, 172.

and outsiders giving harsh condemnation of all social and cultural dimensions of the this-world and 3) a total denial of all other approaches to and claims on the divine, yielding absolute control of access to and knowledge of God. Strategically, a concomitant expository and polemical objective may be detected: lengthy critique of all standing established realities alongside lengthy exposition of the proposed alternative reality. With the prologue, therefore, the Gospel unveils a radical postcolonial alternative—a vision of absolute otherness.[26]

This radical alternative otherworld may be presented in religious terms, yet it affects politics, culture, and society. It extends past the horizon of the Roman Empire and colonial Palestine to encompass all sociopolitical formations in the world below.[27] It is important to note that the alternative imagined reality is not presented as an option, but as uniquely superior, the only true option. John's Jesus as the Word clashes with the evil world governed by Rome and its allies in Palestine. According to Segovia, "such a strategy of absolute opposition, while no doubt reassuring and perhaps most effective as well for hard-pressed believers, in the end borrows perhaps much too much from its target for its own good."[28]

The above quote by Segovia articulates the two different strategic approaches of liberation hermeneutical scholars, which generally includes womanist scholars, and postcolonial scholars. In dealing with the Johannine community's response of absolute opposition to their oppression as excluded and disenfranchised people, which prohibits them from accessing benefits afforded to members of a society, the liberation scholar would highlight the Johannine community's construction of a radical alternative world as absolute opposition to a prevailing oppressive system as an appropriate resistant response. These scholars would typically advocate for a God that is totally on the side of the oppressed or the underprivileged and opposed to the oppressor or the privileged. In other words, the liberation hermeneutic works within an inverted hierarchical binary formation of opposition. In liberation hermeneutics, the binary relationship is reversed with the unprivileged occupying the superior position of the structure and the privileged occupying the inferior position. Therefore, I think it would be safe to say that the liberation scholar who speaks for the impoverished, the marginalized, the politically powerless, would support and maintain the dualistic formation in the Gospel of John, uplifting the sense of a radical alternative

26   Ibid, 169.

27   Ibid., 172–73.

28. Ibid., 192.

universe spearheaded by Jesus, the Son of God, contrasted against an evil world. This is what Segovia means when he says above that a "strategy of absolute opposition is no doubt reassuring and effective for the hard-pressed believer."

In contrast, the postcolonial scholar seeks justice not by working within the binary, but within the tensions and conflicts of life. The postcolonial scholar is intent on exposing the contradictions, and expressing the dangerous possibility of the oppressed morphing into the oppressor because working within the binary presents that possibility. The role of the postcolonial scholar is to deconstruct the dualism, to speak not of this *or* that, but this *and* that. Therefore, postcolonial scholars working on the Gospel of John understand that absolute opposition is dangerous and oppressive when not only practiced by the enemies of the Johannine community but by the Johannine community, itself. This is why Segovia says, "in the end (the radical alternative otherworld) borrows perhaps much too much from its target for its own good."

The quote from Segovia encapsulates the reading strategy of a womanist-postcolonial reading of the Samaritan Women at the Well in chapter 4 and Mary at the Tomb in chapter 20. It appears on first reading that both narratives are in support of the women, that the radical alternative otherworldliness of the Johannine community welcomes the full participation of women (and in the case of chapter 4, ethnic women at that) in matters of communal leadership. This would, of course, be counter to the prevailing societal norms of the evil "this-world." Yet, on a further closer reading of the narratives, it becomes clear that full equality is actually not the case as further events in the text seems to imply that somewhere down the line of communal development the operations of the (once) radical otherworld has shifted to emulate the practices of the oppressive "this-world."

The Samaritan Woman at the Well (John 4:1–42)

Crossing Social Boundaries (4:4–9)

This story, indeed, provides a smooth entrance into the radical otherworldliness of the gospel and is also an excellent example of the interplay of ethnicity and gender in the text. In chapter 4, Jesus is on his way to Galilee after leaving Judea because the Pharisees have been alerted to Jesus "making and baptizing more disciples than John" (4:1). He comes to the Samaritan city called Sychar "near the plot of ground that Jacob had given to Joseph" and sits at Jacob's well where he meets the Samaritan woman. A first-level reading of

Jesus' encounter with the woman acknowledges that the text surely presents Jesus (and by extension, the Johannine community) in direct opposition to the prevailing norms of his society, as he converses, converts, and designates this ethnic other female as an authoritative figure (seemingly) equal to his disciples as he sits and speaks with her about spiritual, otherworldy things. In addition, she performs the action of a disciple when she leaves her water jar at the well (this act signifies that her traditional women's role has come to an end) as she returns to her community and urges them to "come and see a man who told me everything I have ever done!" (4:29). The Samaritan woman's action is directly related to the actions of the men disciples in the gospel. They, too, immediately left what they were doing to follow Jesus.

Many male scholars, past and present, propose that the woman comes to the well at high noon, the hottest time of the day because she was shunned by other women because of her immoral behavior (she has had five husbands and the one she is with now is not her husband [4:17]) and therefore banned from coming to the well in the morning and evening, the usual hours of the day when the women drew water.[29]

White feminist scholars paying close attention to the play on dualistic symbolism throughout the text argue that the time of day in 4:6 must be understood as an intentional contrast to the timing of the Nicodemus narrative in the previous chapter (3:2). The prevalent dualistic theme in the Gospel allows us to note the interplay of dark versus light in these two pericopae. The male Jewish religio-political leader Nicodemus comes to Jesus in the dark, whereas the Samaritan woman's encounter with Jesus at the well occurs at the time of fullest possible light (4:6–7). Nicodemus is denounced by Jesus in 3:20 when he says, "For all who do evil hate the light and do not come to the light, so that their deeds may not be exposed." Jesus continues to say in 3:21: "But those who do what is true come to the light, so that it may be clearly seen that their deeds have been done in God." This verse points ahead to the narrative of the Samaritan woman in chapter 4. The interconnection based on the interplay of binary opposition of the narrative settings in chapters 3 and 4—dark versus light; Jewish, male, privileged, religious leader and Samaritan, female, underprivileged, non-Jewish religious leader—symbolizes the Johannine community's reversal of the "this-world" sociopolitical order and their avowal of a radical alternative world that is in conflict with the social order of the "world" and which welcomes the leadership of women into their radically opposite social order. Literally, it is the Jewish male leader who operates in darkness, and the ethnic female other

29. Craig S. Keener, *The Gospel of John: A Commentary*, vol. 1 (Peabody, MA: Hendrickson, 2003) 584–633.

who walks not only in the light, but at a time when the light has reached its apex at high noon. She is the woman clothed in the sun.

Therefore, in noticing the structure, form, and movement of the Gospel, the common thread that links the chapters together is the crossing of social boundaries detailed in a dualistic literary format. The theme of crossing social boundaries is clearly seen in the Samaritan woman's encounter with Jesus at the well in which there is a crossing of ethnic and gender boundaries. In terms of ethnic boundaries, we realize that the dialogue definitely speaks to a radical otherworldliness of the Johannine community as the narrative dismantles a social taboo that has been practiced for centuries between the Jewish people and their cousins, the Samaritans. In reading chapter 4, Musa Dube states,

> we enter into centuries of imperial subtexts of disruption, alienation and resistance that strains the relationships of the Samaritans and Jews. This tension goes back to the period of the Assyrian Empire. Through intermarriages and the adoption of some of the religions of their Assyrian colonial masters, Samaritans became what some have termed "despised heretics" and "despised half-breeds." As a result, the Samaritan Jewish ancestors distanced themselves from Samaritans on the grounds of religious impurity. Their strained relationship highlights the extent to which imperial domination has affected and influenced the relationship of different people at different centuries in the world.[30]

Gender boundaries are crossed in this narrative by the mere fact that Jesus is conversing publicly with a woman. In the Roman culture, wives speaking publicly with others' husbands was a horrible matter reflecting possible flirtatious designs and subverting the moral order of the state. Even today in traditional Middle Eastern societies, social intercourse between unrelated men and women is almost equivalent to sexual intercourse.[31]

It is recognized by scholars that the story contains elements of a betrothal scene (4:7–16).[32] According to Robert Alter, a betrothal-type scene in the Hebrew Bible occurs when the hero or his surrogate journeys to a foreign land, encounters a girl at a well, and one of them draws water from

30. Musa Dube, "Reading for Decolonization," in *John and Postcolonialism: Travel, Space and Power,* ed. Musa W Dube and Jeffrey L. Staley (Sheffield, UK: Sheffield Academic, 2002) 62.

31. Keener, *The Gospel of John,* 597.

32. Adeline Fehribach, "The Samaritan Woman" in *The Women in the Life of the Bridegroom: Feminist Historical-Literary Analysis of the Female Characters in the Fourth Gospel* (Collegeville, MN: Liturgical, 1998) 45.

the well. Usually the girl rushes to inform her family of the stranger's arrival, and a betrothal is sealed after the future bridegroom has shared a meal with her family (Gen 24:10–61 and Gen 29:1–10).[33] The inference of a wedding between Jewish Jesus and the Samaritan woman is surely a radical other-worldliness that is counter to the prevailing social norm and viewed as a positive and affirming act of inclusiveness and equality.

The narrative displays the audaciousness of the woman in her blunt and forthright dialogue with Jesus (4:17–26). This section of the text presents a bold, outspoken woman, who affirms her culture and her religious heritage. She is totally unconcerned with what Jesus revealed to her about her life. Her discourse with him is intelligent and she proves that she is able to dialogue with him although she does not get it all. The disciples are astonished that he is dialoguing with a woman, but do not interrupt them and continue to let them speak with each other (4:27). Again, an otherworldly reaction, because in the "this-world" the men would have certainly shooed her away. Instead, 4:28 has her leaving her water jar at the well with the men disciples (which as mentioned above symbolizes the abandonment of her traditional women's role) for she is now a disciple who goes back to her community to inform the others about who she found.

While the above interpretations of the narrative highlight the positive aspects of women's role in the Johannine community, a womanist-postcolonial reading also recognizes the dualism at work in the power relationship between Jesus and the Samaritan woman. The womanist-postcolonial scholar, taking the contemporary historical experiences of her community into consideration as an integral part of the hermeneutical process, finds the conversion of the ethnic Samaritan woman to the absolute opposition of Johannine Christianity reminiscent of the conversion practices of the North American slave owner. The womanist-postcolonial scholar understands that binary opposition/absolute opposition justified the North American slave system. The peculiar institution in America, similar to the tactics of colonization, produced an ideology of inferior knowledge and invalid religious faith for those who must be enslaved or colonized.[34] In the early nineteenth century, American slave owners and clergymen were dedicated to the task of Christianizing the slave, the heathen, the uncivilized. Not only did they go about this task with an amazing degree of confidence in the supremacy of Western Christianity, but they were equally confident, if not over-confident, in the Western social and economic order. This sense of certainty not only produced insensitivity to indigenous cultures and religions, but they were,

33. Ibid.
34. Dube, "Reading for Decolonization," 67.

in fact, considered evil.[35] The practice of constructing the slave's ancestral concept of the spiritual world and humanity as ignorant and insufficient aided mightily in their self-demonization. This destruction of the psyche led to the stifling of the impulse of resistance, a stifling made possible by the belief that their African religious system was invalid, and, indeed, impotent. This, in turn, allowed for the formation of a parental relationship between the slave owner and the slave, in which the slave owner believed s/he was called to "parent" the "child-like" slave population.[36] Musa Dube argues that a sharp division exists between the colonizers who know everything and the colonized who know nothing. Therefore, a womanist-postcolonial reading whose aim is to unveil elements of (neo)imperial ideology understands the Samaritan woman as being characterized as lacking. By way of contrast, Jesus is presented as a superior traveler, is knowledgeable and powerful and teaches her people. The dialogue between Jesus and the Samaritan woman unfolds by way of a sharp dualism that subtly diminishes the positive image of her role.

A womanist-postcolonial reading strategy therefore realizes that the woman's position is unstable. Although 4:39 states, "many Samaritans from that city believed in him because of the woman's testimony, 'he told me everything I have ever done'" her privileged status does not last for long. After the Samaritans came to him and invited him back to the city to stay for a couple of days in which more Samaritans believed in him because of his word (4:40–41) they turned to the woman and said to her, "It is no longer because of you that we believe, for we have heard for ourselves, and we know that this is truly the Savior of the world" (4:42). A womanist-postcolonial reading exposes the fact that this radical alternative otherworldliness of the Johannine community that purports to counter the prevalent "this-world" social order has flipped into emulating, mimicking, or reinscribing, the unequal "this-world" social stratification in the end. The otherworldliness signified within this Johannine text has morphed into just another oppressive system that marginalized women. As Musa Dube states, "in this story, patriarchal and imperial rhetorical strategies are intertwined, making a feminist appropriation of the story a precarious and critically demanding

35. Sylvia M. Jacobs, "The Historical Role of Afro-Americans in American Missionary Efforts in Africa," in *Black Americans and The Missionary Movement in Africa*, ed. Sylvia M. Jacobs (Westport, CT: Greenwood, 1982).

36. See also Lynne St. Clair Darden, "Privilege But No Power: Women in the Gospel of Matthew and Nineteenth Century African American Woman Missionaries through a Postcolonial Lens," in *Teaching All Nations: Interrogating the Matthean Great Commission*, eds. Mitzi J. Smith and Lalitha Jayachitra (Minneapolis: Fortress, 2014) 105–26.

exercise."[37] The narrative of chapter 4, in my opinion, reflects that as the Johannine community continued to develop, inclusion became dependent on unequal relationships.

Mary Magdalene at the Tomb and the Other Disciples: 20:1–28

Similar to the Samaritan woman narrative, the beginning of chapter 20 narrates a woman as an equal in status to the men. Yet, on a closer reading of the chapter, again paying keen attention to the action at the end of the chapter, it is possible to discern that Mary, like the Samaritan woman in chapter 4, has her leadership role in the Johannine community stripped away as the community shifts from resisting the prevalent oppressive ethos supported by the evil "this-world" status quo to reinscribing the social imbalance of the "this-world" in the "otherworld" of the Johannine community.

In the beginning verses of the chapter, the narrator presents us with a competition between the male disciples, Peter, and the other disciple, (the one that Jesus loved) as who is the greater one. This is evident as the narrator explicitly states "the two were running together, but the other disciple outran Peter and reached the tomb first" (20:5). The two were hurrying to the tomb at the insistence of Mary who had gone alone to the burial site and noticed that the stone had been removed from the tomb (20:1). She ran to tell Simon Peter and the other disciple what she saw at the tomb. Ironically, although the other disciple reached the tomb first, he did not go into the tomb. He merely bent down to look in and saw the linen wrappings lying there (20:7). So, the other disciple was, indeed, a witness to an epiphany. However, Peter who *followed* the other disciple *passed him* and actually enters the tomb where he saw the linen wrappings lying there just as the other disciple saw, but Peter also saw the cloth that had been on Jesus' head (20: 6–7). Therefore, Peter was afforded a greater vision than the other disciple, thereby connoting an expanded revelation. The text goes on to say in 20:8, "then the other disciple, who reached the tomb first, also went in, and he saw and believed." I suggest that the characters' actions in this scene reflects the jockeying for position that was going on between the disciples in terms of leadership and perhaps also reflects the jockeying of leadership between the Johannine community and other Christian communities, communities who may have supported Simon Peter as the lead disciple.

In continuing the narrative, an interesting development takes place. In 20:11–19, the woman Mary actually receives a greater vision than the two

37. Dube, "Reading for Decoloniation," 70.

men. As she stood weeping outside of the tomb, she bent in to look inside and "she saw two angels in white, sitting where the body of Jesus had been lying" (20:12) and they spoke to her. She is afforded a much more intense and powerful vision than either of the men. The other disciple only saw the linen wrappings, Peter saw the linen wrappings and the cloth, but Mary saw much more than that. In addition, it is Mary who first sees and speaks to the resurrected Jesus (20:14–16). It is her name that he first calls in his newly risen state. Her divine experience definitely surpasses the visions of both Simon Peter and the other disciple. According to Mary Rose D'Angelo, Mary Magdalene appears to fit the Pauline definition of apostle (1 Cor 9:1, 15:3–8); she is accorded the first vision of the risen lord and delivers an apparently oracular message in his person and words (20:17–18). This scene reflects the strong prophetic and visionary element that persists through the stages of communal development from the earliest levels of the tradition through the letters (see 1 John 4:1–2; 5:6).[38]

However, a womanist-postcolonial reading observes that while Jesus forbids Mary to touch him because he has not "yet ascended to the Father" (20:17a) the same is not true for the male disciples. When Jesus appeared to them at the house where they were hiding in fear of the Jews, Jesus *breathed* on them and they received the Holy Spirit (20:22). And, when Thomas doubted his reappearance, Jesus allowed Thomas to touch his hands and his side so that Thomas might believe (20:27). This physical interaction with his male disciples occurred before he ascended to his Father. So, just like the Samaritan woman narrative, Mary Magdalene's leadership authority is affirmed in the beginning of the narrative and then taken away at the end. These males have not only seen and dialogued with Jesus, just as Mary did, but they have been touched by Jesus and have touched Jesus themselves, which Mary was not allowed to do. There is no longer any need for Mary's testimony. Her revelation decreased so that the male disciples revelatory experiences could increase. It is noteworthy that Mary Magdalene does not appear in John 21 with Peter and the other disciple. In fact, 21:14 makes no mention of Mary as a visionary or as a disciple.[39] I agree here with Mary Rose D'Angelo when she claims that the exclusion may reflect a decrease in leadership roles among the Johannine women in the community in its later years, or the desire to restrict women's participation on the part of the author of the appendix or its audience.[40]

38. D'Angelo, "(Re)Presentations of Women in the Gospels," 132.

39. Ibid, 137.

40. Ibid.

Conclusion

The gospel's portrayal of women is fraught with ambiguity; arguments can be mounted for their inclusion among the leaders of the community, and for their exclusion from that group. The question a womanist-postcolonial reading must contend with after examining these two narratives is why does the radical world envisioned by the Johannine community eventually morph into a mirroring of the world they oppose? For seemingly, no matter how determined the Johannine community is in its beginning formation to disconnect from the imperial-patriarchal ethos of the Roman Empire and its Palestinian allies it appears that they eventually revert to appropriating an oppressive ethos in their own world. The Johannine community's replication of patriarchal practices proved that they were not really as isolated nor as non-conforming to the "this-world" as they so passionately proclaimed. A possible answer as to how or why the Johannine community comes to mimic the ideological assumptions and social stratification of empire is that their cultural hybridity as "almost the same but not quite like" resulted in the production of an otherworldliness that eventually reverts to simply a blurred copy of the hegemonic tactics of empire. A womanist-postcolonial reading of the Samaritan woman and Mary at the Tomb in the gospel of John is a cautionary warning to the African American community's potential vulnerability to the subtle ways of the beasts of sexism, racism, and classism when maintaining an absolute opposition that is based on hierarchical binary formation without taking into account a fuller scope of the complexity of communal development.

CHAPTER ELEVEN

Minjung, the Black Masses, and the Global Imperative

A Womanist Reading of Luke's
Soteriological Hermeneutical Circle[1]

MITZI J. SMITH

"I know I got it made while the masses of black people are catchin' hell, but as long as they ain't free, I ain't free." ~ Mohammad Ali

"The concept of love is inextricably interwoven throughout philosophy and religion. And it is in the context of the modern world that faith, love and action based upon one's own personal responsibility to all other [human beings] and to the future of all [hu]mankind becomes most important." ~ Shirley Chisholm[2]

1. Mitzi J. Smith, "Minjung, the Black Masses, and the Global Imperative: A Womanist Reading of Luke's Soteriological Hermeneutical Circle," in *Reading Minjung Theology in the Twenty-first Century*, ed. Yung Suk Kim and Jin–Ho Kim (Eugene, OR: Pickwick, 2013) 101–19. Reprinted by permission of Wipf and Stock.

2. Shirley Chisholm, "The Relationship Between Religion and Today's Social Issues," in *Can I Get A Witness? Prophetic Religious Voices of African American Women. An Anthology*, ed. Marcia Y. Riggs (Maryknoll, NY: Orbis, 1997) 183.

Introduction

I am an African American female employed with Ashland Theological Seminary, which is the graduate branch of Ashland University, both of which are primarily white and rural. However, I teach at the seminary's Detroit metro area center. Most of my students are black females, but I also teach white and Asian students. I grew up in a loving and nurturing single-parent, Christian household. My mother Flora Ophelia Carson Smith (1929–2009) personified and embodied godly ethics and values that I seek to emulate. Flora loved taking care of her four children and her household meticulously and did so even after a debilitating and undiagnosed disease left her wheelchair bound. She could no longer work as a nursing assistant caring for older people or as the "salad girl" in a well-respected, Columbus, Ohio restaurant. My mother also loved other people; she "thought it not robbery" to feed, dress, or encourage others whenever she could. In word and practice, she showed my siblings and me that we should love ourselves, love each other, and other people. My mother embodied, and we inherited, a proto-womanist *materology* (Greek: matēr; translated *mother*) of how to incarnate a living God in a black mother's body baptized in suffering but anointed by an undying spirit of love and perseverance, despite and because of living among the masses. Flora fell into a fireplace, head first, at age five; struggled with narcolepsy in high school; found herself homeless, with one child in her arms and two hanging on her dress-tail, upon returning from work and having failed to get a rent receipt from a unconscionable landlord, to name a few of her experiences.

I grew up poor and many times did not have what I wanted especially as a teenager, yet I remember feeling more slighted by the loss of my mother's presence at school when she could no longer walk than by our economic circumstances. Despite our poverty and my premature determination to forego college and obtain a good paying job, I matriculated at five schools, finally earning my PhD in Religion (specializing in New Testament) from Harvard University. Nobody in my immediate family had yet earned a college degree, but they encouraged, praised, co-signed, and prayed for me. In fact, it was my mother and a former neighbor from the projects, Mrs. Slocum, who made sure I had bus fare and money in my pocket when I first left home for college. You see, out of her own poverty, my mom sometimes fed Mrs. Slocum's children. A proto-womanist materology says I cannot let my neighbor's children starve if I can help it. A circle of people, some we know and some we do not, put their hands, monies, hearts, and prayers together with our dreams and hard work to help us achieve what might otherwise be impossible. So I believe in putting back and paying forward into that circle. I am not free to turn my back to the masses while they stand with their "backs against the wall."[3]

As a black female and womanist biblical scholar, I prioritize black women's experience and artifacts as a starting point for engaging in biblical interpretation and theoethical reflection. In her 1979 essay "Coming Apart," Alice Walker described a womanist as a "feminist, only more common"[4]; that is, I suppose, more like or having more in common with ordinary black women. Walker recognizes that black and white women's experiences differ. Historically, when white women asked black women to choose between the women's suffrage movement and the abolition of slavery, black women chose the latter. They recognized experientially and ontologically the inextricable bond between black men and black women's freedom. In her 1983 book *In Search of Our Mothers' Gardens*, Walker, while defining the terms "womanish" and "womanist," describes black women's individual and communal loyalties:

> Also: A woman . . . [c]omitted to survival and wholeness of entire people male *and* female. Not a separatist, except periodically, for health. Traditionally universalist, as in: "Mama, why are we brown, pink, and yellow, and our cousins are white, beige, and black?" Ans.: "Well, you know the colored race is just like a flower garden, with every color flower represented." Traditionally capable, as in: "Mama, I'm walking to Canada and I'm taking you and a bunch of other slaves with me." Reply: "It wouldn't be the first time." [5]

A womanist perspective is concerned for the masses or the "entire people" but not at the expense of her own health. Black women's concern for self health and for a communal and universal wholeness is the womanist materological interpretative lens through which I shall read the crowds in Luke's Gospel and engage *minjung* theology.

I shall first briefly discuss *minjung* theology and compare it with black and womanist theologies. Second, I discuss some historical ideologies about the relationship between individual mobility or success and the deliverance of the crowds/the masses in terms of black peoples' experiences and history. I further address the contemporary situation of the black masses in America in relation to the success of individual African Americans. Third, I review

3. Howard Thurman, *Jesus and the Disinherited* (Boston: Beacon, 1976) 11.

4. Alice Walker, "Coming Apart," in *The Womanist Reader: The First Quarter Century of Womanist Thought*, ed. Layli Phillips (New York: Routledge, 2006) 7.

5. Alice Walker, *In Search of Our Mothers' Gardens: Womanist Prose* (San Diego: Harcourt Brace, 1983) xi–xii.

Ahn Byong-Mu's observations about the crowds in Mark's Gospel and his literary social construction of *minjung* in relation to Jesus. Finally, I explore some texts in Luke's Gospel where I observe what I call a *soteriological hermeneutical circle* operative; namely, the salvation/deliverance of individuals is inextricably connected with the crowds.

The noun *minjung* is a literal Korean pronunciation of a Chinese word. Generally, *min* means *people* and *jung* connotes *the mass*. Minjung is a difficult term to interpret; it is open to more nuanced translation. *Minjung* signifies the Korean people's history of oppression, colonization, and alienation. Thus, *minjung* as theological reflection is "contextual and indigenous."[6] Indigenous Korean people who compose the *minjung* are the poor, women, ethnic groups, workers, farmers, and peasants who are politically, socio–economically, intellectually, and/or culturally alienated, discriminated against, marginalized, and oppressed masses.[7] The Korean peoples' oppressors have been both foreigners and their own indigenous elite. From 1910 to 1945, the Korean people were feudal peasants under Japanese colonization; from 1945 to 1990 the *minjung* were industrial workers, peasants, and the urban poor under Korean dictatorship; and from 1990 to the present Korean people continue to experience oppression under so-called democratic governments. The *minjung* movement ignited in 1970 when Jun Tae-Ill set fire to himself in solidarity with his fellow exploited factory workers. Consequently, Christian leaders acknowledged the severity of the situation and began to stand for and with the poor and exploited *minjung*.[8] *Minjung* theology is critical reflection on the *minjung's* struggle for liberation.

For minjung theology, the Jesus event is the ultimate liberating phenomenon. The Jesus event is Jesus' suffering, death, and resurrection. It is "holistic, dynamic and changing," unlike the kerygma (proclamation) of Jesus, which is "ideological, static, and unchanging."[9] An inclusive and holistic *minjung* theology incorporates "indigenous cultural and religious elements as part of divine revelation." All of the *minjung's* experiences and/

6. Jung Young Lee, "Minjung Theology: A Critical Introduction" in *An Emerging Theology in World Perspective Commentary on Korean Minjung Theology* (Mystic, CT: Twenty-Third, 1988) 4–5.

7. Chung Hyun Kyung, "'Han-pu-ri': Doing Theology from Korean Women's Perspective," in *Frontiers in Asian Christian Theology. Emerging Trends*, ed. R. S. Sugirtharajah (Maryknoll NY: Orbis, 1994) 56; Lee, "Minjung Theology," 4.

8. Sebastian C. H. Kim, "The Problem of Poverty in Post-War Korean Christianity: Kibock Sinang or Minjung Theology?" *Transformation* 24:1 (2007) 46.

9. Lee, "Minjung Theology," 5, 11, 15; Kwon Jinkwan, "Minjung (the Multitude) Historical Symbol of Jesus Christ," *Asian Journal of Theology* 24 (2010) 155–56.

or history of struggle for liberation are sacred and holy; this includes the good and evil and the moral and immoral.[10] By characterizing himself as the "servant of the minjung," Christ becomes the object of salvation history and the *minjung* become its subject. In or through Jesus, God sides with the *minjung* as the oppressed of society.[11] God's preference for the oppressed *minjung* functions to engender salvation for all of humanity.[12]

Minjung Theology, Black Theology, and Womanist Theology

Both black theology and *minjung* theology emerged in periods of protest. Black theology, as a systematic reflection on and articulation of black people's experience of slavery and oppression in light of their belief in a just and loving God, was constructed during the Civil Rights and black power movements of the 1960s and 1970s. According to James H. Cone, the father of black theology, God stands on the side of the oppressed.[13] The paradigmatic biblical event that demonstrates God's preference for enslaved and oppressed peoples is the Exodus from Egyptian slavery. As James Deotis Roberts argues in his 1988 essay "Black Theology and Minjung Theology: Exploring Common Themes," the Exodus event allows black people to be the subject of God's liberative acts in black religious history. Thus, black people's political liberationist response to oppression should decisively be nonviolent and constructive and seek to make black people the subjects of their own history.[14] Roberts argues that "When a people change from being objects of history to being subjects of their history, they become a force to reckon with. They are motivated from within and are prepared to confront any odds in the quest for liberation."[15] For *minjung* theology the Exodus event is similarly paradigmatic and empowering. Cyris H. S. Moon asserts that in "the Exodus event the *minjung* can be clearly understood as a force that stands in opposition to the powerful."[16]

10. Lee, "Minjung Theology," 20, 21.

11. Ibid., 19.

12. Ibid., 22.

13. James H. Cone, *God of the Oppressed* (Maryknoll, NY: Orbis, 1975).

14. J. Deotis Roberts, "Black Theology and Minjung Theology: Exploring Common Themes," in *An Emerging Theology in World Perspective Commentary on Korean Minjung Theology*, edited by Jung Young Lee (Mystic, CT: Twenty-Third, 1988) 99–105.

15. Ibid., 103.

16. Cyris H. S. Moon, "A Korean Minjung Perspective: The Hebrews and the Exodus," in *Voices from the Margin. Interpreting the Bible in the Third World*, ed. R. S. Sugirtharajah (Maryknoll, NY: Orbis, 1995) 241.

Minjung and black theology, Roberts asserts, focus on the experience of suffering and connected with suffering is the theme of theodicy. Theodicy seeks to understand the justice of God in the context of suffering. "The problem of structural evil and the consequence of mass suffering" are unavoidable.[17] Thus black and *minjung* theologians contextualize suffering and attempt to transform it. The cross is central to both but "the cross is not a symbol of escape; it is rather a symbol of engagement with evil and suffering. Christ's victorious resurrection is seen in relation to the cross as its sequel and ultimate vindication."[18] Womanist theologian JoAnne Terrell cautions against placing too much attention on the cross lest we find ourselves glorifying suffering especially for black people and others who have endured so much unnecessary evil.[19] Suffering can be the consequence of ministry and godlike living, but suffering is not the goal. Some suffering results from evil acts and omission or silence regarding injustice. Not all suffering is redemptive.[20]

Like *minjung* theology, black theology is holistic and inclusive regarding the culture and tradition of indigenous peoples as legitimate sources of theological reflection and divine revelation. This includes black people's religious and/or political histories, traditions, ways of knowing, God talk, and artifacts. Roberts argues that "black theology should be broadly conceived, encompassing a strong emphasis upon history and culture, without toning down the essential, political liberation thrust."[21] This "political liberating" thrust continues to be important since many gains made in the past are being eroded; "blacks still live in the shadow of slavery."[22]

Black people and their allies have won hard-fought Civil Rights battles and other victories since the Emancipation Proclamation, and we have proudly witnessed individual accomplishments (most recently, the first African American President and First Lady, Barack Obama and Michelle Obama). But we continue to live with lagging income, employment, education, and health care statistics as well as the threat of eroding civil and human rights. Black communities struggle with internal and external injustices. Womanist theologians confronted black theology's lack of self-critique

17. Roberts, "Black Theology," 103.

18. Ibid., 104–5.

19. JoAnne Terrell, *Power in the Blood? The Cross in the African American Experience* (Eugene, OR: Wipf & Stock, 2005). See also Raquel A. St. Clair, *Call and Consequences: A Womanist Reading of Mark* (Minneapolis: Fortress, 2008).

20. St. Clair (*Call and Consequences*, 83, 132) distinguishes between pain and suffering as forms of agony.

21. Roberts, "Black Theology," 99.

22. Ibid., 100.

with respect to sexism, classism, and heterosexism. Jacquelyn Grant argued that black men ignored black women's unique experiences rendering them invisible in their theological reflections,[23] a critique to which black theologians conceded and corrected. Womanist theology continues to strive to be an inclusive theology interested in the health and welfare of the whole community.

Given this theological emphasis on inclusivity among black, womanist, and *minjung* theologians (male and female) Jesus' relationship with the crowds in Luke's Gospel provides a useful paradigm for conceptualizing the importance of the masses and for rejecting a concentration on the success of a few as a synecdochical substitute for deliverance of the masses from disease, hunger, and inequalities.

Individual Achievements and the Black Masses

With the election of the first black President of these United States of America in 2008, political pundits and commentators (primarily Anglo) asked whether we could now think of America as a post-racial society. Similarly, one of my white male students asked me whether we should legitimately continue talking about racism as a reality given that he (the student) is sitting in a class taught by an African American Harvard trained PhD and given the election of the first black president. I answered with an unequivocal Pauline "by no means!" When masses of black peoples continue anywhere near the superficial poverty line; are subjected to systemic profiling and racism; do not earn a living wage; have limited or no access to quality education or healthcare; and are inequitably treated within the justice system, we cannot begin to claim that we live in a post-racial America.

The struggle to articulate and address the connection between individual responsibility and the plight of the masses is as old as Moses, the son of Pharaoh, whom God chose to lead a mass of people out of Egyptian bondage in the Old Testament. That struggle has long existed within the black community. Should we encourage those who have been able to achieve a certain socio-economic status despite the status quo to reach back and help elevate their oppressed brothers and sisters while attempting to obliterate oppressive systems? Or should we advocate for a widespread contentment

23. Jacquelyn Grant, "Black Theology and the Black Woman," in *Black Theology: A Documentary History, 1966–1979*, eds. Gayraud Wilmore and James H. Cone, vol. 2 (Maryknoll, NY: Orbis 1979) 418–33. See also Kelly Delaine Brown Douglas, "Womanist Theology: What is Its Relationship to Black Theology?" in *Black Theology: A Documentary History, 1980–1992*, eds. James H. Cone and Gayraud S. Wilmore (Maryknoll, NY: Orbis, 1992) 292.

among the masses without a political liberative agenda to change the status quo, advocating for a "pull yourselves up by your own bootstraps" mentality? Two early twentieth century American "Negro" leaders articulated two different solutions to this dilemma. The sociologist, scholar, author, and political activist W. E. B. Du Bois (1868–1963) the first African American to graduate from Harvard University with a doctorate degree in 1895, wrote: "The Negro race, like all races, is going to be saved by its *exceptional men*. The problem of education, then, among Negroes must first of all deal with the *Talented Tenth*; it is the problem of *developing the best of this race that they may guide the mass away from the contamination and death of the worst, in their own and other races*" (emphasis mine).[24] Du Bois seems to call for the salvation of a representative mass within the masses by the gifted few. Martin Luther King Jr., over 150 years later criticized Du Bois' vision as not for the uplift of the "whole people" but for an "aristocratic elite" who would benefit while they left behind the ninety percent.[25]

Booker T. Washington (1856–1915) was born a slave and became the leading educator among African Americans in the twentieth century, the first principal/teacher of the famous Tuskegee Institute, and author of his bestselling autobiography *Up from Slavery*. Washington, it appears, wished to impact the masses but within the status quo, as reflected in his famous quote "cast down your buckets where you are."[26] In 1949 the theologian, mystic, scholar, author, and pastor Howard Thurman (1899–1981)[27] wrote that masses of people constituting "the poor, the disinherited, and the dispossessed" still "live with their backs constantly against the wall." Thurman ask what does religion or the religious offer them?[28]

Black women activists in the late nineteenth and twentieth century recognized that "their fate was bound with the masses," as expressed by the National Association of Colored Women's Motto "Lifting as we Climb." A prevailing perception existed that black women's "womanhood" was judged

24. W. E. B. Du Bois, "The Talented Tenth," in *The Negro Problem: A Series of Articles by Representative American Negroes of To-Day*, ed. Booker T. Washington (New York: James Pott, 1903) 31.

25. Martin Luther King Jr., *Why We Can't Wait* (New York: Three Rivers, 2006) 19.

26. Booker T. Washington, "Atlanta Compromise Speech," Atlanta, GA, September 18, 1895.

27. Howard Thurman first published an essay entitled "Good News for the Underprivileged" while he was Dean at Howard University's Rankin Chapel in 1935, and that essay became the core of his book *Jesus and the Disinherited* as noted in the foreword of said book.

28. Ibid., 13.

by "the masses of our women."[29] Many black women activists understood from experience that "opportunity and environment" and "not circumstances of birth or previous experience . . . separated them from the masses."[30] Middle class black women could be elitist, but many were guided by a moral imperative to liberate and educate the masses. Rosa Bowser (1855–1931) Richmond, Virginia's first "colored" teacher, wrote in *The Woman's Era* that "Race progress is the direct outgrowth of individual success in life"; "The race rises as individuals rise . . . and individuals rise with the race."[31] Many black women educator-activists, such as Anna Julia Cooper (1858–1964) worked with one high heel planted in the Booker T. Washington camp, supporting industrial education and the other in the Du Bosian school promoting higher education and earning PhDs.[32]

The Rev. Dr. Martin Luther King, Jr. (1929–1968; pastor, Civil Rights leader, theologian, and author) connected injustice perpetrated against black people with its global impact. King famously asserted that injustice anywhere (particular) is injustice everywhere (universal). The transformation of one or a few lives should not excuse or obscure justice everywhere else. In 1963 King expressed his disappointment with both political parties when President Kennedy failed to sign a key housing bill that would end housing discrimination in financing by financial institutions. King wrote that "While Negroes were being appointed to some significant jobs, and social hospitality was being extended at the White House to Negro leaders, the dreams of the masses remained in tatters. The Negro felt that he recognized the same old bone that had been tossed to him in the past—only now it was being handed to him on a platter, with courtesy."[33]

Shirley Chisholm (1924–2005) the first female to seriously run for President of the United States of America, asserted that the Civil Rights movement did not achieve the goal of integration. Individual achievements, she argued, are insufficient and often come at the price of minorities becoming "pseudowhites." Chisholm wrote that "successful blacks who are proud of their own accomplishments should not disregard the fact that despite their own efforts, they owe most of their success to the momentum of their group, to actions taken before they came of age."[34] In order to engender "real

29. Paula Giddings, *When and Where I Enter: The Impact of Black Women on Race and Sex in America* (New York: Bantam, 1984) 97, 98.

30. Ibid., 98.

31. Ibid., 102.

32. Ibid., 105. Ann Julia Cooper earned a doctorate at age sixty-seven after she retired.

33. King, *Why We Can't Wait*, 6.

34. Shirley Chisholm, *Unbought and Unbossed* (New York: Avon, 1970) 151.

progress," Chisholm argues, "we must all move ahead together, and we must do it ourselves."[35] Chisholm referred to Washington's industrial education program as "mind-deadening" and called for fully trained black professionals and black control of black institutions. She advocated nonviolent and pragmatic fighting within the system to change the system.[36]

When he served in the US Senate, President Barack Obama (first African American President of the USA, former US and Illinois State Senator, US Constitution scholar, and author) addressed the state of black masses and other minorities and our continued individual responsibilities to them:

> Still, when I hear commentators interpreting my speech to mean that we have arrived at a "postracial politics" or that we already live in a color-blind society, I have to offer a word of caution. To say that we are one people is not to suggest that race no longer matters—that the right for equality has been won, or that the problems that minorities face in this country today are largely self-inflicted. We know the statistics: On almost every single socioeconomic indicator, from infant mortality to life expectancy to employment to home ownership, Black and Latino Americans in particular continue to lag behind their white counterparts. In corporate boardrooms across America, minorities are grossly underrepresented; in the United States Senate, there are only three Latinos and two Asian members (both from Hawaii) and as I write today I am the chamber's sole African American. To suggest that our racial attitudes play no part in these disparities is to turn a blind eye to both our history and our experience—and to relieve ourselves of the responsibility to make things right.[37]

Black political, educational, and religious leaders have struggled with the plight of the masses that still live with their backs against the wall in light of the few who have climbed over and face the wall. What is the individual's responsibility to the masses from which she emerged and thus to whom she is related by provenance, common humanity, and a remembered oppression? We shall attempt to address these questions through an analysis of the Lukan Jesus' relationship to individuals and the masses. In the process, we shall identify the masses or minjung in Luke. But first we shall discuss Ahn Byong-Mu's characterization of the masses in Mark. Ahn's analysis will serve as a point of departure for our analysis of Luke.

35. Ibid., 154.
36. Ibid., 157, 158.
37. Barack H. Obama, *The Audacity of Hope* (New York: Three Rivers, 2006) 232–33.

Ahn Byong-Mu's Analysis of the Social Construction of the Minjung in Mark's Gospel

In Ahn Byong-Mu's seminal essay, "Jesus and the Minjung in the Gospel of Mark," he attempts to interpret the "crowd(s)" (Greek: *ochlos*, sometimes *pantes*; *laos* is not found in Mark) in Mark from the perspective of *minjung* theology. Ahn's literary reconstruction of the crowds in Mark is foundational for understanding the *minjung* in relation to Jesus. Ahn argues that since little attention has been given to a social construction of the crowds that followed Jesus, his "words and deeds . . . have been desocialized." Much of what Jesus said and did occurred in the context of the crowds.[38]

Ahn observes that the crowds form the background for Jesus' activities as they follow him. The crowds are differentiated from the disciples whom Jesus rebukes.[39] Jesus does not rebuke the crowds even though they consist of the so-called sinners and outcasts. The crowds, the "minjung of Galilee," take an "anti–Jerusalem" stance, according to Ahn, and are distinguished from the Jerusalem ruling class. Finally, the crowds are represented as strong and susceptible to manipulation since the rulers attempt to mobilize them on their side.[40] Despite their attempts to manipulate the crowds, "the unjust and powerful" fear them. Yet, the crowds do not organize themselves into a power bloc, and neither does Jesus. Therefore, Ahn argues, we cannot regard the crowds as "a political bloc," but only "existentially as a crowd. They are minjung not because they have a common destiny, but simply because they are alienated, dispossessed, and powerless."[41]

Ahn found no qualitative evaluation of the crowds and no attempt to judge them on the basis of "an established religious or ethical standard or in terms of a new ethic."[42] Like Jesus, the crowds were peripatetic. Therefore, they likely held no established social positions and were not "members of an identifiable economic class."[43] Nevertheless, "Minjung belong to a class

---

38. Ahn Byong-Mu, "Jesus and the Minjung in the Gospel of Mark," in *Voices from the Margin. Interpreting the Bible in the Third World*, edited by R. S. Sugirtharajah (Maryknoll, NY: Orbis, 1997) 85–86.

39. Lee, "Minjung Theology," 21–22. Lee posits no idealized or romanticized view of the crowds; the minjung are not sinless. Whether Ahn concludes therefore that the minjung are sinless is unclear. Perhaps, the ethical and moral character of the crowds is not the focus since to do so would shift attention from the crowds as victims of oppression to them as perpetrators.

40. Ibid., 88–89.

41. Ibid., 101, 102.

42. Ibid., 90.

43. Ibid.

of society which has been marginalized and abandoned"; they do not belong to the people of God (*laos*) nor are they the baptized crowd.[44]

Mark provides a paradigmatic representation of the crowds that follow Jesus. The crowds are composed of sinners, the sick, the socially alienated, and/or those who committed religious sin. The fact that tax collectors are among the crowds demonstrates the crowds or *minjung* are not limited to the economically and politically alienated.[45] *Ochlos* (Greek translated "crowd") is a relational and fluid concept.[46]

Ahn described Jesus' attitude toward crowds as protective, welcoming, and familial. The crowds are "sheep without a shepherd," a metaphor that served as a critique of the leaders. The crowds were alienated from their rulers. Jesus accepted the crowds as members of his spiritual or fictive family. Jesus took pleasure in teaching the crowds, and they were fascinated by his teachings. Jesus unconditionally accepted and supported the crowds, who were the "alienated and despised class in the community." [47] Ahn asserts that "Jesus' attitude toward the minjung was never limited to people who were politically oppressed," but they included "the aggrieved, and the weak."[48] Jesus promised the future kingdom of God, which represents God's love and justice. God wills to stand with "minjung completely and unconditionally."[49]

The Gospel of Luke and the Crowds/Minjung: A Soteriological Hermeneutical Circle

Much of what Ahn discovered about the crowds in Mark applies to the crowds in Luke, particularly Jesus' attitude toward them. Jesus welcomed them, embraced them, and provided for their needs. The *minjung*/crowds have real needs, which Jesus meets unconditionally. However, I wish to complete the hermeneutical circle that Ahn began. While Ahn examined the crowds solely in relation to Jesus, I analyze the relationship between individuals and the crowds and between Jesus and individuals that Jesus encountered in or out of the crowds. In Luke, I observe an organic or wholistic movement in which the whole gives meaning to the individual parts and individual parts derive meaning from the whole. This does not mean that individuals have

44. Ibid., 101.
45. Ibid., 91–96.
46. Ibid., 101.
47. Ibid., 89–90, 94.
48. Ibid., 95, 96.
49. Ibid., 102.

no identity apart from the *minjung*/crowds, but that without the voice and testimony of individuals who emerge from the crowds we could not know the *minjung*. Protowomanist voting rights activist Fannie Lou Hamer often quoted Luke 4:18 as proof that God was not just interested in liberating black people but the ubiquitous masses: "Jesus . . . was talking about people."[50] Individuals present to us the multifaceted, multidimensional, and human nature of the crowds. From individuals we learn something about the whole. Womanist theologian Jacquelyn Grant argues that "a wholistic analysis is a minimal required for a wholistic theology."[51] A wholistic theology seeks to liberate women, men, and children or the entire black community, as well as the human race. A wholistic theology also recognizes that we live in and are part of the larger world. The Jahwist account of the creation story (Gen 2:4b–24) reminds us that all humans draw substance, meaning, and life from the earth (*adamah*) and from God. Karen Baker-Fletcher argues that our sense of "interconnectedness moves [us] out of prisons of individualism to relearn compassion, to know experientially and to understand that injustice anywhere is a threat to justice everywhere, that when one suffers all suffer, that when one rejoices all rejoice."[52] Womanist biblical interpretation should concern itself with the individuals that emerge out of the crowds to experience wholeness and the crowds they leave behind that continue waiting for their change to come. As Layli Phillips explains, "womanism allows everyone to move toward the same place along different paths: that place is universal community; that path is whatever uniquenesses they have acquired by birth and all their successive travels through different experiences since that time. While this perspective may be unsettlingly nonracial for those who view womanist as merely another name for black feminism or a black women-centered perspective, the reality is that one hallmark of womanist is Black women's and other women of color's expression, vision, and articulation of universal sentiments and aspirations."[53]

50. Jacquelyn Grant, "Civil Rights Women: A Source for Doing Womanist Theology," in *Women in the Civil Rights Movement: Trailblazers and Torchbearers, 1941–1965,* eds. Vicki L. Crawford et al. (Bloomington, IN: Indiana University Press, 1993) 46.

51. Jacquelyn Grant, *White Women's Christ and Black Women's Jesus: Feminist Christology and Womanist Response,* Brown Studies in Religion 64 (Atlanta: Scholars, 1989) 221.

52. Karen Baker-Fletcher, *Sisters of Dust, Sisters of Spirit: Womanist Words on God and Creation* (Minneapolis: Fortress, 1998) 20.

53. Layli Phillips, "Introduction. Womanism: On its Own," in *The Womanist Reader: The First Quarter Century of Womanist Thought,* ed. Layli Phillips (New York: Routledge, 2006) xxxvii.

The womanist interpretive framework I employ is organic. I am concerned with the socio-economic dilemma of the black and human masses (male and female) the *minjung*, and other people locally and globally who live marginalized, alienated, and oppressed lives. My analysis, unlike Ahn's, does not concern redaction criticism. I explore Luke's narrative as an organic whole. Luke provides a literary paradigm for conceptualizing the relationship between the masses/*minjung* and individuals who experience salvation, wholeness, and/or mobility. Most if not all of the individuals who experience God's salvation through Jesus' ministry do so within the context of the masses, as part of the *minjung*. The salvation, deliverance, or wholeness (Greek: *sotēria* or *hygiēs*) of individuals is inextricably connected with the *minjung* and the *minjung* benefit from the salvation or wholeness that individuals receive. I call this phenomena inscribed in the text a *Soteriological Hermeneutical Circle*.[54] The Greek noun *sotēria* is translated salvation. Hermeneutics refers to the art or process of interpretation or translation.

In Luke, as Ahn observed in Mark, much of what Jesus said and did occurs in the context of crowds. Individuals Jesus heals emerge from the crowds and thus were originally *minjung*. When Jesus heals or restores to wholeness an individual, this individual act of deliverance affects the *minjung*. Jesus, in Luke, intends to impact particularly those that some, including the elite religious right(eous) label "sinners." The term "sinners" is a designation that the elite religious right(eous) employ signifying people who do not interpret or practice the Mosaic law and/or religious rituals to the same extent or in the same manner as they prescribe or who belong to groups stereotypically associated with certain socio-political positions (e.g., tax collectors or publicans).

This phenomena of stereotyping and thus categorizing people as "sinners and tax collectors" can be observed in contemporary rhetoric. It casts blame on the masses for their poverty and accuses them of collecting or receiving government tax aid undeservedly. Consequently, many individuals who once lived among the *minjung* will distance themselves from the *minjung* to avoid guilt by association. Recently, some persons associated with the contemporary so-called "religious right" blamed the masses who live in poverty for their situations. For example, Newt Gingrich stated that "Really poor children in really poor neighborhoods have no habits of working and nobody around them who works, so they literally have no habit of showing up on Monday. They have no habit of staying all day. They have no

54. See Martin Heidegger, *Being and Time* (New York: Harper and Row, 1962) 153. Context informs text and text informs context, known as the hermeneutical circle.

habit of 'I do this and you give me cash' . . . unless it's illegal.''[55] And some, like the American Center for Law and Justice's David French, believe people are poor because of deep spiritual deficiencies that result in bad choices and they should not be able to rely on the government or the church for assistance.[56] According to US Census Bureau statistics released September, 2011, 46.2 million Americans live below the poverty line.[57] Currently an estimated 15.7 million American children (ages 0–17 years) live in poverty. These figures do not include those who live near or around the superficial poverty line.[58] White children have the *highest poverty numbers* and black children have the *highest poverty rate* with 25.6 percent children in poverty. Black people are only 14.4 percent of the US population. Black families continue to earn the lowest median income of about two-thirds of the average white family.[59] Globally, billions of people live in poverty. Fallacious and biased ideologies cast masses of people as "sinners and tax collectors" without regard for factors that contribute to mass poverty, such as colonialism, neo-colonialism, systemic racism, sexism (and other isms) deregulation, and capitalistic greed and materialism of which many of their accusers are perpetrators or participants. The circle goes both ways, in the direction of salvation and in the way of destruction.

In Luke, we can observe a soteriological hermeneutical circle operative. I shall analyze seven stories (7:1–10; 7:11–17; 8:19–21; 8:40–56; 9:10–17; 15:1–32; 18:9–14; 18:35–43) through a womanist soteriological hermeneutical lens, which I believe shall assist us in understanding the relationship between the crowds/*minjung* and individuals.[60] At 7:1–10 (Matt 8:5–13) the story about the healing of the centurion's slave is framed by the presence of people/crowds (v. 1, *laos* and v. 9, *ochlos*). Jesus uses the centurion's example of transformative faith to exhort, teach, and rebuke the masses, which

55. Newt Gingrich, Candidate for the Republican Presidential Nominee, Fundraiser in Iowa, December 2, 2011.

56. Kyle Mantyla, "Why the Religious Right Opposes Government Assistance for the Poor," September 19, 2011, http://www.rightwingwatch.org/content/why–religious–right–opposes–government–assistance–poor (accessed December 30, 2011).

57. United States Census Bureau Report, September 13, 2011.

58. Mitzi J. Smith, "The Problem of the Color Line and the Poverty Line," *Womanist Biblical Scholar Reflections*, www.womanistntprof.blogspot.com, February 4, 2011.

59. United States Census Bureau, "Child Poverty in the United States 2009 and 2010: Selected Race Groups and Hispanic Origin," issued November 2011, http://www.census.gov/hhes/www/poverty/poverty.html, (accessed January 6, 2012).

60. I do not generally distinguish between the two Greek nouns *ochlos* (primarily translated crowd) and *laos* (generally translated people) in my analysis of Luke because I am more interested in the distinction between larger groups of people as opposed to individuals.

includes Israelites: "to the crowd that was following him he said, 'I tell you, not even in Israel have I found such faith.'" Because of the centurion's faith, which compels him to enter among the crowds to seek Jesus, his slave was restored. As an oppressed and marginalized person, we would identify the slave with the *minjung*. But since the slave cannot be present to speak and seek Jesus for himself, his master becomes his voice. Similarly, the Lukan story of the encounter between Jesus and the widow of Nain (7:11–17) is framed by the presence of a great crowd/people (v. 11, *ochlos polus*; v. 12, *ochlos*; v. 16, *laos*). When Jesus resurrects the widow of Nain's son, both Jesus and the widow arrive with their crowds. She is a part of the crowds and emerges from the crowds. She speaks for her son. And as one of the most vulnerable in society, subsisting in a patriarchal context without adult male protection, she is the voice and embodiment of *minjung*. After Jesus raises the widow's son, *all* are impacted; the people erupt in praise viewing the miracle as God's favor upon them too. Jesus demonstrates God's solidarity with the *minjung* and God's ability and willingness to meet the needs of the *minjung* who are often voiceless and vulnerable people who need physical and/or socio-economic transformation or wholeness.

At Luke 8:19–21, Jesus' family visits him but cannot reach him because a crowd (*ochlos*) has surrounded him. Jesus takes advantage of this familial visit as an opportunity to conceptually expand family relations beyond biology: "My mother and my brothers are those people who hear and do the word of God," (v. 21). Jesus' biological family, as the particular, becomes a metaphor for a fictive family, the universal or whole. The part informs the whole and the whole informs the part. But the part and the whole are never synonymous and should not be monolithically or stereotypically construed. Jesus neither excludes his family nor prioritizes them at the expense of the masses. Compare this pericope with 11:27–28 where a woman announces that Jesus' biological mother is blessed. Jesus affirms her proclamation, but he exceeds her blessing: it is those who hear and keep the word of God who are blessed. Again, the particular of his biological mother becomes a metaphor incorporating the *minjung*. The *minjung* are Jesus' kinfolk; they are children of God.

The context for Jesus' healing of Jairus's dying daughter and the woman with the chronic hemorrhaging is the crowded city (8:40–56; Matt 9:18–26; Mark 5:21–43).[61] At v. 40 a crowd awaits Jesus' return when Jairus emerges from the crowd seeking Jesus' help for his daughter. Yet Jairus is not the only person in the crowd seeking restoration. While on his way to Jairus' house, a crowd continues to follow and press Jesus. It is as a part of and from within

---

61. Luke follows Mark in this regard.

the crowd that the chronically hemorrhaging woman manages to touch the fringes of Jesus' garment. Despite the crowd's density, Jesus is concerned to know who from among the crowd grabbed the fringes on the hem of his garment. The *minjung* or the masses are the dying and diseased, young and old, with and without advocates who need to be whole.

The woman speaks from the crowd identifying herself. By calling her out, compelling her to identify herself, the entire crowd is made aware of the situation. The crowd is drawn into her story because on some level her story is their story; she is one of them. Thus, all of the people (*pantos tou laou*) are blessed when Jesus makes her whole. Because what Jesus can do for her, he can do for them. God is active in Jesus restoring hope among the *minjung*.

When the apostles return from their commission (9:1–6) Jesus takes them into Bethsaida to spend some alone time with them (9:10–17; Matt 14:13–21; Mark 6:30–44) but the crowds (*ochloi*) find out and invite themselves to the private gathering. Jesus welcomes (*apodechomai*) the crowds.[62] Generally, Jesus does not engage individuals to the exclusion of crowds or vice versa. We move from the particular to the whole again when Jesus takes the one lunch of two fishes and five loaves to feed a crowd. All roads lead back to the crowds. The mention of the leftover twelve baskets full of food also signifies a movement from the universal (the satisfied crowd) back to the particular (the remnants). The story moves from the twelve apostles to the crowds; from the crowds to five loaves and two fish; then from meager lunch to the actual feeding of the multitude; and from the fulfilled crowd to twelve remaining baskets full of food representing several turns of the soteriological hermeneutical circle. We see this pattern in terms of feeding, healing, resurrecting the dead, and teaching. Luke's Jesus creates and maintains a connectedness, rhetorically and pragmatically, between individuals and the masses; the salvation or wholeness of individuals is inextricably connected with the *minjung*.

Only Luke uses three parables to make the point that even if one individual or item is lost, one must attempt to rescue or find him or it (15:1–32; Matt 18:12–14). Luke sets Jesus' sharing of the three parables within the context of a gathering of "*all* the sinners and tax collectors," (15:1). In Luke, the phrase "all the sinners and tax collectors" seems to represent a certain group of people stereotypically understood by some Pharisees and scribes (15:2; cf. 5:29–30; 7:39). The parables show that we should value any individual (or the metaphorical coin or sheep) that is lost or finds herself in an annihilating situation. The lost son, coin, and sheep in this context represent "all the sinners and tax collectors." The gospel is about making people whole

---

62. Mark and Matthew say Jesus had compassion (*esplagchnisthē*).

and not about exalting those we consider whole or who have "made it" as a synecdochical substitute for the suffering or lost *minjung*. This point is also made in the Lukan parable of the Publican and the Pharisee (18:9–14). Jesus chastises the Pharisee not because he lives a good ritual and moral life but because of his attitude toward "the rest of the human beings" (*hoi loipoi tōn anthrōpōn*) (18:11). Jesus is not opposed to the Pharisee's lifestyle. But he singles himself out as the one who has achieved, as opposed to others who have not obtained a certain lifestyle. This sounds all too much like a rhetoric common in contemporary religious circles, especially where the prosperity gospel prevails.

At Luke 18:35–43 (Matt 20:29–34; Mark 10:46–52) even as Jesus journeys to Jerusalem a crowd (*ochlos*) accompanies him. As they pass by, a blind man sitting along the roadway works himself into the crowd. From out of the crowd, the blind man cries out to Jesus for mercy (v. 38). He is part of the crowd; he is *a* voice of the crowd. That Jesus took the time to heal this man on his way to his own death demonstrates the priority Jesus places upon the cries and oppressions of the *minjung*. Again, when Jesus heals the blind man, the *minjung* are encouraged because God has healed one of them. And this event increases the probability of their healing: all the people praise God (v. 42).

The soteriological hermeneutical circle we find inscribed in Luke demonstrates that the *minjung* are the voiceless, oppressed, suffering, and marginalized people who sometimes have advocates and at other times stand alone "with their backs against the wall." They are women, children, and men who need to speak about their conditions, to be heard, and to be made whole. The *minjung* live among the masses, emerge from the masses, and they are the masses. Yet, individuals who emerge from the masses are not synonymous with the masses in a stereotypical sense. The *minjung* are composed of real flesh and blood people with real needs and a desire for wholeness. By journeying among the crowds and allowing the crowds to follow him, Jesus provides space and place for people who makeup the crowds to be seen, heard, and made whole.

God views the *minjung* as part of God's family; they are the children of God. We should view the world and our relationship to it organically regardless of how high we have climbed up the socio-economic ladder. We who arise from the masses should not view ourselves as distinct from the masses. The wholeness that God has engendered through Jesus for individuals that emerge from the masses witness to the possibility of wholeness for all *minjung*. When an individual experiences salvation or wholeness, it is not for the purpose of exalting herself above the local or global *minjung*. The historical and contemporary story of the *minjung* is our story. Yet, no one story exhausts the story or oppressive experiences of the *minjung*. The crowds are not monolithic; their experiences and their socio-economic, ethnic, religious, and gender statuses differ. But they share in common a need to be delivered from some physical, social, and/or spiritual oppression. In Luke 4:18–19, God's Spirit commissions and anoints Jesus to deliver good news among the poor, to announce the release of the colonized and restoration of sight to the blind, and to liberate the oppressed. And the *minjung* will recognize in this the favor of God.

Conclusion

Today God has anointed us to announce the favor of God upon the poor, the marginalized, the neglected, the voiceless, and those who suffer because of injustice perpetrated against them by church and governments alike. We are not anointed to proclaim a gospel of prosperity that demonizes and objectifies the poor. God has anointed us to stand in solidarity with the contemporary *minjung*. Today's *minjung* include people who live in poverty; exist without shelter/homes; suffer without access to (good) medical treatment; are stigmatized and bullied for being different; and are trafficked and sexually abused in church, home, and neighborhood. The *minjung* are people locally and globally who strive to survive in the rubble and ashes of colonization, deracination and enslavement, Apartheid, holocaust and genocide, Jim Crowism, disenfranchisement, racism, sexism, heterosexism, and unbridled capitalistic greed. The *minjung* are flesh-and-blood people cast into the streets and rendered homeless in the midst of a global recovery from a recession caused by Wall Street and disproportionately felt on main street. They are the people who increasingly find themselves languishing on the lower end of a socio-economic gap continually widening in favor of the rich to the detriment of the underemployed and unemployed poor. They are the mothers who are arrested for sending their children across district lines to receive a better education. We continue to live in a racialized society in which one is ostensibly or physiognomically black or white. The *minjung* are people who are more likely to be treated unjustly because of the color of their dark skin and who are the objects of laws like "Stand your Ground" that allow a white Latino to hunt down and kill a young black kid carrying skittles and iced tea. That same law justifies the imprisonment of a young black woman who fires a warning shot into the air to protect herself from an abusive mate. We are called to take a stand with God in solidarity with the *minjung* in the struggle for justice, restoration, and wholeness. I am *minjung*. The *minjung* are God's children.

CHAPTER TWELVE

Wisdom in the Garden

The Woman of Genesis 3 and Alice Walker's *Sophia*

KIMBERLY DAWN RUSSAW

What happens when you are the only one? What happens when you are the only one and you are just as good as the others, but you do not get credit for your contributions because you are not like the rest? You are just as smart—or smarter—than the others, but you do not get recognized for your brilliance. Or maybe, your brilliance is misread, misinterpreted, or misunderstood. Such is the case for many African American women living in a country that has a deeply rooted history of devaluing their intellect, commodifying their bodies, and stereotyping their legacies. In the religious academy, womanist scholars center their scholarship on the concerns of race, class, gender, and heterosexism in an effort to respond to the challenges of the lived experiences of female descendants of Africans now living in America. The work of womanist scholarship is needful, but it can be dangerous. Womanist scholarship can be dangerous because, at its core, it agitates comfortable ideas about the deity (or deities) about humanity and about humanity's relation with the deity (or deities). Even in 2014, womanist scholarship in the religious academy, especially in the area of biblical studies, is revolutionary, destabilizing, and insubordinate.

The work of womanist biblical interpretation is subversive. Womanist ways of reading the biblical text are subversive in that, by and large, they disrupt tightly held images of God and God's relationship to humanity. Womanist biblical interpretation unsettles images that privilege the concerns of males who possess social, economic, and political capital. Womanist interpretations go beyond feminist interpretations that center the concerns of women, to address class and—where the text supports it—race. While inter-disciplinary, womanist ways of reading the biblical text balance precariously on the edges of two realities. Womanist ways of reading balances the reality of patriarchy associated with the text[1] and the very real issues of power dynamics reflected in and ascribed to the text—a text so many hold as sacred.

In this essay, I argue that the woman ('iššā) character of the Gen 3 narrative should be considered among the cadre of wise characters of the Hebrew Bible narratives because she possesses the characteristics of a wise individual as delineated in the ancient Near Eastern wisdom texts and the ancient Israelite corpus. After interrogating the idea of wisdom, I make three moves in this essay. First, I identify the markers of wise individuals in ancient Near Eastern and ancient Israelite literature. Second, I map the markers of a wise individual onto the woman of Gen 3. In my third move, I bridge Wisdom Literature with womanism by considering how the character of Sofia Butler from Alice Walker's book *The Color Purple* meets the requirements for a wise individual.

I borrow Sofia from Alice Walker because so much of her character, which tends to get overlooked in favor of the more popular Celie and Shug, resonates with African American women. Because she resonates with so many, Sofia serves as an accessible conduit between African American female readers and the woman of Gen 3. My hope is that, by connecting Sofia with the woman of Gen 3, I provide for African American women a different way to locate themselves in the biblical text. This connection is womanist because it is courageous, not apprehensive. This way of reading the biblical text affirms, and does not minimize, the personhood of the black female. I do this audaciously womanist work knowing that courage upsets the status quo. It is to this audacious, courageous, and subversive work that I now turn.

Wisdom

We live in perilous times that do not afford us the luxury of being foolish. In a time where reading does not seem to be fundamental, common sense is uncommon and televised reality is unrealistic, we need to be smarter than a fifth grader. After all, fifth graders do not have to make long-term financial decisions while forecasts for the GDP are falling and estimates for inflation are rising. Not only do we need to be smart, we need to be wise. We must possess wisdom. But what is wisdom?

1. This reality includes the patriarchy behind the text, in the world of the text, and in the history of its interpretation.

Wisdom and its definition are illusive. Some say, wisdom is an attitude, a value system or a type of knowledge. Many believe that wisdom is the act of grappling with life's unanswerable questions. Some say wisdom is something passed down through tradition. Others hold that it is connected with prosperity—after all, according to Ben Franklin, "wealthy and wise" go together! Admittedly, wisdom and its literature are full of contradictions about its contours and its character. This situation is complicated by the variety of phenomena that employ the Hebrew word ḥākām (*hokam*, wise, or *hokmah*, wisdom*)* and similar ideas in the ancient Near East. Concepts like bîn (*bin*, to discern or perceive or *binah*, insight, understanding) 'ārûm (*arom*, to be shrewd, crafty or *arum*, crafty, shrewd or sensible) and da'at (*daat*, knowledge) also encompass aspects of wisdom. For the purposes of this essay, however, I define Wisdom Literature as those writings that have as their *telos* or ultimate end the attainment of a life well-lived and rewarded by the Divine. This definition captures both the act and the end of wisdom. Though grounded in an understanding of ancient Near Eastern sapiential (relating to wisdom) material, this definition relies heavily upon the way wisdom is taken up in the Hebrew Bible corpus. It specifically leverages the concepts of the first collection of Proverbs, but also considers the more abstract and enigmatic concerns of Job and Qoheleth (Ecclesiastes).

Modern scholars define and delimit wisdom and its literature based upon the broad corpus of written material from the ancient Near East and the narrower canon of the Hebrew Bible.[2] James Crenshaw suggests that the original authors of wisdom literature pondered life's enigmas in a variety of forms including extensive dialogue, aphorisms, riddles, and popular sayings, but many have bifurcated this unified corpus into the contemporary categories of sayings and instructions.[3] Despite efforts to contemporize the ancient

---

2. For brevity, I engage the work of James L. Crenshaw (*Old Testament Wisdom: An Introduction* [Louisville: Westminster John Knox, 1998]; "The Contemplative Life in the Ancient Near East," in *Civilizations of the Ancient Near East*, ed. Jack M. Sasson [Peabody, MA: Hendrickson, 1995], 2445–57; and "Wisdom," in *Old Testament Form Criticism*, ed. John H. Hayes [San Antonio: Trinity University Press, 1974], 225–264) found in both the ancient Near Eastern corpus and the Hebrew Bible because his treatment of the wisdom material and wise characters reflects the contours and concerns of the current wisdom discourse. For similar treatments of wisdom literature, see Giorgio Buccellati, "Wisdom and Not: The Case of Mesopotamia," *Journal of the American Oriental Society* 101:1 (1981) 35–47; Sara Denning-Bolle, *Wisdom in Akkadian Literature: Expression, Instruction, Dialogue* (Leiden: Ex Oriente Lux, 1992); Michael V. Fox, "Ideas of Wisdom in Proverbs 1–9," *Journal of Biblical Literature* 116 (1997) 613–33; W. G. Lambert, *Babylonian Wisdom Literature* (Winona Lake, IN: Eisenbrauns, 1996).

4. This is similar to Denning's argument that modern scholars' intuitive distinction between two types of wisdom (practical, down-to-earth wisdom and abstract wisdom) is not readily apparent in ancient Mesopotamian texts.

wisdom materials, these scholars rarely take up the concerns of women, who are undoubtedly part of the contemporary landscape. Although the wise, advice-giving tavern-keeper, Siduri in *The Epic of Gilgamesh* and other wise women represent in the ancient texts, prevailing scholarly treatments of Wisdom Literature rarely ascribe wisdom to female characters. Wisdom is personified as feminine in Proverbs, but biblical scholars rarely argue for women as the beneficiaries of wisdom.[4] There is a conspicuous absence of women as the objects and possessors of wisdom in these examinations of the biblical wisdom material. Among the traditional treatments of these wisdom texts, many scholars do not attend to women in the text, the women behind the text or—at the very least—the women sitting in front of the text. And when the scholarship does not consider women, women are relegated to the margins of wisdom. These traditional scholarly treatments of wisdom are overwhelmingly male-centered. It seems to me that if the work of modern scholars is to catalogue, shape, and categorize ancient material, then now might be a good time to revisit wisdom literature, its definition, its markers and contours, its corpus members, and its characters and their concerns. Furthermore, if the work of womanist biblical interpretation is disruptive, this *Womanist Biblical Hermeneutics Reader* seems like a good place to offer my analysis of the woman of Gen 3 as a proto-womanist character.[5]

Markers of Wise Individuals

Throughout the literature of the ancient Near East and the Hebrew Bible, wise individuals are characterized by their skillfulness or craftiness, their ability to see, and their focus on going after what seems good. The first

4. In his *Old Testament Wisdom* Crenshaw defines wisdom as "the reasoned search for specific ways to ensure personal well-being in everyday life, to make sense of extreme adversity and vexing anomalies, and to transmit this hard-earned knowledge so that successive generations will embody it." Looking specifically at wisdom literature as seen in Proverbs, Crenshaw highlights one of its major themes; the wise were righteous because they followed the path of Wisdom, which led to a long, fulfilled life. To this understanding of Proverbs, Fox, in his essay, "Ideas of Wisdom in Proverbs 1–9," adds that in the first nine chapters of Proverbs, wisdom is conceptualized as both earth-bound and lifesaving *and* as other-worldly and transcendental. A critical read of Proverbs, however, yields the shocking observation that within these two worlds (earthly and heavenly) women are missing. Although proverbial wisdom is personified as a female, none of the wise sayings are explicitly targeted towards women. Fathers instruct their sons, but not their daughters. Fathers encourage sons to not reject the teaching of their mothers, but their mothers never speak for themselves.

5. I credit Linda Thomas with the designation "proto-womanist" during a conversation we had at AAR/SBL in 2010.

aspect or indicator of wisdom is its relationship to skill and craftiness. In addition to the variety of words used to indicate wisdom, the ancient world connected the notion of wisdom with that sort of technical skill needed in a particular craft.[6] The wisdom of Atrahasis, whose name is translated, "extra wise," revolves around his devotion to his god and his commitment to his community. In the *Babylonian Flood Story*, he is introduced as one who was exceedingly wise who would dialogue with his god, Enki. Importantly, Atrahasis is the one entrusted with gathering the elders and instructing the men of the city in the building of the sea vessel in anticipation of the deluge. Atrahasis' skill or craftiness is evidenced in his ability to build a structure strong enough to not only survive the watery ramparts, but technically advanced enough to hold the birds flying in the heavens, the cattle of the god, the creatures of the steppe, his family and the people. The story of Atrahasis even suggests he was so savvy that he hosted a feast for all those onboard the sea vessel. Atrahasis is an example of a wise character that demonstrates his wisdom through his skill or craftiness.

The Hebrew Bible material echoes this skilled or crafty aspect of wisdom. One example of this is found at Ex 31:3 where YHWH filled Bezalel "with ability, intelligence and knowledge in every kind of craft" to help build the tabernacle. Another example is that of the man from Tyre whom King Solomon employs. It is said that the man from Tyre is "full of skill, intelligence and knowledge in working bronze" to help build the palace and administrative buildings (1 Kgs 7:14). Wise men like Atrahasis, Bezalel, and the metallurgist from Tyre demonstrate of the relationship between wisdom and skill or craftiness.

The ability to see is another aspect of wisdom found in the sapiential literature of the broader ancient Near Eastern corpus. The wisdom of Gilgamesh revolves around sight.[7] The Babylonia character is introduced as "he who saw the wellspring, the foundations of the land, who . . . was wise

6. Denning-Bolle, *Wisdom*, 33–39. Denning-Bolle sets out to describe the nature of wisdom in ancient Mesopotamia in the third chapter of her book *Wisdom in Akkadian Literature*, but attends to the multiplicity and complexity of the different words to denote intelligence, ability, technical sagacity, understanding, and wisdom by the ancients. Importantly, these words emphasize a required skill or expertise and a sort of knowledge. Here, Denning-Bolle points to Fohrer's and Guthrie's treatment of the Greek, *sophia* (wisdom). In *Studies in Ancient Israelite Wisdom*, Fohrer notes that wisdom/*sophia* can mean cleverness and skill for the purpose of practical action in many biblical texts. In *A History of Greek Philosophy*, Guthrie notes that the words *sophia* (wisdom) and *sophos* (wise) primarily connoted skill in a particular craft and that the word *deinos* (indicating something uncanny and awful connect with the gods) also indicated cleverness in speech and argumentation.

7. An emphasis on seeing, a sight that stems from experience, forms the basis of Gilgamesh's wisdom (Denning-Bolle, *Wisdom*, 47).

in all things." Furthermore, throughout the narrative poem Gilgamesh sees. Gilgamesh sees things in his dreams, sets out to see the giant Humbaba, sees the scorpion monster, looks up and sees Utanapishtim, and finally sees a pond in which to bathe. Interestingly, it is while he is bathing that a snake stealthily steals his plant of immortality—right before his very eyes! Additionally, Gilgamesh's eyes are ultimately opened and he is made aware of the futility of his pursuit of immortality. This is another instance of Gilgamesh seeing.

The idea of illumination or seeing is important in the Hebrew Bible. Many biblical texts take up this notion of wisdom's connection to sight, vision, and mental acuity. As an example, Balaam is described as "the man whose eye is clear . . . who hears the words of God, who sees the vision to the Almighty, who falls down, but with his eyes uncovered" (Num 24:4, 16). This interconnectedness of sight and wisdom is also evidenced in Isaiah when foolish idolaters are described as those who "do not know, nor do they comprehend; for their eyes are shut, so that they cannot see, and their minds as well, so that they cannot understand" (Isa 44:18).

In addition to craftiness and illumination, a wise character goes after what she understands to be good. Wise Gilgamesh sets out on a journey to find Utnapishtim because he wants to know the secret of immortality. Conversely, wise Adapa went after the direction of his lord, Ea, and forfeited immortality when he refused the food of life and the waters of life, offered by Anu, the king.[8] Wise King Solomon asks for wisdom (1 Kgs 3:9–12) and the entire first collection of Proverbs encourages a son to go after wisdom.

Overwhelmingly, wise characters in ancient Near Eastern and ancient Israelite literature are males. Wisdom, however, is not limited to men in the ancient Near Eastern wisdom texts. Characters like Siduri, Utnapishtim's wife, Dumuzid's sister, Geŝtin-ana, and the Sumerian goddess Inana demonstrate that wise women play important roles in the narratives in which they are found.[9] Within the biblical corpus, specifically within Proverbs however,

8. Benjamin R. Foster, *From Distant Days: Myths, Tales, and Poetry of Ancient Mesopotamia* (Bethesda, MD: CDL, 1995) 97. One of the major lessons of this Akkadian myth is, if a man so perfect as Adapa could not obtain immortality, who else could expect to?

9. Gilgamesh travelled to Utnapishtim to learn the secret of immortality. Siduri, the wise tavern keeper, explains the difficulties of such a journey and directs Gilgamesh to a ferryman. Utnapishtim's wife reveals her wisdom when she intervenes on Gilgamesh's behalf and encourages her husband to send him off with a gift that turns out to be the plant of rejuvenation. Dumuzid's sister, Geŝtin-ana, is described as a "wise woman who knows the meanings of dreams." The goddess Inana is wise because she outwits the gods when she ascends from the Underworld after finding a replacement in Dumuzid in the Sumerian folk tale, "Inana's Descent to the Underworld."

the markers of a wise individual are male-specific as if only men can be wise. To counter this long-held presupposition, many scholars highlight the feminine personification of wisdom (Lady Wisdom and her counterpart, Lady Folly) as proof that wisdom is not limited to men in the biblical text. This argument for the presence of women in the biblical wisdom corpus does not suffice for the entire scholarly community, however. When feminist biblical scholars like Athalya Brenner, Lyn Bechtel, Claudia Camp, Carole Fontaine, and Gale Yee examine the wisdom corpus with an eye towards the character and characterization of women, they find women and the feminine in a plethora of places doing a myriad of things. More importantly for our purposes, the wise characteristics of skillfulness or craftiness, seeing, and going after what is good are also found in the woman of Gen 3.

’iššā The Wise Woman of Gen 3

While she is lauded as The Mother of All Living Things, many Christians identify the woman of Gen 3 as the catalyst for the doctrines of the Fall of Man and Original Sin. Tertullian marked third-century women as the first sinners and "the devil's gateway" because they were derivatives of the woman of Gen 3,[10] and medieval artists painted all women as harmful when they depicted the serpent as a female seductress. Even modern images of scantily clad women holding apples conjure remembrance of the woman of Gen 3 for people of the modern age. Although many people remember the woman of Gen 3 as disobedient, defiant, and destructive, a closer reading of the narrative in light of the markers or indicators for wisdom demonstrates that the woman of Gen 3 displays the characteristics of a wise person. The woman of Gen 3 is skillful or crafty, has the ability to see, and goes after what she understands is good.

In Gen 3, wisdom's craftiness takes on aspects of shrewdness. The Hebrew word used to point to the shrewd aspect of wisdom is ʿārûm (arom).[11] This word is used in its adjectival form to describe the serpent and is also found in many places in the Hebrew Bible to indicate the shrewd aspect of wisdom. Two examples include 1 Sam 23:22 in which Solomon refers to his

10. Alexander Roberts, James Donaldson, and A. Cleveland Coxe, eds., *Fathers of the Third Century: Tertullian, Part Fourth; Minucius Felix; Commodian; Origen, Parts First and Second*, 9 volumes (New York: Christian Literature Company, 1885).

11. The verb ʿārûm (arom) means be shrewd or crafty. The Hebrew word, ḥākām (hokam, wise) also carries aspects of shrewdness or craftiness as seen in its use to describe Amnon's friend, Jonadab in 2 Sam 13:3.

nemesis David as "very cunning," and Prov 15:5 where one who heeds the admonition of his parent is characterized as "prudent."

The woman of Gen 3 demonstrates the shrewd or skillful aspect of her wise character in her engagement with the crafty serpent. Although both the man and the woman are present, the serpent speaks directly to the woman. The most subtle or crafty of all the animals engages the woman as an equal. The subtle or crafty serpent does not engage the man. The man has no words and no actions during this skillful interchange. Perhaps the serpent is too crafty or skillful for the man and the interrogation is beyond his capabilities. The woman's ability to engage the one described as "more subtle" or crafty however, speaks to her equal craftiness.

Another indicator of the woman's skillfulness, craftiness, or dexterity is the way the woman treats YHWH's directive. The woman states, "but God said, 'you shall not eat of the fruit of the tree that is *in the middle of the garden, nor shall you touch it,* or you shall die'" (Gen 3:3). When challenged by the subtle serpent, the woman shrewdly modifies the original directive in at least three ways. First, she adds logistical specificity when she distinguishes the tree of the knowledge of good and evil as being in the middle of the garden. The original instruction found in Gen 2 identified the tree with no reference to its location. In the original command God states, "You may freely eat of every tree of the garden; but of the tree of the knowledge of good and evil you shall not eat, for in the day that you eat of it you shall die" (Gen 2:16–17). Secondly, she inserts a prohibition regarding physical touch. The original directive did not include any information about touching the tree. Finally, the woman increases the chronological distance between the pairs' actions and its death-dealing consequences. The original directive simply states that "in the day" that they eat, they shall die. Until this point in the story, no other character has extended the dialogue in this explanatory manner.

Interestingly, the crafty serpent, who seems well versed in the elements of the prohibition, does not challenge the woman's interpretation of the directives. The serpent simply presses his point about death and provides rationale when he states, "you will not die . . . you will be like God" (Gen 3:4–5). I read this to mean that the serpent knew that the skillful woman would require more than a simple, "because I said so" to induce her to take action. I disagree with the writer of 1 John 2:16 who argues that the woman ate because of physical cravings, an aesthetic attraction to the fruit, and a pride of life. The serpent knew that the Godly creation was simply too astute, too subtle, too clever, too skillful, too shrewd, and too crafty to naively eat without a good reason; without having *seen* something worth going after in the fruit.

Sight is the second marker of a wise individual, and sight and seeing are important elements of the character of the wise woman of Gen 3.
The serpent exploits her ability to see when it argues that her eyes will be
open when she eats the fruit. The serpent states, "you will not die; for God
knows that when you eat of it your eyes will be opened, and you will be like
God." The serpent shrewdly mitigates the last element of the divine directive
(death) and moves swiftly to introduce the concept of God-like seeing. I
find it interesting that the serpent introduces this concept with the Hebrew
conjunction, kî (ki, "for" or "because"). In one way, the serpent positions
the God-like illumination as rationale for the prohibition, but in another
more subtle way the serpent dangles the illumination as literal, low-hanging
fruit. It is easy! Presented with such an obvious proposition, who would not
want to be like God? Any self-respecting creation of the Creator would eat!
The introduction of the illumination rationale is an important move by the
subtle serpent, but the crafty woman does not move on the serpent's suggestion. It is only after she sees for herself that she acts.

Only *after seeing* that the tree is good for food, and that it is a delight
to the eyes, and that the tree is to be desired to make one wise does the
woman eat (Gen 3:6). This portion of the text presents a tiered or sequential
act of seeing. In much the same way that many of the sayings of the wisdom
literature corpus are numerical and build upon each other,[12] the woman does
not simply eat because she sees. She eats because what she sees is beneficial,
pleasant, and efficacious. Conceivably, a less astute, skillful or crafty person
may have eaten simply at the suggestion of the serpent.[13] This wise woman
thoughtfully considers her options before acting. It is only *when* the woman
sees that the fruit is good, after she assesses the situation, only then does
she act. Further, she seems motivated by something grander than hunger,
desire, or pride.

Building upon the ancient Near Eastern examples, a wise person would
not only be skilled and knowledgeable, but would undoubtedly recognize
(or be able to *see*) objects for their usefulness. Importantly, they would go
after those things that they understand to be good. Going after what is good
is the third marker of a wise individual. The woman was intentional about
seeking and attaining (more) wisdom through the consumption of the fruit.
The woman's stated goal or motivation was to be wise like God and she
believes she will attain this goal by consuming the fruit.[14] In this respect, the

12. See Prov 6:16 for an example of numerical sayings in the Wisdom corpus of the
Hebrew Bible.

13. In Gen 3:6 the man eats the fruit without question.

14. Knowing good from evil may be considered a God-like quality and I acknowledge this potential epistemological aspect of wisdom. Though it illumines another

wise woman is similar to the wise Gilgamesh who journeyed to the home of Utnapishtim—the one who was granted immortality. She also shares qualities with the wise Adapa who approached Anu in heaven and declined what he thought was the "food of death and waters of death," seemingly in an effort to secure long life. In each of these examples, the wise characters are intentional about seeking and going after that which they understood to be prudent.

Like other wise characters, the woman goes after wisdom. The woman identifies that which is beneficial for life and living and acts upon her assessment; she goes after that which she understands will make her wise like the gods. Furthermore, the woman unselfishly ensures others benefit from her assessment when she gives some to the man who is with her. Although the act of eating from the tree has been treated derogatorily by many interpreters, the women of Gen 3 is motivated to eat in order to be like the gods and to sustain her life and the life of her companion. The fruit *is* good for food and its consumption does not result in death.

The ancient Near Eastern and Israelite sapiential corpora mark wise individuals as skilled, crafty and shrewd, able to see, and focused on going after that which is good. Atrahasis is skillful, Gilgamesh sees, and Adapa goes after what he believes is good. Likewise, the woman of Gen 3 is crafty, can see, and goes after wisdom or that which is good. In addition to meeting the general criteria for wise persons and wisdom literature, the woman and her story as found in Gen 3 also align with my definition of wisdom. I consider the woman wise because, as her words and actions demonstrate, her *telos* or ultimate concern was the attainment of a life well-lived and rewarded by the Divine. Despite this, she and her story have not been included in the traditional list of wise characters. Based upon her crafty or skillful actions, her sight and her intentionality in going after wisdom, the woman of Gen 3 should be given her rightful place among the other characters lauded for their wisdom and her story should be chronicled within a more broadly defined list of wisdom literature.

Not only does the woman of Gen 3 fit the characteristics of a wise individual, she can be understood as possessing the characteristics of a wise individual in a positive, affirming, and empowering way. The story of this woman can be read in such a way that those heretofore relegated to the margins of wisdom and wisdom literature because of their gender (and perhaps their race, class, or sexual orientation) might find themselves closer to the center of the text. To that end, I place the woman of Gen 3 in conversation

---

aspect of the wisdom of the woman of Gen 3, for brevity, I have chosen not to explore this particular aspect of wisdom in this essay.

with Sofia Butler, a wise and womanist[15] character from Alice Walker's novel, *The Color Purple*.

The Womanist Sofia Butler is Wise

Though generally overlooked by readers in favor of the more popular characters Celie or Shug, Alice Walker's womanist character, Sofia Butler, is wise. While no one calls Sofia Butler skillful or crafty, Harpo does call her smart, and her actions demonstrate her shrewd character. Sofia is industrious and strategic. She reveals her survival strategy to Celie when she says that in order to survive the harsh prison conditions she acted diminutive like Celie.[16] Later, readers learn that even Sofia's mother understood that her daughter had a mind of her own. When Sofia was in jail, Harpo asked her mother why she always had to have things done her own way. Sofia's mother said Sofia thought her way was as good as anybody else's. Plus, it was hers.[17]

Because sight and seeing are markers of wise individuals, it is not surprising that Sofia's assailants target the vision of the wise womanist Sofia. The Mayor's wife insulted Sofia by patting her children and marveling at how well-kept they appeared, seemingly questioning Sofia's material possessions, and asking if she wanted to be her maid. When the self-confident Sofia asserts her personhood by answering, "Hell no," the Mayor slaps her. This slap initiates a fight between Sofia and the police. When Celie visits Sofia in prison, she cannot believe she is alive. Celie describes her as so badly beaten that she is swollen, has a cracked skull and ribs, is discolored and has two little slits for eyes. Celie reports, "they blind her in one eye."[18] The police have literally beat Sofia's eyes shut. Although her physical vision is impaired, her psychological vision is clear.

Sofia bore the brunt of her audacious actions with a slap in the face by the Mayor, a beating by the police, a stay in prison courtesy of the local sheriff, and a prolonged stint watching the children of the woman whose

---

15. For treatments of *The Color Purple* as womanist literature, see Goda Baltrusaityte, *Breaking the Boundaries of Masculinity: Men and Women in Alice Walker's Novel The Color Purple* (Saarbrücken, Germany: Lambert Academic, 2012); Harold Bloom, *Alice Walker's The Color Purple*, Bloom's Modern Critical Interpretations (New York: Chelsea, 2008); Cynthia Crosser, "Critical Companion to Alice Walker: A Literary Reference to Her Life and Work," *Booklist* 15 (2011) 44. Rachel Lister, *Alice Walker's The Color Purple: A Reader's Guide to Essential Criticism* (Hampshire, UK: Palgrave Macmillan, 2010).

16. Walker, *The Color Purple* (Amazon Digital Services, 2011) 85.

17. Ibid., 215.

18. Ibid., 84.

insulting offer to become her maid resulted in the "hell no" that instigated the slap in the first place. Despite all this, Sofia triumphs in the end. Celie writes: "She reach for a biscuit and sort of root her behind deeper into her seat. One look at this big stout graying, wildeyed woman and you know not even to ast. Nothing. But just to clear this up neat and quick, she say, I'm home. Period."[19] Or as Oprah Winfrey's Sofia exclaimed, "Sofia's back!" The wise Sofia's blindness is temporary. At the triumphant dinner scene, Sofia is described as wildeyed.[20] When her eyes were once beaten shut to the point that she could not see in one eye, she now has evolved into one whose eyes are wide open. The journey of the wise womanist, Sofia involves a literal opening of the eyes. As a wise individual, Sofia has sight.

Finally, like the wise characters before, Sofia goes after that which she believes is good, and for Sofia dignity is what is good. In addition to her love of her family, Sofia is driven by the preservation of her dignity. She reveals her overarching concern in her conversations with Celie. Readers are familiar with Sofia's "all my life I had to fight" speech in which she claims her willingness to fight for her wellbeing. When she reflects upon her twelve-year prison sentence, Sofia also reveals the tension she lives. Celie writes: "Good behavior ain't enough for them, say Sofia. Nothing less than sliding on your belly with your tongue on they boots can even git they attention."[21] Sofia understands that fawning over others in order to win favor, groveling, and begging may be the only way to stay alive in prison. While maintaining her dignity is what is good for Sofia, she is forced to navigate a power system that seeks to strip her of her dignity. Sofia employs a paradoxical strategy in order to maintain her dignity. Sofia pretended to be passive, submissive, and docile in order to meet her goal of dignity.[22] She tells Celie that while she was in prison, she pretended to be her (Celie) in order to earn her freedom.

The writer of Gen 3 and Alice Walker tell the stories of two women who sought lives well lived. According to my definition, this material can be categorized as wisdom literature and these characters can be considered wise. Wise and womanist. Reading the woman of Genesis 3 as a womanist character can be positive, affirming, and empowering. In this essay I have offered such a reading of the woman of Gen 3 and argued for her inclusion among the cadre of wise characters in the Hebrew Bible narratives and her story's inclusion within the corpus of biblical Wisdom Literature. This reading disrupts the tendency to make the woman of Genesis 3 the origin

19. Ibid., 202.

20. Ibid., 197.

21. Ibid., 85.

22. Ibid.

of "sin" and invites those who read this text for theological, moral, or ethical grounding to find themselves among all of creation that is very good. This reading challenges the affinity of many in and outside the academy to relegate wisdom, its literature, and its characters to prescribed portions of the biblical canon and in so doing expand our critical inquiry beyond the bounds of what may be considered safe, or even good for us.

In *In Search of Our Mother's Gardens* Alice Walker offers a four-part definition of a "womanist." The first part of her definition includes, "wanting to know more and in greater depth than is considered 'good' for one." In many ways, that definition fits the character of the woman in Gen 3. The woman of Gen 3 demonstrates audaciously womanist tendencies in her willful quest for wisdom or knowledge, which is presented as transgressive or beyond the limits of what was "good" for a human being. The woman also displays courageously womanist characteristics in her commitments to the survival and wholeness of an entire people. To that end, my affirming reading of the female character aligns with the vision of Alice Walker's womanist, and should therefore serve as a womanist reading of this all-important foundational text of faith. My reading adds a new voice to the on-going womanist discourse that contributes to notions of moral fulfillment and human flourishing as it offers power and voice to those heretofore marginalized by familiar readings of the text. By connecting the woman to *The Color Purple* I graft her into a womanist tradition that includes renown womanist (and womanish) characters like Celie and Shug from Alice Walker's *The Color Purple*, Janie Crawford from Zora Neal Hurston's *Their Eyes Were Watching God*, and Frieda and Claudia from Toni Morrison's *The Bluest Eye*.

CHAPTER THIRTEEN

"Knowing More than is Good for One"

A Womanist Interrogation of the Matthean Great Commission[1]

MITZI J. SMITH

Introduction

The naming of Matt 28:19–20 as the Great Commission has had the impact of delimiting and orientating how readers should understand that passage and the entire gospel of Matthew.[2] This act of labeling has so constrained how we interpret that text that most readers find it difficult, if not impossible, to read it and Matthew through any other hermeneutical framework. Jesus (and God) is perceived chiefly as the one who sends his disciples to teach other nations. And teaching becomes the primary and essential goal of missions.[3] Matthew and Matthew's Jesus are interpreted pre-

---

1. Excerpted from *Teaching All Nations: Interrogating the Matthean Great Commission*, eds. by Mitzi J. Smith and Jayachitra Lalitha (Minneapolis: Fortress, 2014).

2. For similar final and/or summary commissions in other gospels, see Mark 16:14–18; Luke 24:44–49; John 20:19–23; cf. Didache 7:1.

3. For example, see Christopher J. H. Wright, *The Mission of God: Unlocking the Bible's Grand Narrative* (Downer's Grove, IL: InterVarsity, 2006); John Piper, *Let the Nations Be Glad!: The Supremacy of God in Missions* (Grand Rapids: Baker Academic, 2010); Francis M. Du Bois, *God Who Sends: A Fresh Quest for Biblical Mission* (Nashville: Broadman, 1983); Ross Hastings, *Missional God, Missional Church: Hope for Re-Evangelizing the West* (Downer's Grove, IL: InterVarsity, 2012); M. David D. Sills, *Reaching and Teaching: A Call to Great Commission Obedience* (Chicago: Moody, 2010); Adam Greenway and Chuck Lawless, *The Great Commission Resurgence: Fulfilling the Great Commission in Our Time* (Nashville: Broadman & Holman, 2010); W. Stephen Gunter and Elaine Robinson, eds., *Considering the Great Commission: Evangelism and Mission in the Wesleyan Spirit* (Nashville: Abingdon, 2005); Mike Barnett, ed., *Discovery*

dominantly through the lens of teaching; that is, Matthew's Jesus becomes the quintessential teacher. This results in the exaltation of teaching and the subordinating or rendering invisible any emphasis in Matthew on acts of social justice. And the type of teaching that is exalted as a result of the Great Commission nomenclature is that in which the student (paganized others) is the passive recipient of knowledge, and is seldom, if ever, treated as a producer or originator of legitimate and authoritative knowledge. The legitimized and authoritative disseminators of such missionizing knowledge have historically and traditionally been European missionaries and other approved agents in partnership with colonialism and neo-colonialism.[4]

In Professor Katie Cannon's article, "Cutting Edge: Christian Imperialism and the Transatlantic Slave Trade," she coins two womanist terms that signify how European missionaries employed the great commission together with other theological constructs with deleterious effect upon the Africans to whom the missionaries were sent to Christianize. The two terms are "missiologic of imminent parousia" and "theologic of racialized normativity."[5] The former phrase refers to the synchronization of the so-called Matthean great commission with the belief in the imminent return of Jesus, which served to legitimize the urgent conversion of Africans by any means necessary (including by torture, rape, perpetual slavery, and murder) to transform the "enemies of Christ" into the friends of Christ, the church, and the crown.[6] The latter term, "theologic of racialized normativity," signifies how European missionaries and imperial colonists claimed that God made black people naturally inferior and innately servile to whites. Thus, some missionaries indoctrinated Africans by imposing upon them the belief that they were obliged to serve Jesus Christ *and* their earthly mas-

---

the Mission of God: Best Missional Practices for the 21st Century (Downer's Grove, IL: Intervarsity, 2012); Jedidiah Coppenger, Retreat or Risk: A Call for a Great Commission Resurgence (Nashville: Broadman & Holman, 2010). Also, see Rohan Gideon's article in Teaching All Nations on the Edinburgh 2010 conference and its continued focus on the great commission.

4. Kwame Nkrumah, the first post-independence president of Ghana, coined the term "neo-colonialism." It refers to the practice of using capitalism, globalization, and cultural forces to control a country (usually former European colonies in Africa or Asia) in lieu of direct military or political control. Such control can be economic, cultural, or linguistic; by promoting one's own culture, language or media in the colony, corporations embedded in that culture can then make greater headway in opening the markets in those countries. Thus, neocolonialism would be the end result of relatively benign business interests leading to deleterious cultural effects.

5. Katie Cannon, "Cutting Edge: Christian Imperialism and the Transatlantic Slave Trade," Journal of Feminist Studies in Religion 24:1 (2008) 128.

6. Ibid., 128–30. According to Cannon this form of missionary activity started in Africa in the fifteenth century.

ters.[7] Many missionaries, in collusion with European colonizers, separated the physical unjust, inhumane treatment and oppression of Africans and slaves from the saving of their souls. It was more important for colonized Africans and enslaved blacks to submit to missionary teachings, to learn to recite Scriptures and creeds, and be added to the membership to expand the church's geographical presence as evidence of the successful propagation of the gospel among them and in foreign lands. Teaching and baptizing black souls trumped the liberating of black bodies from the shackles of their white oppressors. While oppressing black bodies, colonizers and missionaries sought to save black souls for the peace of mind of white bodies. Colonizers, missionaries, and slave owners (who were sometimes one in the same) ensured that Africans and enslaved blacks knew only enough to make them good slaves who remained loyal to their oppressors as unto Jesus. By keeping blacks docile and prohibiting them from learning to read and write and/or by controlling who could preach or teach them and the content of that teaching/knowledge, the slavocracy (the system of slavery) attempted to prevent blacks from constructing knowledge of their own. Nevertheless, some black people rejected colonizer-missionary knowledge and relied on their own ways of knowing.

The iconization of the missional preeminence of Matt 28:19–20 as the Great Commission, apparently in the nineteenth century, effectively provided the theological rationale and metanarrative for the prioritization of teaching and the subordination of social justice, permitting strict control of sacralized knowledge (secular knowledge christened as sacred truth).[8] While many missionaries and colonizers had generally privileged Matt 28:19–20 (and 24:14: "this good news of the kingdom will be proclaimed throughout the world, as a testimony to all the nations; and then the end will come," NRSV) scholars and missionaries would eventually extoll it as the magna Carta of missions and name it the Great Commission. And the nomenclature became putative, iconic, and universal knowledge.

Knowledge plays a significant role in the disempowerment (and empowerment) of oppressed peoples, particularly when it is inscribed in sacred and authoritative texts (i.e., the Bible, commentaries, and human bodies).[9] A critical epistemology assumes that knowledge is "value laden and shaped

7. Ibid., 130–32.

8. For a discussion of the religio-political processes of *sacralization* and *secularization* of biblical narratives see Cain Hope Felder, *Troubling Biblical Waters: Race, Class and Family* (Maryknoll: Orbis, 1989).

9. See Vincent Wimbush, ed., *African Americans and the Bible: Sacred Texts and Social Textures* (New York: Continuum, 2003). Wimbush describes black people's experience as texts to be read, the "reading of the *self* (not the text[s]!)" 29.

by historical, political, and social concerns stemming from conditions and positions of power based on race, gender, and socio-economics."[10] When knowledge is oppressive or used to oppress, new knowledge construction is essential for the transformation of individual consciousness and social institutions.[11] Womanists and others must become iconoclasts, breaking up, deconstructing oppressive iconic knowledge, but also constructing, resurrecting, retrieving, and affirming epistemologies that allow black women and other oppressed peoples to survive and thrive.

In this essay, I shall interrogate the so-called Matthean Great Commission (Matt 28:19–20) and its elevation as an iconic and universally putative, authoritative epistemological framework for understanding and implementing Christians missions. As a womanist iconoclast, I shall examine the Great Commission through a womanist epistemological lens critically engaging it as constructed, oppressive epistemic iconography. This womanist lens privileges and considers legitimate black women's experiences and ways of knowing or epistemologies. A womanist framework honors black women's concern for the survival and health of the entire community. First, I shall describe the womanist lens or framework for interrogating the Great Commission and for critically reading Matthew. Second, I shall discuss the prioritization and exaltation of the Great Commission by biblical commentators as iconic, authoritative, and putative knowledge. And finally I shall suggest other ways to know/read Matthew and Matthew's Jesus that shift from a characterization of Jesus as a paradigmatic teacher of passive recipient-paganized-other-nations to a focus on Jesus as God with us. In Jesus, as God with us, social justice and teaching do not strive for mastery over each other. But Jesus' practice of social justice and teaching organically constitute the incarnate, interactive presence of God with us.

The Womanist Lens: Knowing More than is Good for One

In her 1979 short story "Coming Apart," Alice Walker introduces the word "womanist" and describes a womanist as a "feminist, only more common." Walker expands this definition in her 1983 book *In Our Mothers' Gardens: Womanist Prose* as follows:

10. JoAnne Banks-Wallace, "Womanist Ways of Knowing: Theoretical Considerations for Research with African American Women (2000)" in *The Womanist Reader: The First Quarter Century of Womanist Thought*, ed. Layli Phillips (New York: Routledge, 2006) 317.

11. Patricia Hill Collins, *Black Feminist Thought: Knowledge, Consciousness, and the Politics of Empowerment* (New York: Routledge, 1991) 221.

Womanist is "from *womanish*. (Opp. of 'girlish,' i.e. frivolous, irresponsible, not serious.) A black feminist or feminist of color. From the black folk expression of mothers to female children, 'you acting womanish,' i.e., like a woman. Usually referring to outrageous, audacious, courageous or *willful* behavior. Wanting to know more and in greater depth than is considered 'good' for one. Interested in grown up doings. Acting grown up. Being grown up. Interchangeable with another black folk expression: 'You trying to be grown.' Responsible. In charge. *Serious*."[12] (Walker's emphases)

Walker's definition of a womanist as "wanting to know more and in greater depth than is considered 'good' for one" was/is for black women more than a "*wanting*," but a necessity. It is a subversive, zoetic (life giving, saving, and sustaining) and sometimes necessarily belligerent knowing. It is about developing a mature way of knowing, being "grown," before one reaches the age or seasons of maturity, relative to certain experiences. Slavery, racism, sexism, classism, heterosexism, and other isms have necessitated that black women "know more and in greater depth than is consider 'good' for one'" and to teach their children, grandchildren, sisters, brothers, nephews, and nieces to do the same. Black women have had to teach their children to know that white mobs have and will lynch any black male, regardless of age, for looking at a white woman the wrong way or for too long; to know that white men who raped black women were seldom prosecuted, and therefore black women had to walk in numbers and their paths were limited; to know that black men falsely accused of raping white women were more likely to be prosecuted and executed;[13] and to know, among other things, that they will be more likely to be imprisoned and given longer sentences than their white counterparts for the same crimes, if their peers serve time at all.[14]

On the one hand, black mothers chide their children for acting womanish. Conversely, black mothers realize that black children living in a racialized, gendered, classicist world must know more than their white counterparts; and that black children must be prepared to live in a world where they will often be treated according to the color of their skin and not the content of their character. Children are impacted early by racial

12. Alice Walker, *In Search of Our Mothers' Gardens: Womanist Prose* (San Diego: Harcourt Brace, 1983) xi–xiii.

13. See Danielle L. McGuire, *At the Dark End of the Street: Black Women, Rape, and Resistance—A New History of the Civil Rights Movement from Rosa Parks to the Rise of Black Power* (New York: Vintage, 2010).

14. See Michelle Alexander, *The New Jim Crow: Mass Incarceration in the Age of Color Blindness* (New York: New Press, 2012).

attitudes in home, school, and the media. The subtle racial messages that Dr. Melanie Kellen of University of Maryland calls "implicit bias" are picked up by children very early. In CNN's 2011 study of race and children, Dr. Kellen found that African American parents prepare their children early to know about racial discrimination and a world of diversity.[15]

This need to prepare young black children and adults to know more than their racial counterparts has seen a renaissance among some blacks and has become a new reality for others with the recent not guilty verdict rendered by a nearly all-white female jury in the George Zimmerman (a white Latino) trial. Zimmerman murdered seventeen-year-old Trayvon Martin while he walked toward his father's home with a bag of skittles, a can of soda, black skin, and a hoodie. Zimmerman was protected under Florida's Stand your Ground law, despite the fact that Trayvon Martin had every reason to be where he was, was unarmed, and posed no imminent threat to Zimmerman who chose to pursue Martin contrary to the police dispatcher's request that he not do so. Also Marissa Alexander, who was serving a twenty-year mandatory sentence in Florida, now knows, and she and other black mothers must teach their children, that they cannot fire a warning shot into the air to keep a physically abusive husband at bay and expect the same protection that Zimmerman received from Florida's Stand your Ground law.

Acting "womanish" at home is not always acceptable, but acting "womanish" away from home is a necessity. This womanish consciousness is akin to that *double-consciousness* about which W. E. B. Du Bois wrote.[16] My mother, Flora Smith, schooled my brother Fred about what to do should he encounter the police. She had this talk with Fred twice; the second time was just before he entered the Marine Corps: if the "cops" stopped him, he should not "sass" (talk back) keep his hands out of his pockets, and do whatever the "cops" ask him to do. In the 1955 trial of the white men charged

15. See CNN report: http://www.youtube.com/watch?v=GPVNJgfDwpw&feature =youtube. CNN studied one hundred and forty-five children in six schools in three states, they found that white children were far more negative in their interpretations of a picture depicting a white and a black child. White children were more likely to think the white and black child in the picture were not friends and that their parents would not approve of such interracial friendships. Young black children were more positive when shown a picture depicting a black and a white child; only 38 percent of black children viewed the picture in a negative light.

16. W. E. B. Du Bois, *The Souls of Black Folk* (New York: Bantam, 1989) 3. This double-consciousness is described by Du Bois as "this sense of always looking at one's self through the eyes of others, of measuring one's shoulder by the tape of a world that looks on in amused contempt and pity. One ever feels his twoness—an American, a Negro; two souls, two thoughts, two unreconciled strivings; two warring ideals in one dark body, whose dogged strength alone keeps it from being torn asunder."

with brutally lynching her fourteen-year-old son, Emmett Till, in Money, Mississippi for allegedly whistling at a white woman, Mrs. Mamie Mobley Bradley testified that "she warned Till 'to be very careful' in Mississippi, cautioning him to 'say *yes sir* and *no, ma'am*' and 'to humble himself to the extent of getting down on his knees' to whites if necessary."[17] Mrs. Bradley had to prove that she had taught her son to "know his place" or to "know his race."[18]

Black women must know more, and in greater depth, in order to teach their children to know more than the status quo allows or makes known. Knowing more than is good for one signifies knowing beyond the boundaries set for one because of one's race, gender, sexual orientation, education, class, or age. It also connotes knowing beyond the intellectual, religious, and political boundaries established by the status quo, to transgress iconic epistemological borders designed to control, restrain, and subordinate. Womanism does not simply espouse knowing more for knowledge sake, but knowing more so that black women can survive and thrive; so that they can be outrageous, audacious, courageous, and willful in the face of oppression; and so that they can grow up, be responsible, and take charge of their lives instead of relinquishing their voices and allowing others, who do not necessarily have black people's best interest in mind, to determine what is "good" for them.

Persons, institutions, traditions, and resources that we consider authoritative and allow to dominate our lives determine our epistemological limits, to a large degree. And those limits are often expressed in terms of authorized vocabulary and nomenclature, acceptable modes of training, and prescribed individuals authorized to disseminate knowledge or to teach us, as well as what constitutes legitimate hermeneutical frameworks for interpreting authoritative knowledge. Dominant powers in our families, institutions, and communities decide how much we should know, when we should know it, and how we learn what we know. And too often those dominant powers and authorities only act in the interest of the dominant culture. It is up to the marginalized, dominated, or oppressed to critically assess and audaciously reject oppressive, biased epistemologies; to transcend the

17. Ruth R. Feldstein, "I Wanted the Whole World to See: Race, Gender, and Constructions of Motherhood in the Death of Emmett Till," in *Not June Cleaver: Women and Gender in Postwar America, 1945–1960*, ed. Joanne Jay Meyerowitz (Philadelphia: Temple University Press, 1994) 280. The justice system let his murderers go free. See also Stephen J. Whitfield, *A Death in the Delta: The Story of Emmett Till* (Baltimore: John Hopkins University Press) 1988.

18. Ibid.

boundaries of what we have been told "is good for" us to know; and to construct more liberating epistemologies.

A womanist who knows "more than is 'good' for one, and in greater depth" is aware that traditional interpretations of sacred texts and interpretive frameworks constructed by *malestream* biblical scholars[19] and religious specialists, including missionaries, primarily serve the self-interests of men and the white majority. Black women and others have too often been the object of and borne the brunt of oppressive biblical interpretations and theologies that permit, justify, or ignore violence perpetrated against their bodies, against their souls. The naming and iconic elevation of Matt 28:19–20 as the Great Commission with its concomitant emphasis on teaching to the exclusion or subordination of social justice action has encouraged, supported, ignored, and sanctioned violence against black women and others. As womanist scholar Linda E. Thomas has argued, Matt 28:19–20 as the missio Dei has been about, and continues to be so among some Christians, telling "others that we have the keys to the kingdom" and others must get on board so that "we can teach 'them.'"[20] Religious or missional specialists, primarily European white males (and/or their Victorian wives) consecrated and entrusted with the task of teaching "pagans" have been considered the sole authoritative spiritual and intellectual producers and disseminators of religious truth. The truths or teachings of these missional and/or religious specialists have primarily consisted of creeds, rituals, and doctrines either detached from social justice concerns and/or indifferent to violence, such as slavery.[21]

The naming of one text as the Great Commission implies that other commissioning texts are less significant, not worthy of sustained hermeneutical attention, and/or are only to be engaged within the hermeneutical framework already created by the approved specialists, primarily

19. Mary O'Brien (*The Politics of Reproduction* [Boston: Routledge, 1985], 5) coined the term "malestream." It describes the type of sociology that concentrates on men, is mostly carried out by men, and then assumes that the findings can be applied to women as well. It is also a reminder of how completely our cultural discourse is influenced by patriarchal institutions and attitudes.

20. Linda E. Thomas, "Anthropology, Mission and the African Woman: A Womanist Approach," *Black Theology* 5:1 (2007) 13. Thomas prefers the Lukan version of the Great Commission and argues that when we engage in the *missio Dei* we can "forget our mission bag with Jesus in it," (ibid., 18).

21. John Chrysostom (*Homilies on the Gospel of Matthew,* Homily XC, Matt 27:11–14, *Ante-Nicene Fathers* [Peabody, MA: Hendrickson, 2004], 10:531) sums up Matt 28:18–19 as concerning doctrines (baptizing) and commandments (teaching). See also the other essays in *Teaching All Nations* written by Dave Gosse, Beatrice Okyere-Manu, and Mitzi J. Smith.

malestream. By naming Matt 28:19–20 as the Great Commission, some interpreters have hijacked some readers' ability to read Matthew in any other way than through that conceptualized iconic epistemological framework. Also, by putatively accepting the Great Commission as the iconic metanarrative (commonly held and controlling grand narrative)[22] for missions and for reading Matthew, some readers are conditioned to read Matthew with the presupposition or expectation of the (hyper/über-importance of teaching, specifically teaching doctrines and dogmas, and to understand Jesus as the consummate teacher, with whom they should self-identify in relation to others. Thus, readers are blinded or indifferent to the text's pervasive emphasis on incarnational justice and the integral relationship between incarnational justice and teaching. I disagree with David Bosch's statement that "Matthew's entire gospel can only be read and understood from the perspective of the final pericope [i.e., Matt 28:18–20]."[23] The conceptualization of Matt 28:19–20 as the Great Commission has been seared into many Christians' hearts and minds, treated as if written by the very finger of God, accepted by most malestream scholars, in commentary or in practice, as iconic tradition, and exhibited as the objective hermeneutical framework for reading Matthew.

The epistemological challenge for womanists to know more "than is 'good' for" her "and in greater depth," relative to black women's experience, requires that womanists expose, transgress, break down, and counter oppressive epistemologies as the subjective and political constructs that they are. This is not to say that womanist epistemologies are not subjective and political as well; we acknowledge this. But womanists must construct other more liberating ways of knowing, epistemologies, that prioritize the justice needs of black communities and other oppressed groups.

22. Jean-François Lyotard (*The Postmodern Condition. A Report on Knowledge* [Minneapolis: University of Minnesota Press, 1984]) coined the term "metanarrative." A metanarrative is a grand narrative that constitutes false appeal to universal, rational, and scientific criteria, which are actually very particular.

23. David J. Bosch, *Transforming Mission: Paradigm Shifts in Theology of Mission* (Maryknoll, NY: Orbis, 1991) 91. Bosch does articulate this differently earlier in his book, in my opinion, when he says (p. 57) that contemporary scholars agree that "Matthew 28:18–20 has to be interpreted *against the background of Matthew's gospel as a whole* and unless we keep this in mind we shall fail to understand it," and he argues that the language in that text is the "most Matthean in the entire gospel" (Bosch's emphasis).

The Hermeneutical Iconization of Matt 28:19–20
as the Great Commission

It is difficult to know the exact origin of the naming of Matt 28:19–20 as the Great Commission. According to Robbie Castleman, the term may have been coined in the seventeenth century by the Dutch missionary Justinian von Welz (1621–88) but James Hudson Taylor, the great missionary to China, may have popularized it two hundred years later in the nineteenth century.[24] It appears to be in the nineteenth century that the label surfaces in commentaries. Matthew Henry's eighteenth-century six-volume commentary on the Bible, which first appeared in 1706, but was revised after his death in the early to mid-nineteenth century does not name Matt 28:19–20 as the Great Commission.[25] But in the late nineteenth century, John Broadus, in his 1886 Commentary on Matthew (a little over twenty years after Lincoln signed the Emancipation Proclamation in 1863 legally freeing the slaves) asserts that in Matt 28:20a, "teaching them to observe all things whatsoever I have commanded you," we find the "great missionary idea."[26] In his commentary on v. 20b, Broadus refers to Matt 28:18–20 as the "Great Commission" where he states, "obedience to the Great Commission is based on [Jesus'] universal and complete authority. . . . And this applies, not merely to the apostles, but to the disciples of every period."[27] Thus, it appears that in the nineteenth century, the Great Commission as an iconic interpretive framework was born; every person subsequently deemed a disciple possessed the authority granted thereby; and no other commission was so highly valued. Some twenty-first-century commentators have gone so far as to call Matt 28:19–20 "Jesus' Great Commission,"[28] thereby sacralizing the hermeneutical nomenclature itself.

This iconic interpretive naming tradition continues in use by many scholars and Christians, if not the majority, in the twentieth and twenty-first centuries. Some commentators have identified the Great Commission as the distinguishing feature and the interpretive key for understanding Matthew. For example, Edward Blair (1960) called Matt 28:18–20 "the key passage of

24. Robbie F. Castleman, "The Last Word: The Great Commission: Ecclesiology," *Themelios* 32:3 (2007) 68.

25. Matthew Henry, "Matthew," in *Matthew Henry's Commentary on the Bible*, vol. 5 (Old Tappan, NJ: Revell, 1853).

26. John A. Broadus, *Commentary on the Gospel of Matthew*, ed. Alvah Hovey (Philadelphia: American Baptist Publication Society, 1886) 596.

27. Ibid., 596–97.

28. For example, Tim Stafford, "Go and Plant Churches for All Peoples," *Christianity Today*, September 2007, 69.

this Gospel."[29] Oscar S. Brooks (1981) argues that since the pericope stresses authority and teaching, themes found throughout the Gospel, it is "basic to the narrative framework of the entire Gospel."[30] Donald A. Hager (1994) asserts that it has "become the hallmark" of Matthew, that more than any other words, these verses "distill the outlook and various emphases of the Gospel."[31] H. Eugene Boring (*New International Bible Commentary*, 1995) gives Matt 28:16–20 the traditional title the Great Commission and asserts that before the resurrection the disciples had not been commissioned to teach; their teaching will consist of "all of Jesus' teaching contained in the Gospel."[32] Interestingly, even the editors of the *Jewish Annotated New Testament* (2011) are putatively, if not hermeneutically, tied to the nomenclature the Great Commission, asserting that the label derives from v. 19 where Jesus directs the disciples to go to "all nations."[33] But I contend that while the Greek adjective *pantes* ("all") is absolute and inclusive, it is not evaluative in the same sense as the Greek word *mega* ("great") is in Matthew, despite the expansive note it strikes (see discussion below). These and other commentators, including some feminist and liberation scholars, treat the naming of Matt 28:18–20 as the Great Commission as universal, objective, putative, and iconic knowledge.[34] And that knowledge circumscribes how one ought

29. Edward P. Blair, *Jesus in the Gospel of Matthew* (New York: Abingdon, 1960) 45.

30. Oscar S. Brooks, "Matthew xxviii 16–20 and the Design of the First Gospel," *Journal for the Study of the New Testament* 10 (1981) 2–18.

31. Donald A. Hagner, *Matthew 14–28*, gen ed. Bruce M. Metzger, David A. Hubbard and Glenn W. Barker (WBC: Dallas: Word, 1995) 33B:881. See also Douglas R. A. Hare, *Matthew*, ed. Paul J. Achtemeier, Interpretation (Louisville: Westminster John Knox, 1993) 333.

32. Boring, *The Gospel of Matthew*, 503, 504.

33. Gale, "The Gospel According to Matthew," 54, n. 28:16–20.

34. See Robert Jamieson, A. R. Fausset, and David Brown, "Matthew," in *Commentary on the Whole Bible* (Grand Rapids: Zondervan, 1961); Homer Kent, Jr., "Matthew," in *The Wycliffe Bible Commentary*, ed. Charles F. Pfeiffer and Everett F. Harrison (Chicago: Moody, 1962) 985; Ralph Earle, "Matthew," in *Beacon Bible Commentary* (Kansas City, MO: Beacon Hill, 1964) 254; Ralph Earle, "Matthew," in *The Wesleyan Bible Commentary*, gen. ed. Charles W. Carter (Peabody, MA: Hendrickson, 1986) 4:122; D. A. Carson, "Matthew," in *The Expositor's Bible Commentary*, gen. ed. Frank E. Gaebelein (Grand Rapids: Zondervan, 1984) 8:594; Douglas R. A. Hare, *Matthew*, ed. James Luther Mays, Interpretation (Louisville: Westminster John Knox, 1993) 333; M. Eugene Boring, "The Gospel of Matthew" in *The New Interpreters' Bible*, ed. Leander E. Keck (Nashville: Abingdon, 1995) 8:89–505, 503; Donald Senior, *Matthew*, ed. Victor Paul Furnish, ANTC (Nashville: Abingdon, 1998); Manlio Simonetti, ed., "Matthew 14–28," in *Ancient Christian Commentary on Scripture*, vol. 1 (Downer's Grove, IL: InterVarsity, 2001); Aaron A. Gale, Notes and Annotations for "The Gospel According to Matthew," in *The Jewish Annotated New Testament, New Revised Standard Version*, ed. Amy-Jill Levine and Marc Zvi Brettler (New York: Oxford, 2011); Amy-Jill Levine, "Gospel of

to read Matthew. As Vincent Wimbush argues, the commentary as a genre "necessarily forces a certain delimitation"; it forces the interpreter to begin at a place other than "his or her own time . . . or with his or her own world situation."[35]

A few commentators have, to varying degrees, broken with this iconic interpretive tradition. W. F. Albright and C. S. Mann (*Anchor Bible*, 1971) call Matt 28:16–20 "Jesus' Final Commission."[36] This interpretive titular break could be because the *Anchor Bible* series claims to not "reflect any particular theological doctrine."[37] Albright and Mann note that of the other three Gospels, only Matthew "has anything that can properly be called an ending."[38] Matthew's "final commission" or ending may in fact be a summary or synopsis of what is made explicit in the text, according to Albright and Mann.[39] Albright and Mann assert that Jesus commanded his disciples to heal and proclaim during his ministry, but now that it is over he commands them to *teach*[40] (emphasis mine). While Albright and Mann dropped the iconic label, they continue the interpretive practice of subordinating healing and proclamation, to teaching.

Like Albright and Mann, Daniel J. Harrington (*Sacra Pagina*, 1991) sees Matt 28:16–20 as a summary for Matthew, and he argues that Jesus is "the teacher par excellence," sending his disciples to continue "his teaching mission."[41] Thus Harrington also reiterates and exalts Jesus as the paradigmatic teacher in Matthew, encouraging readers to read the entire Gospel through that lens. I propose that this epistemological and hermeneutical practice obfuscates the holistic and incarnational justice ministry of Jesus to which he called and calls his disciples. In Matthew, teaching is embodied;

Matthew," in *Women's Bible Commentary: Twentieth Anniversary Edition*, revised and updated, third edition, ed. Carol A. Newsom, Sharon H. Ringe, and Jacqueline E. Lapsey (Louisville: Westminster John Knox, 2012) 477.

35. Vincent L. Wimbush, "'We Will Make Our Own Future Text': An Alternate Orientation *to* Interpretation," in *True to Our Native Land: An African American New Testament Commentary* (Minneapolis: Fortress, 2007) 43–53, 44.

36. W. F. Albright and C. S. Mann, *Matthew*, ed. William F. Albright and David Noel Freedman (Garden City, NY: Doubleday, 1971) 361.

37. Albright and Mann, *Matthew*, introduction.

38. Ibid., 361. Luke seems to continue in the book of Acts; John (chapter 21) and Mark (chapter 16) have more than one ending.

39. Ibid., 362.

40. Ibid., 363.

41. Daniel J. Harrington, S.J., *The Gospel of Matthew*, ed. Daniel J. Harrington, Sacra Pagina 1 (Collegeville, MN: Liturgical, 1991) 416. See also Donald Senior, *Matthew*, 349.

it is God-with-us teaching. Similarly, Bosch argues that Jesus' teaching in Matthew combines words and deeds.[42]

Donald Senior (*Annotated New Testament Commentary*, 1998) calls Matt 28–16:20 "the Finale." Nowhere in Senior's notes does he use the phrase *the great* commission. In fact, Senior calls vv. 19–20 a "new commission" that fulfills Jesus' words at 8:11–12 where he states that many will come from the east and west to eat with Abraham, Isaac, and Jacob in the kingdom of heaven.[43] Thus, the dropping of the iconic title allows senior to read Matthew somewhat differently.

Ulrich Luz (Hermeneia, 2005) intentionally breaks with the iconic tradition of labeling Matt 28:16–20 as the Great Commission. He provides the interpretative label, *The Commission of the Lord of the World for All Nations*.[44] Ulrich gives a brief interpretive history of those verses. He asserts that the famous Baptist missionary William Carey and his 1792 publication *An Enquiry into the Obligations of Christians to Use Means for the Conversions of Heathens* is responsible for making Matt 28:19 the "Magna Carta of mission."[45] Luz writes the following:

> Through Carey 28:19a became "*the* mission command" that influenced the church and evangelical missionary societies of the nineteenth and twentieth centuries that grew out of the revival movements. I cite as an example the Dutch Calvinist Abraham Kuyper. For him, as for many, 28:19a is an absolute *command*. He understood mission as issuing from God's sovereignty rather than from God's love and correspondingly as "obedience to God's command," "not an invitation, but a charge, an order."[46] (emphasis Luz's)

In the latter part of the nineteenth century, according to Luz, Gustav Warneck, the father of modern Protestant mission scholarship, reiterated the idea of Matt 28:19 as the "charter of missions." Warneck articulated missions as primarily the task of making disciples, "Christianizing" non-Christian nations or of compelling people to submit to Jesus as their teacher and savior, as Luz puts it. Warneck's perception of mission became foundational

---

42. Bosch, *Transforming Mission*, 66–70.

43. Senior, *Matthew*, 347.

44. Luz, *Matthew 21–28*, 614. According to Luz, Matt 28:18b–20 is a "'logion of the Lord' that Matthew composed." He argues that since commissioning narratives have no fixed pattern that would enable Matthew to duplicate it, the form is uniquely Matthean. Verbal agreements with Dan 7:13–14 (LXX) demonstrate familiarity with the passage.

45. Ibid., 627.

46. Ibid.

for the Catholic understanding of missions with the subordination of papal and episcopal succession to Jesus' mission, as articulated in Matt 28:19.[47] In fact, Warneck argues that the Reformation raised the consciousness of the church with regard to "mission-preaching," but he criticizes Martin Luther for not taking the Great Commission seriously. Thus, Warneck asserts that "the great reformer's view of the missionary task of the church was essentially defective," having been distorted by his eschatology.[48] Further, Warneck wrote: "With all earnestness he urges the preaching of the gospel, and longs for a free course for it. But nowhere does Luther indicate the heathen as the object of evangelistic work."[49] And so also were John Calvin's missional views defective because he and his co-laborers, according to Warneck, failed to focus on "the mission to the heathen world" as required by the "missionary commission" that states "make all nations my disciples."[50] Warneck wrote that "inside of Christendom [Calvin] missionarized [sic] with demonstration of the Spirit and of power, but the mission to the heathen world had no interest for him or his fellow-labourers."[51]

Luz, by way of Ceslas Spicq, provides the Catholic view of missions that Jesus authorizes his apostles to teach through the power he received from his Father. Further quoting Spicq, Luz writes, "this authority is unlimited. The hierarchy has the right to promulgate the doctrine and the precepts of Christ."[52] This last statement is fundamental for understanding the impact of this "charter of missions." Jesus' authority is filtered through the institutional hierarchy of the church and so-called "secular" or "mundane powers," which control the hermeneutical construction and dissemination of Christian doctrines and precepts. Warneck argues that the missions command is to "make all nations my disciples"; this does not just mean people within all nations, but "the nations in their entirety."[53] He recognizes that it is impossible to Christianize nations without joining forces with "mundane power." While the missionaries are to dedicate themselves to the spiritual

47. Ibid.

48. Gustav Warneck, *Outline of the History of Protestant Missions from the Reformation to the Present Time: A Contribution to Recent Church-History*, trans. Thomas Smith (Edinburgh: James Gemmell, 1884) 17. Warneck argues that Luther believed that because the last day was at hand, there was no need or hope for converting heathens (ibid., 19).

49. Ibid., 12.

50. Ibid., 4, 18. Interestingly, Warneck cites initially cites Matt 24:14 and not Matt 28:29–20.

51. Ibid., 18.

52. Luz, *Matthew 21–28*, 627.

53. Warneck, *Outline of the History of Protestant*, 4.

component, God will orchestrate the cooperation of mundane power, for example, through the conversion of an emperor or local influential chiefs. Warneck claims that both the apostolic and medieval church periods ended with the Christianization of all nations within their territories.[54]

The focus was squarely placed on teaching others or so-called heathen or pagan nations in conjunction with mundane powers; this agenda has basically remained unchanged. However, Luz argues that beyond "evangelical movements" many are more cautious about using Matt 28:19 as "the missions command" that has served "for a kind of militarization of the practice of missions."[55] It has been a matter of building and expanding churches and not of establishing the kingdom of God in the world.[56]

Nation building and missions were bed fellows (and this continues to some extent in various ways) and the iconic interpretative tradition of Matt 28:19–20 as the Great Commission supported and justified this union. In fact, in the book of Matthew itself we find collusion between missions and nation building. As Musa Dube argues, Matthew "is one of those postcolonial texts written by the subjugated that nevertheless certifies imperialism."[57] But we might attribute this collusion we see to a double-consciousness often developed (consciously and unconsciously) as a survival mechanism among colonized peoples,[58] as discussed in Lynne Darden's essay in *Teaching All Nations*.[59] To name it is not to condone it, but to define and critique it.

While acknowledging Matthew's privileging or at least appeasing, at times, the Roman Empire, we can attempt to extrapolate from Matthew a more liberating, social-justice oriented reading of Matthew,[60] and particu-

54. Ibid., 6.

55. Luz, *Matthew 21–28*, 627.

56. Ibid.

57. Musa W. Dube, *Postcolonial Feminist Interpretation of the Bible* (St. Louis, MO: Chalice, 2000) 135.

58. In addition to being oppressed by the Roman Empire, Matthew's community may have been a Jewish minority who experienced rejection and perhaps persecution from Israel's majority.

59. Also interesting is Matthew's use of the master-slave relationship as an analogy (perhaps further evidence for the double-consciousness that Lynne Darden speaks about in her article in *Teaching All Nations*) for the relationship between the disciple and his teacher. In Matthew, the student does not exceed the teacher, as in John's Gospel (14:12) but it is sufficient "for the disciple to be like the teacher" (10:24–25; cf. 6:24).

60. Warren Carter ("Matthew and the Gentiles: Individual Conversion and/or Systemic Transformation," *Journal for the Study of the New Testament* 26:3 [2004] 216) argues that Matthew evaluates the Roman Empire and the Gentile world as a whole throughout his narrative and characterizes it as "contrary to God's just purposes" and that God's design as manifested in Jesus "will finally subordinate the Roman-dominated world to God's purposes."

larly of Matt 28:19–20, and also break with the naming of the text as the "Great Commission." I agree with Luz that contemporary churches and Christians "can no longer read this text uncritically as the Magna Carta of their missionary proclamation" for reasons external to the Scriptures, particularly given "our modern understanding of the relationship between missions, colonialism, and the export of Western civilization and of the more intensive contacts with non-Christian religions."[61] I propose, however, that for reasons *both* internal (Matthew's literary context) *and* external (historical context of missions, colonialism, and neo-colonialism) to the Scriptures, womanists, feminists, liberationists, and other justice-minded scholars and readers should no longer apply this nomenclature to or read Matt 28:19–20 uncritically as the "Magna Carta" of what it means to engage in missional work or as the iconic hermeneutical lens for reading Matthew.

The Womanist as an Iconoclast: Smashing the Icon and Knowing More

Another Way of Knowing Matt 28:19–20

The naming on Matt 28:19–20 as the Great Commission and the resultant exaltation and myopic focus on "teaching all nations" has supported and provided theological and/or scriptural justification for subordinating, eclipsing, and/or obliterating the centrality of social justice acts and incarnation theology in Matthew and for the Matthean Jesus. Matt 28:18-20 reads as follows:

> And when he came Jesus spoke to them saying. All authority [*exousia*] is given to me in heaven and on earth. Therefore, as you continue to go [*poreuthentes*] make disciples [*mathēteusate*] of all peoples [*ethnē*] baptizing [*baptizontes*] them in the name of the Father and of the Son and of the Holy Spirit, teaching [*diaskontes*] them to keep all that I have commanded you. And know that I am with you [*ego meth' humōn eimi*] all of your days [*pasas tas hēmeras*] until the consummation [*sunteleias*] of the age. (Translation mine)

The end of Matthew is not the first time Jesus bequeaths authority to his disciples. It is the substance of the discourse on the mount that evokes the comparison between Jesus' "teaching" and that of the scribes: "for he taught them as one having authority, and not as their scribes" (7:29). Jesus

61. Luz, *Matthew 21–28*, 628.

concludes his discourse on the mountain with a triple admonition about the importance of practice or manifesting the Father's will in one's life (7:15–20, 21–23, 24–27). When Jesus declares at Matt 28:19 that God has given him authority in heaven and in earth, it is an authority granted to Jesus based on a lived life and a dynamic, organic ministry characterized by congruity between his acts of justice and the words he spoke. And so the authority he gives to his disciples to "teach" refers to the continuation of an interplay, an intricate marriage of just practice and words, without which there is no participation in the kin*dom[62] of heaven (7:21). Otherwise, one has a teaching consisting of rhetoric only and detached from just acts.

The second time that Jesus' authority is mentioned is when Jesus demonstrates to his detractors that he has "authority on earth" by causing a paralyzed man to walk, and not merely by the rhetoric that his sins are forgiven. The just act of healing the man serves as confirmation of the authority of Jesus' speech act forgiving the man's sins; otherwise where is the visible proof? And for the crowds, what Jesus has done demonstrates that God has given "such authority to human beings" generally (9:2–8). This final phrase is absent from the other synoptic accounts (Mark 2:1–12; Luke 5:17–26). This is the kind of authority that Jesus bequeathed to his disciples, one that is manifested by just acts and concomitant words. At Matt 10:1–4 Jesus gave authority to his disciples to do what they witnessed Jesus do (an embodied pedagogy)—cast out unclean spirits and heal diseases and sicknesses or as Michael Joseph Brown puts it "to meet the needs of the 'crowds,' specifically the poor."[63]

God gave Jesus the authority to commission disciples to continue to replicate what they witnessed Jesus do: "all authority is given to me in heaven and in earth," (v. 18).[64] But we cannot understand those words without placing them in the context of Jesus' relationship to authority in Matthew. Unlike Herod, Jesus never used his authority to kill innocent children (2:16). When tempted to abuse the power and authority God had given him, Jesus refused to make bread (bread that would not grace the tables of the hungry) for the sake of proving his authority or power. Jesus refused to af-

62. "Kin*dom" is Ada Maria Isasi-Diaz's replacement for the traditional phrase "kingdom of God" in her article, "Solidarity: Love of Neighbor in the 1980s," in *Lift Every Voice: Constructing Christian Theologies from the Underside*, ed. Susan Brooks Thistlethwaite and Mary Potter Engel (San Francisco: Harper, 1990) 31–40, 303–5. The term signifies relationship as opposed to "kingdom," which connotes hierarchy.

63. Michael Joseph Brown, "The Gospel of Matthew," 99.

64. This phrase is possibly influenced by Dan 7:14, Exod 19–20, and 2 Chron 36:23. See Jane Schaberg, *The Father, Son and the Holy Spirit: The Triadic Phrase in Matthew* (Chico, CA: Scholars, 1982) for a discussion of the connection between Dan 7:14 and Matt 28:18–20.

firm that the authority and presence of God should be demonstrated by the ostentatious display of that power by the powerful (4:3–10). Jesus does not begin his ministry before he has shown that he will not abuse the power and authority God entrusted to him. Unlike many European missionaries, Jesus did not find it necessary to enter into alliances with mundane, evil, and (neo)colonizing powers, in order to own or make disciples of "all the kingdoms of the world and their splendor" or to hasten his mission (4:8–10). Musa Dube argues that when Jesus counsels his disciples to give to Caesar the things that belong to Caesar and to God the things that God requires (22:15–25) Matthew has presented the two on par "without suggesting any incompatibility."[65] I would argue differently that Matthew has demonstrated incompatibility by establishing a dichotomy between what belongs to God and what clearly bears the emperor's imprint. The disciples are to imitate Jesus' relationship to authority thereby maintaining continuity with Jesus' example.

Returning to Dube's contention that Matthew promotes an imperialist agenda of entering foreign lands, with Jesus' authority, and possessing them, Matthew certainly lends itself to such a reading; and missionaries have and continue to read Matt 28:19–20 accordingly. But it is also possible that the first-century apostles read the text differently, particularly given the reality of the Roman Empire lurking over their shoulders. Most of the apostles, according to the Acts of the Apostles, did not initially travel into foreign lands to preach/teach the gospel but stayed in Judea even after the persecution following Stephen's death (Acts 7:54–8:3) where they formed communities that took care of the least among them (2:44–45; 4:32–5:11).[66] Also, if we read the Greek phrase *panta ta ethnē* as *all peoples*,[67] rather than as "all nations" (28:19) then we might understand Matthew as attempting to transcend nationality, and not to subordinate all nations;[68] issues remain.

65. Dube, *Postcolonial Feminist Interpretation*, 133.

66. Although the programmatic verse 1:8 in Acts sets the stage for geographic expansion of the gospel to the ends of the earth, the author does not tell us exactly how that will happen. And, indeed, it happens in a number of ways.

67. The following commentators translate *panta ta ethnē* as all peoples: Eduard Schweizer, *The Good News According to Matthew*, trans. David E. Green (Atlanta: John Knox, 1975) 527. Schweizer also does not label the passage as the great commission.

68. It is interesting to note that in Acts, Peter's first missional speech takes place among many different nationalities who have entered Jerusalem, and of course, later as a result of some apostles entering into foreign lands (i.e., the Apostle Paul and Thomas). Two stories are placed in relief in Acts: the Ethiopian Eunuch traveled to Jerusalem and on his return home the angel of the Lord orchestrates a meeting between the eunuch and Philip (8:26–40); Peter and Cornelius are brought together for Cornelius's conversion and baptism (10–11). Significantly, for modern missions into Africa, the pattern

Matthew's Jesus may also attempt to present an innocuous view of his disciples in light of the Roman Empire. The tendency of Matthew, as Dube demonstrates, to paint the Roman Empire in a more positive light than the Jewish leadership and Israel's faith[69] may constitute an attempt to placate the Roman Empire. Or again as Lynne Darden argues in *Teaching All Nations*, it may be, more specifically, a symptom of the double-consciousness that colonized peoples have had to construct for themselves—a contextual epistemological consciousness that impacts and governs one's mundane existence and survival.

In Matt 28:19–20 we also find a semantic and grammatical continuity expressed by the three verbal participles directed at the eleven disciples. The first verbal participle or action directed at the disciples (as objects of the participle) is translated by scholars not as a participle but as an imperative, "Go!" This is a translation of the Greek aorist passive nominative plural participle form of *poreuomai* (*poreuthentes*, "going"). There is good reason to translate the participle this way. However, it is also possible to translate that Greek participle differently, perhaps as a semantic and grammatical bridge evoking continuity between other commissions in Matthew and the final summary; as a participle that casts a shadow backward and forward. Understood this way, we would translate the participle as "as you continue to go, make disciples." The participle in relation to its immediate context and in relation to the larger context is one of continuity of movement. The disciples have already been commissioned to go; they will continue that commission, and it will become more expansive.

We find a grammatical construction similar to v. 19 at 2:8. At 2:8 Herod instructs the wise men to "Go and search diligently for the child; and when you have found him, bring me word so that I may also go and pay him homage" (NRSV). Here again, we have the aorist passive participle nominative plural of the Greek deponent verb *poreuomai* together with an aorist imperative verb. And again, both verbs are translated as imperatives by most translators. The participle may again function in Matthew as a referent to past action (i.e., the wise men were already searching for the baby Jesus

in Acts is for persons from the African content to travel and seek as subjects rather to wait passively for missionaries to transgress and possess their lands. However, unfortunately the pattern is for the two Africans (the Ethiopian eunuch and Apollo from North Africa) to be taught more (8:26–40; 18:24–28); but they maintain their dignity, agency, and culture. Of course Acts 1:8 set a course for the apostles to travel beyond Judea to Samaria and "toward the ends of the earth," but none of the twelve go the distance, at least not in the canonical gospels (see for example the apocryphal *Acts of Peter*). The Apostle Paul crosses over into Europe and travels to Rome, as a Roman citizen and to Spain (16:1–15; 28:14; Rom 15:14, 28).

69. Dube, *Postcolonial Feminist Interpretation*, 140.

by following his star, 2:2). The participle also constitutes a grammatical and semantic bridge between the journey, the going, they had already embarked upon and the present command to continue the journey, but with the added task to bring back word to Herod.

Similarly, when Jesus commissions the twelve disciples in chapter 10, we find the same grammatical construction with the present tense participle form of the deponent Greek verb *poreuomai* ("going") and the imperative verb *kerousette* ("proclaim") (10:7): "*As you go*, proclaim the good news," NRSV (emphasis mine). The words they will proclaim, "the kingdom of the heavens has drawn near," as they are going constitutes good news. But it is good news because it is connected with "going," and "going" points back to the commission to heal, resurrect the dead, cleanse from unclean spirits, perform exorcisms, and liberate the people (10:5–8). The news is good because it redresses the people's specific needs. (I will say more about this connection between words and acts below.)

Thus, the use of the aorist or present tense participle of the Greek verb *poreuomai* together with the imperative finite verb is not unusual in Matthew to express continuity and to connect the past, present, and future. And the final or summary commission at 28:19–20 is generally no different grammatically than other commissions in Matthew. On the other hand, when Jesus gives a command that is more narrowly construed and directed at an individual or fewer people, a one-time command, Matthew employs an imperative Greek verb translated "Go," usually *hupage* (8:4, 13, 32; 9:6; 18:15; 19:21; cf. 8:9) but sometimes the finite present middle imperative *poreuesthe* ("go!") (21:2).

The other participles in Matt 28:18–20 can definitely be understood as subordinate to the aorist active imperative Greek verb *mathēteusate* translated as "make disciples." Subordinating all participles to the one finite Greek verb in the sentence (*matheteusate*, make disciples) is not the only legitimate way to read the text. Discipling consists of baptizing and teaching, but not only of baptizing and teaching.[70] Some scholars express surprise that baptism is mentioned here,[71] but Matthew seems to mention baptism no less often than the other synoptics. Nevertheless, the teaching should be

---

70. Hagner (*Matthew 14–18*, 887) argues to make disciples in Matthew means foremost "to follow after righteousness as articulated" in Jesus' teachings, and I can agree if we understand righteousness as justice. See H. Kvalbein, "Go Therefore and Make Disciples: The Concept of Discipleship in the New Testament," *Themelios* 13 (1988) 48–53.

71. Luz (*Matthew 21–28*, 631–32) finds it significant that Matthew mentions baptism rather than circumcision since very little is said about baptism in the gospel, but it is important that they follow Jesus' example and submit to baptism and demonstrate such for others.

understood in a way congruous with the manner in which Jesus taught in Matthew. But teaching in Matthew has been diluted to reflect modern understandings of teaching and to support the traditional missionary agenda to teach doctrines. Teaching has come to reflect a colonial mindset and the drive to delimit and control the type of knowledge particular converts (i.e., slaves, Indians, Africans, Asians, women and children) received.

When Jesus commissions his disciples, their going is never limited to teaching, per se, but includes healing and other miracles that redress physical and spiritual needs and brokenness; although it seems that healing is not always accompanied by teaching (10:1–4). As Luz argues "the disciples' 'teaching' is also accompanied by their good deeds."[72] Also, "the content of teaching is described as 'keeping the commandments.' Thus at issue is an initiation into praxis."[73] But one cannot initiate into praxis if one does not already practice or embody what one proposes to teach. The evidence of the nearness of God's kin*dom is the powerful acts of justice Jesus performs, not simply the words Jesus spoke (12:22–32, 13:54–58; Mark 3:22–29, 6:1–6; Luke 11:14–23; also Luke 4:16–30). In fact, Herod thinks that Jesus is John the Baptist resurrected from the dead because of the powerful deeds (*hai dunameis*) he performs (14:1–12; Mark 6:14–29; Luke 9:7–9). John the Baptist was considered to be an Elijah type (17:11–13) known also for his miraculous deeds. And Jesus was like John the Baptist about whom Jesus said there was no greater human being born (11:11).

The Great, Greater, and Greatest in Matthew

While most missionaries, scholars, and Christians have seen fit to continue this iconic tradition of naming Matt 28:19–20 as *the great commission*, the author of Matthew has not called his summary *great*. And Matthew is not reluctant to allude to or single out individuals, commandments, and activities as *great*, *greater*, or the *greatest*. Jesus' withdrawal to Galilee of the Gentiles, after John the Baptist's death, is considered a fulfillment of Isa 9:2: "a great light has dawned" upon a people who sat in darkness (4:12–16). In the context of Isaiah, the coming King will establish and maintain his kingdom "with justice and with righteousness (9:7)." The phrase *justice and righteousness* constitutes a hendiadys or two synonymous terms joined with a conjunction.[74] Doing justice is inherent in the royal office.[75] Matthew, of

---

72. Ibid., 634.

73. Ibid., 633.

74. José Miranda, *Marx and the Bible: A Critique of the Philosophy of Oppression* (Maryknoll: Orbis, 1997) 112.

75. Volkmar Herntrich, *krinō, TDNT,* 3:924.

course, introduces Jesus as coming through the royal lineage of David; he is the anointed, the son of David (1:17–18). As "a great light," we would expect that Jesus would be preoccupied with doing justice.

What is considered great in Matthew is only so in relation to doing justice towards the least. The people who hunger and thirst for justice (*dikaiosunē*) will receive justice (5:6). Those who are bullied and defamed, as were the prophets, will receive a great reward in the heavens (5:12); the kin*dom of the heavens has drawn near in Jesus. The kin*dom does not signify an otherworldly justice; the kin*dom of the heavens is imminent and present in Jesus. Jesus came to fulfill the law and the prophets, which he has summed up as loving God (the *greatest* commandment) and loving neighbor (the second *greatest* commandment) (5:17–20; 22:34–40; cf. 5:44). Anyone who does not love God or neighbor and teaches others to do likewise are least (*elachistos*) in the kin*dom. Notice that *doing* (or not *doing*) is preceded by the teaching; we are to teach the justice we do; and not teach the justice we fail to practice (5:19). So if one teaches doctrines, rules, and standards and yet does not exhibit love, that one or what that one does cannot be considered great. One cannot teach an individual about the golden rule without first practicing the golden rule, as former African slave Linda Brent, aka Harriet Jacobs, recognized.[76] Brent's American slave masters taught a gospel that separated teaching from doing justice, spiritual conversion from physical freedom—at least for the black slaves. Linda Brent, a proto-womanist, knew "more than was 'good for her and in greater depth"; she understood what the status quo would rather she did not know. Brent acted *womanish* when she rejected and wrote about the hypocrisy, the dissonance or disconnect between what her slave mistress taught her and how she treated her. Linda thought that her mother's service as a faithful slave to the mistress would guarantee that her mistress would free Linda by legal will upon the mistress's death. Instead, the mistress bequeathed Linda to the mistress's five-year-old niece. This is Brent's response to the injustice within the atrocity of slavery:

> So vanished our hopes. My mistress had taught me the precepts of God's Word: "Thou shalt love thy neighbor as thyself." "Whatsoever ye would that men should do unto you, do ye even so unto them." But I was her slave, and I suppose *she did not recognize me as her neighbor*. I would give much to blot out from my memory that *one great wrong*. As a child, I loved my mistress; and, looking back on the happy days I spent with her, I try to

76. For more on Linda Brent's (aka Harriet Jacobs) use of Scripture, see Emerson B. Powery, "'Rise up, ye Women': Harriet Jacobs and the Bible," *Postscripts* 5:2 (2009) 171–84.

think with less bitterness of *this act of injustice*. While I was with her, she taught me to read and spell; and for this privilege, which so rarely falls to the lot of a slave, I bless her memory.[77]

Linda Brent recognized that even as her mistress taught her to love her neighbor, her mistress did not consider Brent as her neighbor. Knowing the difference between rhetoric and practice, knowing when good doctrinal teaching obfuscated and/or became a substitute for just practice meant that Linda was not naïve about the injustice and hypocrisy of those who held power over her and about the inherent relationship between just action and right teaching. *Just teaching is not just until it is incarnate as just practice.* And Brent's knowing meant that she held her mistress and herself to a greater accountability. Brent's womanish ways of knowing, her womanist epistemology, compelled her to act courageously and audaciously to name her mistress's duplicity and define for herself the relationship between doctrine or teaching and just practice. Linda Brent's mistress propagated the royal law as dogma or doctrine to be taught and not as a mandate for how to live, to be embodied in relation with others.

The least (*elachistos*) who fail to love God and neighbor are not the same as the kin*dom least (*mikroteros*)[78] who are more significant (*meizōn*) than the greatest man, John the Baptist, born to a woman (11:11). Jesus considers himself, as God with us, to be greater than rites, traditions, and laws; mercy and compassion for human beings, which he embodies, is to be valued above sacrifices and ritual (12:1-7; cf. 12:38-42).[79] While sacrifices constitute symbolic rituals, mercy has to do with just and empathetic engagement with people (and creation). Matthew continually demonstrates, with concrete examples, how compassion should trump a strict, inhumane observance of ritual and doctrine, even with regard to cattle (12:9-14; Mark 3:1-6; Luke 6:6-11).

The Canaanite woman would certainly qualify as least among the least, and yet the Matthean Jesus acknowledges and concedes to the Canaanite woman's great faith (*megalas pistis*) a complement missing from Mark's version of the story (15:21-28; Mark 7:24-30). Jesus does not require that the

77. Linda Brent, "In Incidents in the Life of a Slave Girl" in *The Classic Slave Narratives*, ed. Henry Louis Gates, Jr. (New York: Penguin, 1987) 344 (emphasis mine).

78. Although, Matthew seems to use the two Greeks words translated least, *elachistos* and *mikroteros*, interchangeably.

79. The Matthean Jesus' statement about mercy being preferred above sacrifice, as well as Jesus' explicit and direct indictment of the priests for breaking the Sabbath are absent from both Mark (2:23-27) and Luke (6:1-5). Matthew quotes Hosea 6:6, God requires mercy and not sacrifice, in the context of feeding his hungry disciples (12:1-7) and in the context of the criticism that he eats with "tax collectors and sinners" (9:9-12).

Canaanite woman submit to baptism or become Jewish; in fact, she seems to school, or at least convict, Jesus with her persistence and her audacious words, even as she humbles herself for the sake of her child, willing to assume the role of a dog to retrieve the *crumbs* for her sick child. Significantly, the greatest (*meizōn*) in the kin*dom are those who humble themselves like a child (18:1–5). Michael Joseph Brown asserts that to become like a child means to "renounce their privileges" and to "make themselves some of the most vulnerable people in society."[80] The Canaanite woman exceeds the "requirement" for kin*dom membership. And Jesus as God with us is not above being *taught* or challenged by a Canaanite woman. Jesus' practice of responding to questions with questions, and of acknowledging the opposition to and the production of knowledge by people like the Canaanite woman (15:21–28; cf. Mark 7:24–30) demonstrates that Jesus did not practice a pedagogy in which his disciples, the crowds, or those who sought him were passive recipients of rhetoric.

Conversely, the sons of Zebedee presume that they can be made great (*mega*) in the kin*dom by obtaining seats on Jesus' right and left (20:20–28). Not only does Jesus not possess the authority to grant such a request (it is antithetical to what constitutes authority in Matthew) but greatness comes not from position, but from ministry (*diakonos*); greatness is inherently service-oriented (20:20–28) having more to do with just practice than with empty, disembodied rhetoric.

The Matthean Jesus addressed the dissonance between teaching and practice when he saw that certain scribes and Pharisees taught one thing but practiced another (23:1–36; Mark 12:37–39; Luke 11:39–41, 46–51; 20:45–46). And in response to this dissonance, Jesus reiterated what he told the sons of Zebedee that the greatest (*meizōn*) among them will be the one who engages in a ministry (*diakonos*) of justice (*kristis*) mercy, and faith (23:11, 23). The kin*dom of God will consist of people from every nation who practice justice among/for the least (*elachistoi*) (25:31–46) and who do not consider themselves to be just simply because they mention or preach the name of Jesus wherever they go. The least are the hungry, thirsty, strangers, resident aliens, naked, impoverished, sick, and oppressed. And it is in doing justice to and for the least, that the kin*dom is nearest, takes on flesh or is embodied. It is as we see Jesus in the bodies of the least and respond with justice that we embody the justice of God's kin*dom. By imitating Jesus, we become God-with-us disciples and make God-with-us disciples.

80. Michael Joseph Brown, "The Gospel of Matthew," 108.

God with Us as the Justice of God

Matthew's Jesus is first named Immanuel, which is translated "God with us" (*meth' hēmōn ho theos*) (1:23).[81] Matthew concludes with Jesus' promise to be present with (*egō meth' humōn eimi*) his disciples until the end (28:20).[82] Andries van Aarde argues that Jesus, as God with us, is the viewpoint character in Matthew, and as the viewpoint character he manifests the narrator's ideological perspective, which is also the dominant perspective.[83] The ideological perspective is integrally connected with the interpersonal (the level at which Jesus interacts with others).[84] Jesus as God with us means that God can be experienced (conceived of, spoken about, imitated, or obeyed) concretely anew because of Jesus' flesh and blood presence.[85] This God-with-us experience evokes womanism's insistence on the interdependence of experience, consciousness, and action. As JoAnn Banks-Wallace asserts "the interdependence of thought and action allows for the possibility that changes in thinking will be accompanied by changes in actions and that altered experiences may be a catalyst for a changed consciousness."[86]

This designation of Jesus as Immanuel or God with us, derives from First Isaiah (7:14; 8:8, 10) where the prophet's child is born and named as a sign from God for King Ahaz (7:10–12). Matthew quotes the prophet Isaiah more than any other prophet for a total of ten times, and five of those occurrences are distinctive to Matthew.[87] But Matthew also draws from Isaiah

81. See Barbara E. Reid, "Which God is with Us?" *Interpretation* 64 (2010) 380–89 for a discussion of the tension between the image of a gracious God who is with us in Jesus and the image of God as a harsh punisher of those who do evil in the parables in Matthew. See also Barbara E. Reid, "Violent Endings in Matthew's Parables and Christian Nonviolence," *Catholic Biblical Quarterly* 66:2 (2004) 237–55.

82. Andries van Aarde (*God-with-Us: The Dominant Perspective in Matthew's Story and Other Essays*, Hervormde Teleogiese Studies Supplement 5 [Pretoria: 1994], 34–43, 3) argues that this motif of presence occurs as well in the middle of Matthew at 18:20 where Jesus asserts that where two or three gather in his name he will be among them.

83. Ibid., 34–35.

84. See Brian K. Blount, *Cultural Interpretation. Reorienting New Testament Criticism* (Minneapolis: Fortress, 1995) 11.

85. See JoAnne Marie Terrell, *Power in the Blood? The Cross in the African American Experience* (Maryknoll, NY; Orbis, 1998). Dr. Terrell argues that the crucifix is the greatest reminder of "God's *with-us-ness*," 125.

86. JoAnne Banks-Wallace, "Womanist Ways of Knowing: Theoretical Considerations for Research with African American Women (2000)" in *The Womanist Reader: The First Quarter Century of Womanist Thought*, ed. Layli Phillips (New York: Routledge, 2006) 316.

87. M. Eugene Boring, "The Gospel of Matthew," in *The New Interpreter's Bible*, ed. Leander E. Keck (Nashville: Abingdon, 1995) 151. As with other Gospels, Matthew

an emphasis on teaching that promotes and results in justice (Isa 1:10–17; 10:1–2) the synonymous relationship between justice and righteousness, the embodiment or fulfillment of justice/righteousness, and the emphasis on all nations receiving the teaching of God as justice (2:1–3). In Isaiah, the only way Judah can be redeemed is by justice and righteousness (1:27). When justice is established, all nations will seek to be taught God's ways so that they might also walk in justice (2:1–3); justice is first established before justice is sought or taught. Justice/righteousness exalts Yahweh, and by justice God demonstrates that he is holy (5:16–17; 9:7). As mentioned above, by doing justice God's people demonstrate greatness. In both Isaiah and Matthew righteousness and justice are at least organically interconnected (at most synonymous) (Isa 5:7, 16; 9:7; Matt 25:31–46). As in First Isaiah, when injustice abounds, the people need to know that God is with them and will usher in justice/righteousness.

From the beginning of the birth narratives justice as a character trait and as an ethical practice is valued or evoked, explicitly and implicitly. Matthew embeds the story of Jesus' birth, as Immanuel, God with us, within the historical and political framework of the Roman Empire and its control over Judah through Herod (chapter 2). Prior to the introduction of Herod, Matthew establishes for his readers the character of Joseph as a just (*dikaios*) man who is engaged to the pregnant young girl, Mary; and Joseph is not the father. Implicitly, the justice of God prevails in the wise men's decision not to report back to Herod upon finding the baby Jesus (2:12). Conversely, injustice is committed when Herod orders the murder of all children in and around Bethlehem that are two years old and under (2:16). Acts of justice and injustice are weaved, implicitly and explicitly, throughout the story, the narration of the story, and in the words and practices of Jesus.

The presence of God in Jesus ushers in the justice of God, and the justice of God is evidenced in those who engender justice. When Jesus is tempted by the devil in the wilderness (4:1–11) he chooses not to transgress the boundaries of his humanity (his incarnate God-with-us-ness) while he defies epistemological boundaries by knowing more and in greater depth than the devil would like for him to know: "A human being does not live by bread alone but by every word that proceeds from God's mouth" (4:4).[88] Knowing more is a divine trait here, so as not to commit an injustice, be the victim of injustice, or to be complicit with injustice. It is also an act of justice to act (or refuse to act in this case) contrary to the justice one knows.

---

cites Scripture from the Psalms most frequently.

88. van Aarde (*God-with-us*, 40) argues that in the temptation scene Jesus acts "from a conscious position of power, being *God-with-us*."

It is a refusal to be duplicitous, to lean clearly toward justice rather than injustice. It is also a womanist's necessity. In choosing not to transgress the boundaries of his humanity (trying to be God) Jesus engenders and embodies the justice of God in the wilderness and in his ministry (being like God).[89]

Jesus demonstrated his God-with-us-ness in his dealings with the crowds and some Jewish leaders and sects whom he encountered and who pursued him. Richard Beaton argues that 12:15–21 (including the embedded Isa 42:1–4 quotation) and its immediate context, demonstrate "a developed contradistinction between injustice and justice, namely, the Pharisees' concern for strict halakic observance and their concomitant unjust treatment of the people versus Jesus' own conceptualization of Torah observance and the justice" he engendered among the people.[90] Beaton notes how texts from Deutero-Isaiah's servant songs (Isa 53:4; 42:1–4) which focus on the justice of God and the unjust treatment of the servant, are quoted after Matthean summaries (8:14–17; 12:15–21).[91] In both 8:14–27 and 12:15–21, a summary of Jesus' healing and/or exorcism activities is said to fulfill a portion of the servant songs (Isa 53:4; 42:1–4). In fact, José Miranda notes that Matt 8:17 presents an alternative reading of Isa 53:4 contradicting the "customary interpretation" wherein the Servant takes our pains and sufferings upon himself. But, Miranda notes that in Matthew the Servant takes our pains and sufferings away;[92] Jesus fulfills Isa 53:4 by healing the people of their pains and sufferings, which are acts of justice. Jesus did not require that the crowds listen to his teaching as a pre-requisite for receiving healing and wholeness. His acts of justice constitute embodied, incarnational pedagogy. However, teachings and proclamation did at times accompany Jesus' healings and exorcisms (4:23–25).[93]

The Matthean Jesus taught that the poor/impoverished/broken in spirit will not be excluded from the kin*dom of heaven that has been brought near in Jesus (5:3) as God with us. The insertion of the words "in spirit" after

---

89. Ibid. van Aarde describes Jesus' God-with-us-ness as total obedience to the will of God.

90. Richard Beaton, "Messiah and Justice: A Key to Matthew's Use of Isaiah 42:1–4?," Journal for the Study of the New Testament 75 (1999) 6.

91. Ibid.

92. Miranda, Marx and the Bible, 129.

93. van Aarde (God-with-us, 36) speaks in terms of Jesus' "concrete proclamation," which is manifest in two inseparable ways, by actions (preaching, teaching, healing) and by attitude (love and compassion). This concretized proclamation is intended to liberate the people from the impact of the Jewish leaders' teaching and thus from Satan's temptations.

the word "poor" do not need to be understood as a spiritualizing of poverty. The experience of being trapped in poverty can break one's spirit so that one loses hope of ever changing one's impoverished existence. Conversely, a bankrupt spirit can lead to economic poverty. The fourth beatitude assures that those who hunger and thirst for justice (*dikaiosunē*) will be satisfied (5:6; also 5:10). It is no coincidence that the beatitudes are followed by two significant metaphors admonishing the crowds that they are "the salt of the earth" and the "light of the world" (5:13–14). This connects the promise of justice for the poor in spirit with the global responsibility to impact the world or to engender justice globally. No other synoptic Gospel makes this connection between justice for the poor in spirit and personal and/or corporate responsibility to the rest of the world (Mark 4:21; 9:50; Luke 8:16; 11:33; 14:34–35).

Also, in his discourse on the Mount (5–7) Jesus informed the crowds and his disciples that God cares that they are clothed and have food to eat; that if God clothes and feeds the birds, certainly God cares about human beings and their temporal needs (6:25–34; cf. 7:9–10). In other words, God cares about social justice; God cares that people are fed and clothed; that they do not go hungry or go without proper clothing. Therefore, the disciples can with confidence seek the kin*dom of God first, because justice is an inherent and organic goal of the kin*dom; the mandate does not create a dichotomy between temporal needs and the kin*dom. The gospel is lived and manifested in liberating, just acts (10:40–42; 11:2–6).

As the beloved son, Jesus will bring and proclaim justice (*krisis*) to the nations (12:18–21;[94] Isaiah 42:1–4[95]). It is only in Matthew's version of the commissioning of the twelve that "judgment" or the execution of justice is inserted in the phrase comparing the rejection of the gospel by the cities to which the disciples travel with the fate of Sodom and Gomorrah: "it will be more tolerable for the land of Sodom and Gomorrah on the day of justice [*krisis*] than for that town" (10:16, NRSV; cf. Luke 10:12). Matthew repeats it again but in the context of the failure of cities to respond to Jesus' powerful deeds (11:20–24). José Miranda argues that at 12:20 Matthew has "powerfully" reformulated Isa 42:4 as: "till he has led *mishpat* [justice] to victory,"

---

94. Carter ("Matthew and the Gentiles," 271) translates *krisin* at 12:18, 20 as justice for the nations.

95. Some OT scholars argue that the theme of justice is the key to understanding Isa 42:1–4, as well as the beginning chapters of Deutero-Isaiah. See M. C. Lind, "Monotheism, Power, and Justice: A Study of Isaiah 40–55," *Catholic Biblical Quarterly* 46 (1984) 432–46; D. Kendall, "The Use if Mishpat in Isaiah 59," *Zeitschrift für die Alttestamentliche Wissenschaft* 96 (1984) 391–405; H. Gossai, *Justice, Righteousness and the Social Critique of the Eighth-Century Prophets* (New York: Peter Lang, 1993).

and proceeds to use *mishpat* three more times to refer to a final judgment.[96] Miranda further argues that this reformulation and repetition obliges "us to think that according to Matthew the triumph of *mishpat* will be the Last Judgment."[97] Matthew sees in "Christ's works of justice [*mishpat*] on behalf of the poor and helpless" the "definitive realization of Judgment."[98]

In chapter 25 of Matthew, in the final judgment (execution of justice) God will distinguish between those who act justly toward the hungry, thirsty, imprisoned, and sick (not exhaustive categories) since Jesus considers such people to be the "least" among us; to treat them justly is the same as acting with justice toward Jesus (25:21–46). But those who consider themselves righteous/just and never engender justice, but merely *teach* about righteousness/justice will not comprise the kin*dom of heaven on earth or in heaven. In Matthew, as Alejandro Duarte has argued, "justice is fulfilled when the law, as interpreted by Jesus is fulfilled"[99] (i.e., in sum, treating others as we would like to be treated, 7:12; cf. 5:17–48). Significantly, Matthew's Jesus prefaces the royal law with the words "in everything"; Luke does not (7:12; Luke 6:31). The royal law of doing to others as one would have them do to us is a summation of God's instruction and commandments in the Torah and in the prophets. As Luz asserts, Matthew's Jesus embodied his message and thus his life was the model for his disciples and for readers, one that inspired and encouraged and who is worthy to be imitated.[100] Through and in Jesus, the presence of God becomes concrete and visible, and as such we are able to see how God would or should function on earth and in human relationships.[101]

Conclusion

God is not only or primarily a God who sends, a God of missions.[102] God is a God who is concretely present, intervening in the lives of the oppressed. And Jesus as God with us is chiefly concerned with justice. Oppressed peoples have experienced and need to know that God is a God who was

96. Miranda, *Marx and the Bible*, 129.

97. Ibid.

98. Ibid.

99. Alejandro Duarte, "Matthew," in *The Global Bible Commentary*, gen ed. Daniel Patte (Nashville: Abingdon, 2004) 350–360, 352.

100. Luz, *Matthew 21–28*, 639, 644.

101. Ibid., 644.

102. See Michael Barram, "The Bible, Mission, and Social Location: Toward a Missional Hermeneutic," *Interpretation* 61:1 (2007) 42–58.

present with them before the missionaries arrived and is present with them after the missionaries have left; that God is a God who authors, engenders, and embodies justice. The naming and iconization of Matt 28:19–20 as the Great Commission subordinates the characterization of Jesus in Matthew as God with us and continues the missional agenda of elevating the teaching of doctrines and subordinating social justice.

Additionally, this iconic nomenclature has blinded us to more liberating ways to read the gospel that demonstrate God's care and concern for the oppressed and marginalized. It matters how we read, because how we read impacts how we interact with one another. The execution of an embodied, incarnational pedagogy that privileges justice should flow from the just. The authority of an incarnational, embodied pedagogy rests with the just; those who allow the Spirit of God to transform them into the likeness of Jesus as God with us.

If we understand that God has imprinted his image, the *imago Dei*, on African and African American peoples as well as on any other peoples, then we can acknowledge that even, or especially, black bodies can testify to and/ or embody God's image and be God with us. Others can be visited and "missionized" by black women[103] and other peoples of color, by people with no power or authority, and by Haitian women who praise God from beneath the rubble of an earthquake. Thomas argues that a womanist approach to missions calls us to be "missionized"; to be present, with humility, "to listen to the testimony and to witness to the Spirit of God in action, while resisting the desire to proclaim, tell, or contest."[104] We must embody the justice of God so that our actions and words are in sync. We must be open to learning to be just from those who need justice; we must remain open to seeing God's presence in others, because in others God has also imprinted God's image and commissioned them to be God with us.

103. Thomas, "Anthropology, Mission and the African Woman," 13.

104. Ibid., 14.

CHAPTER FOURTEEN

Silenced Struggles for Survival

Finding Life in Death in the Book of Ruth

YOLANDA NORTON

Womanist hermeneutical analysis of any material compels the reader to
interrogate the ways in which race, class, and gender intersect in narrative. As a result, they force the reader to be attentive to concentric circles
of oppression. Traditional exegeses of the book of Ruth endorse concepts of
loyalty, faith, trust, and genuine love. The text masquerades as a treatise on
the inclusion of the other, instead the book seems to be more of a commentary on the assumed virtue of membership and participation in the Israelite
community. The plot implies that it is a worthy endeavor to sacrifice your
land, your people, your god, and even yourself for the supposed privilege
of participating in what the texts depicts as the most desirable community.

Most often popular interpretations of this novella[1] suggest Ruth's
blind, audacious faith exists in harmonious relationship with Naomi's wisdom and care for her daughter-in-law and Boaz's generosity and concern.
However, a womanist reading of Ruth exposes the assimilationist tendency
of the text while simultaneously highlighting the power, agency, and authority that Ruth takes in the narrative despite the embedded oppositional
forces at play. As such, it becomes necessary to examine what the words and
narrative moves of the text mean for women who live on the margins of
society. I propose that the book of Ruth was intended to serve the purposes
of normative power structures. In its original context this would have meant

---

1. A novella is a historical, episodic, fictional short story with an ideological purpose. For more see: Howard Campbell, Jr., *Ruth*, Anchor Bible Commentary, (Garden
City, NY: Doubleday, 1975) 3–6.

Israel; throughout the history of its reception the text has been used overtly and surreptitiously to enforce white, male norms to the detriment of black women in particular.

The book of Ruth proffers ideologies of "appropriate behavior" and exceptionalism. In response, the power of womanism is its resistance to an impulse that attempts to "explain away elements of biblical literature that modern sensibilities might find problematic or objectionable in order to produce a more congenial text."[2] Instead it exposes those realities and places them in tension with contemporary societal constructions that are relevant today. The power of Ruth's story is that while it is a paradigmatic representation of the hegemonic impulse to promote social accommodation and subservience on the part of the oppressed, the narrative also demonstrates the ways in which the marginalized take agency and save themselves.

It would not be difficult to engage in a debate about whether Ruth's character in this text is liberating or subjugating for black women. On the one hand it could be argued that she is a woman who forsakes her own people and tradition during a time of economic depravity for the sake of self-preservation. On the other hand it might be reasoned that in a difficult situation the character and fortitude that Ruth demonstrates exhibits the resilience and courage of her people. Either way the book of Ruth, despite its apparent simplicity, is a complicated narrative. The embedded ideological messages in the text leave contemporary readers to grapple with the dichotomies and social constructions that it promotes. Readers must simultaneously deal with the ways in which the plot is read in various contexts and what such readings reveal about the social dynamics at play in that setting. As such, it is necessary to deal with the messiness of the ethnic and gendered relationships that develop throughout this narrative.

It would be irresponsible to suggest that there is a direct correlation between Ruth's experience in the biblical narrative and the realities of the black female experience. There is clear dissidence between the social realities that permeate Ruth's world and those that are paramount both in the historical and contemporary every day, "real-lived"[3] happenings of black women. Most obvious among the differences is the ease with which Ruth is able to articulate and superficially transcend her social, political status as a Moabite in the text; that level of social transience is not available to diasporatic black women. For Israel and the biblical world, ethnicity was a

2. Bible and Culture Collective, *The Postmodern Bible* (New Haven, CT: Yale University Press, 1997) 227.

3. Stacey Floyd-Thomas and Anthony Pinn, eds., *Liberation Theologies in the United States: An Introduction* (New York: New York University Press, 2010) 50–51.

matter of social organization around particular norms.[4] While race is in fact a modern construct that centers on creating a particular social order, there are phenotypical signifiers that assist in the substantiation of the organization and formation of norms. The same would not have been true of ethnicity in the biblical world. Thus, it is more difficult if not impossible for black women to transcend their social location with vows of allegiance as they always maintain markers of their race that reify their oppression.

In the first six verses of the book of Ruth, "Moab" is mentioned five times. While on the surface the repetition seems like superfluous excess, in reality this literary move serves a purpose. The proper noun "Moab" literally translated from Hebrew means, "from the father." The ethnic signification of Moab points the reader back to Gen 19:30–38 where Lot's daughters intoxicate their father for the express purpose of having him impregnate them. The insidious actions of Lot's daughters establish a depiction of the Moabites as a perpetually sexual and perverse people. This theme is one that is perpetuated throughout the biblical narrative. In Numbers 25 while Israel dwells in Shittim, Israelite men engage in sexual relations with Moabite women. This sexual interaction precipitates Israelite sacrifice and devotion to foreign deities, particularly Baal of Peor. The Moabites are thus associated with the defilement of Israel and compromising their relationship with YHWH. In Deut 23:3 it is clear that "no . . . Moabite shall be admitted to the assembly of the Lord."[5]

The construction of the Moabite as enduringly carnal reflects the way in which black female embodiment persists in modern society. There is no place where the black female body is not constructed as both ontologically and biologically sexual and deviant. Such depictions are exacerbated in the United States, where images of black women as sexual objects are historical and persistent. From the coopting of our bodies for the sake of sexual relief of white men during slavery and the Jim Crow era to the proliferation of black women as the "side-piece" in popular culture, black women find it difficult to transcend external attempts to commodify our sexuality by depicting it as a compulsory aspect of our beings. Mary Douglass argued that "the social body constrains the way the physical body is perceived."[6] Understanding the black female body as transactional, in the way that Ruth's body becomes transactional based on her depiction throughout the text

4. F. W. Riggs, ed., *Ethnicity, Concepts, and Terms Used in Ethnicity Research*, International Conceptual Encyclopedia for the Social Sciences 1 (Honolulu: COCTA) 4.

5. All biblical citations are taken from the New Revised Standard version unless otherwise noted.

6. Mary Douglas, *Natural Symbols: Explorations in Cosmology*, 2nd ed. (London: Routledge, 1996) 73.

propagates, not only rhetorical constructions of black women as subhuman, but also manufactures the need for white saviors to facilitate the legitimacy of those who have been deemed aberrant.

The excessive mention of Moab in the first six verses of the book of Ruth is particularly significant when placed in contrast with certain Israelite names mentioned at the onset of the text—Elimelech ("God is king") Naomi ("sweetness") and Bethlehem ("house of bread")—all of which allude to a generative setting. Moab is the site of so much spiritual depravity and physical death and lack. Naomi and her family leave their homeland because there is lack in the land; they come to Moab full. Elimelech and Naomi were not the first characters in the Hebrew Bible to migrate in order to escape famine. In Gen 12 Abram and Sarai migrate to Egypt to avoid famine. In Gen 26 Isaac flees famine, travelling to Gerar after receiving the command from God to do so. Later, in Gen 43, Joseph's brothers find themselves in Egypt encountering the brother that they betrayed in an effort to stave off famine in Israel. Given the trajectory of individuals who have been able to escape scarcity, Naomi and Elimelech's ability to escape Bethlehem during its period of economic lack insinuates that they are people of means. However, when Naomi leaves over a decade later, she leaves having lost everything.

Creating a distinct dichotomy between Israel and Moab sets the stage for Ruth to be established as an exception to her people. The pinnacle of her distinction from her people comes in a liminal space between Moab and Bethlehem. In verse 8 Naomi tells her daughters to go back to their "mother's house," and Orpah complies with her mother-in-law's demand with some consternation; "but Ruth clung to her" (1:14). With Ruth's single act of defiance in v. 14 she establishes herself as contrary to all of the preconceived notions that a hearer/reader of this text might have about the Moabites. What follows next is Ruth's uncompromising articulation of loyalty and devotion not only to Naomi but also to YHWH and all of Israel. In Ruth's assimilationist articulation, she simultaneously disavows herself from any Moab allegiance and claims unwavering allegiance to everything Israel. The irony of the story is that Ruth never successfully achieves the status after which she so desperately seeks. In the narrative, Ruth's identity and presence is either interrogated or ignored. Either way, the characters of the text more often than not fail to show her genuine hospitality.

In 1:18 after Ruth conveys her intractable allegiance to Naomi, the author reveals that Naomi "said no more to her." Naomi seems unmoved by Ruth's steadfastness. Naomi's silence is more than deference to Ruth's assertion; her silence measured in conjunction with what follows can easily be read as bitterness and anger. There is no way to know the root of Naomi's resentment; it is possible that her emotions were motivated by the social liability Naomi knew she was going to face by bringing a foreign woman with her back to her people after she and her family had abandoned them years before. It is also possible that she felt entitled to Ruth's deference and thus it held no value for her. The complexity of the interaction between Ruth and Naomi is indicative of how interpersonal relations impact and are influenced by larger social and political dynamics in ways that are emulated throughout the Hebrew Bible and in the modern world within the context of racial and ethnic exchanges.

Next, when Naomi and Ruth arrive in Bethlehem the author suggests that "the whole town was stirred because of them" (1:19); however the women's line of inquiry never seems to acknowledge Ruth's presence. Further, in Naomi's response to the women in 1:21 she communicates that the source of her bitterness is that the Lord has brought her back to Bethlehem empty. The emptiness that Naomi expresses seems contrary to her reality, especially given that she has Ruth with her. This perpetual ignoring of Ruth's presence and/or value carries the message of her insignificance and/or irrelevance to the Israelites.

As if in response to Naomi and the Israelite communities' failure to acknowledge her presence, chapter 2 begins with Ruth's bold pronouncement of initiative and agency, "Let me go to the field and glean among the ears of grain, behind someone in whose sight I might find favor" (2:3a). Each moment that follows in Ruth's journey through Bethlehem seems to be her quest for legitimacy in this society that refuses to accept or acknowledge her. In an attempt to provide additional depth to Ruth's character, to snatch her back from the hands of elite Israelite interests for the sake of marginalized women, it is fruitful to diverge from traditional depictions of Ruth as docile and innocent.

In contrast, Ruth's character must be examined as representative of a resilient trickster. The "trickster" is a biblical motif prevalent in the Hebrew Bible and black culture. The motif is based on the premise that all communities have "rites of passage" between the social roles within which dynamics of class/status, ethnicity, and gender are encompassed. These rites are meant to guide and safeguard the individual through the dangerous "liminal space" when he/she sheds a previous identity and takes up a new one with different responsibilities to the community. When the community is in a powerful, assured or secure situation, these periods of transition are brief and individuals are not allowed to linger in this fluid, indeterminate condition too long; they are ushered rather promptly into their new social roles where they are encouraged to discover their new identities. When a society is undergoing stress and confidence in the efficacy of traditional social hierarchy is waning, individuals occupy such liminal space for longer periods of time.

The community is unable to rely on its traditional wisdom-providers and so, in desperate and/or dangerous situations individuals are given freedom to explore options on their own, unencumbered by conventional structures. In these moments those who are experiencing marginalization are forced to find a new "wisdom" in order to ensure survival.[7]

In this narrative Naomi is ensconced in her grief. She, as the native of Judah, should have provided more wisdom and guidance for Ruth to ensure their survival. Naomi would have been more aware of the laws operative in that day. For example, levirate marriage laws would have required a goʾel ("redeemer") to beget a child for the deceased male to preserve the deceased's name and nahala ("inheritance"). The very connotation of this term, goʾel, suggests that redemption and healing are to occur—if only in terms of reclamation of societal status and property. The idea of the goʾel is to sustain the endogamous (marriage within the family or clan) system promulgated in biblical law; the goʾel's duty is to protect and sustain the mispaha (family). Understanding this system allows the reader space first to recognize that Naomi would have been aware of this system of redemption, and thus she could have negotiated the terms of this restoration upon her return to Bethlehem. Naomi's failure to do so triggers an impulse in Ruth for survival.

Similarly, African American women have no choice but to adopt a "trickster" posture in the midst of tenuous social constructs. In a world where black men are systemically removed from our communities and survival is predicated on participation in a majority, capitalist society, black women have no choice but to find ostensibly deferent but naturally subversive modes of navigating foreign spheres for the sake of their own survival.[8] Our subversive acquiescence is understood as necessary for the survival of our people and our ideals. The compulsion towards long-term endurance of our worldview correlates with the impulse embedded in Ruth's persistent modality.

While the Israelite author clearly sponsors the idea that Ruth continuously seeks inclusion in the community, there is something to be wretched away from the writer that promotes agency in her character. Womanist biblical hermeneutical analysis must engage Ruth's actions as a perfect expression of "traditional communalism."[9] Traditional communalism asserts that

7. Susan Niditch, *Underdogs and Tricksters: A Prelude to Biblical Folklore* (San Francisco, Harper and Row, 1987) 1–22.

8. See Robert D. Pelton, *The Trickster in West Africa: A Study of Mythic Irony and Sacred Delight* (Berkeley, CA: University of California Press, 1980).

9. Stacey Floyd-Thomas, *Mining the Motherlode: Methods in Womanist Ethics* (Cleveland, OH: Pilgrim, 2006) 9.

there is always intentionality in one's actions; the individual is concerned with her communal history, considering the gifts, talents, limitations, and understandings of all people around her and acting out of that awareness. From the perspective of this narrative, it suggests that ingrained in this Moabite woman's consciousness is a concern for her familial community. She does not have the luxury of caring only for herself.

Similarly, there is a dangerous tension that exists for black women in America; we, as Alice Walker suggests are "committed to survival and wholeness of entire people, male and female."[10] Black women have a history of demonstrating a wholehearted commitment to the survival of others. For African American women trauma is not only a function of individual moments, it is a byproduct of our identities as we are unable to claim for ourselves space that is not infringed upon by stereotypes of black women as mammies, Jezebels, angry black women, and a myriad of other pernicious tropes. African American women have inherited a legacy of visceral attacks against our person. Pamela Trotman Reid, in the foreword to *Psychotherapy with African American Women*, proposes that there is a mythical binary for African American women, "either good or bad. The 'good' African American woman is strong, maternal, hardworking, devoted to family, and quiet."[11] This characterization of the "good" African American woman is borne out of the significant burden they have carried in the history of the United States. In the nearly four hundred years since Africans arrived in the colony of Jamestown,[12] they have endured the hardship of being black in America, struggling to survive in a society that continues to implicitly and explicitly reject their identity, having to:

> come to terms with an impeccably hostile and exploitative environment. Black women played their part bearing and rearing children, often working to support them, educating them for their dual roles in white and black society. . . . Survival meant scrounging for food and curing sickness with home remedies, building schools and hospitals and orphanages out of pennies and nickels saved, scrubbing white people's floors and laundry

10. Alice Walker, *In Search of Our Mothers' Gardens: Womanist Prose* (San Diego: Harcourt Brace, 1983) xi.

11. Pamela Trotman Reid, "Foreword" in *Psychotherapy with African American Women: Innovations in Psychodynamic Perspectives and Practice*, eds. Leslie Jackson and Beverly Greene (New York: Guilford, 2000) xiii.

12. In 1619 the first slaves arrived in Jamestown. Approximately twenty Africans arrived. See James Rawley, *The Transatlantic Slave Trade: A History* (New York: Norton, 1981).

... it meant daily living in danger and hardship, swallowing anger and repressing rage.[13]

Consequently, African American women are socialized to assume and maintain an image of strength and resiliency at all costs. There is no margin of error; there is no room for mistakes. It is the women of the community who have raised children alone, often playing both mother and father, as African American men have been ripped from the home—first through slavery and now as a result of unjust laws and the prison industrial complex. African American women endure such hardships all the while projecting an image of imperviousness in order to steel themselves against attacks on their moral character as characterizations of them as "welfare moms" and mammies persist. While bearing substantial societal burden and projecting the image of the "Strong Black Woman," the black female body and being experience both violence and rejection. These images persist in media in the same way that they are handed down across generations. Beverly Wallace, in her article, "A Womanist Legacy of Trauma, Grief, and Loss," explains the ways in which African American girls are raised "to be independent and confident and are taught to survive and adapt."[14] Wallace describes this process as "armoring,"[15] insinuating that there are both intentional and inadvertent moves to raise young black girls to endure the social and political aggression that they will experience. The very definition of womanism—a major classification of black female identity and scholarship—is rooted in the ability of African American women to be audacious and courageous and to exhibit willful behavior.[16] The risk of such "armoring" is that it inherently conditions young black girls to internalize pain, suffering, and oppression, and accept the trauma of their life experiences as an inevitable phenomenon while simultaneously promoting beliefs that they are responsible for the well-being of the very people who consciously or inadvertently do them harm.

Alice Walker, in *In Search of Our Mothers' Gardens: A Womanist Prose*, describes poet Jean Toomer's perception of African American women of the South in the post-Reconstruction Era (post 1877). Toomer saw these women as "exquisite butterflies trapped in an evil honey, toiling their lives in

13. Gerda Lerner, ed. *Black Women in White America* (New York, Vintage, 1992) 287.

14. Beverly R. Wallace, "A Womanist Legacy of Trauma, Grief, and Loss," in *Women Out of Order: Risking Change and Creating Care in a Multicultural World* (Minneapolis: Fortress, 2010) 49.

15. Ibid.

16. Walker, *In Search of Our Mothers' Gardens*, xi.

an era, a century that did not acknowledge them, except as the 'mule of the world.' They dreamed dreams that no one knew—not even themselves, in any coherent fashion—and saw visions no one could understand."[17] Toomer's depiction of African American women still rings true today for "within history and culture in the United States, the competing moral influences of racial and ethnic prejudices supportive of white dominance are often welded to Christian beliefs."[18] As a result, black women are the surrogates for the redemption of others at the expense of their own capacity to receive redemption and healing.[19]

Understanding this social construction of African American female identity and its implications on the space they occupy in society colors the way in which we approach Ruth. If we, as readers, re-approach the larger narrative of Moab understanding Ruth's character to be representative of her people rather than contradictory, it forces us to re-examine the actions of Ruth's ancestors. Lot's daughters must then be understood not as aberrant but as women who pragmatically assessed the best way to maintain their world. It forces us as readers to interrogate the Israelite writer's failure to attend to the full emotional range wrapped up in the decision that the daughters made to preserve Lot's blood line. Reading the text backward from a womanist perspective, we give new life to the Moabites, and Ruth carries the attributes of her people.

Further, when Ruth professes her intention to go into the fields and glean, Naomi's response is perfunctory at best. Naomi fails to acknowledge and/or articulate either the potential dangers that exist for Ruth in the fields, or the potential that exists in Boaz's field. The glaring irresponsibility or short-sightedness of this failure to act is punctuated by the narrator's revelation in 2:1—"Naomi had a kinsman . . . a prominent rich man." The reader is privy to information that Ruth is not and that Naomi seems incapable or unwilling to share. The juxtaposition between Ruth and Naomi's behavior and between Ruth and the people of Bethlehem becomes more suspicious when evaluated within Carol Myers's understanding of family and communal units in biblical Israel. Myers maintains that "In the merging of the self

17. Ibid., 232.

18. Traci West, "Using Women: Racist Representations and Cross Racial Ethics," in *Creating Ourselves: African Americans and Hispanic Americans on Popular Culture and Religious Expression*, Anthony Pinn, ed. (Durham, NC: Duke University Press, 2009) 95.

19. See Delores Williams, *Sisters in the Wilderness: The Challenge of Womanist God-Talk* (Maryknoll, NY: Orbis, 1998) in which she addresses the surrogacy of black women through a womanist reading of the Hagar story.

and family, one can observe a collective, group-oriented mind-set, with the welfare of the individual inseparable from that of the living group."[20]

Throughout the narrative the only person who shows genuine concern for the family is the person who exists outside of the normative tradition of the text. Naomi and Elimelech do not seem to have genuine concern for their larger family, or clan, when they abandon their homeland for Moab, and allow their sons to marry foreign women. Next, Naomi seems to have little regard for the sustenance of the family unit when she is consumed with her grief, and more specifically she shows little regard for Ruth's well-being throughout the entirety of the story. Boaz demonstrates concern for Ruth and Naomi once he encounters Ruth in the field, but there is no character who takes the initiative to care for Naomi upon her return to Bethlehem outside of Ruth. We see this neglect of concern play out throughout the narrative ark. In this context, Ruth is not an exception to her people as much as she is a contrast to the people with whom she finds herself surrounded in the text.

As the narrative transitions to the threshing floor in chapter 3, Naomi prepares Ruth to seduce and entice Boaz in order to secure a better future for them both. Stacey Floyd-Thomas argues that central to the task of womanist ethical inquiry is the quest to "demystify the perception of black women's bodies, ways, and loves as vile."[21] The same tactic is necessary for understanding Ruth as a Moabite in this narrative. There is an imperative to demystify her sexuality and become somewhat suspicious of the Israelite writers and audience by, for, and with whom this story was constructed and transmitted. Interestingly enough the same insidious sexual tactics that define the Moabites as perverse are here being offered as a necessary means to ensure the maintenance of a Yahwistic social order. Ruth's sexuality now becomes not only necessary but ideal.

Little mention is made in the text about the potential dangers that Ruth faces, once again, as Naomi sends her out to the threshing floor. Jennifer Koosed highlights a linguistic incongruence in Naomi's instruction to Ruth; the Masoretic text reads: "go and uncover his feet, and *I will* lie down, and he will tell you what to do" (3:4).[22] While Koosed fails to further attend to the potential significance of this perceived grammatical glitch, I believe that the original language bears some theological and ideological significance. If Ruth's purpose is to serve as a surrogate for Naomi's redemption, then in

20. Carol Myers, "The Family in Early Israel," in *Families in Ancient Israel*, Leo G. Perdue et al., eds. (Louisville: Westminster John Knox, 1997) 21–22.

21. Floyd-Thomas, *Mining the Motherlode*, 9–10.

22. Jennifer Koosed, *Gleaning Ruth: A Biblical Heroine and Her Afterlife* (Columbia: University of South Carolina Press, 2011) 59–60.

fact Naomi does perceive herself as being represented in the actions of Ruth without having to suffer the danger and risk associated with the action.

There is substantial consternation concerning Naomi's words to Ruth in 3:3: "do not make yourself known to the man until he has finished eating and drinking." Andre LaCocque contends that "Naomi was possibly sending her daughter-in-law to her destruction. . . . Ruth was perhaps going to be mistaken for a prostitute. Boaz was perhaps going to do irreparable harm." There was great potential that any Israelite, Boaz included could have taken advantage of Ruth sexually without having to accept responsibility for any child that she bore. As a result, Naomi could have left Ruth vulnerable not only to sexual violence but also to further social ostracizing. Jack Sasson argues that there is no way to ascertain Boaz's potential state of mind because of the hour at which Ruth would have encountered him. As such, Naomi may have been cognizant and intentional about how best to minimize the risk for her daughter-in-law. Either way, Ruth is literally laid down as a sacrifice for the social mobility of Naomi.

Despite the apparent regard for her well-being, maybe out of naiveté or perhaps out of a willful intention towards survival, Ruth presses on. So audacious are Ruth's acts of loyalty that Boaz acknowledges it as *ḥesed* in 3:10. While English translations of the Hebrew Bible often reduce *ḥesed* to "loyalty," the translation fails to encapsulate the depth of the terminology. *Ḥesed* is a contractual term that speaks to mutuality and reciprocity; Nelson Glueck, in his seminal work on the term, signifies that the secular use of *ḥesed* requires mutual assistance and duty.[23] What makes the use of the terminology questionable here is that the security that Boaz seeks ultimately ends up being for Naomi, not necessarily for Ruth. Boaz is a *goʾel*, which means that he is the next of kin who is responsible for redeeming the lineage within the *mispaḥa* ("clan"). Within the levirate tradition that is operative within the social material world of this text, Levirate practices, in particular, required that the *goʾel* produce a child to maintain the deceased male's line. It is important to note that within this tradition the lineage that was being maintained was Elimelech's, and thus the Ruth simply serves as a surrogate for the child who is ultimately Naomi's.

23. Glueck offers three different forms of *ḥesed*—secular, religious, and divine. According to his definition religious *ḥesed* centers on justice and righteous and is concerned with the broader human condition. Divine *ḥesed* focuses on the action of the divine and/or deals with the ways in which human beings mirror the divine in their actions. Thus, the secular use of the definition seems most appropriate here in Ruth because it is concerned with more intimate, individual human interaction. For more information see Nelson Glueck, *Ḥesed in the Bible* (Cincinnati, OH: Hebrew Union College Press, 1967).

Lest there be any doubt that Ruth is purely a function[24] of the narrative, her character lacks any significant growth in the plot. We are not privy to her cognitive evolution or emotional development. Ruth is there to serve Naomi's purpose for redemption and restoration; she is there to highlight the ostensible altruism of Boaz, who serves as an eponymous representation of Israel. The reader has no concept of her as having fear, contempt, or anxiousness or even her mourning. It is as if Ruth is only "safe'" if she is void of emotion. Contrary to the Israelite characters in the narrative—Elimelech, Chilion, Mahlon, Naomi/Mara, and Boaz—we have no concept of her history or identity outside of the fact that she was a Moabite. In a context where name and history are so important, the failure to provide her with any roots or redemptive distinctiveness further sustains an argument for her alienation and subjugation in the story.

Again, we find correlating space for Ruth and black women; it is found in the failure of public script to give voice to their pain. Shoshana Felman suggests that texts that testify to trauma are those that are "composed of bits and pieces of a memory that has been overwhelmed by occurrences that have not settled into understanding or remembrance . . . events in excess of our frames of reference."[25] As such, what is important for this narrative is not necessarily what is said but what goes unaddressed. A failure to examine Ruth's past paired with the lack of attention paid to her emotional well-being situates Ruth as a woman mired in persistent trauma. The inattentiveness to Ruth's being is especially highlighted when read in contrast with the consideration given to Naomi's emotional well-being at the beginning of the text. While Naomi demonstrates her bitterness in her silence towards Ruth in 1:18 and subsequently in her purposive re-naming of herself as Mara ("bitter") the reader is made aware of her emotional and psychological state. Ruth is not granted the space in the text. The narrative ends with slightly more regard for her personhood than it had in the beginning.

At the beginning of chapter 4 Boaz interacts with the next-of-kin who, according to levirate practice, has legal claims and social obligations to marry Ruth and maintain Elimelech's familial line. In Boaz's communication with this unnamed relative, it is clear that Ruth is a liability. Once Mr.

---

24. Adele Berlin describes a function as an individual whose character is there for the purpose of the moving the plot forward. See Adele Berlin, *Poetics and Interpretation of Biblical Narrative* (Winona Lake: Eisenbrauns, 1994) 23–24.

25. David G. Garber, Jr. "A Vocabulary of Trauma in the Exilic Writings," in *Interpreting Exile: A Displacement and Deportation in Biblical and Modern Contexts*, eds. Brad Kelle, Frank Ames, and Jacob Wright (Atlanta: Society of Biblical Literature, 2011) 310.

So-and-So[26] has agreed to redeem Elimelech's land, Boaz makes it clear that the redemption comes with the procurement of Ruth, the Moabite. Upon learning that his inheritance is saddled with the inclusion of the Moabite woman who has intruded upon their community, the unnamed man declines. What is poignant about the man's response is his pronouncement that the transaction will "damage" his inheritance (4:6). There is no clear explanation given for how his heritage will be damaged by the matter but it is obvious that he has great concern about Ruth's impact on his family system.

Despite all of Ruth's efforts, despite her sacrifices, and despite the superficial acknowledgment from both Naomi and Boaz of her faithfulness, Ruth never achieves the inclusion that she seeks. Even as the narrative concludes with the birth of Obed, the words of Bethlehem's women expose the true exclusionary proclivities of Israel and its narrative; the women speak to Naomi and say, "Blessed be the Lord, who has not left you this day without next-of-kin . . . your daughter-in-law who loves you, who is more to you than seven sons, has borne him" (4:14–15). The child belongs to Naomi not to Ruth. Ruth is merely a surrogate, she is a valuable surrogate, given more distinction and worth than her counterpart, Hagar,[27] but she is a surrogate nonetheless.

Black women have been subjected to similar gradations of the same objectification throughout history. There are numerous stories throughout history that bear witness to this surrogacy. It is so engrained in the black conscious that it appears palpably in black popular culture in the cultivation of the "mammie." Take for example the tension that surrounds Sophia from *The Color Purple*; there is tireless effort on the part of the white mayor's family to make Sophia an invested part of their familial unit. Sophia is supposed to serve as a surrogate for the mayor's children and then for the grandchildren, and she is supposed to faithfully love them. In constructing this narrative Alice Walker creates a depiction that calls upon the history of the slave narratives for women like Elizabeth Keckley.[28]

---

26. Several scholars have postulated theories about the significance of the next-of-kin not having a name, but instead being referred to simply as *pělōnî' almōnî*. Jack Sasson suggests that the phrase is not intended to embellish the anonymity by terming him Mr. So-and-So but instead is a circular reference to the space that Boaz wanted him to occupy. See Jack Sasson, "Farewell to Mr. So-and-So" in *Making a Difference Essays on the Bible and Judaism in Honor of Tamara Cohn Eskenazi*, eds. David J. A. Clines, Kent Harold Richards and Jacob L. Wright (London: Sheffield, 2012) 251–56.

27. Hagar too serves as the initial surrogate for the social and religious ambition of Israel. See Gen 16 and Gen 20.

28. Elizabeth Keckley, *Behind the Scenes in the Lincoln White House: Thirty Years a Slave and Four Years in the White House* (London: Penguin, 2010).

Conclusion

While the social parameters of the biblical world, more specifically the social world that surrounds the characters in the book of Ruth, are vastly different from our own what is consistent between the modern world and the biblical world is the construction of "insider" vs. "outsider" dichotomy. The book of Ruth inaugurates a world order in which outsiders are manipulated, whether intentionally or inadvertently, to protect and promote certain norms. Further, the text as part of a larger social ethic simultaneously lauds the utilization of one's sexuality to achieve means that are deemed expectable by one group while eschewing other groups for their sexual lasciviousness. At the same time the narrative assumes that certain groups of women carry no emotional or spiritual burden for having to provide for the salvation of others. Ruth stands perpetually outside of the communal structure of Israel, only able to achieve superficial recognition for her fertility and devotion. Consequently, at the end of the narrative she is still a Moabite acquisition (4:10) in a public transaction.

This is the legacy that black women have inherited from the reception of texts like the book of Ruth. The ways in which this narrative has been proliferated as an ideal paradigmatic representation for a faithful, Christian woman does harm to our collective and individual psyche. While the book of Ruth should not and cannot bear the burden alone, the rhetoric of the reception history facilitates constructions of tropes like the "Strong Black Woman" and the hyper-sexualized embodiment of black women in the public sphere. The narrative correlates with our realities in ways that initiate our exploitation. Such exploitation is further enabled by the moral messages of loyalty and fidelity interlocked with such narratives. Beyond that the book of Ruth, when read through a womanist perspective, challenges the reader to evaluate the ways in which the oppressed interact with those people who are oppressive. We understand from the text and from life that there are no clear lines that separate these two groups of people. Often the lives of power-brokers and marginalized people are inseparable in ways that compound despotic environments. That complicated dynamic influences the final pivotal questions in the text: Where is God in all of this? To whom does this God belong?

It must be noted that in the only Hebrew Bible text attributed to an outsider God does not directly appear in the narrative. Instead, God/YHWH is mediated through God's people. There is no theophany, no burning bush; God's provision manifests in the acts of righteousness/justice demonstrated by humanity. Ruth is never really able to retrieve the God to whom she professes such unfiltered loyalty. The distance manufactured between the eternally Moabite woman and YHWH harkens more contemporary tensions that arise out of the black people's interactions with Christianity.

Gerald West acknowledges that in our current age the Bible has been a tool for both liberation and excessive oppression. He conveys an anecdote about exchange of power, authority, and land for the message and possession of the Bible, saying, "When the white man came to our country he had the Bible and we had the land. The white man said, 'Let us pray.' After the prayer the white man had the land and we had the Bible."[29] The illustration carries a great deal of power but it fails to acknowledge the way in which the Bible, in the hands of the oppressed, continued to be mediated by the oppressor. As a result, many of the ways that black people, particularly black women, interact with the text and with God are influenced by Eurocentric male norms. Consequently, it is easy for us to acknowledge and understand the obvious ways that YHWH acts through Boaz for the supposed elevation of Ruth. We are even capable of seeing the ways in which God uses Ruth to provide for Naomi. However, we fail to acknowledge the ways that God empowers, informs, and emboldens Ruth in ways that allow her to be her own change agent, even when the author fails to acknowledge such characteristics.

29. Gerald West, "Reading the Bible Differently: Giving Shape to the Discourses of the Dominated," *Semeia* 73 (2001) 21.

CHAPTER FIFTEEN

"Give Them What You Have"

A Womanist Reading of the Matthean Feeding Miracle
(Matt. 14:13–21)[1]

MITZI J. SMITH

One Psalmist testified that he had not seen the just (*dikaios*) forsaken (*engkataleipō*) nor his seed seeking (*zēteō*) bread (*artos*) (Ps 36:25 LXX).[2] I have recited and invoked that testimony, as a memory verse and as a promise, despite the fact that it did not represent my reality. As a professor in the classroom, seeking to make the gospel relevant to contemporary concerns, I began to think more critically about the Psalmist's testimony and how its particularity had been universalized. We, our family, did beg for food. When my mother was ill and could no longer work because she could no longer walk, we had to subsist on a welfare check of $110 per month for a family of four children and one adult. Needless to say, that money lasted maybe a good week. Mom would purchase beans and grains that she would stretch to feed us for two to three weeks of the month. When the food was gone, we hunted for empty pop bottles to exchange for the deposit at the corner store so that we might buy food. Or we would comb a nearby field for dandelion or polk salad greens. But sometimes toward the end of the month, we became desperate, and we had to ask the lady we called "the babysitter"

    1. Mitzi J. Smith, "'Give Them What You Have': A Womanist Reading of the Matthean Feeding Miracle (Matt. 14:13–21)" *Journal of the Bible and Human Transformation* 3:1 (September 2013) 1–22. Used by permission of Sopher Press.

    2. Of course, during my childhood we quoted the KJV, which reads, "I have not seen the righteous forsaken nor his seed begging for bread." (Ps 36:35)

(she used to babysit for my younger sister when my mother worked) if she had any leftovers she could give us. She would give us frozen leftovers that sometimes tied us over until the last of the month. Like the Syrophoenician woman (Mark 7:24–30; Matt 15:21–28) my mother did not begrudge the scraps or crumbs when it came to saving her children's lives. Even the scraps can function as a lifeline to sustain a person from one day to the next, from hope to hope. Historically, black people and families have been sustained and have succeeded by being "able to take advantage of the most minimal scraps of opportunity and convert them into outstanding achievement."[3] Our own poverty does not excuse us from sharing what we do have with others who also find themselves in dire situations.

Many African Americans that achieved any socio-economic success or mobility or who for whatever reason barely survived "did not make it alone," and they were "not alone in making it," as Andrew Billingsley demonstrates.[4] My mother always insisted that people need one another to survive. She admonished me and my siblings to love one another because we would need each other. My mother was an intelligent, gifted, just, and god-fearing and godly-living woman, who loved her children and her neighbors. Despite the early death of her mother, a serious childhood head injury, and her struggle with narcolepsy (sleeping sickness) in high school, she was valedictorian of her high school class. She finished two years of nursing school before lack of money forced her to quit. Therefore, my mother made little money as a salad girl in a respectable restaurant or as a nursing assistant in a hospital or nursing home. And when her leg muscles constricted, leaving her confined to a wheelchair, we sunk deeper into economic poverty. Yet despite her own poverty, we witnessed how she shared the pot of chili she cooked for her own children with some of the hungry neighborhood children. She traveled to Tennessee and brought her sick grandfather, Daddy George, to Columbus, Ohio, so that she could care for him in our two bedroom apartment. And my mother told the elderly Trent sisters who lived a few doors from us that they could call her anytime of night when they needed her. My mother knew, and taught us by word and example, that people don't make it alone. Many people, including significant numbers of children, go to bed and wake up hungry in this country and globally, despite that many may have neighbors who choose not to share or to limit their sharing. According to Feeding America, in 2011 50.1 million Americans lived in food insecure

3. Andrew Billingsley, *Black Families in White America: The 20th Anniversary Edition of a Modern Classic by a Preeminent Afro-American Sociologist* (New York: Touchstone, 1988) 100.

4. Ibid., 103.

households, 33.5 million adults and 16.7 million children.[5] Most hungry folks are good and just people who could not testify as the Psalmist has because they have had to beg or depend on others for sustenance.

There is no shame in begging, especially when we have done all we can to survive. What difference would it make in people's lives if we all lived in a sharing mode grounded in a compassionate consciousness of the existence and impact of unjust systems and situations, of human error, of hardships that can befall any of us, and an understanding of our human connectedness? In her 1983 book *In Search of Our Mothers' Gardens*, Alice Walker describes a womanist as "committed to survival and wholeness of entire people, male and female . . . traditionally universalist . . . traditionally capable, as in: 'Mama, I'm walking to Canada and I'm taking you and a bunch of other slaves with me.' Reply: 'it wouldn't be the first time.'"[6] "The first time" signifies Harriet Tubman's escape from slavery and her work to free other slaves. A womanist ethic asserts that we cannot free ourselves without freeing other folk too. We cannot liberate ourselves and our children and leave other folks and their children to themselves without the proverbial boots or bootstraps, if we can help it. Human beings need other human beings to survive. When Harriet Tubman, also known as "Moses," the conductor of the underground railroad, "crossed the line" to freedom in 1849, a deep loneliness enshrouded her because "there was no one to welcome [her] to the land of freedom." Consequently, she resolved to lead her family and other slaves to freedom.[7] Within a space of ten years, Harriet made about nineteen trips from southern slave states to northern free states liberating over two hundred slaves. "Moses" freed her siblings, her parents, and slaves with whom she shared no biological connection. Harriet was of small build and only five feet tall and suffered from seizures that rendered her unconscious as a result of a childhood head injury.[8] Yet Harriet did not count it

5. www.feedingAmerica.com.   http://feedingamerica.org/hunger-in-america/hunger-facts/hunger-and-poverty-statistics.aspx (accessed March 8, 2013).

6. Alice Walker, *In Search of Our Mothers' Gardens: Womanist Prose* (San Diego: Harcourt Brace, 1983) xi. Walker first defined a womanist in her 1979 play ("Coming Apart," in *The Womanist Reader: The First Quarter Century of Womanist Thought*, ed. Layli Phillips [New York: Routledge, 2006], 7) where she asserts that "'womanist' is a feminist, only more common."

7. Jessie Carney Smith, *Epic Lives: One Hundred Black Women Who Made a Difference* (Detroit: Visible Ink, 1993) 529. The underground railroad was a secret and illegal route through which abolitionists (black and white) helped slaves to escape from southern slave states to northern free states.

8. Ibid., 529–30. Harriet was injured at age thirteen while trying to protect a fellow slave from a whipping by the overseer for leaving work early to go to the general store, 532. Dorothy Sterling, ed., *We Are Your Sisters: Black Women in the Nineteenth Century*

robbery to use what she had—courage, audacity, ingenuity, leadership skills, memory, and knowledge of nature (she was illiterate) *and* a long rifle—to relieve others of their suffering and oppression.[9] She spent the money that she saved from working as a cook and domestic in Philadelphia to support herself and others on her trips down and up the Underground Railroad.[10] Harriet used her meager resources to free others. And the threat of losing her own hard-won freedom, did not keep her from risking the depletion of her own social, economic, and physical capital to help free other slaves. Womanist biblical scholar Renita Weems argues that women should pool their resources, gifts, and energies, "so that each of us has the opportunity to grow."[11] As Harriet jeopardized her own freedom and spent her resources to free other slaves, other abolitionists pooled their resources to cover any deficits and to meet Harriet's needs. The eighteenth-century abolitionist William Still wrote of Tubman that "in point of courage, shrewdness, and disinterested exertions to rescue her fellow-man, she was without equal."[12]

I propose to read the Matthean story of the feeding of the five thousand besides (*chōris*) women and children (a detail mentioned only by Matthew, 14:21)[13] through the lens of this womanist legacy of sharing what we have to help others survive and thrive, despite our limited resources. Reading through this womanist lens allows us to focus on our theo-ethical responsibility to share what we have to help others, particularly when to do so would seem unreasonable in the context of our own sense of insufficient resources. I argue that the Matthean feeding story demonstrates a transformative moment wherein the disciples transition from a sense of deficiency to a place of agency in relationship to Jesus and to the hungry multitude.

Other than the resurrection narratives, the feeding of the great crowd (*polus ochlos*) is the only miracle recorded in all four Gospels (Matt 14:13–21; Mark 6:32–44; Luke 9:10–17; John 6:1–14).[14] Only Matthew directly

---

(New York: Norton, 1997) 69.

9. Harriet Tubman probably got her courage from her mother. Her mother, Harriett Ross, modeled remarkable audacity when she refused to let her master take her youngest son whom her master had sold to a Georgia trader. When Mrs. Ross's master attempted to retrieve the boy by deceit, she vowed to split open the head of the first man to enter her house to take him. She hid her son until the trader left. See Sterling, *We Are Your Sisters*, 59.

10. Smith, *Epic Lives*, 531, 533.

11. Renita Weems, *Just a Sister Away* (New York: Warner, 2005) 50.

12. Smith, *Epic Lives*, 534–35.

13. Mark only states that five thousand men (*andres*) were present (6:42).

14. Matthew and Mark include a second story of the feeding of a multitude (Matt 15:32–39; Mark 8:1–9).

links the news of John the Baptist's death with Jesus' decision to withdraw to a deserted place (14:11–13) where he feeds the large crowd.[15] Thus, as Amy-Jill Levine states, "the meal of horror yields to the foreshadowing of the messianic banquet."[16] Herod commanded (*keleuō*) that John the Baptist should be beheaded out of regard for his guests or those that had gathered to recline (*tous sunanakeimenous*) at the table, v. 9. But Jesus commanded (*keleuō*) that the crowds whom Herod feared become his dinner guests by reclining (*anaklinō*) on the grass (v. 19). J.R.C. Cousland characterizes Matthew's crowds as part of the Jewish masses who are the victims of "bad leadership" and as awaiting "divine intervention."[17]

The crowds, unaware that Jesus is grieving, follow him so that he might heal them and/or their ailing relatives or neighbors. Although all Gospel accounts introduce the story by informing the readers that a large crowd (*polus ochlos*) followed Jesus (Matt 14:14; Mark 6:34; Luke 9:11a; John 6:5a) only Matthew inserted the Greek noun *ochlos* (crowd) three times in the story (14:15b, 19a, c).[18] Luke added *ochlos* twice (9:12, 16) and Mark prefers the pronoun instead of the noun.[19] Thus, Matthew seems to humanize the crowds more throughout the narrative by not reducing them to a pronoun as does Mark. Despite his own grief, Jesus had compassion on the crowds and took the time to heal them,[20] as he has previously done (4:25). The crowds to whom Jesus preached and upon whom he had compassion consisted of the physically ill, economically poor, and "the harassed and

15. Matthew follows the order of Mark's Gospel (as does Luke with a short, less detailed version, 9:7–10) by placing the narrative about Herod's beheading of John the Baptist prior to the feeding, but Mark does not make a direct link between news about it and Jesus' retreat to a desert place (Mark 6:14–30).

16. Amy-Jill Levine, "Gospel of Matthew," in *Women's Bible Commentary. Twentieth-Anniversary Edition*, eds. Carol A. Newsom, Sharon H. Ringe, and Jacqueline E. Lapsley, revised and updated (Louisville: Westminster John Knox, 2012) 473.

17. J. R. C. Cousland, "The Crowds in the Gospel of Matthew," *Novum Testamentum* 102 (Leiden: Brill, 2002) 98, 122. Cousland also argues that Matthew has irrevocably severed ties with the Jewish leadership, but maintains a connection with the masses, 304.

18. Cousland (ibid., 39, 45) notes the *ochlos* is virtually the only Greek word Matthew employees to designate the crowds, to which he attributes a "distinctive and unified persona."

19. John refers to the crowds as people (*anthrōpoi*) rather than as *ochlos* (crowd) in the story of the feeding (6:5, 10).

20. Matthew follows Luke stating that Jesus had compassion on the crowds, but Mark states that Jesus welcomed (*apodechomai*) them (6:34). Joseph Fitzmyer (*The Gospel According to Luke I–IX* [New York: Doubleday, 1981], 764) argues that Luke "suppressed" the compassion motive initially expressed by Mark's Jesus toward the crowd.

helpless" (6:31–33; 9:36; 11:5; 26:11).[21] Because of the large crowd and their needs, Jesus stretched the healing service into the evening. Consequently, Jesus' disciples suggest that Jesus send the crowds into the nearby villages to buy food for themselves. The Greek verb *apoluō* translated as "send away" can denote a releasing of the people and thus ending their access to Jesus (14:15; cf. 15:32, 39).[22] This Greek verb *apoluō* is used again at v. 22 when Jesus dismisses the crowd after the feeding and in preparation for his retreat up the mountain to pray. However, when Jesus rejects the disciples' suggestion that he dismiss the crowd, stating that they do not need to go away, the Greek verb employed is *aperchomai*. Jesus had not finished demonstrating compassion for the crowd, but when he has finished with them after the feeding, he releases (*apoluō*) them.

The past and present intertwine; the present is impacted by and borrows from the past. The Gospel feeding of the multitude scenes recall the Old Testament wilderness feeding narratives where God provides manna from heaven and quail meat. But the situation in Matthew is different in that the crowd is not a group of renegade slaves without homes or a homeland. The Matthean crowds have traveled without pursuit into the wilderness to be healed by a man named Jesus with a reputation for working miracles. The historical situation is different, but the human predicament, desperation, and remedy are similar. In this first-century CE wilderness setting, the food that Jesus will use to feed the crowds is in their midst—five loaves and two fish. Jesus confronts his disciples, forcing them to articulate clearly their own sense of lack in relation to the needs of the crowd.[23] The disciples respond negatively to Jesus' command to provide food for the crowd, and their response is based on the reality of their own limited provisions: they have nothing except (*ouk echomen ōde ei mē*) five loaves and two fish

---

21. Leslie J. Hoppe (*There Shall be No Poor Among You: Poverty in the Bible* [Nashville: Abingdon, 2004], 149) rejects the assertion that Matthew spiritualizes the word "poor." The word "poor" signifies one group that existed on the margins of first-century Palestinian Jewish society. "Matthew's eschatological vision sees that the circumstances of the poor and others on the margins will be reversed soon because Jesus is inaugurating the reign of God on earth."

22. At 15:32, Matthew's Jesus expresses a desire not to send the crowd (four thousand plus women and children) away (*apoleuō*) hungry after they have been with him for three days. Jesus appears to make that statement at a point when he is ready to dismiss the crowd. In Mathew's story of the Canaanite Woman who asks the "son of David" to have mercy on her and to deliver her daughter from a demon, the disciples urge Jesus to dismiss (*apoleuō*) the woman, 15:21–23 (cf. Mark 7:24–30 where the disciples are not present).

23. In John's Gospel the narrator informs the reader that Jesus is testing Philip, 6:5–6.

(14:17). In other words, what they do have they believe to be insufficient to deal with the situation.

The feeding of a hundred people by Elisha in 2 Kgs 4:42–44 also provides a literary foundation for the feeding stories in the Gospels.[24] During a famine, Elisha commands a man carrying twenty barley loaves and ears of corn from his first fruits to feed a hundred people. Like the disciples in Matthew's story, the man questions his ability to feed a hundred people with the food he totes. Elisha repeats his instructions to feed the people, and he adds that there will even be some left over. Finally, the man obeys Elisha's command and the result is as Elisha prophesied ("according to the word of the Lord," 4:44, NRSV). In both the Matthean and the Elisha feeding stories, the miracle produces leftovers. In the Matthean story, the number of baskets left over coincides with the number of disciples and not with the amount of bread they started with as in Matthew's second feeding story (14:32–38; Mark 8:1–9). In the latter, the disciples had seven loaves and end up with seven baskets full. By connecting the twelve baskets of leftover fragments with the number of the disciples in the first feeding miracle, Matthew implicitly situates responsibility for future distribution of food to the hungry with Jesus' disciples.

Incarnating Heaven on Earth

Both the miracle of manna in the Wilderness of Sin and the feeding of the great crowd in our text connect the earthly miracle with heaven. In the desert, Jesus looked to heaven before (or as) he blessed and broke the bread.[25] In the Wilderness of Sin, Yahweh promised to rain down bread from heaven for the congregation of Israel. In Matthew, both John the Baptist and Jesus announce (and commission his disciples to proclaim) that the "kingdom of the heavens [*ouranoi*][26] has come near" (3:2; see also 10:7). The kingdom

24. Roger David Aus (*Feeding the Five Thousand: Studies in the Judaic Background of Mark 6:30–44 par. and John 6:1–15* [Lanham, MD: University Press of America, 2010], 26–40) demonstrates that the feeding of the five thousand Gospel stories are based largely on postbiblical Jewish traditions about Elisha's feeding of one hundred men in 2 Kgs 4:42–44. Those traditions show that although Elisha was historically, according to Jewish tradition, the greatest miracle worker, greater miracle workers, like Jesus, have arrived.

25. Daniel J. Harrington, S.J. argues (*The Gospel of Matthew*, ed. Daniel J. Harrington, S.J. [Collegeville, MN: Liturgical, 1991], 221) that the wording of our text— "looked up to heaven and blessed, and broke and gave to his disciples the loaves," 14:19—"prepares the reader for Matt 26:26" where Jesus took, blessed, broke and gave the bread to his disciples.

26. The author of Matthew's Gospel employs the plural "heavens" in the phrase "the

of heaven has drawn near in the person and ministry of Jesus; he embodies the kingdom and encourages his disciples to do the same. Matthew's Jesus is God with us (1:23). The food that fed the multitude was multiplied in the human hands of the earthly Jesus in whom the kingdom of heaven is brought near. "The source of the feeding is God, but the resources are human."[27] As Cheryl Sanders states, "God feeds the poor in our kitchens"; we must make "God's kingdom come alive on earth."[28] The kingdom of God is near; it is incarnate in us. A womanist theo-ethics recognizes that we are called to embody the God-with-us-ness of God exemplified in Jesus' birth, life and ministry. Womanist theologian JoAnne Terrell argues that Jesus' crucifix is a reminder that God is "*at-one* with us" or of God's "*with-us-ness*."[29]

Jesus Engenders Holistic Transformation

In our text, Jesus engenders, what Yung Suk Kim calls holistic transformation.[30] By commanding the disciples to feed the crowds from their own resources, Jesus forced the disciples to confront and to articulate their own sense of insufficiency or what Kim calls an *I-am-no-one* existence.[31] In dia-

---

kingdom of the heavens (*ouranoi*)" (5:3, 10, 19, 20; 7:21a; 8:11; 10:7; 13:11, 24, 31, 33, 44, 45, 47, 52; 16:19; 18:1, 3, 4, 11, 23; 19:12, 14, 23; 20:1; 22:1; 25:1). He sometimes uses the singular "heaven" (*ouranos*) in the phrase "the kingdom of heaven" when referring to God or the Father in heaven (5:16, 45) to God's throne in heaven (5:34) or the father as Lord of both heaven and earth (11:25). Exceptions include the Lord's prayer where the petitioners are to address "Our Father, the one who is in the heavens" (6:9; also 10:32, 33; 12:50; 18:19). It seems when the author wants to make a spatial distinction between the heaven where God's throne sits and the earth, the singular is also used (6:10). Matthew prefers the phrase "kingdom of heaven" to "kingdom of God," but he does use the latter on occasion (6:33; 12:28; 19:24) which is not present in all ancient authorities. It also seems that the author uses the plural in connection with the father, "father in the heavens," when comparing the heavenly father with earthly parents who give good gifts to their children (7:10; cf. 7:21b). The image is of a heavenly father who can inhabit both an other-worldly heaven that is beyond and remote from earth (11:23) and a heavenly space that is near or touches the earth allowing the God-human encounter through which God impacts the lives of human beings. And what impacts humans in the kingdom impacts God. The kingdom of the *heavens* suffers violence when prophets like John the Baptist are killed (11:11–13).

27. Boring, *Gospel of Matthew*, 326.

28. Cheryl J. Sanders, *Ministry at the Margins. The Prophetic Mission of Women, Youth and the Poor* (Downer's Grove, IL: InterVarsity, 1997) 30.

29. JoAnne Marie Terrell, *Power in the Blood? The Cross in the African American Experience* (Maryknoll: Orbis, 1998) 125.

30. Yung Suk Kim, *A Transformative Reading of the Bible: Explorations of Holistic Human Transformation* (Eugene, OR: Cascade, 2013).

31. Ibid., 12–23. The corresponding mode of human existence is *autonomy* and the

logue with Jesus, a tension develops between the presenting predicament or life experience (the hungry multitude and the small amount of food available) and Jesus' command to feed them. The disciples recognize in this life moment that they are but dust and cannot adequately respond to the need. In his homily on Matthew's feeding of the multitude story, John Chrysostom (c. 349–407) describes the disciples as being in an "imperfect" state.[32] In this state of conscious imperfection or an *I-am-no-one* existence, the disciples humble themselves and follow Jesus' instructions to distribute the small amount of food that they have to the crowds. In the process of trusting and responding to Jesus' commands, the disciples enter into what Kim calls the *I-am-someone* mode of existence, recognizing that in and with them is the breath of life, or as we shall see below, the Son of God.[33] The disciples respond to God (through Jesus) by feeding the hungry crowd out of their own poverty.

The experience of having twelve baskets of food left over after the feeding miracle, one for each disciple, ushers them into the final phase of this particular transformative moment, which is called "I am for others." The leftovers symbolize and tangibly represent the future work of feeding that the disciples can or will undertake. The fragments signify that future miracles can occur even if all they have are small fragments and/or leftovers. Having fed this hungry multitude out of the paucity of their resources, the disciples know, experientially, that they can with God's help exist for others, regardless of how little they possess, that God will replenish and multiply whatever they submit to God for the fulfillment of justice. Here, this life moment correspondences to a mode of existence called relationality; one enters into a transformative relationship with the neighbor. In the *I-am-someone-for-others* life moment one feels "committed to service, willing to become any-body for others," because one is aware that one is a living, dynamic being,[34] even as God is a living, powerful, dynamic God. Conversely, in the Wilderness of Sin, the congregation of Israel—who have no part in feeding one another but are solely dependent on God—are instructed to expect no leftovers and not to take more than a day's ration.

Holistic transformation is relational (impacts and involves neighbor, God, and self). It is circular and recurs throughout a person's lifetime as we enter into complex life experiences in the context of our faith in God. Yung

---

subject is the *self.*

32. Saint John Chrysostom, *Homilies on the Gospel of Saint Matthew*, Nicene and Post-Nicene Fathers 10, ed. Philip Schaff (Peabody, MA: Hendrickson, 2004) 304.

33. Kim, *A Transformative Reading*, 12–23. The corresponding mode of human existence is heteronomy and the subject is God/Jesus, as holy and wholly other.

34. Ibid., 18, 29.

Suk asserts that according to the insights of political theology the three subjects of a holistic transformation—self, neighbor, and God—should enter into or participate in "'inconvenient' tense relations so that healthy transformation might take place."[35] Further, holistic relational transformation entails movement from *I am no-one* (autonomy and the old sinful self) to I am some-one (the new creation of Christ). And becoming *I am some-one* results in becoming *I am one-for-others* (relational and exhibiting neighbor love). These transformative and revelatory cycles are repeated throughout one's life, and each moment of transformation from one moment or mode of existence to another occurs in "conversation with God and neighbors" including our so-called enemies. Transformation takes place as we move through ordinary life experiences, as we struggle with issues of theodicy, meaning, faith, and an imperfect existence in an imperfect world. Each mode stands in tension with the others and informs the other; transformation occurs as humans move through the three moments of life, from autonomy (*I am no-one*) to heteronomy (*I am someone*) and to relationality (*one for others*).[36]

This entire transformative event involving the taking/giving, blessing, and sharing of a small meal with a large multitude ushered the disciples into the very mystery of God and life. In the Matthean feeding story we witness what happens when human need intersects with divine mandate and what occurs when a human faith response to the divine mandate engenders human transformation. Through the feeding miracle, Jesus taught the disciples the art of "radical sharing."[37] Womanist scholar N. Lynne Westfield argues that sacrament broadly defined occurs when profound experience connects us with "the very mystery of life, thus putting us in touch with God."[38] We experience God through Jesus. For Christians, Jesus constitutes "the ultimate sacrament of God."[39] In sacramental events, lives that have touched, experienced, and encountered God are changed.[40] Lives are transformed not just for themselves but for others. Matthew's Jesus encourages the crowds to strive for the kingdom of heaven that is near or present and that fulfills justice in the present, rather than to worry or cause others to fret about food and clothing. Matthew's Jesus models for his disciples how the nearness of

35. Ibid., 17.

36. Ibid., 27, 31.

37. Samuel Kobia, "What's in a Miracle? Feeding the Five Thousand," *Ecumenical Review* 59 (2007) 534.

38. N. Lynne Westfield, *Dear Sisters: A Womanist Practice of Hospitality* (Cleveland: Pilgrim, 2001) 81.

39. Ibid.

40. Ibid.

the kingdom is incarnate in human flesh and for the benefit of human flesh. This is radical justice (6:31–33).

Besides (*chōris*) Women and Children

In an androcentric text created in a patriarchal context, to focus our imagination on justice for women and children constitutes a radical shift. Shifting our imagination may enable Matthew's "story to be re-read and re-told differently and so shape a new and more inclusive praxis."[41] As noted above, of the four Gospels that record this story, only Matthew mentions the presence of women and children among the great crowd. This Matthean addendum may highlight the androcentric focus of the text and thus the marginalization of women and children.[42] Yet, it simultaneously creates "fissures, however slight in the androcentric world created by the text."[43] The mention of the women and children might also constitute an attempt to evoke realism and/or to humanize the crowd.[44] The inclusion of the women and children may show that Matthew's Gospel is from and for the marginalized.[45] Several images of women and children are invoked in Matthew beginning with Mary and her child Jesus fleeing from Herod and his decree to kill all children under two years (2:11–16, 20). The murder of the children in Bethlehem fulfilled Jeremiah's prophecy about Rachel crying for her children (2:17). Jesus healed the Canaanite woman's daughter, and praised the woman's great faith (*megalē sou hē pistis*) which stands in contrast to the disciples' little faith (*oligopistos*) (15:21–28; cf. 8:26; 14:31; 16:8; 17:17–20).[46] Noting the history of interpretation of this text, Ulrich Lutz notes that Anselm of Laon (?—d. 1117) asserts that "the women are 'pampered and given

41. Elaine M. Wainwright, "Tradition Makers/Tradition Shapers: Women of the Matthean Tradition," *Word & World* 18 (1998) 381. Wainwright explores the participation of women in the making and shaping of early Christian tradition, including the "incorporation of women into that tradition," (382).

42. Mark 6:44 makes no mention of women and children.

43. Wainwright, "Tradition Makers," 382.

44. M. Eugene Boring (*The Gospel of Matthew, VII* [NIBC: Nashville: Abingdon, 1995], 325) argues that the inclusion of "women and children" serves to "expand the numbers of people present and thus the greatness of the miracle . . . and to evoke the image of the people of God in the wilderness."

45. See Warren Carter, *Matthew at the Margins. A Socio-Political and Religious Reading*, Bible and Liberation (Maryknoll: Orbis 2000).

46. Mark's story of the Syrophoenician woman does not mention the woman's faith (7:24–30).

to vices."[47] Matthew has no such negative view of the women and children, generally, or the ones whom Jesus fed.

Whenever men and women are sick, hungry or impoverished, it follows that children are starving and sick. More than sixteen million children (under eighteen years) lived in poverty in the US in 2011 or one in five children, which is higher than any other age group. Three other countries have higher poverty rates than the US, and they are Mexico, Chile, and Turkey. In the US, black children are more likely to live in poverty than other racialized groups with 38.2 percent living in poverty. And children living with a single mother experience poverty at higher rates than children in two–parent households.[48] Since women do not receive equal pay for equal work, as single mothers they would automatically have fewer resources with which to feed and clothe their children. And because minority women make less than their white counterparts, they will have even fewer resources to feed and clothe their children. Hunger should be a priority because all human life is precious. And the most vulnerable among us—our children, the elderly and the sick—will be more adversely impacted by hunger and poverty. The kingdom of heaven belongs to the children (19:14). Matthew's Jesus does not, in the same rhetorical breath, reduce his pronouncement about the children to a spiritual metaphor signifying how adults must enter the Kingdom, as does Mark and Luke (cf. Mark 10:13–15; Luke 18;15–17).

Bread and Water Miracles, Justice Fulfilled, and the Son of God

In the text that follows our Matthean pericope, Jesus again seeks alone time apart from the crowds to pray, and joins the disciples on the sea where their boat is being battered by a violent storm. At dawn, Jesus walks to the disciples on the sea. Because they fear Jesus is an apparition, Jesus identifies himself and admonishes them not to be afraid. As proof that it is Jesus, Peter asks to join Jesus on the stormy waters, but when faced with the strong winds, Peter begins to sink. Jesus saves Peter from his sense of deficiency or insufficiency (*I am no-one*) in the face of a daunting situation. Once Peter safely exits the life-threatening sea, he identifies Jesus as the Son of God (v. 33). In Mark the feeding of the five thousand is followed by the similar story of Jesus, but in that story Jesus alone walks on the water, identifies himself,

47. Ulrich Lutz, *Matthew 8–20*, ed. Helmut Koester, Hermeneia (Minneapolis: Fortress, 2001) 315.

48. James M. Breslow, "By the Numbers: Childhood Poverty in the US," *Frontline*, November 20, 2012, http://www.pbs.org/wgbh/pages/frontline/social-issues/poor-kids/by-the-numbers-childhood-poverty-in-the-u-s (accessed March 4, 2013).

and no title is attributed to him (6:45–52). Also, Mark notes that the disciples did not understand about the feeding (6:52). John's Jesus also walks on water after the feeding, but there is no declaration about Jesus' identity nor any title attributed to him (6:16–21).[49] In Luke, Peter identifies Jesus as the Messiah (*christos*) of God after Jesus interrogates the disciples about Jesus' identity (9:19–20; cf. 16:16 where Matthew's Peter declares Jesus to be the Messiah, the son of the living God). Thus, Matthew's story alone is followed by another episode in which the disciples express their sense of deficiency when confronted with a daunting situation. And in that episode Jesus is declared to be the Son of God. In Luke the feeding miracle decisively leads to a conclusion that Jesus is the Christ of God,[50] but in John we have an intervening miracle followed by a declaration of Jesus as the Son of God.[51] Matthew draws a more direct literary link between the feeding miracle and Jesus' identity as the Son of God,[52] which is the primary title for the earthly and the exalted Jesus in Matthew.[53] What does this title mean in Matthew and how does it relate to our text?

The first time that Jesus is called the Son of God in Matthew is at 3:15–17[54] where the fulfillment of justice (*dikaiosunē*) is connected with Jesus' identity as the beloved Son of God at his baptism. The Father rec-

---

49. However, later Jesus identifies himself as the "bread of life" (6:35).

50. Wilson C. K. Poon argues ("Superabundant Table Fellowship in the Kingdom: The Feeding of the Five Thousand and the Meal Motif in Luke," *Expository Times* 114 [2003] 224–30) that when read in the context of food and meals in Luke, Luke's feeding of the multitude is "primarily a miracle of superabundance," is about God's inclusivity and "unconditional acceptance" of the "sinners and outcasts" for table fellowship, and it points forward to the Emmaus road rather than to the upper room. By pointing to the Emmaus Road or the mission of Jesus' followers to eat and feed others as Jesus did.

51. I. Howard Marshall, *The Gospel of Luke* (Exeter: Paternoster, 1978) 357.

52. Andrew R. Angel ("*Crucifixus Vincens*: The 'Son of God' as Divine Warrior in Matthew," *Catholic Biblical Quarterly* 72 [2011] 299–317) argues that in the temptation narrative Matthew raises the question about whether and/or how Jesus is the Son of God. Matthew answers the question in the crucifixion narrative (27:40, 43, 54) which is connected to the episode about Jesus' walking on the water (14:33). The latter episode is rhetorically linked with the crucifixion scene where the soldiers exclaim that Jesus *was* truly the Son of God. In the story where Jesus walks on water, Peter affirms that Jesus *is* truly the Son of God. There Matthew depicts Jesus as the Son of God, the divine warrior who conquers the forces of chaos (the stormy seas). At the crucifixion Jesus as the Son of God is the divine warrior who conquers the forces chaos and evil.

53. Jack Dean Kingsbury, "The Title 'Son of David' in Matthew's Gospel," *Journal of Biblical Literature* 95 (1976) 591–92. W. D. Davis ("'The Jewish Sources of Matthew's Messianism," in *The Messiah*, ed. James H. Charlesworth [Minneapolis: Fortress, 1992], 500) argues that Son of David is the designation for the earthly Jesus most characteristic of Matthew.

54. The last time Jesus is called the Son of God is after his crucifixion (27:54).

ognizes Jesus as the Son of God before he performs any miracles, as do the demoniacs (8:28–29) but the disciples do not make this connection until after Jesus feeds the multitude and walks on the water (14:33). In the wilderness (*erēmos*) temptation scene, the devil asks Jesus to prove that he is the Son of God by turning bread (*artos*) into stones (4:3).[55] Jesus refuses to do so because "humans do not live by bread alone but by every word that proceeds from the mouth of God" (cf. Deut 8:3). That Scripture, recontextualized in Matthew, is part of the Torah. Torah is translated *nomos* ("law") in the Greek New Testament. Jesus did not come to destroy the *nomos* and the prophets but to fulfill it (5:17). And the fulfillment of the *nomos* and the prophets is the golden rule that requires us to do to others as we would have them to do to us (7:12; 22:38–40). Thus, in Matthew when Jesus performs the bread (*artos*) and the feeding miracle in the desert (*erēmos*) out of compassion for the large crowd, he is fulfilling the *nomos* and the justice of God as God's son. Matthew brings together the bread miracle, Jesus as the Son of God, and the fulfillment of the *nomos* or the golden rule in demonstrating God's compassionate justice in feeding the hungry crowd through Jesus. As the Son of God in Matthew, Jesus embodies or incarnates the compassion of God, the justice of God and the power of God to perform miracles within the framework of God's compassion and justice. Humans neither live by bread alone nor by God's word alone. "The gospel is never offered as a substitute for the fundamental needs of human survival."[56]

Conclusion

I have attempted to read the Matthean story about the feeding of the five thousand including women and children through a womanist hermeneutical lens—a lens that has historically valued and encouraged black women to give what they have, regardless of how small their resources, to help others. By reading this feeding story through this womanist lens, we highlighted the significance of the disciples' giving what they had and the holistic transformation that Jesus engendered in the process. Womanism values and seeks to engender the holistic transformation of black women, the community, and the world. We can make a difference, individuals and groups, sharing what we have through individual and collective effort for justice, for the elimination of hunger. Chrysostom asserts in his homily on Matthew that "we should be taught, that though we have but little, this too we ought to

---

55. At 7:7–11 Matthew makes the connection again between bread and stone.
56. Kobia, "What's in a Miracle?," 535.

give up to them that are in need."[57] The fact that Jesus used the food already in his disciples' possession to feed the masses shows by uniting their efforts Jesus' disciples can have a significant impact on alleviating hunger. As long as we insist on someone else doing what we can do for ourselves and others, it will not happen. Michael Joseph Brown asserts that it was not unusual for early Christians to combine their resources to feed enormous crowds as the sixth-century Alexandrian Christians did under the leadership of Bishop John the Almsgiver; together they fed seven thousand people.[58] The Acts of Apostles presents what some consider to be an ideal community[59] in which the early believers shared all things in common so that none were indigent (*endeēs*) (4:34). Certain ideals are worth striving for, and ideals can be achieved. At least we claim that with God all things are possible (Matt 19:26; Mark 10:27; Luke 1:37; 18:27).

The disciples initially were unwilling to give up their food for the crowds. They assumed that everyone in the crowd would have the financial means, the cultural resources, the physical ability, and the psychological aptitude to purchase food, but Jesus did not. They did not think of sharing their food even with the most vulnerable individuals in the crowds or those in closest proximity to them. Women (married, single and widowed) and children were inevitably among the hungry crowd and likely accounted for a significant portion of it. Perhaps, the crowd had grown so that it became easier for the disciples to see them as a faceless, insignificant statistical mass. Perhaps they conceived of the needy crowds as a monolithic whole instead of a collective of individual human beings. If they did not have enough to help them all, they resolved not to share their meal with any of them. I recall the story of Elijah and the widow of Zarephath who Elijah expected to give her last meal to God's prophet (1 Kgs 17:8–16). Should not the disciples of God be expected to exercise a similar trust in God? When human beings fail to respond to hunger, to dismantle injustice, and use what we have for the sake of others, then even the righteous will be forsaken and its seed begging

57. Chrysostom, *Homilies*, 305.

58. Michael Joseph Brown, "The Gospel of Matthew," in *True to Our Native Land: An African American New Testament Commentary*, ed. Brian Blount (Minneapolis: Fortress, 2007) 105.

59. For example, Joseph Fitzmyer (*Acts of the Apostles* [New York: Doubleday, 1998], 268) asserts that the first major summary in Acts (2:42–47) "is an idyllic description of the life of the primitive Christian community in Jerusalem, its spontaneity, harmony, and unity, its devotion to prayer and Temple worship. The picture it presents is a foil to the scandal and the squabble to be recounted in Acts 5 and 6." Gerd Lüdemann (*The Acts of the Apostles: What Really Happened in the Earliest Days of the Church* [New York: Prometheus, 2005], 57) states that Luke "presents an utopian portrait" of the primitive Jerusalem church and simultaneously "recalls Greek ethical ideals."

for bread. It was in "circumstances of poverty and powerlessness that Jesus and his followers found it essential to struggle to practice" liberality, cooperation, and sharing of resources.[60]

Sharing does involve the redistribution of resources in order to meet basic human needs; it is about demonstrating compassion for the poor and homeless, an embodied compassion. Laura Stivers asserts "there is no perfect response to poverty and homelessness, but any adequate response must include both compassion and justice. It is vitally important that we disrupt the causes of poverty and homelessness and advocate for alternative visions and policies that promote flourishing lives for all. Neither disruption nor advocacy will help individuals or communities to flourish, however, if we do not have a deep level of compassion for *all* of our neighbors."[61] It must be the practice of both individuals and communities to demonstrate compassion and justice toward the poor and hungry.

Some people take pride in saying that they never had to beg or receive government assistance (even those for whom it is not true). Everyone does not have the luxury to live on pride, nor should they be bullied or shamed into going hungry because others choose to judge them as unworthy simply because they seek help or resort to begging. Many people never resort to begging but quietly go without and die like stray dogs on the street because we have shamed them into believing that their poverty is a sin. And if we can convince ourselves that everyone who is down and out is there because of their own sinfulness, we absolve ourselves of any responsibility to others. The channel or medium through which Jesus fed the masses was tangible, visible, earthly, available or accessible material substance common to humans: bread. The imminent and the ultimate expectation that God has of us is for God's people to be able to testify that when we saw the least of these hungry, we fed them; when we saw them thirsty, we gave them something to drink; and when we saw them naked, alone, estranged, or imprisoned, we responded according to their needs (Matt 25:31–45).

60. Richard A. Horsley, *Jesus and Empire: The Kingdom of God and the New World Disorder* (Minneapolis: Fortress, 2003) 128.

61. Laura Stivers, *Disrupting Homelessness. Alternating Christian Approaches* (Minneapolis: Fortress, 2011) 123.

CHAPTER SIXTEEN

Acts 9:36–43

The Many Faces of Tabitha, a Womanist Reading

FEBBIE C. DICKERSON

Emilie Townes, in describing womanist thought, calls the particularity of African American women's experiences a symphony that at times may move to a marvelous and creative cacophony.[1] Thus there is not one voice in womanism, but sometimes even discordant voices. Womanist discourse, then, should be accountable to Marissa Alexander, who fought a twenty-year sentence for firing warning shots at her abusive husband, as well as Mellody Hobson, the Senior Vice President of Ariel Investments in Chicago and the wife of George Lucas. Often, however, womanist discourse erases these distinctions in favor of a strategic essentialism that associates black womanhood primarily with the struggle against racism, sexism, and classism. In so doing, it gives the impression if not insists upon common experiences and common responses.[2]

To continue to make suffering, resistance, and survival the essential marks of a black woman's experience erases our various subject positions.[3] Moreover, it brackets us into the roles of victim and survivor when these

1. Emilie M. Townes, "Ethics as an Art of Doing the Work Our Souls Must Have," in *Womanist Theological Ethics: A Reader*, ed. Katie Geneva Cannon, Emilie M. Townes, and Angela D. Sims (Louisville: Westminister John Knox, 2011) 36–50.

2. Monica A. Coleman, "Introduction: Ain't I A Womanist Too?," in *Ain't I A Womanist Too? Third Wave Womanist Religious Thought*, ed. Monica A. Coleman (Minneapolis: Fortress, 2013) 16.

3. Victor Anderson, *Beyond Ontological Blackness: An Essay on African American Religious and Cultural Criticism* (New York: Continuum, 1995) 112.

categories do not ring true, at least for some of us, to our own, personal experiences. We are products of our cultural legacy, and we recognize that struggles will continue as long as racism and sexism exist. But if we foreground victimization and struggle, we limit other possibilities. Womanism, as a way to make central the lives of African American women in public discourse, cannot exemplify a one-size-fits all model. It must acknowledge our various subject positions, and in doing so, it has a better chance of pursuing both social transformation (the result of the struggle) and personal and communal wholeness that moves us from survivor to creator to celebrant.[4] A womanist hermeneutic, then, is accountable to the variety and complexity of black womanhood, which can and should be celebrated rather than muted.[5]

The Marvelous Cacophony of the Bible

A commonality for many Christian African American women is the import of the Bible in our everyday lives. Through the word from the pulpit and the study at the table, black church traditions locate the Bible as the absolute source for righteous living. The Bible allowed me to connect to God; I not only memorized verses, I internalized the narratives. Hannah's earnest and fervent prayer to God became my instruction on how to communicate with the holy (1 Sam 1:1—2:10). Although I did not choose to pray for a child, I decided which details of the character spoke to me, and which could be set aside. I saw myself as a trailblazer like the judge Deborah (Judg 4:4–10) but I never thought of the need for a Barak to help me wage whatever battle needed fighting.

The Bible gave comfort by providing the answers to life's challenges, and it gave me assurance that God was always present. I even listened to some of what Paul taught: I tried to rejoice always, pray without ceasing, and give thanks in all circumstances because that was the will of God for me (1 Thess 5:16–17).

Later, I both recognized and finally had the words to express the disjuncture between my personal experiences with the Bible and what I was taught in my church: the same text I found freeing was also used to limit my options. As I studied this guide that was my standard for determining what was right and wrong (Matt 5:21–26) I came to realize how the Bible is used to

---

4. Coleman, *Ain't I a Womanist Too?*, 19. Coleman argues that womanist thought, if it is going to be an agent of change, must be able to make alliances with black, white, women of color, global, and third world feminisms.

5. Townes, "Ethics as an Art," 36.

constrain people, particularly women. I heard that women should be silent in the churches (1 Cor 14:34); wives are to be subject to their husbands (Eph 5:22); and women are not permitted to teach or have authority over men (1 Tim 2:12). We could sing in the choir, do fund-raising activities, and serve the food, but we weren't allowed in the pulpit. We women, no matter our accomplishments, were all the same: we were to be taught and not to teach; we were in need of the pastor's instruction, the deacon's guidance. We were weak and they were strong.

I turned again to the Bible, this time to see what it had to say, specifically, about women. There was no single teaching and no general mold. The Bible offers a marvelous cacaphony. Women in the Bible are single (Luke 8:2, 3b) married (Matt 27:19; 1 Cor 16:19; 2 Tim 4:19) and widows (Mark 12:41–44; Luke 7:11–17; 18:1–8; 20:47; 21:1–4); mothers (Matt 20:20–23; John 2:1–11) and sisters (Luke 10:38–42; John 11:1–45); homeowners (Luke 10:38; Acts 12:12; 16:15; Col 4:15) and business women (Acts 16:14); upper (Acts 17:4, 12) and lower class (Mark 12:42–43; Luke 21:1–4); Jewish (Luke 1:5, 27, 2:36–28; 10:38–42; Acts 12:13; 16:1; 2 Tim 1:5) Samaritan (John 4:1–42) and gentile (Matt 15:21–28; Mark 7:24–30); vengeful (Matt 14:3–4; Mark 6:17–20) and collaborative (Acts 18:2, 26); sick (Matt 8:14–15; 9:20–22; Mark 5:25–29; Luke 8:43–44) and healthy (Matt 8:15; Mark 1:31; Luke 4:39; 8:44); adulterous (John 8:3–4) and faithful (Matt 25:1–13; 27:55–56, 61; 2 Tim 1:5); slaves (John 18:16–17) and free (Gal 4:31); prophets (Luke 2:36–38; 1 Cor 11:5) deacons (Rom 16:1) and apostles (Rom 16:7). Yet preaching and teaching in my church did not acknowledge this plurality.

This same lack of acknowledgement threatens some womanist biblical interpretation, and not just womanist interpretation but feminist and so-called "objectivist" or "malestream" interpretations as well. Biblical women are read through stereotypes; widows are vulnerable and needy; women's lives are ravaged by a patriarchal society. Rather than promote stereotypes—all widows are poor and sympathetic; all upper-class people are the enemy of the poor, all Christians are good—we should interrogate them.

Womanist Biblical Hermeneutics

Womanist thought found its way into biblical studies in the early 1980s. Renita Weems (OT) and Clarice Martin (NT) both used a womanist lens, although differently, to interpret the biblical text. Weems combined the fruits of early feminist biblical criticism with its passion for reclaiming the stories of biblical women with a rereading grounded in the African American gift for storytelling.[6] Martin's focus on race, gender, and class as well as on linguistic sexism found both problems and possibilities in translation and interpretation.[7] More recent womanist biblical scholars have focused on the racial, ethnic, and gendered nature of the work of black mothers and on the benefits and potential difficulties in African American women's traditional understanding of Jesus as cosufferer.[8]

Most womanist biblical interpretation begins with the reader, or contemporary black experience (however understood) or various forms of critical theory, rather than with the biblical text itself. This focus is in part a product of the academy. Womanist thought developed primarily in the fields of ethics and theology, and thus the questions it brings tend to be located in the ethical-experiential or theological-constructive areas rather than in historical-critical ones. Moreover, with its increasing interest in readings "in front of the text" and in avoiding any falsely objectivist conclusions, biblical scholars respond by foregrounding the autobiographical or the present problem, to which the text then responds. Consequently, the historical-critical method as well as attention to, e.g., the biblical author's perspective (redaction criticism through literary approaches) is underutilized in womanist biblical hermeneutics. There are additional reasons for this lack of precise exegetical work aside from disciplinary divisions. I have heard, in my church and in the corridors of Vanderbilt Divinity School, the standard complaints about historical-critical or rigorous exegetical work: it is elitist; white feminist biblical interpretation erases our experiences; this stuff won't preach; we need to read the text as it is translated today rather than learn Hebrew and Greek; we cannot deconstruct oppressive systems with the master's tools.

6. Renita J. Weems, *Just a Sister Away: A Womanist Vision of Women's Relationships in the Bible* (San Diego: LuraMedia, 1988) ix. While Weems identifies as a black feminist, she links herself to womanism by way of Alice Walker's definition, which asserts that a womanist is a black feminist or feminist of color. See Alice Walker, *In Search of Our Mother's Gardens: Womanist Prose* (San Diego: Harcourt Brace, 1983) 18–38.

7. Clarice J. Martin, "Womanist Interpretations of the New Testament: The Quest for Holistic and Inclusive Translation and Interpretation," in *Black Theology: A Documentary History, 1980–1992*, ed. James H. Cone and Gayraud S. Wilmore, vol. 2 (Maryknoll: Orbis, 1993) 225–44.

8. Stephanie B. Crowder, "BMW: Biblical Mother Working/Wrecking, Black Mother Working/Wrecking," in *Mother Goose, Mother Jones, Mommie Dearest: Biblical Mothers and Their Children*, ed. Cheryl Kirk-Duggan and Tina Pippin (Atlanta: Society of Biblical Literature, 2009) 157–67. See also Raquel St. Clair, "Womanist Biblical Interpretation," in *True to Our Native Land: An African American New Testament Commentary*, ed. Brian Blount et al. (Minneapolis: Fortress, 2007) 54–62; Raquel A. St. Clair, *Call and Consequences: A Womanist Reading of Mark* (Minneapolis: Fortress, 2008) 1–18.

If we do not use these tools—if we do not use whatever resources available to us—we are not bringing out of our treasure houses both what is old and what is new, and thus we cannot be scribes for the kingdom of heaven. If we start with, or at least treat as a primary concern, the Bible as understood in its own context, we can better put the text into dialogue with our contemporary experience. With this approach, the Bible becomes more than a prooftext used to validate our views or a foil against which we struggle and prevail. Historically informed womanist biblical hermeneutics can uncover and debunk cultural constructs concerning women—and men—by including in its analysis what is found in the library, what is heard from the pulpit, and what is heard in the women's room after the sermon. It can put the fruits of historical-critical exegesis, both sour and sweet, into dialogue with African American women's experience and the black church tradition to show how the biblical text helps us envision different social realities and challenge stereotypes.[9]

Such concern for the ancient context should reinforce the import of womanist work. A womanist reading necessarily interacts with the situations in which African American women find ourselves. This situatedness means awareness of our own history, and our own experiences. We celebrate our particularity. We should do the same for that of Jesus and his follower. They too lived in particular times and circumstances, and they too were part of a larger story. I am an African American woman, born in Atlanta and living in Tennessee. Jesus was a Jewish man living in the land of Israel; his followers, Jewish and gentile, had their own contexts, and their own stories. A womanist biblical hermeneutic, informed by attention to literary and cultural construct, can help retell those stories, and from these womanist informed stories, we have much to learn.

In turn, by attending to the various forms of biblical scholarship, womanist readings are more likely to impact biblical readers outside of our own field. Our central audience remains African American women, but what we have to say should prove instructive to men in our churches and communities, and to all readers. The point is not to sell out to the academy; it is to participate more broadly within it. Here in the field of biblical studies with all of its approaches we can both sharpen our womanist instincts and instruct others who come to the text with different experiences and agendas.

My test case is Acts 9:36–43, the story of Tabitha/Dorcas, a Jewish woman living in Joppa, on the border between predominantly Jewish and predominantly gentile areas. Her situatedness impacts her story, and that

9. See Eboni Marshall Turman, *Toward A Womanist Ethic of Incarnation* (New York: Palgrave Macmillan, 2013).

context must be respected. Her story is also embedded in Luke's narrative, and we should attend both to how Luke presents her and how Luke's narrative has been understood. We do the same for our own lives: even as we construct our own stories, so we recognize that others are also constructing our biographies. We may find such constructs harmonious or discordant, but we should not ignore them. I put into the same quire/choir biblical exegesis, black church sermons, responses from a women's ministry, and womanist thought to show how a womanist biblical hermeneutic opens the potential for both biblical affirmation and biblical critique, and for social visions seen both with clarity and perhaps, through tears.

Tabitha's Story

Tabitha, also known as Dorcas, a "disciple" in Joppa devoted to "good works and acts of charity," becomes ill and dies. An unknown "they" prepares her body by washing it and placing it in an upper room. Hearing that Peter is in the nearby town of Lydda, the disciples in Tabitha's community send two men to urge Peter to hasten to Joppa. Peter accompanies the men and, upon arriving goes to the upper room to see Tabitha's corpse. Hearing the widows weep over Tabitha and seeing them display the clothes Tabitha had made, Peter says nothing. Instead, he puts everyone out of the room. He kneels, prays, and then commands, "Tabitha, get up." Tabitha opens her eyes, sees Peter, and sits up. Taking her hand and helping her stand, Peter calls the "saints and widows" to show them Tabitha lives. News of her resuscitation spreads and, because of it, many believed in Jesus.

Luke provides little information about Tabitha. We know neither her family nor her socioeconomic status; we do not know her occupation; she may be in the textile business as is Lydia (Acts 16:14) or she may have made clothes as part of a charitable concern. We do not know if she is from Joppa or whether she moved there, as Lydia moved from Thyatira to Philippi and as Peter and Paul will move from place to place. We do not know when or under what circumstances she joined this community. Although Luke calls her a "disciple" (Greek, *mathētria*)—she is the only woman in the New Testament accorded that designation—we do not know if she had ever met Jesus.

Lack of textual evidence rarely stops biblical readers from filling in the gaps. We are told, for example, that Tabitha's story is one of several to bolster Peter's identity: he is the miracle worker who carries on Jesus' work. Like Jesus who commands Jairus' daughter to "get up," Peter also commands

Tabitha to "get up," and so displays the same resurrection power.[10] Readers also suggest that her story is the vehicle to move Peter towards the ends of the earth (Acts 1:8); for this movement outward from Joppa on the border of Jewish and gentile areas anticipates Peter's conversion of Cornelius in Caesarea.[11]

Reading Tabitha's story as part of a Petrine cycle reminds me of how the work of African American women can be primarily looked upon as lifting up the church and the family rather than about the actual good work of women. Women become the anonymous wives of Proverbs 31: their names are lost; their life and work are in service to others. The communal focus in the black church can suggest to women that it is not our role to stand out. We are to be humble rather than proud; because we know in our hearts how much we have accomplished, we do not need public accolades. Christ knows our service. While the result is progress for the community, the idea of working in service to a greater cause can obscure the work of individuals.

To see Tabitha's story as a vehicle to uplift Peter masks the importance of Tabitha herself. Luke took the time to mention her; we should pay more attention. Further, Luke mentions that she is a "disciple" (*mathētria*); she is the only named woman in the New Testament to be accorded that title. One of the women in the Just A Sister Away Women's Ministry of the Ray of Hope Community Church (JASA) shared that she didn't know that women were disciples; she thought men were the only disciples.[12] Androcentrism in the Bible, preaching, and Bible studies can lead to skewed understandings of the biblical text and culture. I do wonder what a sermon on how Peter's role is to promote Tabitha's discipleship would sound like. I wonder even more what would happen if preachers learned Greek and so recognized that Tabitha's identification as "a certain female disciple" (*tis ēn mathētria*) probably indicates that she is one of many female disciples.[13]

Other gap-filling suggests that Tabitha's value to the Joppa community comes from her good works and acts of charity.[14] The expression *ergōn*

10. F. Scott Spencer, *Journeying through Acts: A Literary-Cultural Reading* (Peabody, MA: Hendrickson, 2004) 116.

11. Charles H. Talbert, *Reading Acts: A Literary and Theological Commentary on The Acts of the Apostles* (New York: Crossroad, 1997) 104.

12. Just A Sister Away Women's Ministry, Ray of Hope Community Church, Nashville, 2014.

13. Mikeal C. Parsons, *Acts*, Paideia Commentaries on the New Testament (Grand Rapids: Baker Academic, 2008) 138.

14. Gail R. O'Day, "Women in Acts," in *The Women's Bible Commentary*, ed. Carol A. Newsom and Sharon H. Ringe, 2nd ed. (Louisville: Westminster John Knox, 1998) 398–99.

agathōn (good works) can, and perhaps in the case of Tabitha, should suggest deeds that exhibit a consistent moral character; *eleēmosunōn* (almsgiving) connotes her compassion. Yet readers are inclined to reduce Tabitha's discipleship to forms of volunteerism. The good works become distinct from anything requiring technical skill or business acumen. We do not typically think of Tabitha's good works as instruction, or financial management of the community, or promoting an early version of union organizing (i.e., a voluntary association) by uniting the widows in the community. The focus on her good works and acts of charity also keeps her within the confines of women's work: she then easily epitomizes the pastoral epistles' ideal widow; "she must be well attested for her good works [*en ergois kalois*] as one who has brought up children, shown hospitality, washed the saints' feet, helped the afflicted, and devoted herself to doing good in every way" (1 Tim 5:10). The disciple has become the mother, the humble hostess, and the helper. We can fill in the gaps by reading Tabitha in light of Peter, or in light of the Pastorals, but surely there is more to be mined from her story.

Tabitha, also known as Dorcas, lives in Joppa, a seaport city thirty-five miles from Jerusalem and close to the border between Judea and Samaria. The setting in Joppa may explain Tabitha's double name. Established as a Jewish port after Simon Maccabeus occupied it in 145 BCE (1 Macc 12:33–34; 13:11) Joppa remained a significant Jewish center until its destruction by Cestius Gallus in 66 CE.[15] Josephus reports that the Jews rebuilt Joppa only for it to be destroyed a second time by Vespasian.[16] Vespasian then built a Roman camp so that the Jews would not rebuild the city again.

Tabitha's story is set prior to the Jewish War of 66–70, but Luke's readers in Luke's own time would likely know the history of the city. Tabitha/Dorcas may provide Luke, and us, an alternative to battles fought over ethnic, or religious, or racial differences. She tells us that even when empires try to prevent us from flourishing, that as long as we remember the stories, we can prevail.

Like Saul/Paul and John Mark she has both Aramaic and Greek identifications (Acts 12:12, 25). The Aramaic Tabitha can be seen as looking back to the early Jerusalem community with its Jewish base; the Greek Dorcas

---

15. Veronica Lawson, "Tabitha of Joppa: Disciple, Prophet and Biblical Prototype for Contemporary Religious Life," in *Transcending Boundaries: Contemporary Readings of the New Testament*, ed. Rekha M. Chennattu and Mary Coloe (Liberia Ateneo Salesiano, 2005) 287. See also Ute E. Eisen, "Boundary Transgression and the Extreme Point in Acts 10:1–11:18," in *On the Cutting Edge: The Study of Women in Biblical Worlds*, ed. Jane D. Schaberg, Alice Bach, and Esther Fuchs (New York: Continuum, 2004) 161.

16. Josephus Flavius, *The Wars of the Jews*, trans. William Whiston (New York: Dutton, 1928) book III, chapter 9, 245.

foreshadows gentile persons who will become a part of the growing community (Acts 10:17–33). Tabitha/Dorcas is more than a reminder and a harbinger; in her own person she can be seen as showing the unity of the Jewish and gentile church. Each group keeps its own identity, its own name, but they function as a body working together. Thus, Tabitha/Dorcas reminds us of our multiple identities; she celebrates what should be multiculturalism in the church.

The name Tabitha/Dorcas comes into English as "Gazelle," a wild, graceful creature found mostly in the African Savannahs. Some preaching traditions in the black church interpret her name as suggesting that Tabitha was quick to help others.[17] We can do better. To African American women, she may have a special message: we are both heirs to our African heritage, with names that may have been lost, but we are also part of our American settings. We may be fully home in neither location, but we nevertheless thrive. The word "gazelle," which comes from the Arabic, connotes in Arabic poetry the ideal of female beauty. Thus we African American women recognize ourselves as beautiful, but not as domesticated. We can find ourselves in her story, and we can better tell that story if we respect its own language and context.

Tabitha may have been "quick to help others." Again, we can do better, since this "helping" in the black church must be specified. It was the women in the early women's club movement of the black church who led fund-raising efforts to build schools, provided food and clothes to the poor and established nursing homes and orphanages.[18] These efforts go well beyond washing the feet of the saints. African American women continue to be the backbones of our communities. Without us a lot of charitable work would not get done, social justice on the ground would be diminished, and outreach to poor people would be severed.[19]

Under debate is the nature of Tabitha's work; most readers assume that she made clothes "for" the widows. The Bible, however, does not support this assumption. The underlying Greek suggests that Tabitha made clothes

17. David Watson, "Position Yourself for a Blessing" at Tower of Power Ministries, 2012, https://www.youtube.com/watch?v=KVc1FIJSozU (accessed April 16, 2014). See also Brian Nelson, "Stop Praying For It and Start Talking To It" at Jericho City Houston, 2010, https://www.youtube.com/watch?v=uzdL7KGthT8 (accessed April 16, 2014). Nelson suggests that the mourning widows were put out of the room because they were making the wrong sound.

18. Evelyn Brooks Higginbotham, *Righteous Discontent: The Women's Movement in the Black Baptist Church, 1880–1920* (Cambridge: Harvard University Press, 1993) 2.

19. Liane Membis, "Does the Black Church Keep Black Women Single?," CNN. com, http://www.cnn.com/2010/LIVING/08/10/black.church.women.single/ (Accessed May 5, 2014).

"with" the widows. Thus, Tabitha may be in the textile business similar to Lydia (Acts 16:14) who is a seller of purple cloth. If she is in the textile business, she perhaps has a degree of wealth and independence.[20]

Mikael Parsons suggests that although Luke knows of women of independent means (Acts 17:15, 12) Tabitha cannot be classified in this category. He notes that Tabitha made clothes by her own hand and thus, while she may have been a benefactor toward widows, she was not herself wealthy.[21] He does not consider the possibility of a wealthy woman working with her own hands, such as Penelope, the wife of Odysseus, who weaves each day,[22] or of a business woman working in a guild with others.

The possibility that Tabitha is in the business of making clothes can serve as a reminder of African American women who had successful lives as entrepreneurs. Ms. Chloe Spear, an African-born slave residing in Boston, operated a boarding house with her husband. Spear, a woman of industry, worked days and nights supporting prominent families and washing the laundry of boarders.[23] Her ability to save some of her earnings allowed her eventually to purchase a home. She then rented out rooms in her home as a source of income.[24]

Madame C. J. Walker was a businesswoman and philanthropist. Walker, who was instrumental in developing hair care and cosmetic products for black women, was also a benefactor to Tuskegee Institute.[25] Through her hair care empire, Walker was able to build factories, salons and cosmetology schools to train African American women for jobs in the hair and cosmetics industry.[26]

The subject positions of African American women are limitless and different images of Tabitha can be a resource for seeing different possibilities for the lives of women in general and African women in particular, more clearly. When we do the history of women in antiquity, we see multiple possibilities for Tabitha, in the business world as well as in charitable work.

20. Spencer, *Journeying through Acts*, 175.

21. Parsons, *Acts*, 138.

22. Homer, *The Odyssey*, trans. Martin Hammond (London: Duckworth, 2000) book 2, 93–111, 12.

23. A Lady of Boston, *Memoir of Mrs. Chloe Spear, A Native of Africa, Who Was Enslaved in Childhood, and Died in Boston, January 3, 1815 . . . Aged 65 Years* (Boston: James Loring, 1832). Documenting the American South, University of North Carolina at Chapel Hill, http://docsouth.unc.edu/neh/brownrw/brownrw.html, 53.

24. Ibid., 57.

25. A'Lelia Bundles, *On Her Own Ground: The Life And Times of Madam C.J. Walker* (New York: Scribner, 2001) 60, 151.

26. Ibid., 97–99, 105.

Her story can then lead us to see the multiple roles of African American women—and indeed to see that entrepreneurial work and discipleship are complementary. To be celebrated for "service" should not erase the celebration of keen business acumen, or of diagnosing a community need.

After Tabitha becomes ill and dies, persons in the community wash her body and place her in an upper room (Acts 9:37). We might take a moment to be with Tabitha's body. Jesus' body is anointed before burial; Tabitha's body is washed. It is honored, treated with compassion, and cleansed. Given the social prominence today within many African American communities of the funeral home director, that an unknown group within the community prepares Tabitha's corpse suggests that social prominence gives way to a service all in the group might perform.

The upper room *(hyperōon)* where Tabitha is placed evokes its own set of associations. Commonly understood to be a meeting place for Jesus and his disciples (Mark 14:15, Luke 22:12, Acts 1:13, 12:12) the upper room *(hyperōon)* is the place for prayer as well as preaching/teaching (Acts 20:8). Old Testament mentions of upper rooms *(hyperōon,* LXX) suggest that they were places for the restoration of the sick. Both Elijah and Elisha perform healings in an upper room: Elijah heals the son of the Widow of Zarephath (1 Kgs 17:19) and Elisha heals the Shunnamite woman's son (2 Kgs 4:8–37). It is in an upper room where David mourns Absalom (2 Sam 18:33). And it will be in an upper room where Paul will preach, Eutychus will fall out the window, and Paul will raise him from the dead. Since the early church in Acts typically gathers in private homes (Acts 2:46, 5:42, 8:3, 12:12) and since the original disciples met in an upper room in Jerusalem (1:13) the upper room in Joppa can be seen as a place of mourning, of prayer, and of healing.[27] Thus a location in Joppa reminds us of other sacred sites, in Zarephath, in Jerusalem, and wherever the community is gathered to remember those who have passed.

Although the narrative does not indicate who owns that upper room, there is the possibility that Tabitha is the homeowner. Upper rooms were frequently built onto houses in order to accommodate either growing families or guests, tenants, and meetings.[28] New Testament evidence supports the plausibility of Tabitha as a homeowner. Mary and Martha host Jesus in their home (Luke 10:38–42) while Mary the mother of John Mark hosted the early community that gathered to pray for Peter's release from prison (Acts 12:12). Lydia, of Thyatira, invites Paul to be a guest in her home after

27. Spencer, *Journeying through Acts,* 117.

28. Hilary Le Cornu and Joseph Shulam, *A Commentary on the Jewish Roots of Acts* (Jerusalem: Academon, 2003) 535.

she and her household were baptized (Acts 16:14–15). Nympha owns her home in Colossae where Jesus' followers worshipped (Col 4:15). There is no mention of a husband or male authority in the cases of Mary and Martha, Mary, Lydia, and Nympha; the women, like Tabitha, are independent participants in the church.[29]

Tabitha can be a businesswoman and a homeowner, and a woman of independent means. However, readers tend to tie Tabitha's resources—whatever they may be—to that of widowhood. For some readers, Tabitha is the heir to her husband's estate; she inherited her resources rather than earned them on her own. Even were this the case, however, Tabitha should still be commended for managing those resources. For other readers, it was Tabitha's husband's money that gave her the leisure to do the "good works and charitable deeds" for which she is famous. The explanation that Tabitha can do "volunteer" work because she is living off her husband's investments can prompt resentment among those of us who do not have such "leisure" time because we are working sixty hours a week in the attempt to become partner in a law firm, or even longer, in the attempt to earn the PhD, or longer yet, because along with needing to earn a living, we are also raising children.

One of the JASA members, while acknowledging that the Bible does not indicate that Tabitha is a widow, was pleased to think Tabitha was continuing to do good works in the community despite of the loss of her husband.[30] Still others wondered if her good works were prompted by her widowhood: the loss of her husband prompted Tabitha to find solace in the company of the widows and meaning for her life in helping to support them.

The absence of the mention of a husband should not presume widowhood. Luke is one among many New Testament writers who recognize the contributions of women who are not identified as having a husband or male counterpart. Mary Magdalene and Susanna (Luke 8:1–3) Mary and Martha (Luke 10:38–42) the Canaanite/Syrophoenician woman (Matt 15:21–28, Mark 7:24–30) Phoebe, Junia, Tryphaena and Tryphosa (Rom 16:1–2, 7, 12) and Euodia and Syntyche (Phil 4:2) all stand on their own. They may have been widows, or divorcees, or single women, or women who left their husbands. Thus, women without the mention of husbands or other males could be an affirmation of singleness in the community. Remarkably, although the story of Tabitha is paired with that of Aeneas (Acts 9:32–35) whom Peter also raises, no one speculates as to whether he is a widower.

29. Carolyn Osiek, Margaret Y. Macdonald, and Janet H. Tulloch, *A Woman's Place: House Churches in Earliest Christianity* (Minneapolis: Fortress, 2006) 158.

30. Just A Sister Away Women's Ministry.

When the subject is a woman, somehow commentators all want to know about her marital or sexual status; for men, the question is infrequently asked. Even in contemporary church settings, marriage and children are the markers of "real" womanhood. I have been asked if I want to be married and I have been told that I was not a woman because I don't have children. Retelling Tabitha's story provides me a response to such charges.

In church spaces, single people are often relegated to the margins. A fundamental problem for single women and single women with children in the African American church tradition is that their family structure does not mirror what is thought to be proper.[31] Church tradition favors the hierarchal and male-ruled family. Contemporary configurations of the family, however, show a multitude of models: kin, both blood and fictive, extending beyond the nuclear ideal.[32] Rather than relegating Tabitha to the margins of the community by depicting her as single, Luke appears to boost her status. Moreover, Tabitha's work in the community and her relationships with the widows, men, and other disciples of the community may very well signal her family unit. Not every woman needs a husband or children in order to feel complete, be a disciple, do good works and deeds of charity, run a business, or be respected in her community.

The Joppa widows take center stage in the narrative as they weep over Tabitha. Luke's depiction of these widows is consistent with the overall depiction of widows in Luke-Acts. Luke typically undercuts indications of their independence or agency. Rather than living on her own like the widow Judith, Anna, a prophetic widow, lives in the temple where she worships day and night with fasting and prayer (Luke 2:36). She conforms to Luke's sense that widows should pray rather than speak. The widow of Nain remains the object of Jesus' compassion, but not a subject in her own right (Luke 7:11–15). Widows are victims to rapacious scribes (Luke 20:47); Jesus commends to the disciples a poor widow who offers all she had (Luke 21:1–4); the widow embedded in Levirate marriage is objectified. The Hellenist widows need to be fed (Acts 6:1–4); but they do not open their mouths. Likewise, the independence or agency of the widows in Joppa is also undercut; Luke shows the widows crying rather than praying for Tabitha themselves.

Widows, however, are the most unconventional of conventional figures: expected to be weak, they move mountains; expected to be poor, they prove savvy stewards; expected to be exploited, they take advantage

31. Febbie C. Dickerson, "The Canaanite Woman (Matthew 15:22–28): Discharging the Stigma of Single Moms in the African American Church," in *Matthew*, ed. Nicole Wilkinson Duran and James Grimshaw, Texts @ Contexts (Minneapolis: Fortress, 2013) 66.

32. Ibid., 66.

where they find it.[33] Biblical and post-biblical images of widows show us that widows are more than monodimensional images of need (Tamar, Ruth and Naomi, Widow of Zarephath, Judith). Luke may attempt to contain and constrain widows, but the biblical tradition overall challenges this view. Tabitha herself, if she is a widow, is one such challenge.

Quickly dismissing the widows, Luke and Luke's readers quickly turn their attention to Peter as the one through whom the power of the Lord is truly at work.[34] Sermons take the point and extend it. Some preach that Peter knew the power of Jesus; therefore, we should desire people around us who not only act like Jesus, but also know the power of Jesus.[35] The problem here is that Peter was not the only one who knew this power: all the people in the church knew it. Not everyone has the gift of being able to raise others from the dead. Peter's apostolic credentials should be acknowledged, but not at the expense of the beliefs of others in the church.

In some sermons, the widows are sometimes used as a negative foil for Peter, who is placed in the role of emulating Jesus. The widows, because of their weeping, are seen to be a distraction and, so the logic goes, Peter needs to have them removed. The message to the congregation is if one is a believer, he or she shouldn't weep as someone who has no hope.[36] Thus the women are negative exemplars. The secondary message is even less encouraging: weeping women get in the way; active men fix things. Conversely, the JASA women were intrigued with Peter's putting the widows out of the room. They noted that Luke suggests the widows' love for Tabitha in that they washed her body and laid her in the upper room.[37] Here we see more gap-filling: for these modern women, it was the widows who cared for the body: they do more than weep—they are ancient funeral directors. One person asked how did the widows' presence hinder Peter. She also strongly

33. Amy-Jill Levine, "This Widow Keeps Bothering Me (Luke 18:5)" in *Finding A Woman's Place: Essays in Honor of Carolyn Osiek*, ed. David L. Balch and Jason T. Lamoreaux, Princeton Theological Monograph Series 150 (Eugene, OR: Pickwick, 2011) 124.

34. See Luke Timothy Johnson, *The Acts of the Apostles*, Sacra Pagina, vol. 5, ed. Daniel J. Harrington, S.J., (Collegeville: Liturgical, 1992) 178.

35. Horace A. Hough, "A Strong Team" at Messiah Baptist Church, 2011, https://www.youtube.com/watch?v=TmfZKIxTODo, (accessed April 16, 2014).

36. Aaron Louis Purham, "Tabitha Was Dead, But Presented Alive" at Freedom Baptist Church, 2013, https://www.youtube.com/watch?v=JY01_yWvgVo, (accessed April 16, 2014). See also Brian Nelson, "Stop Praying For It and Start Talking To It" at Jericho City Houston, 2010, https://www.youtube.com/watch?v=uzdL7KGthT8, (accessed April 16, 2014). Nelson suggests that the mourning widows were put out of the room because they were making the wrong sound.

37. Just A Sister Away Women's Ministry.

identified with the widows by saying "she couldn't get over being put out." Not all women identify with these widows; some find them negative exemplars not because they got in Peter's way, but because they moved when he commanded them to go.

Another JASA member suggested that it was fine for Peter to put the widows out of the room because sometimes one has to do things alone.[38] Yet another suggested the widows' continuous involvement in the narrative signified that Tabitha had a special connection to them.[39] She identified with Tabitha because "seeing someone widowed as herself reminds her of the sacrifice of Jesus." For this reader, it is not Peter who is in the role of Jesus, but Tabitha herself, who sacrificed for others, died, and was raised.

We can view the widows as the women who take care of others in the church, from birth to death, and so tell the stories of the congregation: these are the church mothers. Perhaps they are the other women disciples hinted at in Acts 9:36. The title of "church mother" is often given to older women who act as leaders in the black church; they recall the history of their communities and set the cultural and behavioral standards for their congregations.[40] Church mothers have tremendous authority in the midst of patriarchal church settings. They reign over the moral standards within the church and are the link between the ordained men and the women they lead.[41] They are often the church's financial pillars; when the community is financially insecure, the church mothers provide the bailout. We can see Tabitha as such a mother, or as a benefactor, but there is no reason to limit the role of church mother just to her. The Joppa Widows as church mothers are the link between Peter and the community. Margaret Aymer argues that the widows' mourning and tending to Tabitha's corpse suggests that these women had clear and respected roles within the community.[42] They give the good report about Tabitha when Peter comes to the upper room by displaying the clothes Tabitha made with them. They perhaps communicated with the disciples who sent the men to Lydda to find Peter. They are the forces that drive the plot. Rather than being incidental, or annoying women who get in the way, these are church mothers, and they must be not only noticed, but also respected.

38. Ibid.

39. Ibid.

40. Anthea D. Butler, *Women in the Church of God in Christ: Making A Sanctified World* (Chapel Hill: The University of North Carolina Press, 2007) 2.

41. Ibid., 3.

42. Margaret Aymer, "Acts of the Apostles," in *Women's Bible Commentary*, ed. Carol A. Newsom, Sharon H. Ringe, and Jacqueline E. Lapsley, 3rd ed. (Louisville: Westminster John Knox, 2012) 541.

This positive view of the women need not suggest a negative view of Peter. Womanist thought should not be a zero-sum game in which the elevation of one group or individual means the marginalization of another.

Another preaching theme suggests that Peter knew what to do for Tabitha because he saw Jesus raise Jairus' daughter (Mark 5:40–42).[43] As Jesus asked everyone to leave the room at the raising of the dead girl, Peter puts everyone out of the room as he resuscitates Tabitha. Jesus allowed the girl's parents and the disciples to remain, but Peter was alone with Tabitha. Peter says "Tabitha, get up," just as Jesus says, "Talitha cum" to Jairus' daughter. One might wonder if Peter wanted this setting because he was unsure that he could perform the miracle.

Women in the JASA ministry also linked Peter with imitating Jesus. One of the members suggested that Tabitha may have appeared to be dead, but because Peter walked with Christ, he recognized, similar to Lazarus, that Tabitha's illness wasn't unto death (John 11:4). In my response to this participant, I suggested that it might be better to acknowledge Tabitha's death since the text says Tabitha became ill and died (Acts 9:37).

The resuscitation of Tabitha links Peter's miracles with those of Jesus (Luke 5:17–26; 7:11–16) Elijah (1 Kgs 17:17–24) and Elisha (2 Kgs 4:32–37).[44] All three interpretations, however, put Tabitha's story in service to edifying Peter. More, they put Tabitha in the position of a child. It might be more helpful to compare the raising of Tabitha to that of Lazarus, in that in both cases the one doing the raising had to travel a distance, there was no question of the death, and the corpse is that of an adult loved by other adults (indeed, especially by women: Mary and Martha for Lazarus; the widows for Tabitha). It might be more helpful yet to see the raising of Tabitha as a reminder of the resurrection of Jesus, also known for his "good deeds." Her description as *plērēs ergōn agathōn kai eleēmosunōn* ("full of good works and almsgiving") should be linked to Jesus who is full of the Holy Spirit as well as other disciples such as Stephen who is "full of faith and the Holy spirit" and Barnabas who is also "full of the Holy Spirit and of faith."[45] Being "full" is not a term to be quickly dismissed.

Conclusion

My interest in Tabitha's story is undergirded by my subject position as a single, African American woman who has worked ministry in Christian

43. Hough, "A Strong Team."
44. Johnson, *Acts*, 178.
45. Lawson, "Tabitha of Joppa," 291.

faith communities. I've been a church administrator, Christian education director, pastoral assistant, and associate minister. Like Tabitha, I have been a visible leader within my community. I resonate with Tabitha because she appears to live into her particularity even when readers attempt to minimize it. They read her as a good worker in the community rather than a good worker who is a leader in the community. They see her as a widow and by default see her resources as an inheritance from a deceased husband. Readers also prefer to see the widows as vulnerable rather than viable participants in the community. While readers celebrate Tabitha, they also suppress her. Our meaning making in the Bible should spur readers to see past stereotypes.

I also understand how the church can be both liberating and oppressive. Churches establish a right and wrong way to live, and anything outside of the prescribed norms is anathema. All too often African American women attempt to fit into these oppressive strictures of the church and lose all sense of particularity and uniqueness, of beauty and freedom. Tabitha, then, is a model for the marvelous and creative cacophony of womanism. Her story is the seed for encouraging not only African American women, but also all women to look for the variety in women's experience.